English Ministry Crisis in Chinese Canadian Churches

"Ably applying the theory and practice of transformational leadership to the urgent problem of poor retention of the local born in Canadian Chinese churches, Todd's book breaks new ground in the advanced study of this crucial issue. Todd examines a number of models proposed by veteran practitioners of North American Chinese ministry and argues forcefully for one particular model based on his decades of ministry experience and up-to-date research. While readers may or may not agree entirely with him, no one who cares about this topic can afford to ignore his significant contribution to this conversation."

—Marcus K.M. Tso
Assistant Professor of Biblical Studies,
Ambrose University College Seminary, Calgary, Canada

"Todd's work in this book elicits a deep sense of gratitude within me. He has done a great service for the Canadian Chinese Christian community by documenting, analyzing, and reflecting upon a reality that has troubled the Chinese Christian church in diaspora for decades; namely, the loss of their next generation. Through his research he has recorded the heartfelt experiences of those who have become culturally displaced and disenfranchised and given them a voice. Having identified the felt needs and perspectives of the next generation and their relationship with the first generation, Todd not only provides insightful observations but suggests a practical road map for a healthy future direction through tangible forms of transformational leadership."

—Ted Ng, Dmin.
Executive Lead of F3C; affiliate with Shepherd's Circle Network Group,
Vancouver B.C., Canada

English Ministry Crisis in Chinese Canadian Churches

Toward the Retention of English-Speaking Adults from Chinese Canadian Churches through Associated Parallel Independent English Congregational Models

Matthew R.S. Todd

WIPF & STOCK · Eugene, Oregon

ENGLISH MINISTRY CRISIS IN CHINESE CANADIAN CHURCHES
Toward the Retention of English-Speaking Adults from Chinese Canadian Churches through Associated Parallel Independent English Congregational Models

Copyright © 2015 Matthew R.S. Todd. All rights reserved. Except for brief quotations in critical publications or reviews, no part of this book may be reproduced in any manner without prior written permission from the publisher. Write: Permissions, Wipf and Stock Publishers, 199 W. 8th Ave., Suite 3, Eugene, OR 97401.

Wipf & Stock
An Imprint of Wipf and Stock Publishers
199 W. 8th Ave., Suite 3
Eugene, OR 97401

www.wipfandstock.com

ISBN 13: 978-1-4982-0884-0

Manufactured in the U.S.A.

Dedicated to my biracial granddaughter Jessica; may your years discover the advantages in-between cultures; may God show you the most excellent way.

Dedicated to the many English ministry and Chinese church Pastors who have, and are still, struggling in the trenches To see Christ formed in the lives of the next generations.

What you have done and are doing has eternal significance. Therefore, my dear brothers and sisters, stand firm. Let nothing move you. Always give yourselves fully to the work of the Lord, because you know that your labor in the Lord is not in vain.
—1 COR 15:58

Contents

Acknowledgments | ix

Abbreviations | xi

Glossary | xiii

Abstract | xvii

1 Introduction of the Problem | 1
2 Literature Review | 12
3 Context of Ministry | 43
4 The Biblical and Theological Basis | 62
5 Methods of Research | 75
6 Findings and Results | 77
7 Desired Outcomes | 123
8 Summary and Conclusion | 138

Appendices

1 "A Synopsis of the Silent Exodus Research Design" | 151
2 "Sample Research Survey Form and Questions for Dropouts" | 154
3 "Clergy Data" | 163
4 "Dropout Data" | 165

5 "Sample Research Survey Form and Questions for Remain-Ins" | 242

6 "Remain-In Data" | 251

7 "Letter to Focus Group Leaders / Focus Group Responses" | 351

Bibliography | 363

Acknowledgments

For six years, I have carried a research burden to contribute to the health of English-ministry congregations in Chinese churches in British Columbia. It is my intention that this book project would be a resource for the many servant leaders in Chinese (and other) bicultural churches who sincerely desire to empower their English-ministry congregations to fulfill the mission of Christ. I am grateful for the grace that has been given to me to be passionate and persistent in this effort and to have been given the privilege to share the insights gleaned from years of praxis and research, including an extensive survey process. This manuscript is my doxology, for I fully recognize that every grace to articulate something good comes from above (James 1:17). *A Dio sia tutta la gloria.*

In August 2010, when the last of sixty surveys of CBCs (Canadian-born Chinese) was completed, I thought this project would die a stillbirth due to several family deaths that occurred within an eighteen-day span and the announcement that another family member had short-range terminal cancer. I stepped away from an unfinished DMin program and a twelve-year pastorate (initially perceived as further losses) to manage grief and work toward a new normal in my family life. This period of my life was a discouraging time.

After a break, I felt a sense of incompleteness, not knowing what to do with the research I had not finished. Then I was gifted with a recommendation from Dr. Ward Gasque to consider finishing my research with Bakke Graduate University, which offers an inclusive doctoral program that serves not just clerics but the whole people of God. I had no idea of the extent to which Dr. Gasque had been involved in BGU's history or that he would later, providentially, become my local dissertation advisor; I have deeply appreciated Ward's encouragement along the way.

This book has caused me to reflect on the experiences of my son, who was a statistic in his formative years, departing from the English ministry congregation in a Chinese church. I hope this book might also make it easier for people from other cultures/races in English ministries in Chinese churches.

I want to especially thank my wife and soul-mate, Linda, with whom I have been in a cross-cultural marriage for over thirty years; she, too, has been an English ministry leader and a solid partner in serving where transition and change is messy. I appreciate her for patiently listening to me talk about this topic for so many years and for giving me space to travel, research, and write.

Thanks also go to my old friend Willie Kwong, who shared the burden with me in 2008 and suggested that qualitative surveys could be a means for moving past anecdotal reporting on the silent exodus from Chinese churches.

In addition to Dr. Gasque, I thank Lowell Bakke, my university liaison, for his cheerful availability in handling my many inquiries and in being a source of encouragement. In this regard, I also want to thank Judi Melton.

I want to extend my sincere gratitude to Dr. Randy White. I have been enormously blessed by his hospitality and leadership. I was deeply impacted by the principles for reflection and action he communicated in the courses Overture 1: Fresno and Overture 2: China. This project resonates with the vision he imparted for the leaders who serve in urban ethnic settings and for the things that matter to the heart of God.

I want to express my appreciation to my Personal Learning Community composed of Rev. Doug Friesen, a denominational unit supervisor; Rev. Kum Seng Fang; and Pastor Raymond Seetoh, who would meet with me at some strange hours to interact on my progress and encourage me. To Nick Suen, I just want to say thanks for the many phone conversations over the years we've shared trying to solve the EM problems. I am also grateful to Dr. Joyce Chan for being my second reader and recommending ways to help provide this manuscript as a resource.

I want to gratefully acknowledge that without the sacrifices of the founders of the Chinese church there would be no English ministries. Last, I thank the many English ministry and Chinese clergy who shared their burden for mission to CBCs. I am thankful for the many English-speaking CBC adults who were spiritually nurtured in the womb of Chinese bicultural churches and who poured out both their hurts and their hopes for a brighter future. I wish I could express the many tears, heaviness, joys, and amusement that I experienced in reading their surveys. It is to them and others like them that I offer these findings as a gift of love – I hope that I may be remembered as a friend of the Chinese. As all of us in the faith family must press into the life of Christ; may we be encouraged by Jesus' promise: "I will build my church and the gates of hell shall not prevail against it" (Matt 16:18, ESV).

Abbreviations

A	Alliance
ABC	American Born Chinese
ACC	Anglican Church of Canada. The Anglican participants in this study were from Anglican Network in Canada (ANIC) churches.
B	Baptist
CBC	Canadian Born Chinese (this term can also sometimes refer to those who are ethnic Chinese but who are disposed to accept the dominant culture)
CCC	Christ Church of China
CM	Cantonese Ministry
CRC	Canadian Raised Chinese
EFC	Evangelical Free Church of Canada
EM	English Ministry – ministry to Canadian Born Chinese, Canadian Raised Chinese, and non-Chinese who attend the English congregation in Chinese churches
I	Independent church
LBC	Local Born Chinese
L	Lutheran
MB	Mennonite Brethren
MM	Mandarin Ministry

NACC	North American Chinese Churches (comprising various Chinese ethnicities, languages, and generations)
OBC	Overseas Born Chinese; first generation immigrant Chinese
P	Pentecostal
PC	Presbyterian
R	Reformed
TCK	Third Culture Kids; *also* adults who have grown up as part of a third culture
U	university age

Glossary

acculturation. a) Cultural modification of an individual, group, or people by adapting to or borrowing traits from another culture; *also* a merging of cultures as a result of prolonged contact b) the process by which a human being acquires the culture of a particular society from infancy.

alienated ethnics. People who are culturally estranged from their culture of origin due to acculturation into another dominant culture.

assimilation (cultural). A process by which members of an ethnic minority group lose cultural characteristics that distinguish them from the dominant cultural group or take on the cultural characteristics of another group.

bicultural churches. Churches with two congregations with distinct languages and cultures (e.g., Chinese language and English language congregations).

biculturalism. Having one's foot in two cultural worlds, also known as 'cultural juggling.'

cultural pluralism. A condition in which minority groups participate fully in the dominant society, yet maintain their cultural differences; *also* the belief that a community benefits from this.

diaspora Chinese churches. Churches with members that are dispersed from their country of origin (Hong Kong, China, etc.) and yet continue to identify with their country of origin and retain emotional ties to it.

Hakka Chinese. The Hakka, sometimes Hakka Han, are Han Chinese who speak Hakka Chinese and have links to the provinces of Guangdong, Jiangxi, Guangxi, Sichuan, Hunan, and Fujian in China. The Chinese character for Hakka literally means "guest families." The Hakka's ancestors were often said to have arrived from what is today's central China centuries ago. In a series of migrations, the Hakkas moved, settled in their present locations in southern China, and then often migrated overseas to various countries throughout the world.

marginal ethnics. A cultural minority within a similar race.

mono-cultural/mono-ethnic churches. Churches with a single, homogeneous, unilingual culture without (or resistant to) diversity or dissension; sometimes referred to as a homogeneous unit or segregated church.

multicultural churches. Churches which understand their mission as expanded beyond just reaching immigrant families of the same ethnic group; churches with a theological recognition that the Great Commission and God's kingdom transcend a limited focus on the preservation of ethnic and cultural piety; a model which pays attention to promoting full cultural diversity within a congregation and values unity in diversity, justice, racial reconciliation, and authentic community.

multiracial church. A church where no one racial group is 80 percent or more of the membership; a church whose participants have observable physical differences, not just cultural differences.

pan-Asian multi-ethnic English language congregation. An autonomous, Asian congregation connected by a shared language (English), vision, mission, direction, set of values (e.g., community), and set of resources, with a preference for shared leadership rather than a hierarchical model of leadership.

parallel associated dependent English ministries congregation.
- "Parallel" refers to dual, separate, side by side congregations in one church.
- "Associated" refers to family and cultural heritage links between the two congregations.
- "Dependent" refers to the fact that the English ministries congregation is an unequal partner and is governed and controlled, in its operational, financial, ministry (mission and vision), and structural dimensions, by overseas-born Chinese; any autonomy granted to the EM congregation can be withdrawn; the EM congregation remains dependent, often for decades, up to the point it matures into an interdependent congregation.

parallel associated interdependent English ministries congregation. A mature EM congregation that has a greater degree of autonomy from the dominant Chinese congregation and shares with that congregation a mutual/reciprocal/shared partnership in the decisions and direction of the church.

parallel associated independent English ministries congregation.
- "Parallel" refers to the EM congregation sharing (through sponsorship or a negotiated agreement on rental costs) a facility or congregational meeting place with the Chinese congregation of origin.
- "Associated" refers to the fact that the congregations are linked by family, cultural heritage, a sense of affinity, intentional voluntary joint ministries, and relationships.
- "Independent" refers to the EM congregation being registered as a separate legal entity with full autonomy in all matters of governance, operations, finances, structures, and ministries; these congregations usually have an inclusive, multi-ethnic/multicultural mission and vision.

sinocentrism. The tendency in certain Chinese churches to apply a Chinese cultural lens to church work, seeing the Chinese cultural way of doing church as the correct way and resisting culturally diverse ways of doing church. That is, the cultural ingroup beliefs and attitudes become the reference point, a situation experienced by many CBCs.

transnationalism. Feeling a belongingness to two cultures; holding stakes in two or more cultures.

tricultural churches. Churches with three congregations with distinct languages and cultures (e.g., Cantonese, Mandarin, and English).

xenophobia. The irrational or unreasoned fear of that which is perceived to be foreign or strange. Xenophobia can manifest itself in many ways involving how an ingroup perceives and relates to an outgroup, including a fear of losing identity, suspicion of its activities, aggression, and a desire to eliminate its presence to secure a presumed purity. Xenophobia can also be exhibited in the form of an uncritical exaltation of another culture in which that culture is ascribed an unreal, stereotyped, and exotic quality.

Definitions of Qualities of Transformational Leadership

The definitions of transformational leadership come from Randy White's "The Eight Qualities of Transformational Leadership" taught in the Bakke Graduate University Doctor of Transformational Leadership program (lecture Overture 2: China course, Hong Kong, April 11, 2012 and Overture 1, Fresno course, Fresno, CA, October 20, 2012).

incarnational leadership. The leader pursues shared experiences, shared plights, shared hopes, in addition to shared knowledge and tasks.

servant leadership. The leader's behavior and priorities are primarily focused on servanthood. In the style of Jesus, the leader leads by serving and serves by leading.

prophetic leadership. The leader speaks truth with love to and through power. With sacrifice and humility, the leader pursues change in the broken systems and practices in the political, economic, social, and religious life of the city and the world. The leader gives voice to those who have no voice (Proverbs 31:8).

reflective leadership. The leader lives in reality, reflects on its meaning, and catalyzes others with courage, symbols, and examples to make meaning in their own lives.

shalom leadership. The leader pursues reconciling relationships between people, between people and God, between people and their environment, and between people and themselves. The leader works toward the well-being, abundance, and wholeness of the community, as well as of individuals.

calling-based leadership. The leader seeks to understand God-given gifts, experiences, and opportunities in understanding his/her unique role as a called instrument of Christ's transforming work in and above world cultures.

Abstract

THIS STUDY RECOMMENDS SOLUTIONS towards the retention of Canadian Born Chinese (CBC) adults in Chinese bicultural churches through empowerment. To address retention, the key risk factors and common dynamics that contribute to a "silent exodus" of CBC adults were established through qualitative research, including a survey of participants from diverse church affiliations. A literature review was conducted of a) various models and proposed solutions the Chinese church has used to retain its English-speaking congregants and b) research on leading change and transformational leadership. Attention was also given to a theological basis for being inclusive in mission initiatives and for empowerment through passing the leadership baton. The research included an action-oriented step of convening leadership focus groups with Chinese church leaders to obtain feedback on the hypothesis and survey findings. Based on an analysis of the literature review and survey results, this study advocates working toward the retention of English-speaking adults from Sino-centric Canadian churches through associated parallel independent English congregational models; this approach recognizes a link between the process of acculturation and the imperative to leverage mission. The recommended solution requires negotiation with Chinese church leadership to give power away to English ministry leaders and congregations. It is anticipated that this would create a governance framework capable of strategizing to address the spiritual life stage needs of CBCs, reduce the exodus, and maximize mission/vision potential. In other words, it would permit transformational leadership practices that contribute to shalom, community transformation, and lasting congregations.

1

Introduction of the Problem

And once the storm is over, you won't remember how you made it through, how you managed to survive. You won't even be sure, whether the storm is really over. But one thing is certain. When you come out of the storm, you won't be the same person who walked in. That's what this storm's all about.

—HARUKI MURAKAMI

Statement of the Problem

THE INTENTION OF THIS study is first to identify key factors why English-speaking Chinese adults exit (defect from, apostatize from, leave) Canadian Chinese bicultural[1] churches—a problem Helen Lee has termed a "silent exodus."[2] The second intention of this study is to recommend some leadership strategies toward the longitudinal retention[3] of these adults through English ministry congregations. Transformational leaders can develop healthier congregations that maximize missional capacity. The model and

---

1. Biculturalism is defined as having one's foot in two cultural worlds and "navigating through the hills and valleys of each." Dennis, *Biculturalism*, 6. The book notes that "being bicultural means theoretically [that one is] not [yet] being assimilated" (5).

2. Helen Lee, "Silent Exodus."

3. This objective resonates with Jonathan Wu's question: "Is there anything [English-speaking Asian adult] home congregations can do or could have done to serve better or retain them longer?" Jonathan Wu, "Trusting Households," 107.

structure for English ministries is an area of concern. Almost all Canadian Chinese churches operate their English congregations as a youth ministry or as an "associated dependent parallel congregation." This system can also be called a "parent-child model," in which the Chinese congregation is the parent and the English congregation is the child. However, once the English congregation matures into adulthood and becomes intergenerational, enforcing a "systemic dependence on the Chinese-speaking congregation"[4] is a significant factor in the silent exodus phenomenon. If these churches switched to an "associated independent parallel congregation model," more people would remain in these maturing English congregations, and fewer of them would leave the church.

Audience/Ministry Opportunity Addressed

This book should be of primary interest to Chinese church pastors and leaders. This is not a homogeneous group, as it includes Chinese pastors, multiethnic English ministry pastors, lead and associate pastors, elders, church boards, and lay leaders of English ministries. This project would benefit lead pastors who want to have their bicultural churches adopt the associated independent parallel English congregation model. This project would also benefit English congregation pastors who want to guide their emerging English congregations into becoming mature associated independent parallel English congregations.

Second, this book is also directed to theologians who are interested in the transformation of their own associations, religious nonprofit organizations, or denominations and the expansion of missional capability. Faculty in theological institutions should be on the "cutting edge" of equipping parish leaders to steer through change.

Third, this book should also be of interest to leaders in multicultural churches. Multicultural churches are often the recipients of many of the wounded who exit English ministry congregations in Chinese churches. Having an understanding of some of the causes of their woundedness can help multicultural churches contribute to the healing process. In addition, many multicultural churches today are exploring the "churches-within-a-church" concept and could benefit from understanding the associated independent parallel congregation model with its potential for church planting. Leaders in multicultural churches are in denominations with leaders of

---

4. Tso, "English Adult Ministry," 6–8. The author points out that with this model "the Chinese-speaking board continues to be the real decision maker, without any plan for a cultural/language and generational transition."

Chinese bicultural churches and could have fruitful dialogue with them on transformation and the use of different church models.

Fourth, this book should be relevant for denominational leaders in the religious nonprofit sector. Denominational leaders want to encourage the missional activity of their Chinese bicultural or tricultural churches, but many of these leaders do not comprehend the complexity of why emerging generations of Canadian-born English-speaking Chinese are leaving the church. These denominational leaders should be interested in trying to promote the development of a healthier church model.

Fifth, this volume will be useful for leaders of other Asian churches. Because many Asian church pastors have similar exodus issues[5] with their English-speaking adults, some may want to smoothly transition their churches into incorporating the model recommended in this study.

Sixth, this research could be relevant for leaders of non-Asian immigrant ethnic churches. The pastors of many of these churches are experiencing similar exodus issues with their English-speaking adults and may find an invitation here to smoothly transition their churches using the model recommended here.

Finally, this book will be of interest to certain other Christian leaders. Those serving in leadership positions that can influence bicultural and tricultural Chinese churches (e.g., those producing denominational journals and resources) may find in this study a means to address the exodus of English-speaking people from bicultural Asian churches.

Purpose Statement

This research on the silent exodus is based on a qualitative study using sixty in-depth, open-ended questionnaires emailed to former church dropouts and remain-ins selected from a wide spectrum of circumstances and bilingual church affiliations. The goal was to identify common patterns and risk factors (cultural, organizational, spiritual, and personal) that may contribute to the silent exodus. It is recognized that there will likely be multiple "causes" or factors; each church may have its own unique circumstances due to its own history and cultural practices. However, the desired outcome for this project is (1) to identify patterns and common dynamics in Chinese

---

5. Consider the following: Chai, "Competing for the Second Generation," 300–301; Witham, "Minority Challenge." Witham cites the challenge for second generation Koreans struggling in a dual bilingual and bicultural world, experiencing "the tug-of-war between isolation and assimilation" (114), and living with "an ambiguous [ethnic] vision of ministry"; though "some lament a silent exodus" (119), it stems from a desire "to avoid the ghettoization and cultural isolation" (117).

bicultural churches that are contributing to a silent exodus, and (2) to compile a list of risk factors.

My action-oriented step is to provide to transformational leaders substantiated data on why Chinese bicultural churches are losing numbers from their English-language congregations. My intention is to summarize the survey findings into a short document to share with three leadership groups/teams that either are in Chinese bicultural churches or have left Chinese bicultural churches. My objective is to test the survey findings with them, get their feedback, and create a way to address a reoccurring problem. I will be looking to these leadership groups to see what they recommend could be done differently. Many Canadian bicultural Chinese church teams have been through the silent exodus, know of it, or were part of such an exodus. I will be asking particular leadership teams for their advice and wisdom on the idea of giving permission to their English congregations to have decision-making powers—which is sometimes called "leading without power."[6] This action-oriented step will culminate in a written piece based on the feedback from these leadership focus groups. It is my intention to publish this material and circulate it among local Chinese churches to enhance their current models. The ultimate goal of learning from past unfavorable experiences is to prevent history from repeating itself and to go forward with healthy transformational leadership insights into the future.

The Background of the Project

Since 1977, I have been a practitioner serving in English ministries in bicultural and bilingual settings as a volunteer, vocational youth worker, community service worker, and English ministries associate track leader. Furthermore, I have served during the year 2010 in the executive leadership of the Mennonite Brethren Chinese Churches Association (MBCCA)[7] as the elected English clerics' liaison. I also served in the former Greater Vancouver English Ministries Fellowship (VCEMF),[8] helping to plan joint min-

---

6. Bakke, *Joy at Work*, 139. Bakke discusses the need to give people freedom in the exercise of their unique gifts without trying to control them (25). There is a need to distinguish between advice giving and decision making. I want to introduce the concept that just as children should eventually make their own decisions, the senior leaders are called to give permission to their English congregations to make independent decisions. Theologically, this is rooted in an understanding of how God operates with humanity; God could make all human decisions—so that humans function like puppets or robots—but God gives people the power to make independent decisions.

7. This group is a Canadian association of Chinese churches within the denomination.

8. This group was an association of English ministries pastors that engaged in joint

isterial initiatives and next generation Chinese Canadian events in southern British Columbia. Study travel in Hong Kong and cities in China (Shanghai, Beijing) gave me greater experience with issues pertaining to culture and identity. Altogether, these experiences provided me with over thirty years of exposure to the issues addressed in this book. Anecdotal reporting on the exodus of English-speaking adults from Chinese churches is abundant, but I wanted to establish the facts through qualitative research and then provide some leadership strategies toward minimizing the problem and maximizing mission potential. The background theory that provides the context for this enquiry is in the fields of immigration, sociology of religion, and ethnicity as they relate to the topic of cultural assimilation and integration of Chinese ethnic communities into the mainstream of North American society.[9]

This research looks into an emerging conversation regarding the interrelationship between religion and ethnicity.[10] It is natural for Chinese immigrant groups to selectively assimilate/acculturate[11] into Canadian culture while also preserving Chinese values and cultural practices. For Chinese immigrants in particular, some of the focus on identity and resistance to cultural assimilation, in both the past and the present, has been due to the negative impact of prior discriminatory immigration legislation.[12] Guest, Bramadat and Seljak, and Yang, have focused on religion among Chinese immigrants and the historical issues related to assimilation and adhesive identities.[13] Current research on Chinese Christian communities continues to identify resistance to the process of incremental cultural assimilation.[14] It has been noted that large-scale sociological studies on Canadian religion have overlooked the tensions that occur regarding identity and assimilation within Canadian Chinese bicultural churches.[15] It seems rather idealistic to assume, from general discussions on the functional role of religion in

---

citywide ministry ventures. I served as chair one year and was on the committee for annual citywide evangelistic initiatives. This association has evolved into being called Shepherd's Circle Fellowship.

9. See Ebaugh and Chafetz, "Passing It On," in *Religion and the New Immigrants*; Min and Kim, *Religions in Asian America*; Alumkal, *Asian American Evangelical Churches*.

10. Lai et al., "Chinese in Canada," 1–2, 5.

11. Yang, *Chinese Christians in America*, 10, 183, 187–98.

12. Jonathan Tan, *Asian American Theologies*, 59–60; Lai et al., "Chinese in Canada," 90, 106.

13. Guest, *God in Chinatown*, 2, 4, 7, 9; Bramadat and Seljak, *Christianity and Ethnicity*, 1–5; Fenggang Yang, *Chinese Christians in America*, 27–28.

14. Leonard et al., *Immigrant Faiths*; Yoo, *New Spiritual Homes*; Wing Chung Ng, *Chinese in Vancouver*; Chai, "Competing for the Second Generation."

15. Bramadat and Seljak, *Religion and Ethnicity*, 5, 21; Bibby, *Restless Gods*, 6–7, 9.

culture, that religious ethnic communities always facilitate healthy group cohesion, community, and social integration into mainstream society.[16]

There is often a significant amount of tension in the transmission of religious and ethnic identity from one generation to the next.[17] This research explores the tensions surrounding the differences between first and next generation members within Chinese churches.[18] A focal point in this study is the theoretical debate regarding maintaining Chinese identity versus assimilating into Canadian culture. This debate plays itself out in Chinese Christian churches in Canada, too often with adverse outcomes for some next generation Chinese Canadians from the English-speaking congregations of bicultural churches. There are enormous challenges in a Chinese faith context when a first generation takes an uncompromising posture with a second generation that has been selectively adapting to Canadian society.

In particular, this research is concerned with probing the allegation by Helen Lee of a contemporary unresolved issue referred to as the "silent exodus." The term refers to the high dropout rate of second generation English-speaking young adults from Asian North American bilingual, bicultural churches.[19] US studies indicate that from 75 to 90 percent or more of second generation Chinese and Asian young adults leave their churches,[20]

---

16. Emile Durkhiem assumes that religion plays a functional role in being a conduit into mainstream society for people on the fringes: Durkheim, *Elementary Forms of the Religious Life*. Bryan Wilson assumes that as one becomes more integrated into society, there is a move from a communally based to a societally based disposition: "Secularization and Its Discontents," in *Religion in Sociological Perspective*, 148–79.

17. Zhou, "Conflict, Coping, and Reconciliation." Zhou notes that the family relationships between OBC and LBC in Chinese immigrant families are "characterized by intense bicultural and intergenerational conflicts" due to the "different pace of acculturation" (21). The LBC "find themselves straddling two social-cultural worlds . . . which is at the core of head-on intergenerational conflicts" because of filial piety (29). Zhou argues that "social and cultural institutions" (which could include Chinese churches) help reinforce the cultural expectations of the OBC (22).

18. Additionally, my experience working with Italian churches in Canada, serving in the Mennonite Brethren denomination that only recently (late 20th century) transitioned from its German roots to the mainstream, and being present with a Latino pastoral panel in Fresno, California, (2012) have deepened my conviction that transitioning a cultural church is a common challenge with ethnic congregations.

19. Helen Lee, "Silent Exodus."

20. Esther Liu, in "Cultural Tensions," provides statistical data that Chinese churches in North America have been consistently losing 80–90 percent of their youth and young adults. Ken Fong noted that "well over 75 percent of the [LBCs] end up leaving the Chinese church . . . something is not right." Fong, "Rejuvenating Sick Bodies," in *Pursuing the Pearl*, 175. See also Cha, "Finding a Church Home," 146; Joseph Wong, "Bridging the Gap," 1–2; Cha et al., *Growing Healthy Asian American Churches*, 148. In 1986, Gail Law set a precedent in citing longitudinal data on the silent exodus, stating,

compared to 51 to 77 percent of the younger generation in Euro and multicultural Canadian church communities.[21] Finding comprehensive data[22] for non-Asian young adults in the Canadian context is not easy. This difference is between 24 and 39 percent. Primary interviews with clerics and leaders from a heterogeneous spectrum of denominations lend further support to the conclusion that there is an ongoing "silent exodus."

From a cultural and sociological perspective, the silent exodus poses the challenge of bridging familial and ethnic values into a new philosophical and cultural context. Furthermore, it raises questions about the possibility of gracefully expressing some community ideals cross-generationally and cross-culturally. Whether this can be achieved has implications for the future harmony, direction, growth, and leadership development of these faith communities and families.

As stated, the purpose of this study is to establish the facts about a silent exodus, identify some of the factors that contribute to it, and provide some recommendations to stakeholders in these communities. Anecdotal contributing factors to be explored include philosophical and theological disparity, identity issues, socio-cultural elements, intergenerational conflict, life stage transitioning, the influence of a shame culture, developmental views of autonomy and religious concepts, and a postmodern orientation.

The Contribution of the Project to Transformational Leadership

It is my intention to help transformational leaders move beyond anecdotal knowledge of why English-speaking adults have been leaving Chinese bicultural churches and to provide them with some solid qualitative research outlining key factors on why the exodus happens. This research should

---

"It has been estimated the dropout rate among [LBC] Christians for the past 40 years has been as high as 95%." Law, "Model for the American Ethnic Churches," 131.

21. *Focus on the Family*, July 2005, 17. Also see Breaux, "Mad Multi-Gen Strategy," 44. Breaux cites George Barna that there is up to a 58 percent drop in church attendance during the 20-something years. Sociologist James Penner did a study of Canadian young people between the ages of 18 and 34, commissioned by the Evangelical Fellowship of Canada's Youth and Young Adult Ministry Roundtable, and found that "only one in three Canadian young adults who attended church weekly as a child still do so today." Penner, *Hemorrhaging Faith Report*.

22. The problem with the following authors is that they don't cite where they are obtaining their data. David Kinnaman speculates that about 37 percent of those aged 18–41 in the United States are outsiders to Christianity. Kinnaman, *UnChristian*, 18. In Canada, David Sawlers speculates that "over seventy percent . . . leave by the time they reach the age of eighteen." Sawlers, *Goodbye Generation*, 6, 7.

provide insights to leaders on how to do a spiritual health check, where to focus intervention, how to equip staff, and how to empower English ministry congregations to flourish. Included in this book is a recommendation for a church model that could provide a strong governance framework for strategic planning, reduce the exodus, and achieve a transformation that will potentially hold greater promise for the future. In the words of Randy White, I'd like to "create a few onramps for others"[23] toward shalom and "to go where God is going."[24]

In broad terms, transformation starts with transformed people,[25] who can then be conduits of "transformational influence on their surroundings."[26] "Transformation [is] an ongoing process" that addresses change, "creat[es] what isn't," and builds shalom.[27] White defines *shalom* as "making things as they ought to be for people, in people and between people."[28] Therefore, "transformational relationships cannot be one-way [but] bring change to both parties."[29] Transformational leadership, then, is a God-given, servant-based call to collaboratively engage others in God's work to the end of attaining shalom.

Here are some indicators that can be used to measure the receptiveness to transformation in a bicultural Chinese church context.

Transformational Leadership

There should be a called, mature, stable transformational leader or leadership cluster motivated to conduct some focused strategic assessment and envision the possibilities.[30] Possibility leadership is a by-product of reflective leadership.[31] On the basis of reflection, there should be recognition by the leadership that where the church is today is a result of the decisions made in the past, that a change of dynamics and trends has occurred, and that it is

---

23. White, *Encounter God in the City*, 18.
24. Ibid., 104.
25. Ibid., 119.
26. Ibid., 121.
27. Ibid., 124.
28. Ibid., 126.
29. Ibid., 148–49.
30. Lewis, *Transformational Leadership*, 36, 49, 71.

31. Leadership should reflect on means to retain adults but also on how to reach others who are not being reached, as outlined in Gail Law's bicultural continuum scale (DBC model): Law, "Model for the American Ethnic Churches," in Yau, *Winning Combination*, 134–36. Reflective leadership "spend[s] time anticipating issues to adapt to." Yancey, *One Body One Spirit*, 149.

INTRODUCTION OF THE PROBLEM

now time to plant the seeds of change. There should be a willingness to engage in transformational conflict (prophetic leadership) with the board and church—which can be healthy conflict[32]—and a willingness to face areas of misunderstanding (regarding values, interests, and mission) in introducing the need for change.[33] Transformational leaders use their power to motivate others "to do more than they envision by raising awareness of different values" and thereby work toward a more preferred future.[34] Prophetic leadership speaks into the future since "the shape of some future events can be calculated from trend data."[35] Prophetic leadership "can accurately sense what is going on . . . and foresees what is likely to happen next."[36] In fact, visionary and prophetic leadership is about taking a realistic appraisal of reality, dreaming about what might be possible in moving into "uncharted territory," faithfully applying the promises of the canon, and strategically setting some "specific and attainable objectives."[37] Prophetic leadership will help to educate and prepare both the English ministry and the Chinese OBC leadership board for what's needed to progressively move ahead. Prophetic leadership provides a relevant application of biblical teaching that aids in hearing God clearly. In order to do effective biblical mission, there needs to be an appropriate, clear, consistent vision.[38]

Reconciliation and Shalom

In a bicultural church where Spirit-guided transformation is occurring, there should be greater shalom, including renewed intergenerational relationships (Eph 2:14–17). Reconciliation can be the outcome of shalom leadership; true understanding comes out of being truthful, and active listening to discover barriers—what could be called transformational communication.[39]

---

32. Consider the conflict/disagreement that Paul and Barnabas experienced in Acts 15:36–41: the positive result was inclusion and the expansion of mission.

33. Lewis, *Transformational Leadership*, 149.

34. Ibid., 21, 232.

35. Greenleaf, *Power of Servant Leadership*, 129.

36. Ibid., 124.

37. Lewis, *Transformational Leadership*, 94–95.

38. Alfred Lam, former pastor of East Toronto Chinese Baptist church in Canada, notes that an emerging frustration develops in English congregation adults over a too narrow mission and vision in the Chinese church; he states: "They are not frustrated because they want to rebel against the church or that they don't care about the church. Rather . . . because God has given them a vision for ministry that is greater than the preservation of the Chinese church . . . a dream to extend His kingdom to the ends of the world." Lam, "Backwards Way of Developing."

39. Lewis, *Transformational Leadership*, 175–76.

Equality and Empowerment

Where there are reconciled relationships between the generations, God's resources (blessing) will be released, and there will be a recognition of the potential of the collaboration that can occur with an associated independent model. One by-product of the reconciliation between generations should be the promotion of equality and empowerment, including trust in transferring the leadership to a younger generation. Good things happen when "transformational leaders develop trusting relationships"[40] and "create an environment of trust . . . by demonstrating constancy, congruency, reliability and integrity."[41] A "considerate, consultive, participative, consensual and collaborative transformational leader"[42] should aid in moving the English ministry toward structural and ministry autonomy; this autonomy would include giving the English ministry leadership the freedom to flourish. More autonomy would advance the possibility of acquiring additional culturally relevant staff (calling-based leadership) and further development of the independent structure. The English ministry would benefit from more culturally relevant mentors and coaches and increased investment in discipleship (incarnational leadership).

Inclusiveness

A by-product of shalom leadership is the development of a safe, inclusive environment for all races and diminishing segregation. There would be a growing multicultural vision that supports interaction with other nationalities and with mainstream society; greater respect and inclusiveness, regardless of culture or socio-economic status; and more intercultural and intergenerational programs to aid in building relationships. Life stage transition needs would be addressed. There would be a greater focus on relationships and less focus on pragmatic programming. As a result, there would be a greater community connection and authenticity and increased openness, honesty, and sensitivity between associated congregations. Real Christian character will produce greater empathy and supportiveness, improved communication, and more sharing.

The theological foundation for these transformational indicators might be Matthew 20:25–28:

---

40. Ibid., 233.
41. Ibid., 215.
42. Ibid., 234.

Jesus called them together and said, "You know that the rulers of the Gentiles lord it over them, and their high officials exercise authority over them. Not so with you. Instead, whoever wants to become great among you must be your servant, and whoever wants to be first must be your slave—just as the Son of Man did not come to be served, but to serve, and to give his life . . . for many." (NIV)

The transformation that is being advocated in this book will not be achieved quickly, and those who attempt it should be mindful of being journey oriented, knowing that they are not yet what they shall be, but that they are moving in the direction of experiencing greater fullness in Christ (1 John 3:2).

2

Literature Review

I can do things you cannot, you can do things I cannot; together we can do great things.

—MOTHER TERESA

IT SHOULD NOT BE overlooked that the transition in Chinese church models has some relationship to congregational life cycles in general, specifically that congregations pass through the stages of "emergence, growth, maturity, and decline."[1] Partly because they are largely composed of relatively recent immigrants, most Chinese churches in Canada seem to be in the first three life cycle stages and are thriving at this time. Many of the church models discussed here also find a place in a broader discussion on the life cycle of the ethnic church and theories on ethnic church development.[2] In reference to the growth of the Canadian Chinese church, many practitioners

---

1. Lewis, *Transformational Leadership*, 37.

2. See Min and Kim, *Religions in Asian America*, 217; Mullins, "Life-Cycle of Ethnic Churches"; Law, "Model for the American Ethnic Chinese Churches"; Gordon, *Assimilation in American Life*. Robert Ezra Park, spoke of the progressive and irreversible process of acculturation and assimilation in *Race and Culture*. Those in the Intentionally Multicultural church movement see the ethnic church as stage one on a continuum of becoming an intercultural church, moving from exclusive to inclusive. The stages are: stage 1 (an excluding church), stage 2 (a club church), stage 3 (an open church), stage 4 (an awakening church), stage 5 (a redefining church), and stage 6 (a transformed church). See Intentionally Multicultural Churches Conference, "Continuum on Becoming an Inter-Cultural Church"; Sheffield, "Becoming a Multicultural Leader," in *Multicultural Leader*, 92.

and scholars have discussed models intended to maintain the unity of the church and help churches retain their English ministries and their adult members;[3] these practitioners and scholars include David Chan,[4] Victor Lee, and Morgan Wong. Early conversations have focused on how to create an improvement in the church model used to transition English ministries in Chinese churches.[5] Ng analyzed five different church models for Chinese ministry,[6] pointing out that each model has strengths and weaknesses, and a model that works in one church may not be transferable to other churches.[7] The first, the Absorbing House Model, is monolingual and exclusive.[8] The second, the In-House Model, is often represented by a bilingual service with the English ministry as a subordinate ministry.[9] The third, the Separate House Model, is the start of a separate, parallel, dependent English ministry, with both the Chinese and the English congregation under one senior pastor and governing structure.[10] The fourth is the Autonomous House Model; Ng speaks of this model as the coexistence of different congregations within a single church environment:

> They *all* may contribute to the *umbrella church* in finance and *government*. But at the same time each group has its own pastor, lay leadership and budget. Each lives and moves in proximity but *autonomously . . . one governing board* oversee[s] the *general direction* of the church. However, each congregation has its own pastor and executive committee who make *all decisions* pertaining to its defined ministry.[11]

If this was how this model actually worked, it would be ideal; however, the italicized words point out key areas where these idealistic statements are not what English ministry clergy universally experience or report. Furthermore,

---

3. Victor Lee, "Models of Ministry in Chinese Churches." Morgan Wong comments that as the Chinese church evolves, it will be necessary to talk about church models. Wong, "NACC Church Models."

4. David Chan (a professor at the Alliance Bible Seminary in Hong Kong) is quoted in Matthew Todd's article, "Development and Transition of English Ministry," 18. The discussion centers on the kind of "house model" the Chinese church will operate with and how the growth momentum of the English-language congregation will affect the form of governance.

5. Matthews, "Poised for Impact," 14–24.

6. John L. Ng, "Church Models for Chinese Ministry," in Yau, 145–50.

7. Ibid., 145.

8. Ibid., 146.

9. Ibid., 146–47.

10. Ibid., 147.

11. Ibid., 148, emphasis added.

although the word *autonomous* is used, this model does not offer full legal-constitutional empowerment or full independence in operations, finances, ministry, or mission/vision. Ng's fifth form is the Mixed House Model; the goal in this model is "to reach out to as many culture groups as are in the community" (although Ng only includes Cantonese, Mandarin, and English Chinese in his example).[12] Not one of Ng's models grants full independence operationally or in governance to the English ministry; he recognizes "there is more than one type of Chinese church,"[13] but he doesn't articulate a future for more acculturated EM models. Jeung, however, alluded to various second generation models, including English ministries within immigrant congregations, Asian pan-ethnic congregations, Asian American-led multiethnic congregations, mega churches, and second generation hybrid congregations.[14] Jeung's first model appears to be still a dependent model, and the latter four models are disassociated from the Chinese church.

The models described by Lee, Wong, and Chan are summarized and compared in the following table.

Table 1. Church Models

Victor Lee Models of Ministry		Morgan Wong NACC Church Models		David Chan EM Develops Like a Housing Configuration	
Parental Father/ Son Model	The predominant model	**Monocultural Model**	Homogeneous OBC	**Private Residence**	One language service
Stage 1	Cultural preservation	**Bicultural Model (stages) or Tricultural Model**		**Room to Let**	EM children/youth program
Stage 2	EM started Translation	**Parent/ child Model**	Dependent	**The Duplex**	OBC leadership: "I am still the boss and call the shots"

12. Ibid., 148.
13. Ibid., 149.
14. Jeung, "Emerging Second Generation."

Parallel Model of Ministry		**Parallel Model**	Interdependent "chopstick model"	**The Hotel**	Co-existence: "You go in and everyone has their own room"
Stage 3	OBC leadership and board in control	**Multisite Model**		**The Lodge**	EM has its own place
Stage 4	CBCs' participation encouraged / lack of ownership	**Multicultural Model**		**The Town House**	Two churches under the same roof; EM has its own board.
Partnership		**Church planting**	Multicultural Monocultural Bicultural Tricultural	**The Private Residence**	EM is church planted out.
Stage 5	Structures modified				
Stage 6	Dual/multi church building model "if financially able and spiritually ready"				
The focus is on an ideal achievement of a partnership model under a shared board within an associated dependent or interdependent model—support for this is a challenge to achieve at the board and Chinese congregation level.		These options do not include a registered parallel independent model that is operationally, financially, and ministerially independent, yet still associated in some ways.		This model appears to show EM becoming independent only possibly in the last stages.	

Yang has documented that regardless of which model the immigrant Chinese leaders in a Chinese church are using, they are tenacious in trying to avoid divisions that stem from cultural differences.[15] It is recognized that "cultural heterogeneity is the most prevalent dividing factor" that OBC leadership must counter in order to uphold the unity of being one church.[16] The attempt to hold the various language groups together in the Chinese church, under various models, for as long as possible, is based on the fact that the "Chinese culture highly values harmony" and on the complementary "ideals of Christian unity"; these "mutually reinforcing" ideas are evoked to diffuse dissention.[17] This approach also reflects the tendency to run the church the way the Chinese family functions.

With increased waves of Chinese immigration and the coming of age of North American–born Chinese, the topic of church models for English ministries has garnered a great deal of attention.[18] There are a variety of models in the literature,[19] yet the long-term sustainability of English ministry congregations in Chinese churches has only recently come into question.[20] Many early studies concentrated on how to either maintain a mono-ethnic church or operate using a parallel associated dependent model, with the congregations divided along cultural lines.[21] Later there was more discussion on the move toward more autonomous models. For example, Fong

---

15. Fenggang Yang, "Tenacious Unity," 347, 350, 352.

16. Ibid., 354.

17. Ibid., 354–56. "Unity and harmony are highly valued." Yang, *Chinese Christians in America*, 171.

18. Wayne Wong's 1998 thesis on "Chinese Ministries in Greater Vancouver" represented an era of discussion when the Chinese churches in that area were still envisioning the future needs for English ministry and considering pan-Asian and multicultural models. Wong, "Current Challenges of Doing Inter-Generational Chinese Ministries," 119–21. Wong's focus then was also on CBCs as an emerging "unreached people group in Canada" (86). Now, in 2014, the Greater Vancouver area has seen the emergence of models that go beyond an associated parallel dependent English ministry model. These include The Tapestry, a multicultural intergenerational community of different ethnic groups, http://www.thetapestry.ca; Faith Werks, a multicultural church plant led by Nick Suen, http://faithwerks.org; F3C, a predominantly Asian English-speaking church planted by Ted Ng that values empowerment, authenticity, and ethnic and cultural diversity, saying, "We are willing to build a multi-ethnic pastoral team and leadership," http://f3c.ca/f3c/welcome-to-faith; and Urban Village, a church plant using the English language that wants to engage the surrounding culture and reflect the diversity in the neighborhood, http://www.urbanvillagechurch.ca.

19. Carlson, "Patterns in Development," 121–26.

20. Evans, "Impending 'Silent Exodus.'"

21. Wayne Wong, "Current Challenges," 118–20. His argument is that the choice of model depends on which "Chinese subgroup they can best reach" (119).

sees the Chinese churches transitioning through a series of models: mono-ethnic, multilingual/bicultural, LBC English, and finally multi-Asian and multiethnic kingdom communities.²²

Although practitioners may discuss multiple models,²³ most of the research has focused on five categories:

1. the retention of English speakers in Chinese mono-ethnic church models and structures

2. the retention of English speakers in parallel associated dependent church models

3. the retention of English speakers in independent church plants (pan-Asian or predominantly CBC)

4. the retention of English speakers in mainstream multicultural churches

5. the retention of English speakers in parallel associated independent church models and structures.

The following diagram illustrates the process of a mono-ethnic church model evolving into a parallel associated independent church model.²⁴

---

22. Fong, *Pursuing the Pearl*, 216. The model the author aims at is a multi-Asian, multiethnic, multi-socioeconomic, multigenerational church (95).

23. I will not deal with all possible English-speaking models (such as integration into mainstream /community church models, which represents a form of assimilation), just those that are the most common results of the development of English ministries and the most popular destinations of those who exit English ministries in Chinese churches. The survey work in this book demonstrated that CBCs who exit their churches choose the following church models, in order of preference: (1) multicultural, (2) mainstream community, (3) CBC/pan-Asian, (4) other healthier Chinese churches with associated dependent parallel English ministries.

24. It is acknowledged that there are other kinds of English-speaking Chinese churches such as first generation and 1.5 generation Chinese English-speaking congregations. However, they generally have a different history and power base than what most LBCs experience in a bicultural Chinese church. For example, they either started off as English-speaking churches (such as Lord's Peace Chapel in Vancouver, BC) or historically were launched from a Euro-based church (e.g., Church of Zion, Surrey, BC). Perhaps an entire OBC/CBC church could choose to do church together (or merge with an existing community church) using only the English language and thus helping to accommodate the second generation; however, I am unaware of many immigrant Chinese church leadership groups that have made such a move.

Figure 1. Process of Chinese church models with local-born Chinese (LBC)

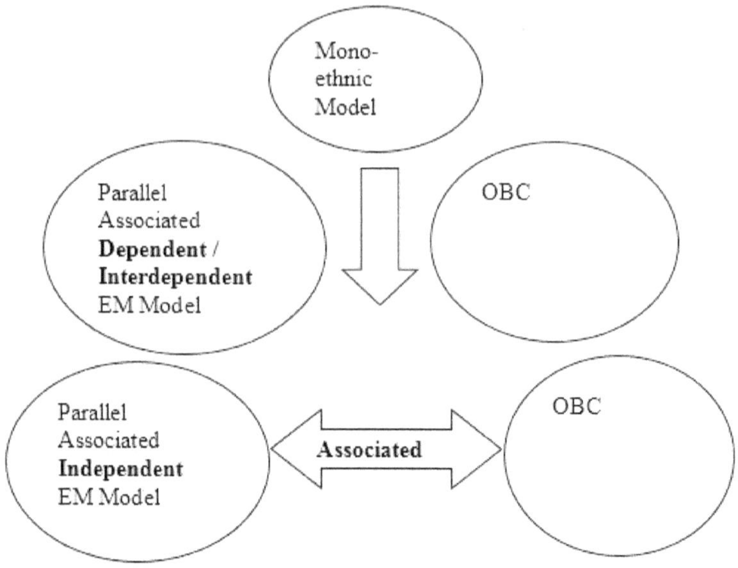

```
                    Mono-
                    ethnic
                    Model

    Parallel                        OBC
    Associated
    Dependent /
    Interdependent
    EM Model


    Parallel                        OBC
    Associated      Associated
    Independent
    EM Model
```

Literature Research toward the Retention of English Speakers in Chinese Mono-ethnic Church Models and Structures

Yancey notes that with "ministry to first-generation immigrants . . . monoracial churches . . . can be the best way to go."[25] Mono-ethnic church models exist so that Chinese can hear "Spirit-led and empowered" preaching "in their own language and culture."[26] Tsang points out that the mono-ethnic church model is more often the beginning initiative of a church plant;[27] she notes that because of the process of assimilation, that creates "cultural polarization between OBCs and CBCs," and because the Chinese community is not culturally homogeneous, she is not in favor of exclusively trying to "form more mono-ethnic, culturally homogeneous churches."[28] Clements indicated that because of the high Chinese immigration figures,[29] mono-

25. Yancey, *One Body One Spirit*, 33. Monoracial churches help avoid interpersonal conflict with other races (32), particularly those with Eurocentric values (39) and help avoid "the assimilation of minority groups' cultures by the majority group" (31).

26. Daniel L. Wong, "Toward a Theological Foundation."

27. Gladys Lee Tsang, "Churches in Ethnic Transition," 97, 120.

28. Ibid., 69–73, 56, 102.

29. Evans comments that "the Canadian Chinese-immigrant church is not

ethnic (or homogeneous) church models are necessary but should be seen as a dynamic in need of future transition.[30] Tan is open to mono-ethnic churches staying as segregated homogeneous units; historically, this model has been the status quo.[31] The value of this book to my project is that it explains how the North American Chinese church has historically evolved to keep the English congregation dependent on the Chinese-speaking leadership/congregation. The book is historical, biographical, sociopolitical, and theological. Tan indicates that the origin of segregated Chinese churches was due to historical bigotry and injustice against Chinese. The author also inadvertently admits in a couple of places[32] that some xenophobia[33] toward Caucasians exists.[34] The author favors homogeneous segregated Asian churches "primarily because of discrimination and stereotyping arising from [Asians'] physical inability to blend in with the dominant white American society."[35] However, contemporary Canada has a more egalitarian climate. Canada has legislated multiculturalism and is a cultural mosaic where pluralism[36] and cultural diversity are celebrated and protected by law. Tan sees multicultural congregations as colonial and paternalistic, something to be avoided. He explains why Asian Americans "choose to establish and maintain their own churches . . . rather than assimilating into existing white . . . churches" though they may speak the same language and share the same doctrine.[37] The main reason is that they "provide valuable social functions that help [their] ethnic communities define and sustain their unique identity and cultural traditions."[38] DeYoung et al. also concede that

---

proceeding as quickly through the usual lifecycle path, because there is a seemingly steady supply of Chinese immigrants being accepted by Canada." Evans, "Impending 'Silent Exodus,'" 183.

30. Clements, "Segregated Church." In this regard, Ley concedes that "cultural homogeneity [is] reinforced by a continuing stream of new immigrants" that buttresses a "monocultural institution." Ley, "Immigrant Church," 2006.

31. Jonathan Y. Tan, *Asian American Theologies*, 59–60.

32. Ibid., 111–33.

33. The *Oxford Desk Dictionary and Thesaurus* defines xenophobia as a "deep dislike of foreigners."

34. My book's survey also comments on concerns with xenophobia (e.g., see dropout case 24 in appendix F).

35. Tan, *Asian American Theologies*, 60.

36. Dictionary.com, s.v. "cultural pluralism."

37. Tan, *Asian American Theologies*, 59.

38. Ibid., 60. See also Fenggang Yang, "Chinese Conversion to Evangelical Christianity," 245. Yang comments on how the Chinese church has sociologically functioned to help immigrants find "belonging," "community," solace, and moral support in the development of their families.

even if racism had not been part of the Chinese experience, the move for separation exists because "culture and ethnicity are . . . central concerns."[39] This book helped sensitize me to what some Chinese may be feeling in the Canadian context: marginalized.

Lee also assumes that a mono-ethnic church model is meaningful for the Asian family as it "serves as a refuge" for "comfort, encouragement and aid," a safe liminal space, and a "place of healing" and restoration.[40] Lee indicates that opting for this model stems from the experience of feeling marginalized and distant from the cultural center of society.[41] Although Lee helped me understand the decision of Asian churches to try to retain their English congregations in dependent models, the transformational leader should not be content with sustaining a model over a long term that does not enhance the capacity of the church (the *ecclesia* which is "called out") to accomplish the mission of Christ toward a multicultural faith community.

Often, but not always,[42] churches in this kind of model are holding services in Chinese only, perhaps with translation. Sustaining this kind of model in the Chinese language is possible until the next generation is in children's ministry, at which time the children are using English in the public school system, which increases the difficulty for some children to grasp the teaching in Sunday school. As a result, English language ministry begins,[43] but, as Wayne Wong points out, "the mono-cultural identity of . . . church leaders [is the added factor in causing] alienation."[44] They may, says Ley, "draw in the wagons more closely and pretend nothing has changed."[45] However, "to bring justice mono-cultural patterns and intolerant attitudes need transformation."[46]

---

39. DeYoung et al., "Separate but Equal," in *United by Faith*, 113. The Chinese church "has been the primary means of preserving ethnic/racial identity as well as cultural transmission" (120).

40. Sang Hyun Lee, *From a Liminal Place*, 127–28.

41. Ibid., 36–37; 1–5, 29–33.

42. In the United States and Canada there are mature Chinese congregations which use English yet choose to remain a Chinese faith community.

43. Carlson, "Patterns in Development," 121. William Wong, "Establishing the Need," 1–7.

44. Wayne Wong, "Current Challenges," 18.

45. Ley, "Immigrant Church," 2068.

46. Clark, "Theology in Cultural Context," 124.

Literature Research toward the Retention of English Speakers in Parallel Associated Dependent Church Models and Structures

As youth issues and identity struggles begin to develop, the need for an English language youth worker (mentor, leader) develops. It is usually at this point that a separate English language service is suggested[47] by parents to minimize the resistance of their youth to coming to church.[48] There is a felt need to establish an English congregation (sometimes called the "Room for Rent" model).[49] Some churches may add an intermediary step by creating a translated bilingual service. Often listening to the service via earphones is hard on the ears of some youth, and they may not feel independent enough. When a separate English service is created, it is generally an experimental stage for many Chinese churches as they struggle with how to operate two congregations under the same roof. Gradually, leaders are appointed, and the English ministry becomes a department/subministry. Ley notes that the creation of a parallel dependent congregation is both a "containment strategy" and a means to reduce "strained relations [and] bridge the intergenerational gap."[50] Yuen is credited with pictorially describing English ministry as a *parallel* ministry in the Chinese church.[51] Parallel ministries exist when the church leadership is governing and ministering to the needs of more than one language/cultural congregation. Kong used the analogy of "chopsticks" to depict the parallel relationship of the English and Chinese language congregations.[52]

---

47. Ibid., 122.

48. One of the conclusions of the BC Spring Chinese Conference in 1996 was that a parallel model for English ministries was the best development to date. Wayland Wong, "Towards a Mature English Ministry." The conclusion represented the extent of palatable/tolerable models for English ministry that Chinese bicultural churches could accept.

49. This model is viewed as advantageous because it keeps the family together and helps preserve culture; also it offers opportunities for evangelism to other Chinese. Notable disadvantages are that it does not prepare for the long-term future of the English ministry, and it hinders evangelism to non-Asians. Eng, "Room for Rent." Eng credits this model description to Dr. Benjamin Shin in a lecture in the doctor of ministry Asian American program at Talbot School of Theology.

50. Ley, "Immigrant Church," 2068–69.

51. Peter Yuen, "Parallel Ministry and Oneness," 1, quoted in Daniel L. Wong, "Toward a Theological Foundation," 11.

52. Kong, "English Speaking Ministry," 1, quoted in Wong, "Toward a Theological Foundation," 11. Kong's description of why "chopsticks" represent parallel ministries in the Chinese church is worth noting here: "As Chinese, our cultural pattern is to eat with two chopsticks, while the Caucasians eat with one fork. This analogy applies to

Carlson notes that "many Chinese churches are content to remain in this stage for a long time, even decades."[53] The model of ministry is sometimes called "The Paternal (Father/Son) Model,"[54] and it reflects the hierarchical nature of filial piety and the challenge for the younger generation to mature. Pollock and Van Reken's observations with third culture peoples has a parallel with the CBC experience in that grappling with a multiplicity of cultures can have an impact on the maturing process.[55] The Chinese church wants to embrace the dual-language family under a one-roof model. Ping was an early strong advocate for parallel ministries and sharing the resources.[56] It is at this stage that the church experiences people from the English congregation bringing guests from non-Chinese backgrounds to fellowship events. The church leadership is thrust into recognizing the need to have a posture toward the variant cultures emerging in the church. It is later in this model that "the church needs to ask itself if it is serious about reaching English-speaking adults . . . some Chinese churches never move past this stage."[57] Though the English ministry in this model may be called a parallel congregation (or a "Duplex Model"),[58] it is not treated as an equal partner and is governed by the OBC leaders and board because it is a younger group, with less leadership experience.[59] A majority of authors (including myself in the past)[60] have spoken about the retention of English ministry adults in this associated parallel dependent model through various means.[61] Some

---

our church life. We find it is possible for the Caucasian churches to minister with just one language in the long run. I perceive that the Chinese churches in Canada . . . will always be running a dual (chopstick) ministry. Our healthy and steady growth is hinged upon how effectively the Chinese speaking and the English speaking complement one another in reaching and teaching different generations of Chinese through the local church."

53. Carlson, "Patterns in Development," 123.

54. Ibid., 124. Carlson notes that "most Chinese churches begin with a structure and leadership style influenced by traditional Chinese culture. Often the OBC leaders run the church in the same way as they run their family, with a top down approach . . . paternalistic leadership style."

55. Pollock and Van Reken, *Third Culture Kids*, 143.

56. Ping, "Why Stay in the Chinese Church?," 1–2.

57. Carlson, "Patterns in Development," 123.

58. Although more attention is given to English ministries and the proximity of the English and Chinese congregations helps retention of the family, the maturity of the English ministry and evangelism of non-Asians are still hindered in this parent-child model. Eng, "Duplex." Eng credits Benjamin Shin, a professor at Talbot School of Theology, for this material.

59. Ping, "Why Stay," 123–24.

60. Matthew Todd, "Embracing an Advisory Role," 12–13.

61. These means include getting them involved in serving and engaging them in

authors have tried to articulate a theology for English ministries based on how to be more spiritual or better understanding of Christians inside the dependent model.[62] Eng notes that a Triplex Model[63] can be established at this point by the creation of a third language congregation—most often Mandarin. My personal experience in such a tricultural model was that it presented challenges to the English ministry over shared resources.

The book by Branson and Martinez is important because it provides practical steps for how to transition a church to embracing more than one ethnic culture;[64] the material is highly relevant to OBC and CBC congregations, especially those in a bicultural church where ministry is to one ethnicity (Chinese). The central question of this book is "What is the call of the gospel on churches?"[65] The authors believe that God has called churches to love their neighbors—regardless of what their ethnicity or culture is; to do this requires intentional work and God's grace.[66] The authors' "purpose of writing is to help church leaders to see differently [and] to gain the skills and competencies needed for multicultural contexts."[67] They want to provide understanding and encourage commitment to "engage other cultures."[68] The book is divided into three sections: theology and context;

EM leadership, training, discipleship, and programs. Matthew Todd, "Scripture That Guides."

62. For example, Paul C. Wang wrote about retaining "intergenerational partnership" in the current associated dependent model. He suggested the Chinese church needs to focus on healthy conflict management so as to foster spiritual "unity" and make "ministry partnership" achievable (149). His work has a number of proposals and strategies to accomplish this (179–82). Wang, "Study on Cross-cultural Conflict Patterns."

63. My experience concedes Eng's point that this model still caters to the Asian crowd and creates challenges to church unity in the face of some power struggles. The "parent-child dynamic" is extended to the Mandarin ministry, and the implications are that the "maturity of the EM can be hindered." Eng, "Triplex."

64. Branson and Martinez, *Churches, Cultures and Leadership*. The authors recommend the following five steps to lead change: (1) Name and describe your current praxis. (2) Analyze your praxis to understand influences and consequences. (3) Study and reflect on Scripture and Christian history concerning your praxis and analysis. (4) Recall and discuss stories from your church and your own lives related to your praxis. (5) Discern and shape your new praxis through imagination, prayer, experiments, and commitments (45, 215).

65. Ibid., 17.

66. Ibid., 12.

67. Ibid., 13, 57.

68. Ibid., 28. The authors stated, "We believe that whenever possible churches should pursue cultural boundary crossing with neighbors and intercultural life within their congregations" (89); "we believe that it is important for churches to value and work on ethnic diversity" (92).

socio-cultural perspectives; and leadership, communication, and change. This volume supplies the transformational leader with a five-step practical theology for leading change.[69] The material recommends interactive steps for theological reflection regarding the current practice in the life and ministry of the church. I have always felt that Chinese church leaders and boards have been too busy for the kinds of reflection (reflective leadership) that are needed to bring about change in the church and community. This book is a good resource to use with leaders and laity in transitioning a congregation; the Bible studies that encourage cross-cultural local mission are practical and open-ended for contextual application; the reflection/group exercises are very practical, as are the recommended cross-cultural movies and websites. This book is a positive transitioning resource that can be utilized by transformational leaders serving Chinese bicultural churches who want to see intercultural/interracial life happening. The exercises can be used to shift Chinese churches entrenched in models that keep the English ministry dependent on the Chinese-speaking congregation and move the whole church toward an inclusive theology and practice.

Ling and Cheuk attempt to help both the Chinese and the English congregations to understand one another better and live harmoniously in an associated dependent church model.[70] The authors advocate for the English language congregation[71] and delineate the differences in the experiences of first, second, and third generation North American Chinese. The book focuses on how the Chinese church helps retain Chinese identity and is more sociological than theological.[72] I expect that young adults, by virtue of their life stage, will be working through more identity issues than people at any other life stage. Thankfully, the authors are clear that "God is the defining pillar of identity."[73] Given the maturing of English congregations, the authors ask, "What time is it in Chinese American ministries?"[74] I agree with them that it is time for "parallel ministries"[75] rather than a parent-child congregational relationship (which can be paternalistic and imposing in nature). Ling and Cheuk have pinpointed "the crucial question for the Chinese church in North America": it has to do with English ministries,

---

69. Ibid., 42–45, 215.
70. Ling and Cheuk, *Chinese Way*.
71. Ibid., 119.
72. Ibid., 19, 27, 107, 109–34, 210.
73. Ibid., 24.
74. Ibid., xviff.
75. Ibid., xviii, 206.

and it is a crisis of leadership.[76] There is a shortage and a high turnover of English ministry leaders in the Chinese church,[77] and much of the tension comes from the cultural differences between OBCs and CBCs.[78] The latter experience "the process of assimilat[ion]" quicker.[79] This book is a good resource;[80] it is refreshing that the authors advocate cross-cultural and multicultural mission that includes whatever race one's neighbors are.[81]

Wong went as far as to call for parallel ministries where the EM congregation is independent but related to the Chinese congregation, keeping both under one roof so the Chinese church remains a whole unit.[82] But Wong does not address who is really governing in that model. It is within the dependent model that OBCs have been heard to say, "One day the EM will run the church." Out of that kind of understanding, some have suggested a variation of the associated dependent model by granting the English congregation the status of being a parallel *inter*dependent[83] congregation (having a greater degree of autonomy but still connected).[84] Mak viewed

---

76. Ibid., 102.

77. One report on the English pastoral turnover in Chinese churches in the United States is Justin Der, "ABC Pastor Discouragement." Also see Kang, "Asian American Churches."

78. Ling and Cheuk, 109–34.

79. Ibid., 77.

80. Especially helpful is the authors' attempt to promote understanding between OBC and ABC/CBC Christians sharing the same faith household.

81. Ling and Cheuk, *Chinese Way*, 178, 205. The authors are correct that Chinese churches are multicultural (171), but generally within a Chinese or pan-Asian range. Here is where his promotion of theological and leadership training is needed (194).

82. Wayland Wong, "Towards a Mature English Ministry," 5. Wong noted that changing the structure in "moving toward parallel ministries" (4), "not independence but freedom to develop its own ministries," could be a viable solution for the emerging EM.

83. Where I have seen healthy interdependent CBC/OBC church models is either where the CBCs are parallel in age to the OBCs—which diffuses hierarchical relationships and generates partnership—or where the OBC leadership has been diligent in discipling the OBC congregation so that there is a parallel in spiritual development and maturity with the LBCs, who have had the advantage of spiritual resources provided in English through seminaries, conferences, workshops, and the like. Healthy OBC discipleship is a key factor here. For more on interdependent models, see "Multigenerational Households," in Cha et al., *Growing Healthy Asian American Churches*; Nakka-Cammauf and Tseng, *Asian American Christianity Reader*, 127–37.

84. Tso, "English Adult Ministry," 8. Helen Lee shares a story about an EM that was given autonomy in three areas: "finance, staffing, and ministry direction"; however, after two years, it failed because the immigrant leadership took back control. This highlights why autonomy should be total—and that can never be the case in an associated dependent model because the immigrant leadership holds the greater balance of power

the interdependent model as an ideal to achieve.⁸⁵ Wong recognized that because of the "multiple varieties of Chinese" that are attracted to the EM, a mutual/reciprocal/sharing partnership might best represent the interdependent relationship of two language-based congregations in one church.⁸⁶ There is a vision for a partnership model in theory, but, as Lee's analysis points out, drawbacks to such a model are that it "may not be very appropriate or effective [for] a multicultural, multi-racial setting"; it is a model still at risk of being dominated by a "patriarchal style of leadership," and the "English ministry is usually at a different stage of growth than the Chinese counterpart."⁸⁷ The church board (still predominantly OBC) permits the English ministry to have more ministry autonomy, but it remains legally, operationally, financially, and structurally attached. The challenge here is to give the English ministry space and freedom in ministry and mission and to have an inclusive church vision. Usually, up to this stage, the Chinese church has had a mission and vision focused mainly on the immigrant family already inside the church.⁸⁸ This focus can be problematic for some CBCs, who would like the church to be more inclusive of the multiethnic networks of Canadian-born Chinese. The potential problem for all parallel dependent or interdependent models is that although the church board may "allow for the formation of an autonomous congregation parallel with the OBC congregation . . . with its own leadership team, pastor, budget, and authority,"⁸⁹ the leadership group that legally and constitutionally sanctions the permitted power are the OBCs, and they can veto EM autonomy at their discretion. It is for reasons such as this that Ng does not see "a future in the Chinese church *as it is* [the current paradigm model] for the next generation"; two reasons for this are the Chinese churches' ethnocentric mission⁹⁰ and the

---

to veto EM direction and decisions. "Healthy Leaders, Healthy Households 1: Challenges and Models," in Cha et al., *Growing Healthy Asian American Churches*, 58–59.

85. Wing H. Mak, "Embracing the English-Speaking Ministry," 10. Mak noted that only if both the Chinese and EM made mutual efforts toward mission, trust, and accepting the diverse gifts each contributes could there be a healthy interdependent model (13).

86. Daniel L. Wong, "Toward a Theological Foundation," 11–12.

87. Victor Lee, "Models of Ministry," 3. Lee notes that "the leaders opt for a Parallel Model of Ministry as a mediating position rather than visionary progress" (2).

88. Yang has emphasized that the first generation have a Sino-focused mission (69), based on the "Chinese first" principle. Fenggang Yang, *Chinese Christians In America*, 173–75, 180, 193.

89. James A. Evans based most of his argument on this model in "Impending 'Silent Exodus,'" 184.

90. Ted Ng, "Is There a Future." Ng notes that the Chinese church has "little involvement with the church at large" and "neglects second generation mission." Ng explains that "since the mission of the Chinese church is to reach more Chinese, the

immature leadership in the English ministry due to lack of discipleship.[91] Apart from "a few rare instances," Ng says that attempts to build a healthy Chinese church with parallel interdependent congregations are something that "has been seemingly unsuccessful in Vancouver so far."[92] To be successful would require a "missional vision, beyond ethnocentrism . . . to all people,"[93] a "culture of empowerment,"[94] and "mature leadership that is willing to implement" the needed changes.[95]

Literature Research toward the Retention of English Speakers in Independent Church Plants (Pan-Asian or Predominantly CBC)

An independent model strikes at some Chinese communal cultural values and expectations on intergenerational hierarchical[96] relationships (how the church family maintains order and control). Mak considered an independent CBC church plant to be a consequence of the failure of OBC leadership, occurring because of the "sin [of] spiritual apathy to fully obey the Great Commission"; he would rather the OBC leadership "encourage a daughter church to be formed."[97] Wong points out that "Chinese people

---

English speakers are not encouraged to pursue their own natural missional strengths. Next-generation Chinese Christians find peers to be multi-ethnic and either multi or mainstream in culture. These are the people they want to reach and are prepared to reach but there is no opportunity and no place in Chinese churches for them to bring non-ethnic Chinese" (1). An additional factor is that a "glass ceiling [is created] for next generation ministry and leadership [where] next generation people who may be spiritually mature or effective leaders are passed over" (2).

91. Ibid., 2–3. The deficit in discipleship is due to things such as a programmatic (rather than a relational) approach to discipleship (2), the "lack of long-term pastors" (high turnover) (2), and "unfit leaders."

92. Ibid., 1, 3.

93. Ibid., 3.

94. Ibid. A culture of empowerment is "a church culture that is about letting each congregation find their calling, passion and mission in Christ rather than a system of control. Let congregations use their own methods of ministry while sharing the same mission and gospel. Unity in diversity and freedom of expression is needed rather than conformity to a ruling group."

95. Ibid.

96. Samuel Ling discusses the hierarchical pattern of leadership in the Chinese church in "Chinese Way," 48.

97. Wing H. Mak, "Embracing the English-Speaking Ministry," 16–17. Mak makes a clarion call for the Chinese churches to do mission in Canada to their English-speaking neighbors (18).

fear the individualism of the Canadian culture can threaten the unity of the Chinese family and so will do everything to pass on collectivism."[98] The motion to move to an independent model can also be misread as challenging "other cultural characteristics such as loyalty, obedience, respect for authority and the elders, non-competitiveness [—all aspects that] support the hierarchical social structure."[99] Yang feels that once LBCs have lost their language and culture they will likely leave the Chinese church and a pan-Asian model can be a sought option.[100] However, anecdotal reporting from CBC pastors who have pursued church plants reveals that there was initially no intention to do a church plant; typically, there was an initiative to restructure so that there could be real partnership and shared vision with the OBC congregation. When the initiative to restructure did not succeed,[101] the EM leadership began to see a church plant as being the most integral option. Evans suggested that "invest[ing] in the planting of a CBC church, independent of the OBC church and at a separate location," could curb the silent exodus.[102] However, some CBCs have opted for pan-Asian congregations that are generally an expression of the dissatisfaction of the "second generation with band-aid concessions."[103] Jeung presented a Second Generation Hybrid Model as an American trend that would address the needs of churched and unchurched second generation Asians.[104] This trend has been noted with regard to American Chinese Churches for some time.[105] Chuang has been keeping track of the more recent develop-

98. Wayne Wong, "Current Challenges," 20. Mak comments that "a pan of sand is often used to [negatively] describe individualism among Chinese people." Wing H. Mak, "Embracing the English-Speaking Ministry," 15.

99. Wong, "Current Challenges," 21.

100. Fenggang Yang, *Chinese Christians in America*, 170–71.

101. The failure was often due to factors such as an unhealthy and dysfunctional leadership culture or the inability to achieve the mission and meet the needs of the EM. This raised the desire for a new paradigm of church life that could also serve the next generation.

102. Evans, "Impending 'Silent Exodus,'" 184.

103. Tseng et al., "Second Generation and Beyond," chapter 3 of *Pulpit & Pew Research*, 24.

104. Jeung, "Emerging Second Generation." This model is attractive because of the generational, racial, cultural, and economic similarities and because of the opportunity for the EM to be autonomous operationally and in leadership development; however, the model is limited by generation and class. There is still the question of whether the choice of this model still represents a residual feeling of marginalization (The Orientalist script) and a search for identity and belongingness.

105. Peter Cha, Steve Kang, and Helen Lee have noted a church model transition that began in the "late 1990's and early 2000's" in which many new Asian American congregations were launched to help English-speaking Asian adults come to terms with

ment of next generation multi-Asian churches in North America.[106] These are "autonomous English-speaking churches that are intentionally reaching next gen-Asian Americans"; to date there are 251 in the United States and at least eight in Canada.[107] DeYoung et al. report that "once [the next generation] comes of age there is increasing evidence that [they] become engaged in more racially and ethnically diverse congregations"; language proficiency removes the need to continue in "ethnic segregation" and leads to interethnic and pan-Asian networks.[108] The pan-Asian model seems to crop up in the literature[109] as a solution to the discontent that university, early career, and married mature adults (perhaps with young families) may feel with an associated parallel dependent English congregation model. It arises for various reasons that are identified in this book; these include conflict experiences with Chinese leadership,[110] relational isolation, life stage issues not being met, the direction and vision for the English ministry not being relevant and different values (cultural polarity). Young married adults who grew up as CBCs in the church become concerned about whether their needs (given their stage of life) will be met in their churches. Furthermore, such congregations often have mature married Chinese adults who came from overseas English-speaking places or are more comfortable with the Western/Asian "feel" of the English congregation. Some come from other Chinese churches where the English ministry was less developed. Some come with their own youth, looking for a place where they can grow spiritually together. Fellowship, caring, visitation, and relational needs are a priority for them. They do not appreciate being viewed as the servants of the parents of an OBC Chinese language congregation, which was established primarily to serve the immigrants' youth. They do not want to be judged because they practice faith in culturally different ways (usually with less focus on programs, meetings, and activism). The pan-Asian model is one option, born out of a discontent with being kept systemically dependent

---

questions pertaining to identity, mission, and their faith journey. "Growing Healthy Households of God," in Cha et al., *Growing Healthy Asian American Churches*, 11. Also see Jeung, *Faithful Generations*, 63–45, 169.

106. Chuang, "Next Gen Multi-Asian Churches."

107. Ibid. Three of these pan-Asian churches are in Ontario, and five are in BC. Since 1996, this variety of church has been developing in Canada.

108. DeYoung et al., *United by Faith*, 121–22.

109. Tsang, "Churches in Ethnic Transition," 63. The pan-Asian model represents acculturation but not carte blanche assimilation.

110. They become frustrated with OBC leadership functioning as a "second-house," or senate, vetoing CBC ministry decisions on the basis of OBC values informed by a different cultural lens.

on the Chinese OBC congregational leadership, which insists on making certain key decisions for the English ministry and inadequately developing transitional plans. This dependent relationship can be the downside of filial piety—not letting people "grow up." Nature teaches that the natural propensity of development is to mature and start new families; perhaps considering a church plant is symptomatic of that, since planning a church plant is about a preferred future for ministry and the next generation of children. Options like church planting become a consideration when CBC adults feel they are second class or a minority in their churches. On the other hand, opting for an independent pan-Asian or CBC church plant seems to stem from the comfort felt with other Canadian-born Asians.[111] However, gravitating to a limited assemblage of ethnicities can still be a truncated interpretation of the Great Commission; therefore, Tso is probably correct that, as an option, the pan-Asian church is "a variation of the mono-ethnic model."[112]

Jeung's research shows why North American-born Chinese have opted for pan-Asian church plants instead of assimilating into a mainstream church.[113] Jeung notes that pan-Asian church models are a "radical break from the model of church found in ethnic-specific churches."[114] The high inflow of Chinese immigrants into the Chinese bicultural church heightens the strain between the immigrant first generation, and "later generations," which polarizes the cultural perspectives.[115] Cultural conflicts over decision-making styles, being direct in preaching, authenticity, the implications of filial piety for hierarchical authority and leadership, OBC leaders showing favoritism toward Chinese language ministry in agenda and budget allocations, OBC leaders treating the adult English ministry congregation like "an older version of youth ministries," and the lack of autonomy, resources, and status for the English ministry—all of these feed into the conclusion to start a pan-Asian congregation that does not have to "compete with the

---

111. Fenggang Yang, "Religious Diversity among the Chinese in America," in Min and Kim, *Religions in Asian America*. Continuing to practice faith with "fellow Chinese" can be a growing desire (92).

112. Tso, "English Adult Ministry," 8. Busto also suggested that a downside of pan-Asian organizations can be that "from an evangelical viewpoint they are exclusionist." Busto, "Gospel according to the Model Minority?," 182. Russell Jeung noted that although Asian pan-ethnic congregations gain autonomy in their leadership, the focus is on generational, racial, and cultural similarities, and they have limitations by generation and class. Jeung, "Emerging Second Generation."

113. Jeung, "Asian American Pan-Ethnic Formation," 215–16.

114. Jeung, "Emergence and Institutionalization of Asian American Churches," in *Faithful Generations*, 43.

115. Ibid., 54.

agenda ... [of the] bilingual church. Instead [focus can be given to] the spiritual mission of the gospel."[116]

Jeung states that "the emergence of pan-ethnic congregations does refute theories that assert that Asian ethnic congregations will assimilate after the first generation."[117] In pan-Asian church plants, solidarity is not based on a "common cultural and linguistic" background but "tends to be more symbolic in nature." There is a "feeling of connection,"[118] a social construction. The congregants share various "lifestyle affinities" values, and interests.[119] Jeung points out that "contrary to expectations [many] Chinese Americans" have not been simply moving through a "straight-line assimilation paradigm that accounts for ... acculturation."[120] Pan-Asian church plants are an outgrowth of social networks,[121] many of which began on school campuses.[122] They reflect demographic trends and generational issues. Leong argues it would be incorrect to say these Asians share homogeneous ideas and values; however, they will "reconfigure ... identities" in "individual and collective" ways.[123] The "tension between the immigrant

116. Ibid., 54–56, 58–59.
117. Ibid., 239–40.
118. Ibid., 216.
119. Ibid., 234ff. Jeung notes that these are contexts where next generation Chinese can still "affirm ethnic heritage" (228) and "ethnic-specific" observances (229). Tseng et al., *Pulpit & Pew Research*, note that these kinds of churches "develop their own hybrid spirituality by fusing elements of Confucianism, immigrant Protestantism, and various expressions of Evangelicalism" (24). They have a high Asian value on community over individualism (24) and yet reject aspects of the immigrant church such as "hierarchical notions of leadership and the rigid separation of clergy and laity" (25). Jeung, in *Faithful Generations*, notes that those attracted to pan-Asian churches typically share common "class backgrounds [and] interests," are "similar in ... professional status," and are upwardly mobile (79).
120. Jeung, *Religions in Asian America*, 218. Yang has also noted that the evolution from monolingual to bilingual to monolingual English "pattern of straight-line evolution does not apply to Chinese churches." Yang, *Chinese Christians in America*, 100.
121. Jeung, *Religions in Asian America*, 220.
122. Ibid., 230. Jeung says that pan-Asian churches draw from their former college and campus networks. Jeung, *Faithful Generations*, 43, 160. Busto notes that a high number of English-speaking next generation Chinese have participated in various Asian parachurch campus ministries (180) and contexts that "relegate ethnic difference to secondary importance." Busto, "Gospel according to the Model Minority?," 175–76. It is reasonable to assume that pan-Asian collaborative experiences in parachurch campus organizations and campus life networks provide a basis for planning later pan-Asian church plants. Jeung also points out that "those who go to college discover a different kind of faith experience and want to relive this in their churches." Jeung, "Emerging Second Generation."
123. Leong, "Asian Americans," 10–11. Yang notes LBCs are integrating multiple

and [next] generations has long been the central organizational issue for the Chinese . . . church. Cultural differences and unequal power relations [that] lead to . . . splits [can] spawn new pan-ethnic congregations."[124] The pan-Asian church plant represents those who have "differences in cultural orientation."[125] Wang noted that the initiative to start pan-Asian Canadian churches is an attempt to integrate cultural identity;[126] his research with CBCs discovered that "in spite of their western lifestyle and value system, [many] are still not perfectly comfortable in assimilating into a purely Caucasian church."[127] Because of "generational differences" and a "lack of autonomy, resources, status," and "freedom of ministry," they leave "to begin new congregations."[128] A pan-Asian church plant "attracts members who want to avoid the cultural baggage of ethnic churches . . . what we call the 'Silent Exodus.'"[129]

Literature Research toward the Retention of English Speakers in Mainstream Multicultural Churches

Lee highlighted pilgrimage as one faith response to the experience of marginality: being "ready to leave the present situation toward a God-promised goal."[130] The journey has a purpose since at the margins people may realize "the capacity to recognize others at the margin" and discover that these can be divinely creative places.[131] Jeung notes that over half of Asian English-speaking Christians go to non-Asian churches, which may include multiethnic and mega churches; in many cases, this choice is due to being "burned" in their own ethnic contexts.[132] A high percentage of ethnic churches face the issue of having to eventually address the exodus of their locally born next generations who have a desire to experience greater freedom in ministry, mission, and outreach beyond the ethnic precincts of their

---

identities. Fenggang Yang, *Chinese Christians in America*, 16, 164, 194.

124. Leong, "Asian Americans," 221.

125. Ibid., 222.

126. Paul C. Wang, "Study on Cross-Cultural Conflict Patterns," 34.

127. Ibid., 121, 4, 136.

128. Leong, "Asian Americans," 223.

129. Ibid., 232.

130. Sang Hyun Lee, "Pilgrimage and Home," 219.

131. Ibid., 222. "Pilgrims know that 'here we have no lasting city' and are willing to follow Christ to the margins that participate in Jesus' project" (223).

132. Jeung, "Emerging Second Generation."

mother church.¹³³ For example, the German-speaking Mennonite Brethren churches in Canada battled with this issue for decades, with many congregations finally concluding that if they wanted to retain their progeny, they needed to see what they could "do to reach the neighborhood and plan for the future of [their] children."¹³⁴

For these German-speaking churches, migration came to an end, and it became necessary to "re-vision church life outside the limits of the ethnic church; the German churches are some way down a path that their Chinese . . . counterparts are just contemplating"¹³⁵ Ley pointed out that the German churches made this transition by "mov[ing] towards only English language services [and] extend[ing] their settlement services outside the cultural boundaries of co-ethnics."¹³⁶ There has been little progress toward Ley's 2008 speculation that one day the immigrant Chinese church might move toward a multicultural model, although one Canadian Chinese church and one Mennonite Brethren English ministries Chinese minister are now experimenting with this model.¹³⁷ This "significant and often painful transition takes place, as the cultural cocoon falls away in the attempt to bridge social capital across group boundaries and move towards a multicultural congregation."¹³⁸

---

133. Consider the following Canadian examples: Di Giacomo, "Identity and Change"; Di Giacomo notes that Canadian Italian Pentecostal first generation immigrants have been very resistant to assimilation (104) and limited their mission to the Italian community (105). Di Giacomo documented that "the normal pattern for immigrant churches is to begin as ethnic enclaves but then, as the children and grandchildren identify more with the new world majority culture, they depart from their exclusively ethnic character, undergo transformation, and meld into the wider culture" (83). Also see Guenther, "From Isolation and Ethnic Homogeneity," 138–61.

134. Ediger, *Crossing the Divide*, 187. Ediger, in the entire book, focuses on the transitioning of an ethnic church to stay focused on the mission of Christ to reach all nations. Sara Wenger Shenk demonstrates that negotiating being an ethnic church and doing mission is a current issue with various Euro-ethnic churches: "Should the Mennonite church continue to exist?" Shenk, *Thank You for Asking*, 230–40. Also see Redekop, *Ethnicity and the Mennonite Brethren*. The author felt it was necessary to argue that "the ethnic identity [of believers] with other heritages also be affirmed" (vi). Redekop argued that "mission means the rejection of all ethnocentrism" (5) and that there is a danger in fusing ethnicity and theology because it marginalizes other ethnicities (8, 54).

135. Ley, "Immigrant Church," 2072.

136. Ibid., 2069.

137. North Shore Bethel Church and Faith Werks.

138. Ley, "Immigrant Church," 2071.

Shoemaker and Trieu argued that it is more theologically sound to move "from Chinese church to Multicultural Church."[139] Jeung indicates that the "motivation and vision" for a multiethnic church plant is generally a "reaction to [LBCs'] former work at ethnic-specific churches [and those churches' failure] to meet the needs" of LBCs.[140] The multicultural model circumvents "cultural problems in the ethnic church," such as the immigrant "mission,"[141] and "controlling resources, staff and space."[142] It draws inspiration from the eschatological "heavenly reality,"[143] the multicultural perspective of diversity,[144] and the multicultural values of "inclusivity, affirmation, authentic community,"[145] justice, and racial reconciliation.[146]

DeYoung et al. advocate for churches to move toward a more multicultural model.[147] The purpose of their book was to make a controversial case that "Christian congregations, when possible, should be multiracial."[148] The authors point out that one of the most segregated times in America is Sunday;[149] this book speaks to many CBC experiences, where the composition of the Chinese church is troubled with a "paradigm of separation."[150] They argue that the inertia that keeps Chinese churches culturally homogeneous or ethnocentric has been harmful to people in the English congregations.[151] Although the authors cite the historical reasons for the development

---

139. Shoemaker and Trieu, "Moving from Chinese Church." They make a biblical (Eph 4:4; 1 John 2:2; Gal 3:27–28; Rev 5:7–10), pragmatic, sociological, and theological argument. Preeminent examples given are: Tenth Avenue Church (Vancouver, BC), Richmond Hill Chinese Baptist Church (Toronto, ON), and Evergreen Baptist Church (Rosemead, CA).

140. Jeung, "Conclusion," in *Faithful Generations*, 148.

141. Ibid.

142. Ibid., 149.

143. Ibid.

144. Ibid., 150.

145. Ibid., 151.

146. Ibid., 154.

147. DeYoung et al., *United by Faith*.

148. Ibid., 2. The authors believe that this is what it means to be "the church of Jesus Christ" (185).

149. Ibid., 5.

150. Ibid., 122.

151. Historically, much of the push for intentionally multicultural churches appears to have come from mainstream church leadership, either by establishing multiethnic, multiracial congregations or by renting space to ethnic congregations, as Killarney Park Mennonite Brethren Church in Vancouver did. Dueck, "Bridging Cultures in the Church." It would be hard to cite a Canadian example of a Chinese church initiating a full-blown intentionally multicultural church, beyond daughtering a CBC or Mandarin

of Chinese cultural churches (chap. 7), in Canada the millions of Chinese Christians immigrating in the last several decades have remained separate from other races in congregational life in order to retain their ethnic and cultural identity—there is an eclipsed biblical theological vision in this. In Canada, there are Chinese churches founded in the late 1800s that continue to have thriving exclusive Chinese congregations—despite the multiethnic composition of their surrounding communities. Are these ethnic churches a sign of racial segregation?[152] Some would say yes, but it is difficult to envision the authors' idea of an integrated multiracial congregation[153] as there are so few examples in any Canadian city. The "healing of the nations" is one of the things Christ intended to be first evidenced in the church, a place where people might be compelled to say, "See how they love one another" (John 13:35). The authors' call for a paradigm shift is admirable, as are their call for the church to be biblically intentional and inclusive; their call to rethink what should be normative; and their call to reconsider Jesus' vision for the church to be a "house of prayer for all nations" (Isaiah 56:7). The authors seem to be dreaming of creating "heaven on earth." *United by Faith* is a risky, cutting-edge, prophetic book (looking at what the ethnic composition of churches should be). It is not that far from the vision of this book for associated independent parallel English-speaking congregations associated with Chinese churches, where the outreach and ministry would be to any ethnicity. The authors allow three exceptions for an ethnic church.[154] They concede that homogeneous ethnic churches may be appropriate for first generation immigrants,[155] but they expect that associated second generation English-speaking congregations should reach out to multiracial groups. Their book reinforces a biblical understanding that homogeneous ethnic churches in multiethnic cities should be viewed as a start but a longitudinal anomaly if sustained; it strengthens my resolve to advocate for churches to be places of worship for all people groups (Mark 11:17). However, the authors overlooked my model as a missional possibility for an ethnic church.[156] Their book advocates going from a homo-

---

ministry congregation. The core values of intentionally multicultural churches (such as impartiality to all ethnic groups, unity in diversity, commitment to discipling the nations, and representative leadership) clash with the Chinese church's focus on cultural preservation. Intentionally Multicultural Churches Conference, "Responding to the 'New Reality.'"

152. DeYoung et al., *United by Faith*, 182.
153. Ibid., 169.
154. Ibid., 143.
155. Ibid., 132.
156. We see mainstream churches sponsoring or renting to associated independent

geneous ethnic church to a full-blown multiracial church; it moves from A to C, skipping B.[157] The B option would be a transitional stage in which the Chinese mother church would partner in launching associated independent congregations.[158] The congregations would share a facility, a common history, and a sense of similarity. The entire Chinese family would still be ministered to but in associated independent flocks. Yancey points out that several types of multiracial churches are possible under the umbrella idea of multicultural churches. Surveys of CBCs have often revealed an interest in reflecting neighborhood multiracial demographics (to be a neighborhood church), what Yancey calls "demographic multiracial churches."[159]

Literature Research toward the Retention of English Speakers in Parallel Associated Independent Church Models and Structures

Tsang was an advocate for "different types of churches to suit the needs of different kinds of Chinese in Canada[160] and "diversified models of ministry."[161] She discussed four church planting models used for starting an ethnic church;[162] her description of the multi-congregational model,[163] with complete operational independence for each congregation, contains similar elements to my model of a parallel associated independent English congregation. Research material on such a model is sparse. For example, Kim and Lee talk about their discouraging experience in an Asian context, working an English congregation toward independence but being stalled

---

parallel congregations. Why can't we dream about the Chinese church adopting such a model?

157. Jumping from A to C is too abrupt and doesn't factor in the value of a B model that can serve as a transitional stage for the intergenerational and multilingual Chinese family.

158. Some Cantonese churches do this when developing a Mandarin church plant; the logistics could be similar for an English congregation.

159. Yancey, *One Body, One Spirit*, 56–58. He states, "A multiracial church is not likely to have the emphasis on Chinese culture that a predominantly Chinese church would since a multiracial church has to be mindful of cultural aspects from many different racial/ethnic groups" (32).

160. Tsang, "Churches in Ethnic Transition," 92–97.

161. Ibid., 105.

162. Ibid., 92–97.

163. Ibid., 95–97. Each congregation would be autonomous, with "no responsibility or accountability of the pastor to the church board of the other congregations" (96). The English congregation could negotiate rental costs if using the building or some other location on the property. Some mutual or joint initiatives could be negotiated; however, both congregations would be legally and operationally separate entities.

by the first generation governing board deciding that the English ministry should remain as a sub-ministry within the wider church.[164] The EM continued to be patient as they worked through the process while honoring the intergenerational relationships. Lee notes being in an associated parallel independent church using the same facility as the parent church it had come out of twelve years before. He indicated that "we were financially and operationally independent from our parent church, yet we stayed together because there was no compelling reason to leave."[165] Lee lauded the benefits of this arrangement, including partnership in educational ministry. Tso indicates these associated but independent congregations are "where the autonomy is increased and the interconnection is decreased until the two congregations are virtually two independent churches sharing a building, a common past, and a sense of affinity towards each other."[166] Tso's statement implies a process in which the handover was arbitrarily determined by the OBC leadership. Although some believe that the "Townhouse Model"[167] represents the parallel independent model, it does not—because the English ministry in that model still shares finances, staff, and resources with the Chinese congregation; it is not financially independent, nor fully operationally independent, nor is it registered as a separate legal-constitutional entity. I have come across only two churches that have embraced variations of the associated independent model.[168]

164. Kim and Lee, "Intergenerational Ministry."

165. Ibid., 30. Lee was speaking of Harvest Community Church in Hoffman Estates in Illinois.

166. Tso, "English Adult Ministry," 6–8.

167. In the Townhouse Model, the English congregation has a distinct leadership, pursues its own mission, engages in independent decision making, and is autonomous in its ministry approach. However this model is really an advanced level of the parallel dependent model in that it is operationally, financially, and ministerially connected and the congregations are still legally registered as one entity, not two separate associated churches. See Eng, "Townhouse."

168. (1) Scarborough Community Alliance Church in Ontario, http://scommac.org/about-us/leadership/staff. This church describes itself as being in an "autonomous interdependent" relationship. (2) Everygreen Baptist Church of Los Angeles, http://admin.ebcla.org/history3.php. This church, which began as a Japanese-American church, has gone completely multicultural; Facebook photos indicate it is predominantly Asian. The first associated independent congregation emerged when the English-language congregation became a separate church across the street. Fong notes that this "would later prove to be the key to evangelizing the future generations. Nearly every positive development toward becoming a cutting-edge multi-Asian / multi-ethnic ministry can be traced back to this . . . decision." Fong, *Pursuing the Pearl*, 24. Jonathan Wu states that the leaders of this church recognized that "kingdom purpose transcends ethnic heritage and cultural practices" and "created greater space and freedom for the growing . . . English-speaking congregation by moving their worship service across the street. Although these two congregations remained in close proximity to each other, this marked a watershed moment in the ethos and direction of Evergreen Baptist

Despite the fact that this model is barely explored in the literature, particularly for the Canadian context, I want to suggest that it holds a great deal of potential. Wang notes that "second generation Asians in North America [are] 'on the move' somewhere along their bicultural continuum, ranging from Chinese-ness on one end, to North American-ness or 'hybrid' culture orientation on the other."[169] Models with increasing autonomy embody the increased value placed on independence and empowerment. Cha discusses the stages that a second generation congregation goes through from dependent models to more independent models.[170] However the "associated" factor in the associated independent model I am proposing focuses on the retention of healthy long-term intergenerational ties and a form of unity in the body of Christ that honors God.[171]

The disposition of this book is toward the associated parallel independent English congregation model. To a practitioner, I would advocate making this a third, optional move for the church after the stage of a mature parallel dependent English congregation model (assuming there are cultural obstacles that don't permit an egalitarian interdependent model). I don't think that any particular church model or structure is a final solution. However, I do think that some models/structures can be more liberating (for growth, mission, and vision) since they remove barriers (such as heavy-handed top-down governance) that can limit the empowerment and autonomy of an adult English congregation. To be healthy, associated independent models also need to be informed by a biblical spirituality and maturity and centered on the development needs of those in the EM. The goal in choosing a model should not be cultural preservation but working out God's mission in the present (not one ambiguous day in the future); one should ask how the church is supporting the effort to make disciples of all nations. That is, it is important to ask questions about the ethos behind the model. To endorse this model means that those entrusted with power are seeking to empower the next generation for ministry. Wong is correct that there is a danger of the English ministry being just a clone of the parent church. However, there is also danger in thinking the solution is a model. Models exist to serve the mission.[172] Unlike Evans, who gave his exposition a despairing title,[173] I am

---

Church." Wu, "Trusting Households," 105, 101.

169. Paul C. Wang, "Study on Cross-Cultural Conflict," 65, 135.

170. Cha et al., *Growing Healthy Asian American Churches*, 151. Daniel H. Bays noted that "Chinese culture has hegemonic features." Bays, *Christianity in China*, 117. There are many reports of the oppressiveness of hegemony on CBC and ABC Christians in OBC Chinese diaspora churches.

171. Cha et al., *Growing Healthy Asian American Churches*, 151–52.

172. Hoover Wong, "Contextual or Evangelical?," 169–70.

173. Evans, "Impending 'Silent Exodus.'"

optimistic about God's sovereign use of various models in the transitions of the Chinese church and its English ministries; I see these models as means of grace. However, like a wineskin, a model has a season, and it is only as good as its spiritual content and relevant usefulness. Nevertheless, I agree with Evans that, given the current structural situation, the silent exodus "will continue unless appropriate action is taken."[174] Emerson and Smith make a solid case that "when problems are [partly] structural, they must be addressed at least in part by structural solutions."[175] I am tackling the structural element by advocating the retention of English-speaking adults from Chinese Canadian churches through associated parallel independent English congregational models, which recognize a linkage between the process of acculturation and the imperative to leverage mission.

Literature Research on Transformational Leadership and Leading Change

De Pree puts significant emphasis on the leader giving away power (enabling and empowering) and on servant leadership.[176] The leader is "one who serves" and is a "steward . . . of relationships, assets, legacy, momentum, effectiveness, civility and values."[177] De Pree views the servant leader as one who "liberate[s] people," "enables his or her followers to realize their full potential,"[178] helps "enable [people's] gifts,"[179] and is "responsible for future leadership."[180] The servant leader encourages participation and inclusiveness,[181] is respectful and mindful of beliefs[182] and covenants,[183] and "understands that relationships count more than structure."[184] The servant leader knows that people have a "right to affect [their] own destiny"[185] and the "right to appeal."[186] Servant leaders learn "to recognize the signals of

174. Ibid., 183.

175. Emerson and Smith, *Divided by Faith*, 130. They make a strong case that social structures of inequality (55, 57) create structural conditions (112) and arrangements (154) that cause poor relationships (78) and undermine positive actions (168).

176. De Pree, *Leadership Is an Art*, 11.

177. Ibid., 12–13.

178. Ibid., xxii.

179. Ibid., 10, 78.

180. Ibid., 14.

181. Ibid., 24.

182. Ibid., 26.

183. Ibid., 27, 37–38, 60–61.

184. Ibid., 28.

185. Ibid., 40.

186. Ibid., 41.

impending deterioration"[187] and look to "providing for the future . . . and growing other leaders who will look to the future beyond their own."[188] De Pree's key statement is: "The signs of outstanding leadership appear primarily among the followers. Are the followers reaching their potential?"[189] All of these good leadership practices would prevent the silent exodus and should be the substance of any model.

Schein's research[190] on transformational change shows that if a leader does not promote incremental transition in the organization during his or her tenure, it is a failure to move the organization toward the fullness of its mission; the leader cannot use the excuse "Let someone else do it"; it is a sin of omission. Schein demonstrates that there is a close link between problem solving and culture formation; groups learn particular ways of solving problems which become embedded as culture. An organization may be regressively controlled by the "founder's beliefs and values"[191] when it is in need of responding differently to a changing situation: "Culture [can] become a constraint on strategy."[192] Culture change, therefore, requires learning new ways to solve problems. Schein really is calling for more transformational reflective leadership. He describes culture as being made up of artifacts (e.g., structures), espoused values (e.g., strategies, goals, philosophies), and underlying assumptions (e.g., beliefs).[193] This theory helps explain why church culture can be difficult to change, as it represents a cluster of historic learning that has made a group successful.[194] People in churches find meaning and identity in their cultural assumptions and, therefore, can be resistant to change.[195] They are really being asked "to give up some beliefs, attitudes, values and assumptions [and] learn some new ones."[196] Schein's idea that the achievement of "goals and ideals" will fail unless internal discomfort is created should be applied to the silent exodus problem.[197] Church boards should be made uncomfortable with a reality they can change. Schein is

---

187. Ibid., 111.
188. Ibid., 129.
189. Ibid., 12.
190. Schein, *Corporate Culture Survival Guide*.
191. Ibid., 16. An application here is that we should be asking questions about inherited embedded theology and what needs to be further examined. Deliberative theology then involves careful reflection on embedded convictions to develop a more adequate way of understanding.
192. Ibid., 18.
193. Ibid., 21.
194. Ibid., 28.
195. Ibid., 35, 81.
196. Ibid., 105.
197. Ibid., 107.

realistic in saying that transformational leaders should expect "psychological . . . resistance to change [because of the] fear of loss of power."[198] Transformational leaders should understand that the stronger the organization, the more resistant it might be toward reexamination and renewal.[199] Schein provides eight helpful steps to smoothly move organization members through change and learning[200] and five characteristics[201] that all change agents should exhibit. These are essential tools for transitioning an English ministry to an associated independent model.

Kotter's leadership theory provides an eight-stage "roadmap [for] transformation, change problems, and change strategies."[202] Useful for this book is Kotter's emphasis on "creat[ing] a . . . powerful guiding coalition" that will engage other gifts to overcome tradition and apathy.[203] It is having the right people, a common goal, and trust "that can make things" change.[204] He recognizes the power of vision to inspire and direct people[205] and help them "believe that a transformation is possible."[206] Many in an EM feel overlooked, but Kotter points out that vision should not be ignoring the "long-term interests of anyone."[207] Kotter's category of transformational leadership has a prophetic quality because the leader is trying to change broken systems. Kotter makes a clear distinction between leadership and management. The silent exodus would suggest that many church leaders are just managing and not inspiring change or new directions.[208] Kotter believes that the transformational leader needs to raise the urgency level for making change.[209] Although Chinese churches have envisioned an interdependent model as an ideal, Kotter comments that "interdependencies can seriously complicate change."[210] He warns that there is always the danger of slipping back into the old cultural rut[211] and leaders should not underestimate the power of the previous culture: "When the new practices made in a transformation effort are not compatible with the relevant culture, they will always

198. Ibid., 112.
199. Ibid., 171.
200. Ibid., 115.
201. Ibid., 182.
202. Kotter, *Leading Change*, ix (see exhibit 2, 21).
203. Ibid., 6.
204. Ibid., 66.
205. Ibid., 7.
206. Ibid., 9.
207. Ibid., 73.
208. Ibid., 25–27.
209. Ibid., 44.
210. Ibid., 136.
211. Ibid., 146–47.

be subject to regression. Changes . . . can come undone even after years of effort."[212] This danger of slipping back is why a new independent EM model should have status as a separate legal entity.

Weems recognizes that "the task of leadership is change" and leaders should be "change masters."[213] Particularly relevant is the prophetic element of transformational leadership that Weems addresses; to call for a renewed vision for those who are being marginalized is giving a voice to those whose voice is being suppressed (Prov 31:8). Leadership should be seen as a channel of God's grace.[214] I want to draw from Weems's focus on the role of the leader being to discern and articulate a shared vision,[215] as I see the next few years as a pivotal period that will determine whether a paradigm shift in a church model for English ministry is permitted to happen or not. I resonate with Weems's statement that "God is always pulling us into the future with a call for an order far different from the current state of things."[216] It is the transformational leader's calling to "picture what is possible . . . a preferred future."[217] I particularly appreciated Weems's emphasis on a shared vision focused on the future that advances mission[218] and is a sign of hope.[219] Achieving this "preferred future" will require a look at the English congregation's identity in terms of its core values, history, and cultural heritage.[220] Unfortunately, Weems says very little about cultural heritage—a factor that weighs heavily in a Chinese CBC congregation. English ministry leaders would find useful Weems's recommendations to pay attention to trends and changes,[221] to listen to "feedback regarding the current situation and future needs,"[222] to pay attention to what kinds of developments are going on in the "external environment,"[223] and to "get a sense of how the community" perceives the church.[224] The EM leader and group should be sensing a "rightness" about a discerned vision and what they need to do if they are "to grow and thrive."[225]

212. Ibid., 148.
213. Weems, *Church Leadership*, ix.
214. Ibid., 1–20.
215. Ibid., 21–53.
216. Ibid., 22.
217. Ibid., 23.
218. Ibid., 26, 30.
219. Ibid., 29.
220. Ibid., 33–34.
221. Ibid., 257.
222. Ibid., 36.
223. Ibid., 37.
224. Ibid., 38.
225. Ibid., 43.

3

Context of Ministry

A great wind [of change] is blowing and that either gives you imagination or a headache.

—CATHERINE THE GREAT, 1729–96

Impact of a Segregated Homogeneous Unit Church Model: Brief Overview

It is appropriate to recognize the historical framework of Canadian Chinese diaspora churches[1] in order to understand the context English ministry congregations find themselves in the immigrant experience.[2]

    1. Diaspora churches have members that are dispersed from their country of origin and yet continue to identify with their country of origin. Bramadat and Seljak, *Religion and Ethnicity*, 16. The authors also refer to such peoples as being transnational, "living between two . . . kinds of national ethnic identities often reinforced by frequent travel between such countries" (17).

    2. Walter Brueggemann speaks of the faith in exile experience (the word *exile* being used as a *metaphor*)—many first generation immigrants feel as if they are in exile; they may "grieve their loss and express their resentful sadness about what was and now is not and will never again be"; "there is no . . . old family place . . . [but a sense of] rootlessness." Brueggemann warns that "the danger in exile is to become so preoccupied with self that one cannot get outside one's self to rethink, reimagine, and redescribe larger reality. Self-preoccupation seldom yields energy, courage, or freedom." It is through exemplar cross-cultural lives in Scripture (such as Joseph, Esther, and Daniel) that Christians can discover how to live more "freely, dangerously, and tenaciously in a

Sociologically, first generation Chinese Christians are mindful of not living in their country of origin; this "plays a major role in promoting a sense of solidarity and identity"[3] in the establishment of Chinese churches. Jeung notes that Chinese churches "have established ethnic solidarity around transnational[4] and cultural ties."[5] The immigrant church has fulfilled both a spiritual and a sociological function in the process of doing outreach.[6] By creating ethnic churches "Christian immigrants are able to utilize a well-established infrastructure [such as an existing denomination that the ethnic church can join] that facilitates integration."[7] Ebaugh and Chafetz have noted that immigrant congregations additionally function as community centers that help with resettlement and cultural preservation.[8]

Ley undertook a "comparative study of [immigrant] Chinese, Korean and German Christian churches in Greater Vancouver"[9] to determine if there were similar experiences.[10] Ley concluded that immigrant churches become a "hub in which relations of trust and compatibility generate bonding social capital; from this base a [variety] of social services is provided ... aiding co-ethnic members to adapt to their new conditions."[11] He found some

---

world where faith does not have its own way." Faced with the threat of "assimilation into the dominant culture [these biblical figures] do not forget who they are, with whom they belong, nor the God whom they serve ... [they are living] a life of endless negotiation." The stunning characters in these narratives are indeed "bilingual," knowing the speech of the empire and being willing to use it, but never forgetting the cadences of their "mother tongue." Brueggemann, "Preaching to Exiles," 4, 5, 10, 11.

3. Bramadat and Seljak, "Toward a New Story," in *Religion and Ethnicity*, 229. See also DeVries et al., *Asian Religions*, 9. The authors point out that "ethnically defined religious organizations have several secular functions besides satisfying religious needs of their members." These functions include providing a cultural context to meet social needs, providing "a venue for immigrants to reaffirm their ethnic identity" opening opportunities for service, and providing a place "to attain high-status positions, that might be difficult for them to achieve in Canadian society at large." Furthermore, "they provide an avenue for promoting ethnic consciousness [in the] second and third generations where their ancestral roots lay."

4. Transnationalism is defined as feeling a belongingness to two or more cultures. Dennis, *Biculturalism*, 83.

5. Jeung, *Faithful Generations*, 17.

6. Rah, "Holistic Evangelism," in *Next Evangelism*, 177.

7. Ibid., 231. However, they may remain separate from mainstream churches even if they share an affiliation in the same denomination.

8. Helen Rose Ebaugh and Janet Saltzman Chafetz, "Structural Adaptations in Immigrant Congregations," *Sociology of Religion*, 61:2, (2000): 135, 145, 149–50.

9. Ley, "Immigrant Church," 2058.

10. Ibid., 2072.

11. Ibid., 2057.

similarities with "various immigrant trajectories"; these churches initially function as a "community and spiritual center,"[12] providing "settlement services"[13] and "practical helps,"[14] "primarily to co-ethnics . . . during the immigrant phase."[15] However, these churches are prone to "internal conformity and the exclusion of outsiders."[16] Outreach is directed only to "new co-ethnic immigrants."[17] These churches see "their community in co-ethnic terms . . . [and have a] limited capacity to reach outside the ethnic bubble . . . current immigrant churches are rarely neighborhood based."[18] Jeung mentions that Chinese churches believe that "major denominations and mainstream congregations would treat Asians . . . differently or simply neglect them," so they retain group cultural boundaries for the purpose of reaching co-ethnics and preserving cultural heritage and values for future generations.[19]

This helps to explain why Chinese churches appear to have a disposition toward a homogeneous unit[20] church model that has been inherited in various structural configurations.[21] Most of the early Chinese churches were established by individual and denominational home missionary efforts to reach and assimilate the Chinese.[22] In conjunction with positive changes in Canadian policy and the adoption of multiculturalism (1971), many of

12. Ibid., 2062.
13. Ibid., 2063.
14. Ibid., 2065.
15. Ibid., 2066.
16. Ibid., 2058.
17. Ibid., 2066.
18. Ibid., 2067.
19. Jeung, *Faithful Generations*, 40.
20. The term "Homogeneous Unity Principle" has a history. Donald A. McGavran, founder of the church growth movement, discussed this church growth model in his book *Bridges of God*, published in 1955. His book "shaped the view of the church's mission regarding growth," so churches provided ways where people could become Christians without crossing racial barriers. However, one should ask if this is learned from the life of Christ or if he worked and advocated for mission outside of this theory. Barro, "Unity and Diversity." DeYoung et al. discuss the work of Wagner and McGavran in encouraging the development of "uniracial congregations," contending they are more "socially relevant and biblically based." These church growth theorists did not advise attempting to develop "multiracial congregations." DeYoung et al., "Separate but Equal," in *United by Faith*, 123–25.
21. Yang notes that Chinese churches opt for independent status or less centralized denominations. Fenggang Yang, *Chinese Christians in America*, 33, 63, 126–31, 189.
22. One can access various denominational records to investigate this, but one volume that makes the point is by Jiwu Wang, *"His Dominion" and the "Yellow Peril"*, especially 9–68. Also see Joyce Chan, *Rediscover the Fading Memories*, 20, 21–64.

the "old Caucasian denominational missions . . . turned over their work to their Chinese congregations"; from this time forward, "many self-managed Chinese churches came into being."[23] One can grasp that there are theological justifications for a mono-ethnic church as a logical starting point ("Jerusalem" in Acts 1:8), with the intention to expand the ethnic sphere of mission ("to the ends of the earth," Acts 1:8). The stated intention of this approach is to ensure that each ethnic entity (tribe, nation, people, and people group) has an opportunity to clearly hear the good news in its own language and in its own cultural context.[24] This approach helps make the gospel more accessible by taking into account the worldview of the hearers. Furthermore, it removes some cultural obstacles while bringing clarity to communication of the gospel. Consider the fact that the gospel was first brought to the Jews by Jews (Rom 1:16: "first for the Jew, then for the Gentile"; Acts 14:1: "as usual into the Jewish synagogue"). When Chinese immigrant churches are established, they are successful, in part, because of cultural coherence in the communication of the gospel.[25] However, the perpetual insistence on this model after many decades of existence, especially in Chinese diaspora churches,[26] can over time develop some problematic dynamics for the unity

23. Yu, "Christianity as a Chinese Belief," 239. Yu notes that "the rise of self-managed churches . . . indicate[d] that Christianity had changed from an external assimilating force into a project of the Chinese churches . . . These churches became Chinese ethnic churches [with a] Chinese belief system. This historical transformation is a major factor behind the growth of Christianity in the Chinese community" (240). Jeung similarly attributed the development of independent and segregated Chinese churches in the United States to a reaction to cultural imperialism of white home (local) missionaries and discriminatory laws; he suggested that discrimination and declining denominational support led to the development of autonomous Chinese churches. Jeung, *Faithful Generations*, 18–21. Yang concurs that mission churches had limited success because of "missionaries' racist [and] paternalistic attitudes." Fenggang Yang, *Chinese Christians in America*, 38.

24. Orville B. Jenkins, "People Groups." Jenkins notes that "this is consistent with the earlier popular mission strategy of church starting by the 'homogeneous unit' principle. That is, people can respond and a church can be started best in a context of one ethnic identity where the people share a common worldview, social structure, and decision-making patterns and personal relationships."

25. Guenther points out that "despite Chinese Christian's distribution and involvement in various Canadian-based denominations, common ethnic ties remain a powerful bond reflecting the strong commitment to community that is part of Chinese culture." Guenther, "Ethnicity and Evangelical Protestants," 380.

26. Douglas Todd, "Immigrants' Religions." Todd cites the work of Baker and DeVries in *Asian Religions* as evidence that "Asian immigrants are segregating based on religion, as well as language and ethnicity." He expresses concern "that many immigrants are leaning on religion to strengthen their threatened Asian identities, leading to less creative interaction with broad Canadian culture and values." He indicates that "the same is true among Asian immigrants who are Christian, including 26% of Chinese

of the church across all ethnic and cultural barriers (Gal 2:11–14; 3:1–3, 28). To see the Chinese diaspora church as existing solely to preserve group culture and identity and to defend against assimilation diverges from the Great Commission.[27] Those CBCs on the path to acculturation into mainstream society will most likely feel this acutely.[28]

Too often there is very little place in a mono-ethnic church model for culturally assimilating second or third generation English-speaking adults because the model squeezes out cultural diversity.[29] There can be an un-

---

newcomers. With only a few exceptions, most Asian Christians choose their churches in BC along ethnic lines. There are 110 BC Christian congregations exclusively serving Chinese people (providing services in Mandarin and Cantonese and sometimes English)." Todd notes in his article that "BC Chinese churches began as a way to assimilate Chinese immigrants to Canada, but their new function has increasingly become 'solidifying the Chinese identity.'" Todd asks if this is entirely a good thing.

27. Guenther comments that the issue of "cultural differences between generations [occurs] as gradual integration into Canadian culture takes place. The first generation immigrants often have the most difficulty . . . adjusting . . . and therefore may feel the cultural transitions as a loss of identity." Guenther, "Ethnicity and Evangelical Protestants," 382. See also Tan's proposal "that the church [is] experienced by the migrant generation as a place where they [can] continue to be Chinese [in] . . . language and culture, and . . . find refuge from 'mainstream society'" (52). Any threat to this leads to a defensive posture regarding the church's mission and vision because the church is seen as helping to "sustain . . . Chinese identities." Joshua Weichong Tan, "Cross, Culture, Confusion," 52.

28. The majority immigrant power group, by applying pressure to retain language, culture and traditions, "frequently threatens to jeopardize their relationship with the second and third generation Canadian-born younger Chinese, who have become thoroughly familiar with the English language and Canadian culture through school and work, and often wish to shed an exclusive Chinese identity. Congregations that are slow to adjust often lose a significant proportion of their young people. Inter-generational tensions are sometimes escalated further when the Chinese cultural value of giving honor and respect to the elderly and to community leaders collides with the more individualistic and democratic North American values accepted by the youth." Guenther, "Ethnicity and Evangelical Protestants," 382. Bramadat and Seljak note that "[those] born in Canada to immigrant parents from China are raised in a far more individualistic social milieu than traditional Chinese society. Because these children are raised in Canada they often come to expect more freedom from family expectations than do their parents [or] grandparents." Bramadat and Seljak, "Chinese in Canada," in *Religion and Ethnicity*, 106.

29. Overmyer notes that "there are tensions within some of these religious groups between generations." Dan Overmyer, "Concluding Comments," DeVries et al., *Asian Religions*, 280. See also Dennis, *Biculturalism*. It is noted that the bicultural person who visibly takes on acculturation—visible attributes of mainstream society—may be viewed negatively. Johnstone, "Chinese Churches Thrive," 4–5. The problem was just as prominent in 2002 when Johnstone interviewed leaders in the BC Chinese community who admitted that "reaching Canadian-born Chinese [was] one of the challenges presently facing the church. Raised as Canadians, most second and third generation Chinese find

healthy concern over people bringing multiethnic friendship networks into the church for fear that it will diminish the ethnic identity of the church. The church should recognize the slow transition of cultural assimilation, respect the pace, and not dodge the primary theological and sociological reasons why adjustment happens and why it can be necessary and healthy.

Mono-ethnic churches, over time, can project a prejudicial witness to the community. It has been commented that 11:00 a.m. Sunday is one of the most segregated times of the week in North America.[30] More embarrassing yet is that historically some Christians have tried to establish a theological defense for mono-ethnic churches and racial segregation on various grounds,[31] to "legitimize . . . ideology via theology."[32] Some of the historical theological justification for keeping racial groups worshiping with "their own race" has tended to follow an aberrant theology that puts emphasis on differences between the races as being equally important to what the Scripture proclaims concerning the unity of the human race, reconciliation in Christ, and restoration of human fellowship.[33] One can falsely conclude that the story of the tower of Babel (Gen 11) reinforces the separation of racial groups. This interpretation overlooks the fact that the Babel story does not contain the last word concerning divine intentions with humanity. The last word concerning the divine intentions appears in the vision of the New Jerusalem of Revelation 21 and the command (Jer 29:5–7; Matt 6:10) to begin to build here and now along the lines of this new world-city. Others have misinterpreted Paul's words from either the KJV or NASB that God has "determined the boundaries of the habitations of men" (Acts17:26) to keep people of different races apart. Christ came to break down the walls between the races and integrate redeemed humanity into one body (Eph 2:11–22).[34]

It is a poignant reality that, parallel to the history of the growth of the Canadian Chinese church, many Chinese were the object of discrimination,[35] most blatantly represented by various restrictive immigra-

---

a large culture and language gap in relating to first generation churches . . . many potential young leaders are drifting away uninterested in perpetuating the churches they were raised in. 'As a result of our failure to reach out to these people the last 30 to 40 years, our English speaking congregations are still mainly 30-and-under,' . . . pointing to a lack of second and third generation Chinese in these congregations."

30. Mathabane, "Taking the Measure of American Racism."

31. Ham et al., "Are Black People," 99–103.

32. Verkuyl, *Break Down the Walls*.

33. Erickson, "Universality of Humanity," in *Christian Theology*, 542.

34. Matsuoka, "Stone That Cries Out," in *Out of Silence*, 85–120.

35. Bramadat and Seljak, *Religion and Ethnicity*, 90, 94, 102, 107, 224. Jiwu Wang discusses Chinese Christians historically encountering Sino-phobia, Anglo clergy

tion policies that remained in force until the 1960s.[36] It is not surprising, therefore, that most of the early Chinese churches developed somewhat segregated from mainstream Canadian society.[37] The growth of the Chinese church has been born out of a thorny history with mainstream Canadians in which for decades Chinese were "denied full participation [causing them to] segregate themselves from the rest of Canadian society."[38] The first Chinatowns were a form of "residential segregation [for] mutual protection," and Chinese churches began in such contexts.[39] Often "located in the heart of Chinatowns, the churches had almost no contact with the mainstream"[40] church community—which explains a disconnect some had with the de-

---

ethno-cultural prejudices, and a Protestant mindset favoring assimilation; it was difficult to establish a relationship of mutual trust with white ministers when denominational and clergy initiatives contained an ethnocentric tone of cultural superiority, nationalistic sentiments, and a push toward cultural conformity. Jiwu Wang, *"His Dominion" and the "Yellow Peril,"* 87, 2, 4, 67, 90, 95, 144.

36. Jiwu Wang notes that between the mid-nineteenth century and 1967 the experience of Chinese Canadians was "characterized by legal restriction, cultural prejudice, and public hostility." Chinese were marginalized by the discriminatory practices of the 1885 head tax, 1923 Chinese Exclusion Act, and 1950 amendments to restrict Asian immigrants, which they were finally able to move past with the establishment of the universal point system in 1967. Wang, *"His Dominion" and the "Yellow Peril,"* 9, 12, 52, 69–72. Also see Wing Chung Ng, *Chinese in Vancouver*, 17, 130, 143; and Guenther, "Ethnicity and Evangelical Protestants," 378–79. Lai et al. note that some resistance to cultural assimilation has been because due to "prejudice and discrimination . . . they found it impossible to join mainstream Canadian society." Lai et al., "Chinese in Canada." DeVries et al. note that it is a sad commentary that British Columbia took until 1947–52 to "remove the ethnic voting barrier." DeVries et al., *Asian Religions*, 4.

37. Jiwu Wang notes that part of the segregated nature of the Chinese church "was to maintain their autonomy and cultural identity" Wang, *"His Dominion" and the "Yellow Peril,"* 67. The Chinese church "was part of immigrant heritage . . . In the church immigrants could relive their homeland experience. Their ethnic sensibilities . . . [were] reinforced by exclusive sermons" (133). The Chinese clergy, then, often saw their role as supporting group ethnicity (134). Given this, it's not surprising that CBCs in English congregations experienced conflict with the Chinese leadership. CBCs are going through acculturation to the mainstream while many OBCs were vicariously using the church to strengthen their community-ethnic identity (137). The groups are pulling in two different directions.

38. Jiwu Wang notes that historically mainstream denominational missions and Chinese church planting in Canada were guided by a nationalistic vision of "His Dominion," which implied a definition of Canadian culture as a homogeneous Anglo-Saxon culture; this formed the basis for relations with the Chinese. The segregation of Chinese churches was a move "to defend ethnic solidarity" Wang, *"His Dominion" and the "Yellow Peril,"* 7, 31. Norman R. Yetman notes similar discrimination and antipathy to Chinese immigrants in the United States. Yetman, "Historical Perspectives," 117–18.

39. Jiwu Wang, *"His Dominion" and the "Yellow Peril,"* 55.

40. Ibid., 138.

nominations they were linked with. The phenomenon of Chinese churches dividing along ethnic lines has been partly a xenophobic response to a history of marginalization from mainstream Canadians. The growth of Chinese churches also had a historical impetus from the desire to avoid subtle forms of Anglo ethnocentrism, or the imposition of non-Chinese cultural standards that were historically a part of mainstream Caucasian churches. Historically, mainstream Christians were not a loud enough voice in regards to "fair treatment, justice and fair play for the Chinese."[41] The self-management of Chinese churches helped promote cultural cohesion (Chinese distinctiveness) and the growth of Christianity;[42] out of this soil developed many of the early English ministries congregations. In the western Canadian context, the growth of Chinese churches was accelerated by waves of immigration,[43] the student movement of the 1970s,[44] the transfer of Hong Kong back to China in 1997,[45] and the new waves of immigration out of China.[46] Accompanying this influx[47] has been the "exponential growth" of the English congregations in Chinese churches since 1980.[48] However, the de facto segregation of Chinese churches from the mainstream persists in some variant version of a homogeneous unit model—English ministry congregational experiences are an extension of this dynamic.[49] Some of the survey participants quoted in this book[50] reported that internal diversity

41. Ibid., 72, 102.

42. Yu, "Christianity as a Chinese Belief," 245.

43. Jiwu Wang, *"His Dominion" and the "Yellow Peril,"* 83, 85. Also see: Yu, "Christianity as a Chinese Belief," 234, 235–37; Fenggang Yang, *Chinese Christians in America*, 39–41.

44. Ling, "Perplexities of Chinese Christian Communities," in *Chinese Way*, 96–97. Mennonite Brethren Herald, "We Are in the Same Family."

45. Guenther, "Ethnicity and Evangelical Protestants," 379.

46. Ling, "Perplexities of Chinese Christian Communities," in *Chinese Way*, 101ff. Fenggang Yang, *Chinese Christians*, 84.

47. Gail Law, noted that the "1960's and 1970's [were] a time of unprecedented growth" for Chinese churches in North America. Law, "Model for the American Ethnic Churches," 131.

48. Paul C. Wang, "Study on Cross-Cultural Conflict," iii.

49. Jiwu Wang notes some of the history of English ministries in the 1920s, and later in the period between 1940–1960, and that initially even CBC Christians were "not welcomed in white community." Historically into the 1960s English ministry congregations were a compassionate response for "many young Chinese Christians felt they did not belong to either the Chinese community or the larger society . . . discrimination always affected . . . Chinese Christians." Wang, *"His Dominion" and the "Yellow Peril,"* 110, 139, 138.

50. See appendix D, "Dropout Data"; appendix F, "Remain-In Data"; chapter 6, "Findings and Results."

or cultural heterogeneity can be perceived as an impediment to the cohesion of an ethnic church that is trying to preserve cultural practices and traditions.[51] One can perceive why movement of the English congregation toward multiculturalism could be perceived as a threat to maintaining the ethnic identity of the Chinese church.[52] Wong has pointed out the tension between OBCs and CBCs over the question of either preserving Chinese culture or integrating into Canadian culture:

> [One] conclusion . . . drawn from the history of Chinese people [in BC] that may provide insight to the possible causes of the cultural conflicts within Chinese families and churches [is] the past history of exploitation and prejudice towards Chinese [which] may explain why the past and present generation of Chinese parents have both prejudices towards Caucasians and the instinctual desire to "protect" their children from what they perceive as the negative influence of Canadian culture.[53]

Friedman's family systems theory states that "if a church . . . is part of an ethnic group, general anxiety in that 'extended' system can escalate anxiety over specific issues in the various . . . congregational groupings."[54] Studies have shown that an anxious insistence on imposing cultural homogeneity fails to provide the quality of spiritual life CBCs are seeking within

---

51. See Bramadat and Seljak, "Toward a New Story," in *Religion and Ethnicity*, 227–28. Jiwu Wang discusses how segregation has served to help Chinese churches maintain their cultural heritage and in turn use their ethno-cultural identity to help unite their people. He also notes that sociological conflict theory "suggests that conflict between a dominant and a minority ethnic group will produce internal solidarity in the minority group." Wang, *"His Dominion" and the "Yellow Peril,"* 127, 131, 148. David Ley found that "greater cultural diversity is consistently associated with lower levels of social capital, especially in terms of interpersonal trust." Ley, "Immigrant Church," 2067.

52. One should not overlook the fact that Chinese transnational immigrants coming out of Hong Kong and China have been a part of a country with a colonial and xenophobic history. The national aspirations of China are xenophobic and Sinocentric. Given China's history with foreign imperialists, including the humiliation and loss of control of their country, this is scarcely surprising. It is reasonable to assume the transference of such sentiments to some of the Canadian Chinese immigrant churches, and this may factor into the posture against assimilation. K. K. Chan, "Christianity in China." For a look at China's xenophobic history and the church, see Philip Jenkins, *Next Christendom*, 87; Bays, *New History of Christianity*, 14–15, 17, 20; Bays, *Christianity in China*, 117, 163; Uhalley and Wu, *China and Christianity*; Aikman, *Jesus in Beijing*, 30, 36–37, 42. Aikman points out that the Great Wall of China is in some sense a metaphor for China's xenophobia.

53. Wayne Wong, "Current Challenges," 6.

54. Friedman, *Generation to Generation*, 204.

their faith communities.⁵⁵ Popular articles by CBCs also confirm this concern.⁵⁶ Various international reports reveal that some next generation congregations in Chinese churches in other countries are encountering similar issues.⁵⁷

I want to acknowledge that there have been a number of efforts by people within these contexts and by faith-based organizations⁵⁸ to address this problem, with a goal to liberate those within the model. Many are op-

---

55. Ebaugh and Chafetz point out that "in general it appears that congregations that focus most strongly on recreating ethnic ambience of the old country are most likely to alienate" the next English-speaking generations. Ebaugh and Chafetz, *Religion and the New Immigrants*, 119; also see 133. Intergenerational strains and conflicts that contribute to the alienation and estrangement of the second generation are also partly due to the immigrant adults' "self-imposed segregation from other ethnic groups" (129) and the English congregation being "denied meaningful participation and access to authority roles to which they think they are entitled" (130).

56. Esther Yuen notes that many CBC adults experience "feeling alienated in the struggle between assimilation and cultural preservation." Her article is a call for transformation of Chinese Canadian bicultural churches. Yuen, "Mass Exodus."

57. For Australia, see Hor, "Reforming Church." For the United States, see Lim and Quek, "Silent Exodus." The silent exodus has also been noted as a problem with other Asian churches in Western contexts (e.g., Korean, Filipino). Henry Lu, general director of Chinese Overseas Christian Mission, expressed concern about second generation Chinese growing up in Europe, where language and cultural barriers are a challenge to integration, creating intercultural and intergenerational conflict in the church. Lu states that "it has been observed that many second-generation young adults are alienated from the first-generation immigrant churches and are leaving them in a quiet and silent exodus . . . very few Chinese churches are ministering to this strategically important group." Lu, silent exodus discussion, *Link*, 2011. In my communications with other international English ministry pastors in Chinese churches in the UK and Nordic countries such as Sweden, they have anecdotally confirmed there is a concern with the exodus of second generation Christians in those churches; one can reasonably conjecture that this is an issue in all of the over twenty countries (CCCOWE data) where Chinese diaspora churches have been planted.

58. For example, City in Focus was a part of promoting the vision of *Project Contempo* with local pastors and leaders of the Chinese churches via Dr. Clement Yeung, the national president of the Canadian Chinese Christian Business and Professional Association. The project recognizes that young adult CBCs are "much closer to the mainstream of society than many of their parents and church leaders. Because of their advanced training and professionalism, it is very difficult for them to overlook the mediocrity and inconsistencies in the Chinese churches. Also most of the pastors are not from the North American backgrounds finding it difficult if not possible to bridge the cultural gap." This initiative has been an attempt to "reach out to Canadian born Chinese young career people"; it has been an innovative way of tackling the exodus of Chinese young adults and provide a "better support system" in helping them "see the relevance of their faith in real life." Project Contempo has been intended to be a "national movement among young career people across Canada." Clement Yeung, "Project Contempo," 2005.

timistic that those in English ministry congregations in Chinese churches will reach their mission potential. However, it is important to examine the root causes of why English-speaking adults exit and critically review the role the leadership in the Chinese churches can play to transform the situation. This book project will attempt to point to a way in which English ministry congregations can be more sustainable, be transformed, experience greater integration, and expand mission initiatives. This project will provide some recommendations toward the retention of English-speaking adults in Chinese bicultural churches and a reduction of the silent exodus through transformational leadership approaches.

Understanding How English Ministries Were Bequeathed the Prevalent Associated Dependent Model

English ministries in Chinese churches cannot be understood without understanding this model as a derivative of a historical transformation, a result of what Yu describes as "Christianity changing from a western religion into a Chinese belief."[59] The creation of an English ministries congregation is both a sociological process and a transitional "God thing" (a redemptive work of God).[60] However, there are many life stages such a congregation must pass through if it is to survive and flourish in the long run.[61] English ministries congregations begin with the recognition that there is a cultural and linguistic difference emerging within the church. Ley has documented that "the first and deepest challenge to the immigrant church comes from . . . its own second generation of Canadian-born members."[62] They object "to tradition, to hierarchical and formal social relations, and . . . use of the mother tongue."[63] Subsequently "the challenge of difference pricks the

---

59. Yu, "Christianity as a Chinese Belief," 245. Also see Kwai Hang Ng, "Seeking the Christian Tutelage." Ng discusses how Chinese immigrants, through their churches, blend Chinese culture and Christianity.

60. God has a vested interest in the preservation of his called-out ones. I am of the conviction that the human inspiration for transitional church family models is in fact a providential gift. This conviction is based on an understanding that "God is continually involved with [his creation and] directs [it] to fulfill his purposes." Grudem, *Systematic Theology*, 315; see also 320–21, 171–72. I am of the persuasion that "God [has] intended it for good to accomplish . . . the saving of many lives" (Gen 50:20).

61. Matthew Todd, "Development and Transition," 16–18.

62. Ley, "Immigrant Church," 2068. Fenggang Yang also cites the issue of second generation LBCs pushing for "the immigrant church to give up original language and ethnic values in favor of English and [North] American values." Fenggang Yang, *Chinese Christians in America*, 95; also see 32.

63. Ley, "Immigrant Church," 2068.

ethnic bubble, originating from the acculturation and suburbanization of the second generation."[64] Lee has pointed out that "later generations often feel alienated both from their parents' first-generation church" and from mainstream society, when really the "household of God" should be a place where the next generations should be accepted for who they are.[65]

The English congregations didn't choose or get a democratic vote for the associated dependent model they function in. It was arranged for them by the OBC congregation with Confucian-based cultural assumptions and expectations. Tan presents a case study of a Chinese church with a maturing English ministry where the whole church met to discuss the church's core values and preferred future. When it was made known by the OBC leadership that being Chinese was "a core value" and "defining characteristic" of the church's identity and "ministry direction,"[66] many maturing EM people and leaders left. They would not accept the non-inclusive focus on cultural perpetuation[67] rather than an inclusive mission to the multicultural neighborhood community.[68] The different expectations produced a crisis "over [the] church's identity (e.g., being a 'Christian Canadian Chinese church' versus being a 'Chinese Christian Canadian church')[69] and future."[70]

Nature demonstrates that in order to mature, one must not remain in a dependent parent-child relationship.[71] Continually framing an inter-congregational relationship in dependent terms limits authenticity, growth, leadership development, and mission to associated networks.[72] Policies

64. Ibid., 2071.

65. Sang Hyun Lee, "Pilgrimage and Home," 225. Although this work focuses on the English-speaking second generation in Asian/Korean churches, the cultural dynamics are similar.

66. Joshua Weichong Tan, "Cross, Culture, Confusion," 2.

67. Ibid., 30.

68. Ibid., 35. The CBC's in this study were not comfortable with a "delocalized" mission focus (53).

69. Ibid., 35.

70. Ibid., 30.

71. Over half of the participants surveyed for this book were from western Canadian Chinese churches that were in a mature life stage category. Ten percent of the churches were over one hundred years old; 6.66 percent were fifty to ninety-nine years old; 33.33 percent were thirty to fifty years old; and 46.66 percent were between sixteen and thirty years old. This makes the challenge of vision and the dropout rate of English-speaking adults more disconcerting.

72. The research findings in this book show that the majority exit in the young adulthood stage of life, with some leaving as late as mid-life. Evelyn and James Whitehead say that the young adult period is a stage when there is an egalitarian quest for mutuality, teamwork, and cooperation and a desire to "commit to . . . concrete affiliations and partnerships." Whitehead and Whitehead, *Christian Life Patterns*, 81, 83. Being kept in

to retain the old order ("old wineskins," Matt 9:17) are the flaw that keeps decision making for the English ministry subject to control by the OBC leadership.[73] Reform is needed so that leadership in English ministries is not undermined (a factor in clergy turnover[74]). As I will point out later, after many decades of planting Chinese churches in western Canada, there is still a dramatic exit of English adults going on. Of the many English ministries congregations in Chinese churches in the Greater Vancouver area today, there are scores that have been unsuccessful in developing fully mature, equal partner, associate interdependent congregations.[75] The majority continue to experience a momentous dropout around the university and young adult career stage. Another concern is that many denominations are not looking closely into this debacle even though the silent exodus represents a considerable loss of human resources. The exodus frequently is solely attributed to the exiting CBCs' own identity problem rather than seeing it as the end result of negative experiences that include disempowerment and a lack of value on cultural diversity. Tan has identified that "different generations of Chinese-Canadians" attach to and negotiate "their Chinese, Canadian and Christian identities" uniquely;[76] they imagine different kinds of faith

---

a dependent relationship inhibits this. My research also shows that there is a smaller group who exit in the mid-life adult stage. The Whiteheads say that this is a reflective time when adults reassess commitments (113) and "desire [to take on] responsibility [and] assume leadership" (114). They want to use their influence to create a better future (121). However, "when no [or limited] access to religious leadership is provided for maturing adults their religious maturation can be stunted—by the church" (137), contributing to stagnation (147). Leadership that will not "let go [of] control . . . retards the development of the next generation of ministers" (149).

73. Tseng et al. say that in the United States "tensions revolve around" dysfunctional religious practices and modeling in the immigrant church and "cultural differences in the styles and philosophies of church leadership [and] control." Tseng et al., *Pulpit & Pew Research*, 24.

74. James Andrew Evans notes that there is also a "parallel exodus of English ministry pastors and leaders" from Chinese churches and that many CBC seminarians are repulsed by the idea of serving under the hierarchical model of OBC leadership and therefore choose not to serve in Chinese churches. Evans, "Impending 'Silent Exodus,'" 166, 169, 171. Evans asks a question of interest to this book: "How can the CBC congregation [the OBC board] attract and retain leaders in its congregation?" (172). The fact is that English ministries will be in dire straits without leaders.

75. Marcus Tso asks, "If a healthy, well-established congregation is supposed to be multigenerational, where are the mature English speaking adults (and seniors!) in our English congregations?" Tso, "English Adult Ministry," 6. Wayland Wong says that many EM's have not gotten beyond doing youth ministry because "the Chinese orientation has rendered some churches ineffective in reaching English speaking Chinese." Wayland Wong, "Immigration and the Church—Opportunities and Dangers," *About Face*, February 1985, quoted in Gladys Lee Tsang, "Churches in Ethnic Transition."

76. Joshua Weichong Tan, "Cross, Culture, Confusion," 3–4. Yang has also noted

communities and desirable futures.[77] English ministry leaders may aspire to having a more independent congregation or a church plant, focusing on "the Great Commission . . . outreach, missions, evangelism"[78] and expanding into the multicultural community.[79] They can have this vision because CBCs' "sense of community include[s] Canadian peers, Canadian families of their own, and Canadian futures."[80]

A further aspect of the problem is the perceived favoring of OBC leaders over CBC adult leaders where relationships are based on hierarchal cultural values. This Confucian-based system has shaped intergenerational relationships.[81] Some parachurch organizations have formally recognized the problem;[82] volumes[83] have been written on this matter and the recognition that the OBC senior leaders are the gatekeepers for change. Is there a way to move beyond this impasse and address the silent exodus at its roots? How can the potential of English ministries be harnessed to ensure that such faith communities are transforming for the better?

The Current and Transformational Hopes for the Project

This project recognizes that English language congregations in Chinese churches have their beginnings in youth ministries. English ministries, as I am using the term here, refers specifically to services and ministries provided by ethnic churches in a second language—English. An English ministry finds its entry point in trying to meet the needs of the next generation among families in the church. Its ministry target is youth and young adults raised in the church. It attempts to be relevant to Canadian raised Chinese, whose distinct life experiences are different from the experiences of their parents and the experiences of people from the mainstream culture. Eventually, two

---

that even marginal LBCs "regard themselves as Chinese and feel Chinese in their hearts. Their primordial Chinese identity mostly comes from consanguine or lineal ties." Fenggang Yang, *Chinese Christians in America*, 169.

77. Tan, "Cross, Culture, Confusion," 5–6, 22, 24.

78. Ibid., 19.

79. Ibid., 20, 52–53.

80. Ibid., 55.

81. Yang has made the case that with first generation Chinese immigrants "Confucian tradition is often seen as synonymous with Chinese culture." Fenggang Yang, *Chinese Christians in America*, 44; see also 47–48, 51, 94, 147–56, 161, 199. The challenge comes when religion and culture are indiscriminately fused.

82. For example: Chinese Coordination Center of World Evangelism—USA and Canada, Conference on the Challenges and Future of English Ministries.

83. Foundational books are Min, *Second Generation*; Yep et al., *Following Jesus*.

related congregations are established under one roof to meet the needs of both; they are seen as two ministries but one church. These CBC ministries then proceed to develop CBC leadership. Over time, the English services begin to attract anyone comfortable in English, including CBCs, overseas-born Chinese (OBCs), and even people from non-Chinese backgrounds. As the ministry grows, it draws in young adults and families, which necessitates a broader pastoral response. If the life stage of this ministry is not eclipsed, it invariably becomes intergenerational, intercultural/cross-cultural/interracial, and mature—all characteristics that this project would like to affirm. Such congregations have their own unique collective character; most have a dual cultural identity and have learned to adjust to living in a bicultural context. Common denominators for such congregations are language (English) and the Christian canon. Two issues identified with these English language congregations are high pastoral turnover[84] and the substantial exodus of the English-speaking adults who attend them. These issues threaten to destabilize the mission possibilities of the English language congregations and their potential for reaching the congregants' networks (which are multiracial and multicultural), as well as CBC generations. The question is how to minimize or eliminate these losses and promote the longevity of the mission of English language congregations associated with bicultural churches.

On the basis of the feedback from the qualitative research in this study, it would appear that there are problems with many Chinese bicultural churches' "destiny vision" for their English ministries congregations: Where are these English ministries headed—what is their "port of destination"? The vision for the Chinese bicultural church comes from the OBC lead pastor, the overall governing board, and the Chinese congregation, the majority of whom are not culturally CBC or from the English congregation. Hence, in order for a vision for the whole church to truly include the English language congregation, equal representation and input from the adult leadership in the English congregation need to be included in the conversation. "Can two walk together except they be agreed?" (Amos 3:3). Most English language congregations in Chinese churches were established to accommodate the second generation; in many cases, little thought was put into where the ministry to this demographic group might be headed. When the English ministry congregation was started, parents focused on their immediate need to see their youth become Christians, grow in character, stay in school, and keep out of trouble, but five to fifteen years down the road,

---

84. Hor points out that this is often because of different values and different paradigms for ministry; the English pastor can conceive of being missional with an English-speaking congregation differently than the Chinese leadership in a Chinese church. Hor, "Reforming Church."

the same group starts maturing, and degrees of cultural polarity become evident. (CBCs are being Westernized through the educational system, the media, intermarriage, and other channels.) At this point, the question arises of whether the vision for the English ministry includes a biblical foundation for mission (Matt 28:19). As well, the CBCs are maturing into Christians who want a say in where the OBC leadership wants to take them. In some of this project's survey research with dropouts from Chinese English ministries, people have reported that they left because there was no vision in the church for the future of the English ministries congregation—other than being an appendage (extra) ministry or a youth/young adult ministry. Once they realized this would remain a limited, culturally irrelevant ministry, bound to a future in a church that they could not see themselves in, they exited from that particular Chinese church.

The silent exodus does not have to take place. One place to begin remedying the problem is to take a close look at factors that cause people to leave; review the mission, model, and governance of the English congregation; and establish a long-term, bigger-picture vision for the Chinese church that will include and embrace the English ministry congregation—as an equal partner—with all of its cultural differences.[85]

At this point, the predominant model for an English congregation in a Chinese church still expects and requires systemic dependence on the Chinese-speaking congregation. I am recommending that this model needs to transition to a more egalitarian structure. One question to ask is: Does this dependent model reflect kingdom values or the values of a colony? Do Christians confuse colonizing with kingdomizing? I will provide some definitions.

Colonizing

A colony (often a people of one nationality, race, or culture) is generally a closed community that is intentional in existing as a separate subculture. Colonies are known for their resistance to incremental assimilation and insistence on cultural preservation through initiatives taken to remain separate. The term has often been associated with ethnic ghettos and has a negative history in association with China's foreign treaties system with the practice of overseas expatriates living in compounds. The experience of being colonized is often associated with negative feelings because it is *imposed*; the colony may make decisions which impact those of other cultures in the

---

85. Many mainstream Canadian churches help launch ethnic churches using precisely this model.

surrounding area, but the key decisions are made in a closed, restrictive structure. Those in surrounding cultures are never invited to become citizens of the colony. There are many lessons to learn here.

Kingdomizing

This term stems from a theological understanding that "the earth is the Lord's and everything in it" (Ps 24:1). It also reflects a recovery of the gospel and of the Abrahamic covenant ("All nations of the earth will be blessed through him," Gen 18:18). It reflects a recognition that those within the kingdom are called to extend themselves, be outward looking, and invite others who are culturally different to join the kingdom and become equal citizens. The circle of embrace is to be inclusive. God is interested in the whole world, and his guidance is intended to bring his followers into the bigger dimension of his kingdom that includes all ethnicities.

Why might reflection on these two models matter to a Chinese bicultural church? One answer is to encourage bicultural churches to recognize the preeminence of Christ's mission. The dominant predisposition of any church can be toward colonizing or kingdomizing. It's important for churches to recognize the multiethnic/multicultural masterpiece Christ intends the body of Christ to be.[86] Understanding what God wants can open up new possibilities and opportunities that should compel any church to move from colonizing to kingdomizing. If English-speaking adults are leaving Chinese churches (as this research substantiates that a majority do), there are many losses, one of which is the failure to tap into their potential for the mission of the church. For example, CBCs have a unique ability to reach other CBCs and Asians, either on the campus or in the marketplace. They understand their struggles, values, and particular issues. The majority of those in English ministries in Chinese churches are bilingual as well as bicultural. Their ability to relate to two cultures holds significant potential for the mission of the local church, for community service, and for short-term missions to China to teach English. Chinese English ministry congregations are in a unique position to participate in Canadian evangelism (especially among the large number of immigrants from China and Asia) and in the current shifts in world evangelism. The Chinese are one of the five largest unreached people groups in the world. The emerging generations in Chinese bicultural churches are quite willing to go to places where Caucasian believers experience barriers.

---

86. The New Testament shows the church was to become a collective of many different cultures and nations: Acts 6:1; 11:20; 1 Cor 12:13; Gal 3:28; Rev 5:9; 7:9.

One of the top three ethnic groups immigrating into Canada is Chinese and South East Asians.[87] The fastest growing North American churches (church plants) are Chinese[88] and Asian, yet some of the highest dropout rates are found in Chinese and Asian churches' English ministries.[89] This research helps answer why. It recommends transformational leadership initiatives and a church model modification that will not only assist in "closing the back door" but will also assist in inclusively "opening the front door."

How this Project Might Transform a Particular Aspect of Christian Ministry

The vision of this inquiry is to promote transformation of English ministries in bicultural Chinese churches. Transforming English ministries would first require transforming the maturity, mission, and vision of leaders in English ministries and empowering them (legally-constitutionally, operationally, financially, ministerially, and structurally) to be relevant and inclusive. This project can also potentially transform various Chinese church leadership groups, giving them greater openness to doing ministry and mission associatively and independently. I anticipate that presenting an associated independent model to leaders of a Chinese church will provoke an assessment of how they share power, of their existing church model/structure, and of their focus of mission. Are they promoting the empowerment and mission of the English ministries, and are they promoting good stewardship of the gifts and holistic calling of the English congregation? Is there an unhampered future for the English ministries congregation in policy, structure, and practice, so that the members of that congregation can freely act to carry out Jesus' Great Commission to the nations?

To begin implementing this model will require a change in the training of the English ministries leadership. It will require hiring a transformational leader with executive/lead pastor potential for the EM. The new

---

87. Citizenship and Immigration Canada, "Annual Report to Parliament on Immigration, 2012," 19. Bramadat and Seljak note that over 25 percent of Chinese immigrants become adherents of Christianity in Canada. Bramadat and Seljak, "Chinese in Canada," *Religion and Ethnicity*, 104.

88. Jonathan Y. Tan, 62–63. Bramadat and Seljak comment that "minority religious traditions in Canada are not assimilating in any unequivocal unidirectional manner to an allegedly neutral rational culture"; as a result, I suspect that there is going to be a long future for the Chinese church in coming to terms with the dynamic growth of its English ministry. Bramadat and Seljak, "Toward a New Story about Religion and Ethnicity," in *Religion and Ethnicity*, 225.

89. DeYoung et al., *United by Faith*, 127.

model will require a transformation of strategy and a transformation of how the Chinese and English congregations work together—in association but independently. The training material for understanding and implementing this new model will include some of the theology that is found in chapter 4. With a model that empowers EM self-governance and encourages transformational leadership (calling-based leadership, shalom leadership, reflective leadership, servant leadership, prophetic leadership), I am persuaded that the mission potential of an English ministry will be revitalized, extended, and, by God's grace, sustained. At a minimum, I expect that exposure to this project could cause some ministry development and ministry strategy initiatives to be amended toward greater fairness in response to the English congregation's adults' concerns.

I anticipate that a proposal for significant change and a call for a paradigm shift in the Chinese church model are going to make many in the leadership and Chinese congregation uncomfortable. However, remaining silent won't reduce the problem of the exodus. It is my hope that this project raises the level of awareness of a more liberating and inclusive church model and addresses some of the systemic and structural causes of the silent exodus.

4

The Biblical and Theological Basis

> We now know that human transformation does not happen through didacticism or through excessive certitude, but through the playful entertainment of another scripting of reality that may subvert the old given text and its interpretation and lead to the embrace of an alternative text and its redescription of reality.
>
> —WALTER BRUEGGEMANN, *CADENCES OF HOME*

ADDRESSING THE SILENT EXODUS and promoting the development of a parallel independent congregation model in Chinese bicultural churches is intended to advance the fulfillment of Jesus' Great Commission. In Chinese bicultural churches, the networks of the English congregations tend to be more heterogeneous and multiethnic than those of the OBC congregations. For this reason, bicultural Chinese churches have unrealized potential to reach their communities (the nations) through their English congregations. But what if the resistance toward egalitarianism and the associated parallel independent congregation model creates a barrier that makes it more difficult for the English congregation to bring in other races? The question might be Is Jesus' Great Commission—reaching "all nations"—applicable to ethnic churches?

An emerging area of study has been in the interrelationship between religion and ethnicity.[1] The literature indicates that a major motivation for

---

1. Min and Kim, *Religions in Asian America*; Bramadat and Seljak, *Religion and Ethnicity*.

immigrants to create or join congregations composed of fellow immigrants is to share their ethnic backgrounds, "traditions, customs, and languages" and transmit their ethnicity to the next generation.[2] In other words, there is a vested interest in maintaining a cultural context different from that of the broader intercultural/multicultural society/denomination the church is in. I have spent a good deal of research and ministry time thinking about the question of incremental assimilation versus rigid preservation of a distinctive cultural identity for ethnic churches, about the question of the role religious organizations play in endorsing either assimilation or cultural preservation. Members of ethnic churches in Canada opt to practice their faith in a manner that preserves ethnic identity, or they take an approach that allows incremental, selective adaptation to Canadian culture. While many laud the fact that Canada no longer espouses an assimilationist model for its immigrants, there can be an assumption that immigrant churches are going to be comfortable with practicing *carte blanche* multiculturalism. There is plenty of research available that points out that these churches experience a significant amount of tension in the transmission of their religious and ethnic identity to the next generation.[3] My observation has been that ethnic churches tend to be very successful in reaching immigrants of their own ethnicity. For that I am thankful. It is obvious that an ethnic church will be especially effective in evangelizing unbelievers that belong to its ethnic group (its homogeneous unit). One could think of ethnic churches as mid-wives who help first generation Christians with cultural transition and the transmission of faith. They also try to do a good job of nurturing early faith in their second generation. For example, English language congregations in Chinese churches have been established to "keep their kids" and to transmit faith and Chinese culture. The problem is that for a high percentage of these churches, the immigrant group expects the emerging English language congregations to follow its example in mission, reaching out exclusively to one race, to the same immigrant group—even though the English congregations have wider social networks.

Churches (of any ethnicity) can function partly as cultural societies. Now the question is Because there are ethnic churches that may have such a vested interest in preserving and reproducing their cultural traditions, customs, and language, does Jesus' Great Commission to "go and make disciples of *all nations*" (Matt 28:19) apply to cultural churches? Are ethnic churches "off the hook," so to speak, from participating in, initiating,

---

2. Ebaugh and Chafetz, "Chinese Gospel Church," in *Religion and the New Immigrants*, 180ff.

3. See, e.g., Guest, *God in Chinatown*; Ediger, *Crossing the Divide*. One example in this book is remain-in case 28 in appendix F.

and commissioning cross-cultural, multiethnic, and multiracial outreach, mission, and evangelism? Are they off the hook from establishing parallel associated but independent English congregations that are autonomous in mission?

I find it meaningful to remind myself how Christ started the new era of the church. It was with a more inclusive idea about who the new family of God would embrace.[4] Every human being bears the image of God and, therefore, is eternally valuable to him (Gen 1:27).[5] Every race was precious enough for the Creator of the universe to give his only Son to die (John 3:16). It is wise to embrace the Lord's opinion and the priority he puts on "the world." One of the features of human fallenness/brokenness can be an inability to grasp the scope of who the new spiritual family includes—redeemed people from every nation. In the Old Testament, the Jews frequently seemed to struggle with keeping the faith as an ethnic faith, but God intended them to be a "light to the nations" (Isaiah 42:6). Certainly there is evidence of non-Jews coming to faith, but there is a lot of scriptural evidence that God had to also judge the people of Israel, in part because of their treatment of foreigners (e.g., Malachi 3:1–5, Zechariah 7:10–14). When the Christian church first got started, it was an ethnic church, and there is evidence that many Christian Jews continued to struggle with including people of other ethnic backgrounds (Acts 15). One of the early tensions in the Christian Jewish community was with other Jews who were culturally different. The local-born Jews were having a problem with overseas-born Jews. In the early church, "Grecian" Jews were overlooked in the distribution of food; these "Grecians" looked like Jews but were bicultural,

---

4. My theology also comes from examples in Scripture of the Lord incorporating multiethnic peoples into the family of God. These include Ruth, a Moabite (Ruth 1:4), Rahab, a Canaanite (Josh 6:22–23), Uriah the Hittite (2 Sam 11:3), a Roman (Matt 8:5), a Greek (Mark 7:24–30), and many Samaritans (John 4:39–42). The book of Acts focuses on the spread of the gospel to the world—from one ethnic group to another (Acts 17). Christ's Great Commission and his heart for the ethnic groups of the world is very clear (Matt 28:19; Mark 16:15). Second, my theology for harmonious multiethnic living comes from Paul's teachings, including Gal 3:26–28: "You are all sons of God through faith in Christ Jesus, for all of you who were baptized into Christ have clothed yourselves with Christ. There is neither Jew nor Greek, slave nor free [poor or rich], male nor female, for you are all one in Christ Jesus." In advocating for parallel independent congregations, it is important to also focus on what Christians hold in common: "There is one body and one spirit—just as you were called to one hope when you were called—one Lord, one faith, one baptism; one God and Father of all, who is over all and through all and in all. But to each one of us grace has been given as Christ apportioned it" (Eph 4:4–7).

5. Grudem comments that "this has profound implications for our conduct towards others [that every culture and] race deserve equal dignity and rights." Grudem, *Systematic Theology*, 450.

part of the Jewish Diaspora (Acts 6:1).—Luke points out that they were "Jews from every nation (Acts 2:5).[6] The first generation of Christian Jews also struggled with cultural/racial biases over other Christian Jews taking the gospel to different people groups. Peter struggled with the Holy Spirit over associating with those not of his race—Cornelius (of the Italian Regiment) and other Gentiles (Acts 10:9–48); the impression is that he would have preferred segregation (Acts 11; Gal 2:11–13), but in obeying the Holy Spirit, he witnessed the outpouring of God's presence. Peter said, "I now realize how true it is that God does not show favoritism but accepts men from every nation who fear him and do what is right . . . Jesus Christ . . . is Lord of all" (Acts 10:34). Luke noted the criticism Peter received from the Christian-Jewish ethnic church for focusing gospel initiatives outside the Jewish race and culture (Acts 11). Jewish believers' obedience in sharing the Good News sparked a multiracial/multicultural church in Antioch (Acts 11:19–21). Peter had to "revision and rethink [his] theological paradigm" and make a shift.[7]

Three Observations

The Lord Gave the Great Commission to an Ethnic Group of Jewish Men

Jesus said, "Go into all the world and preach the good news to *all* creation" (Mark 16:15). Jesus' followers were to begin among their own ethnicity, but they weren't to stop there; they were to reach out to "Jerusalem . . . Judea . . . Samaria . . . the uttermost part of the earth" (Acts 1:8.) Despite the fact that Jesus had clearly laid out the logic of the gospel—that it was to be spread to every nation—too many in the first generation Jerusalem Christian-Jewish church were reluctant to be inclusive of other nationalities in evangelism. Many (not all) didn't show a lot of enthusiasm for reaching other races/cultures with the gospel.

---

6. Some CBCs have expressed that their experience with some OBC leaders has some similarities to this story.

7. Ray S. Anderson, "Praxis of the Spirit as Liberation for Ministry," in *The Soul of Ministry: Forming Leaders for God's People* (Louisville, KY: Westminster John Knox Press, 1997), 118.

The Lord Specifically Intervened to Call Out Individuals of the First Generation Ethnic Church

If it wasn't for God's direct intervention (e.g., Peter's vision, Paul's calling), one wonders how long it would have taken for the early church to be mobilized to do world evangelism. However, two persecutions (40 AD and 70 AD) forcibly scattered Jewish Christians from Jerusalem to geographical areas that were more multiethnic.[8] Paul especially found himself challenging people of his own ethnicity about their sin in keeping the gospel ethnic instead of offering it to people of other ethnicities. Paul knew his ultimate identity as a citizen of heaven was greater than his ethnic background (Phil 3:20). On more than one occasion, Paul felt compelled to tell the church that the Lord had made all of the redeemed into one family: "[Jesus] has made the two one and has destroyed the barrier, the dividing wall of hostility" (Eph 2:13–14); "His purpose was to create in himself one new man out of the two, thus making peace and in this one body to reconcile both of them to God through the cross, by which he put to death their hostility" (Eph 2:15–17); "The Gentiles are heirs, together with Israel, members together of one body, sharers together in the promise of Christ Jesus" (Eph 3:6); "We will in all things grow up into him who is the Head, that is Christ. From him the whole body, joined and held together . . . grows and builds itself up in love" (Eph 4:15–16). Paul found himself having to challenge those of his own ethnicity for showing prejudice in evangelism and even for giving different treatment to Christians who did not share the Jewish ethnicity (Gal 1:7–10, 2:11–16). He challenged Peter for behaving as if one race were better than another and for dividing the church (Gal 2:13). This second-class treatment of Gentile Christians (withdrawal/separation during fellowship and hospitality) was basically canceling out all that Peter and Paul had preached to people who were of a different ethnicity—that the gospel was for all ethnicities/cultures/races and that all would become equal in the family of God. Paul did not hesitate to label the second-class treatment of other Christian ethnicities as hypocritical and out of line with the gospel and would not let even Peter go unchallenged on this issue. Paul had to remind the Jewish ethnic church that "there is neither Jew nor Greek . . . for you are all one in Christ Jesus" (Gal 3:28). Jesus spoke of others not yet reached with the gospel and of bringing them together into one flock (John 10:16). Paul taught that the body of Christ was to be racially and culturally diverse ("whether Jews or Greeks," 1 Corinthians 12–13), and that for the Christian to have feelings

---

8. Earle E. Cairns, "To the Jew First," in *Christianity Through the Centuries: A History of the Christian Church* (Grand Rapids, MI: Zondervan Publishing House, 1981), 56, 58.

of ethnic superiority is a sin (Phil 2:1–8). In the Bible God is never found affirming racial (ethnic or cultural) segregation, only religious segregation: "Let us do good to all people, especially to those who belong to the family of believers" (Gal 6:10). It is true that Paul was mindful of his ethnicity as a starting point in evangelism ("to the Jew first," Acts 19:8–10, 26:20), but he didn't stop there, taking the gospel to those culturally removed. Heaven will be multiracial and multicultural (Rev 7:9), and one day all cultures will bow before Christ (Eph 1:10; Phil 2:6–11).

In light of this clear biblical teaching, ethnic churches should be seen as beginnings and not the end of God's vision for his church. Here's the real question: If Christ commanded his Christian-Jewish ethnic followers to make disciples of all nations, how can any Christian individual or church be exempt from the Great Commission today? The development of associated independent parallel English-speaking congregations is one optional step toward fulfilling Christ's mission.

The Gospel Moved from Being an Ethnic Enclave to Crossing Cultural and Ethnic Boundaries

If Christians want to know what they are supposed to be doing, sometimes it helps to see a vision of where they are going. The Apostle John provides a picture of the whole family of God singing before the living God Almighty—a group of worshipers "from every tribe and language and people and nation standing before the throne and in front of the Lamb" (Rev 5:9–10; 7:9). How can heaven be so racially diverse? In part, the people of God are diverse because of the obedience of Christian leaders in every generation to go out of their comfort zones to reach others who are racially, ethnically, and culturally diverse. The will of God is that all of the redeemed would be one on earth as they will be in heaven (John 17:22). Isaiah said that the desire of God for his church is that it be a "house of prayer for all nations" (Isaiah 56:7). When Jesus used Isaiah's quote, the religious leaders feared Christ—they didn't want the nations to worship with them, and so they looked for a way to kill Jesus and his mission (Mark 11:17–18).

How can people who are heavily invested in their cultural identity be brought to a place where they will begin to invest in cross-cultural/intercultural outreach? The place to begin is to do a good job of theologically teaching people that God loves the world—not just their own ethnicities but every nation. They need to grasp the reality that their present and eternal identities are to be found in this multiethnic global family of God. For this reason, church leaders should make certain that their church's mission (expressed in its statement of faith[9]) is biblically based on the Great Commission. It is one thing to talk about these truths and yet another to put them into practice. Church leaders should then ask if their churches are comfortable with multicultural expressions within their particular contexts.

Scripture shows clearly what the new spiritual family of Christ is supposed to look like.[10] Today Christianity is no longer identified strictly with its historic first-century ethnicity.[11] Christianity is a global faith family. Out of many ethnicities and races, God has created a new multiethnic nation (1 Pet 2:9), the family of God. Christians are called to obey the Lord in this area, work for unity in the body of Christ, and advance Christ's kingdom beyond barriers of race and culture.

Since the kingdom of God is to be multiracial, then no ethnic church can relinquish its responsibility to obey Jesus' Great Commission to reach "all nations" (Matt 28:19). In fact, in bicultural Chinese churches—those that have English-speaking congregations—the capacity for evangelism may be even greater because of the members' transnational and multicultural social networks. There is a parallel between CBCs and Timothy, who was bicultural, a hybrid, successfully doing mission among two cultures, Jewish and Gentile (Acts 16:1–5; 1 Tim 1:3). One of the significant ways a bicultural church can carry out Jesus' Great Commission is to release, resource, bless, and affirm its English congregation to do mission in ways that are authentic for that congregation. One way to release, resource, bless, and affirm the English congregation to do mission is to make it an associated independent parallel congregation. As wonderful as the Chinese cultural heritage may be, I hope that every Chinese Christian church has a greater mission for its English congregation than just "keeping our kids with us" and "transmitting our ethnicity" to the next generation. When leaders in Chinese churches see the Holy One face to face (Rev 22:4; 2 Cor 5:10), they will be made keenly aware of whether they have obeyed the heart of God in mission; their "work will be shown for what it is," whether its foundations were in Christ (1 Cor 3:12–13; 2 Cor 5:10; Rom 2:6–11; 14:10, 12; Rev 20:12, 15). An English ministry needs a spiritual vision rooted in Christ's mission. The networks of an English congregation in a Chinese church tend

---

9. Many Chinese churches say in the statements of faith on their websites that they value spreading the gospel and missions. Many of them are in multicultural communities, but the ethnic composition of their churches is not representative of their communities.

10. 1 Tim 5:1–2; 2 Cor 6:18; Matt 12:49–50; 1 John 3:14–18; Grudem, *Systematic Theology*, 858.

11. By the second century, the Christian church was no longer Jewish but predominantly Gentile.

to straddle two cultures. This bicultural reality should be acknowledged, nurtured, commissioned, and released, in many cases through an associated independent parallel congregation.

Further Theology toward the Retention of English-Speaking Adults Associated with Chinese Churches

Theology for Cultural Transition / the Creation of Subcultures

Humanity makes culture because human beings are created in the image of God (Gen 1:26-27; Acts 17:28), who is the Maker of heaven and earth. Humanity has been given a cultural mandate (Gen 2:15) to "take care" of the created order—and this includes culture. Culture, says Rah, "consists of shared, socially learned knowledge and patterns of behavior."[12] Humankind has been given dominion over creation and culture (Gen 1:26-28; Ps 8:6; Gen 9:1), and therefore culture is dynamic, something human beings both generate and change (e.g., Christians are charged with reconciling cultural elements to God: Col 3:23-24). As Niebuhr has discussed, human beings need to recognize that they can co-create with God in the transformation of culture.[13] Yancey notes that the "static notion of culture" needs to be challenged . . . all cultures are constantly changing over time and will change . . . from exposure to other cultures."[14] Christians are reminded that stewardship includes culture (Matt 25:14-30) because culture ultimately belongs to God (Ps 24:1). Certainly "the only way to change culture is to create more of it."[15] Because humanity is given both the imago Dei and common grace to make culture, there can be much of culture which is good.[16] However, all "cultures . . . are an expression by fallen humanity [in the] attempt to reflect God's image through the process of creativity."[17] Therefore, Scripture warns Christians not "to conform to this present age" (Rom 12:2)

---

12. Rah, "Theology of Culture."

13. Niebuhr, "Theological Convictions," in *Christ and Culture*, 194-96. From an anthropological perspective of culture, both theology and culture are things that humans produce, and they only do it well if God is their ultimate point of reference. Tanner, "Nature and Tasks of Theology," in *Theories of Culture*, 63-65.

14. Yancey, *One Body, One Spirit*, 39.

15. Crouch, *Culture Making*, 67.

16. Kersten, *Reformed Dogmatics*, 78. Common grace is given to humanity in all cultural dimensions of life that require gifts and abilities with the accompanying "virtues, graces, wisdom, understanding," capacities, and ethical exercise (78). Common grace is a reflection of God's love, mercy, and preservation (75).

17. Rah, "What Is Culture?," in *Many Colors*, 29.

and to be cautious of "the deception of the world's wisdom (1 Corinthians 3:18–19)."[18] When Christians witness power groups blocking cultural diversity, they should recognize it as a symptom of human depravity. "The gospel destigmatizes and deabsolutizes every culture; no culture can claim it is the full expression of the gospel"; furthermore, Christians should recognize that the "gospel can only advance by being able to take root in every culture."[19] Sugikawa and Wong aptly state that "when Christ is 'born' into each society his presence may oppose, replace, complete, or fulfill various aspects of society's culture."[20] The New Testament shows many subcultures transformed by the gospel. The Great Commission has profound implications for the cultural mandate in terms of how the Good News enters into different cultures (Matt 28:18–20). Only God's people can fulfill this salvific aspect of the cultural directive. Though there is no "culture-free expression of the gospel," Christians are called to be an "alternative culture" that gives witness to the Good News.[21] Rah expressively states, "Our goal [is] to seek ways to honor the presence of God in different cultures."[22] Based on Revelation 7:9 (which refers to cultures and languages) and Revelation 15:2–3 (which refers to cultural forms), the knowledge that Christ's Lordship includes everything, and the understanding that everything will be renewed (Rom 8:19–21), should mean that some human culture-making will have eternal significance.

Theology for Cultural Inclusiveness and Diversity

Rah has made the case that a cultural framework (Western, Eastern, Confucian, etc.) can hold the church captive to a cultural worldview.[23] There are a number of themes in the Scriptures that invite the church to embrace diversity. Genesis 1 repeats five times God's pleasure in diversity. The mention of the various nations in Genesis 10 further reinforces God acknowledgment of ethnic multiplicity. In Genesis 12:2–3, God tells Abram that he plans to bless all the peoples of the earth through him. If a people are redeemed, the cultures they create can be too. The obvious conclusion is that God intended the human family to become multiethnic and multicultural. A divine af-

---

18. Heidebrecht, "Culture Clash," 9.
19. Paul, "Leadership Integrity."
20. Sugikawa and Wong, "Grace-Filled Households," 32.
21. Guder, *Missional Church*, 87, 119.
22. Rah, "What Is Culture?," in *Many Colors*, 29. Rah says that Cultural Intelligence is about being hospitable to different cultures and cultural expressions and "developing a biblical view, rather than a socially derived view of culture" (195).
23. Rah, *Next Evangelicalism*, 207.

firmation of dispersion is reinforced by the scattering after the flood (Gen 7) and after the tower of Babel incident (Gen 11). Sheffield suggests this scattering "was meant as a gift."[24] Cultural multiplicity is the ramification of Genesis 1:28 and 9:1, where humankind is told to "be fruitful and increase . . . fill the earth." Throughout the Old Testament, there are texts that refer to the people of God coming from many cultural backgrounds (Gen 14:18; Exod 3:1; 12:48–49). People from every cultural background are invited into the Good News. In the book of Acts, the trajectory of outreach is toward the nations. Since "from one man [God] made all the nations" (Acts 17:26), therefore, God is the ultimate source of the potential for cultural diversity. In declaring that the gift of salvation is extended to "everyone who calls on the name of the Lord (Acts 2:21)," no matter what culture they may have come from ("for all who are far off," Acts 2:39), God is presenting an inclusive, multiethnic, multicultural, and multiracial template for the church. In the New Testament, the church is reminded of the call to embrace unity in diversity (Gal 3:28; Eph 4:3–6). Furthermore, Christians are called to love their neighbors (Matt 5:44), their enemies (Matt 5:46–48), and those different in the body of Christ (John 13:35).[25] There is nothing the matter with wanting to preserve culture (it's a matter of free choice), but to use that as an excuse to hinder other subcultures from doing culturally relevant mission is an act of suppression. The reason for addressing cultural inclusivity is that some of the impetus for the silent exodus is that many Chinese churches have not come to terms with how to keep the unity of the faith despite cultural diversity. Paul makes a call for unity and maturity in the body of Christ (Eph 4:1–6) and for Christians to "build others up according to their needs" (Eph 4:29). It is wrong to confuse unity with uniformity in the body of Christ (Rom 12:4; 1 Cor 12:13; 4:1–4). Creation shows that the Creator did not make everything the same—there is great variety. Scripture also advocates for cultural diversity (Ezek 47:22; Gal 3:28; Col 3:11; Isa 56:6–8). Therefore, trying to preserve cultural uniformity in the church misses the point that the church in all its cultural diversity finds its identity in Christ. Simply put, "a biblically grounded theology of cultural diversity does not simply inspire us to affirm our differences . . . but also to . . . seek out truly reconciled relationships."[26] Lee offers an "Asian American theology in the context of marginality [as] an invitation . . . to meet as fellow strangers and

---

24. Sheffield, "Biblical Reflection on Cultural Diversity," in *Multicultural Leader*, 28.

25. Clark, "Theology in Cultural Context," 126–28.

26. Ibid., 131.

to stand by each other in solidarity as we join in God's own joyous struggles to build the household of God where [others] can come and be at home."[27]

Theology for Identity

I agree with Wing So that "the quest of identity . . . is also a theological problem."[28] Certainly every wave of new Chinese immigrants has helped reinforce the retention of Chinese culture and kept Chinese communities negotiating identities between two worlds.[29] Ng has noted that historically many first generation Chinese in the immigrant community have taken a dim view of local-born Chinese assimilating into the Canadian/Western culture.[30] One first generation Chinese labeled the acculturation of CBCs as a problem of "the local born, who should be ashamed of their cultural corruption and deficiency."[31] On the other hand, in 1964, a CBC minister "reflected on the fallacy of assimilation and the merits of integration" as being more able to fully "participate . . . as Canadian citizens."[32] Furthermore, "embracing a Canadian identity should not entail the loss of one's ethnic culture."[33] The statements by these two men demonstrate the competing views in Chinese culture of what it means to be Chinese Canadian and what it might mean to be a Chinese Canadian Christian. Neither view makes it imperative that one cease to be Chinese or embrace Chinese culture. Wang notes that because CBCs are a hybrid culture,[34] "the coexistence of Chinese and western (Canadian) identities in the church brings tensions and conflict into this community."[35] My impression is that some OBCs see the

---

27. Sang Hyun Lee, "Pilgrimage and Home," 228.

28. So, "Identity and Identification," 35. This quest asks questions such as "Why am I here?" and "What is the ultimate reference point of my life?"

29. Wing Chung Ng, "Negotiating Identities between Two Worlds, 1945–1970," in *Chinese in Vancouver*, 88.

30. Ibid., 89.

31. Ibid., 89.

32. Ibid., 105.

33. Ibid., 105.

34. Paul C. Wang, "Study on Cross-Cultural Conflict," 6–7. One example of this hybrid feeling is remain-in case 23 in appendix F.

35. Ibid., 140. Wang believes that the coexistence of "interlocking identities of Chinese culture, Canadian values and Christian beliefs induce tensions and conflict" (32). Wang's belief is that CBCs are "a generation in search of its identity" (143). Yang comments that these tensions and conflicts become manifest where "immigrants want [LBCs] to show deference and obedience whereas [LBCs] want more independence and respect." Fenggang Yang, *Chinese Christians in America*, 178.

movement toward acculturation as a "CBC identity problem"; in other words, some OBCs preach a purer form of Chinese culture; they see the cultural drift as a CBC problem and feel that OBCs have an obligation to pull CBCs back to the cultural center. It should be obvious that a bicultural identity is different from either a Canadian or a Chinese culture, and it is true that in the history of English ministries many have had "a difficult time finding a sense of significance, identity, and belonging within the church."[36] However, from a theological point of view, the Christian's identity is given by Christ, not culture (1 Cor 15:10; 2 Cor 5:17). People need to recognize theologically that God did not make a mistake in their faith development or their ethnic identity formation. The canon defines the people of God as members of Christ's body (Eph 4:15–16). The true lineage of faith, according to Romans 4:16–17, is that the descendants of Abraham are those who live by faith. Christians are God's community (John 1:12; Rom 8:14–16), and being "baptized into the body of Christ" (1 Cor 12:27) brings people into this new covenant family of God (Gal 6:10; Rom 11:27). This covenant family of God sets the framework for Christians' identity. The family of God exists to worship God (to be a house of prayer for all nations, Mark 11:17), to nurture the intercultural faith family, and to carry out Christ's mission.[37] For these purposes, all the boundaries of ethnic cultural identity are dissolved in Christ. The cross is the reconciliation point for all nations (Eph 2:11–22). Believers are called to pursue peace in light of the reality of the new family of God (Rom 14:19; Heb 12:14–17). As part of God's family, Christians are recruited to carry out his mission and purpose (John 20:21); "the church's essence is missional for the calling and sending action of God forms [Christians'] identity."[38] Christians share a unity, a common identity that is Christocentric and surpasses all cultural conventions. This common identity is anchored "in the theological claim unity is [a reflection of the] Trinitarian God."[39]

Theology for Passing the Leadership Baton on to the Next Generation of Adults

Some OBC leaders in Chinese churches are suspicious that an acculturating English ministry is a subtle rejection of Chinese identity and culture and

36. Wayne Wong, "Current Challenges," 8.
37. Grudem, "Nature and Purposes of the Church," in *Systematic Theology*, 867.
38. Guder, *Missional Church*, 82.
39. M. Sydney Park, "Theology of the Household of God," in Park et al., *Honoring the Generations*, 9.

possibly a rejection of Christian orthodoxy. In fact, many adult second generation Chinese "find that . . . Christianity reinforces 'Asian' values of family, work and education"; in some ways, "Confucian ideals . . . [are treated] similar to Christian ideals."[40] Back in the 1980s, Ling commented that "the baton belongs to the future leaders."[41] English ministries in Chinese bicultural churches have come of age, and that future is here now. It is time for an expanded model for English ministries. The Scriptures provide various examples of the leadership baton being passed on to the next generation; some of these narratives are messy, and others are intentional and seamless. Moses mentored and commissioned Joshua (Num 27:18–23; Josh 1:1–18). David prepared Solomon (1 Chron 28:1–21). Elijah mentored Elisha (1 Kgs 19:19–21). Jesus trained and commissioned the disciples to disciple other leaders (Matt 28:18–20). Barnabas advocated for Paul's leadership (Acts 9:27–29). Paul cultivated leadership in bicultural Timothy and encouraged him to also pass the leadership baton (2 Tim 2:2). The discerning of such transitions needs to be immersed in prayer (Matt 6:10) and focus on a calling-based leadership. Given Scripture, the literature review, and the survey results in this study, I am advocating the retention of English-speaking adults from Chinese Canadian churches through associated parallel independent English congregational models. These models will require a passing of the leadership baton and empowering EM leaders to authentically leverage mission.

---

40. Busto, "Gospel according to the Model Minority?," 177. Jeung discusses various Confucian virtues, such as family unity, education, a work ethic, a sense of responsibility, duty and obligation that get adapted into the Western Christian context. Jeung, *Faithful Generations*, 33–35. Ruokanen and Huang note that Chinese Christians repeatedly find themselves interfacing Confucianism with a Christian identity; some believe there is little conflict between Christianity and Chinese Confucianism due to the fact that "Confucian thought has a definite religious dimension." Miikka Ruokanen and Paulos Huang, *Christianity and Chinese Culture*, 81ff., 215, 279, 101, 107.

41. Ling, "Chinese Way," 58.

5

Methods of Research

Ignorance is the night of the mind, but a night without moon or star.
—CONFUCIUS, THE ANALECTS, BOOK 11:11

Research Design and Methodology

TO ASCERTAIN THE EXTENT and nature of the problem of the silent exodus, I developed three interviewing guides to use in a series of qualitative research interviews. The guides were designed to reveal the prevailing/dominant cultural values and community practices in Chinese bicultural churches and also discover the empirical reasons and personal explanations for the silent exodus. These guides were developed according to previous theoretical insights, anecdotal observations, and postulates on various contributing factors. I used three information sources (anecdotal observations, responses from dropouts, and responses from remain-ins) to *triangulate* the circumstances for the occurrence (or non-occurrence) of the problem. The goal was to establish an objective analysis of the factors leading to the silent exodus. The results could also set the stage for a larger scale, more in-depth, and more rigorous qualitative survey of the potential risks and contributing factors to the silent exodus of young adults from the bicultural church. It was suggested that this next phase of the research employ a questionnaire to measure quantitatively the prevalence of the risk factors of the silent exodus (established in this, phase 1) among Chinese second generation young adults in local Chinese churches, especially as they relate to the prevalent cultural practices of their churches. See appendices A, B, and E for a further synopsis of the silent exodus research design and a sample of the research form and questions. A two-year collection of surveys was completed at the time of my transfer into the BGU program; thirty were completed with English ministries clergy; thirty were completed with remain-in adults; and thirty were completed with adults who had left Chinese churches. The research highlights the highest reporting convergences.

Subsequently, I provided to three leadership focus groups in Chinese churches substantiated data on the key reasons why Chinese bicultural churches are losing numbers from their English language congregations. I constructed a short document containing my hypothesis and survey findings to share with these leadership groups, who either were in Chinese bicultural churches or had left Chinese bicultural churches. My objective was to test the survey data and findings with them and get their feedback. The aim was also to create a way to address this recurring problem. I was looking to these leadership groups to provide feedback to see what they would recommend could be done differently. In particular, I was asking particular leadership teams for their advice on the idea of giving permission to English congregations to have broader decision-making powers.

It is my intention to publish all of my research material and circulate it among local Chinese churches in hopes of reversing the silent exodus.

6

Findings and Results

> But Jesus has a different vision of maturity: It is the ability and willingness to be led where you would rather not go . . . the servant-leader is the leader who is being led to unknown, undesirable, and painful places. The way of the Christian leader is not the way of upward mobility . . . but the way of downward mobility ending on the cross.
>
> —HENRI NOUWEN

Findings from English Ministry Clergy in Chinese Churches

THIS RESEARCH BEGAN WITH a quest to discover the top factors why English-speaking Chinese adults leave Canadian Chinese bicultural churches; my concern has been with the high dropout rate of second generation adult English-speaking Christians. I began the research by constructing a survey for thirty English ministry pastors serving in thirty Chinese bicultural churches in the Greater Vancouver area of British Columbia. These pastors represented seven denominations and one independent stream[1] (see the

---

1. The denominations represented were Alliance (nine), Mennonite Brethren (ten), Evangelical Free (two), Independent (three), Christ Church of China (one), Reformed (one), Baptist (two), and Presbyterian (two). I intentionally did not include surveys received from four parachurch workers and one church worker so as to narrow the anecdotal feedback to only include pastors directly involved in English ministries.

clergy data graph in appendix C). Seven participants were lead pastors also serving the English ministries; twenty-three were associate English pastors. At the time of the survey, their years of pastoral experience with the English ministries ranged between three and twenty-five years. The age range of the pastors was between twenty-eight and seventy-one, with the average age being approximately forty.

The survey dispersed to these pastors consisted of two questions put into the following statement:

> A number of people have raised the discussion as to whether there is a Silent Exodus of CBC young adults from the Chinese churches here in Canada. In your opinion, would you agree with the observation? If you say yes to the above question, could you give three reasons for the Silent Exodus of some young CBC adults from the Chinese church—what would you say the factors are?

After receiving the feedback from these thirty pastors, I listed the factors, in order according to the number of times each was mentioned. I then condensed the top reasons and developed them into questions represented in appendix B.

In brief, topping the list of the thirty pastors' speculations were the following.

Issue #6: An Overemphasis on Chinese Ethnicity

The problem of overemphasis on Chinese ethnicity was compounded by the church being bilingual (language barriers) and the experience of OBCs trying to keep English ministries Chinese-Christian instead of Christian-Chinese. The experience of cultural dislocation and neglect contributed to a feeling among Canadian-born Chinese of not being at home—but rather being in a cultural bubble, where their faith could not be fully expressed in local church practices.[2]

---

2. Frank Wu's best seller gives the impression that Asian-Americans feel squeezed by mainstream culture, creating identity issues, which is a factor in the OBC disposition toward segregation and putting paternalistic and hierarchical pressures on North American-born Chinese to follow "the way things are done" in the Chinese bicultural church. Wu, *Yellow: Race in America beyond Black and White*.

Issue #10: Leadership Matters, Theological Problems with the Mission and Vision for English Ministries

The leadership issues included frequent leadership turnover, limited leadership opportunities, ineffective leadership, and frustrations with leadership. Many spoke of there being a lack of a clear sense of purpose and mission rooted in the Great Commission. One Chinese pastor, who is currently an executive lead pastor, made a representative statement:

> The silent exodus has happened twice in our church . . . I have concluded after nine years of staying with the English ministries, to mature and develop a vocational English group, that it is not workable because the Chinese churches don't have a vision for the CBCs that drift further away from their culture of origin. The hierarchical, patriarchal nature, lack of vision and leadership style creates a difficult atmosphere for English adults to stay and grow into fully mature and independent adult English congregations. I have now planted a second generation church to reach second generation Chinese, those that have left the Chinese church and those who are of other ethnicities.

Issue #9: Authority, Power, Politics, Control, and Empowerment

The English ministries are in the weaker position in relation to the Chinese congregation. They are kept dependent and not given real autonomy, independence, freedom, and power to make decisions for EM. This lack of power is tied in with organizational structure.

Issue #2: Life Stage Needs

There was a sense that life stage needs were not being met in the EM. A Chinese CBC worship pastor spoke of his past church experience this way:

> The silent exodus has been real for the past thirty years; I've seen it every year. Once young adults finish their education and get married, they have reached the Asian age of independence; after that there is this huge drop in ages over thirty and upwards. I would guess [my church] has lost over 90 percent of this age group. The most obvious part of the silent exodus is the ones you can see. There are fringe people that are harder to track

(e.g., friends who were brought in) . . . At the young adult age the circle of friends of CBCs become culturally diverse. To only reach other CBCs is to ignore the whole world around them. They relate to so many other people they work with and care for (challenge: "it's odd you can't bring them to your church"). The English service in an immigrant church [feels like] an alien anomaly . . . The world outside is so different from our [church] world inside. The motivation for doing ministry with the EM has to not be simply "how can we keep them?" That's not being missional, nor is it based on Scripture or Christ's teachings. It is idealistic but possible for a fully mature English congregation to be nurtured, but it would require a lot of charitable things to be in place (e.g., have to allow people into leadership who don't look like OBC leaders; both sides need to understand that things look different).

Issue #3: Unhealthy Church Community Matters

The consensus here was that problems do arise from intergenerational and intercultural conflicts within the Chinese church family, as the entrenched attitudes and traditional values of OBCs clash with the values of CBCs. Many English ministries pastors felt that CBCs had encountered self-righteousness, hypocrisy, reluctance to listen, and lack of respect from the OBC generation.

Not Inclusive Enough to Bring Non-Chinese Friends

I should note that two of these thirty pastors questioned whether there was a parallel between the Chinese church silent exodus and the exodus of young adults from mainstream churches.[3] The seven lead pastors out of the thirty were the most articulate regarding their concern over the silent exodus and its etiology. One Chinese lead pastor felt that one reason for the silent exodus was that CBCs are questioning whether OBCs really care about them:

> CBCs are wondering why it has taken so long to realize the problem and have been discouraged at their importance to the

---

3. There is some merit to the questions. A 2011 Canadian survey by the Angus Reid forum, commissioned by the Evangelical Fellowship of Canada, has noted the high numbers of people between the ages of 18 and 34 leaving the church: only "one in three Canadians who attended church weekly as a child still do so today." Penner, *Hemorrhaging Faith Report*.

church. Many Chinese churches have been quick to respond to [the many] immigrants . . . and now the flood of Mainland Chinese that are coming. Why have the Chinese churches not responded with as much enthusiasm to the local born? It sends a hypocritical message to them. You don't miss me when I'm gone because someone new has quickly filled my seat from overseas.

Another CBC lead pastor made this statement:

> Personally, I don't think there is anything "silent" about the attrition. It is more than evident over the past twenty years here in the Vancouver area, if we would only admit it. The fact is, most English ministries still look exactly the same (primarily teens/college age with a sprinkling of 35 and up) as when I grew up . . . nothing's changed over the past 20 years. And as I have had the opportunity to speak at various Chinese churches, I find this to be true. The question is, where did all the older ones who grew up in my generation go? Answer: They're all around us. Most of my neighbors are CBC/CRCs with young children. They're just not in the Chinese church for whatever reasons. My heart is not to criticize what we haven't done, but what we can do better to reach the CBC/CRCs. Not just the ones that left the church, but also the younger ones who are there right now. I pray that the Lord will put this burden on more people to see the opportunities and think missionally. Talking and discussions are necessary, but we must act strategically too. I hope we don't keep asking, "Is there a silent exodus" twenty years from now.

These were the thirty pastors' anecdotal speculations on the silent exodus. I turn now to the research findings from the dropouts on why they really left the Chinese church.

Logistical Details

The groundwork for the survey design was challenging. The responses had to be compared against some standard of church health, and, admittedly, I have my Western values and biases[4] of what church health should look like.

---

4. Creswell, "Framework for the Study," in *Research Design*, 6. Dey also discusses the intrusion of a researcher's own values and inclinations. Dey, "Introduction," *Qualitative Data Analysis*, 6. Silverman discusses relating questions to "Standards of Action." Silverman, "Interview Data," in *Interpreting Qualitative Data*, 92. Certainly my questions assume a comparison with what is value-appropriate in a Canadian society that lauds human rights, egalitarianism, and pluralism and what Scripture teaches on building community (Acts 6:1–7; Matt 5:9; Rom 12:14).

The survey questionnaire was designed based on a review of relevant literature and discussions with informants. Careful thought went into the sampling process and data collection method.[5] Along with the questionnaire design, the issues that needed to be addressed included who the participants would be; how large the sample would be; the need to present the questionnaire with a clearly stated purpose and assurances of confidentiality and anonymity;[6] the construction of relevant questions in funneled order; and a method of data collection.[7]

All of the participants were English-speaking adult Canadian-born Chinese. Referrals came through friendship and ministerial networks. The participants were sent a survey by email or were interviewed face-to-face or on the phone. More than fifty surveys were dispersed to CBCs who were from Chinese churches. Over twenty people dropped out (40 percent); three of those indicated the reason was that they were too busy; seventeen never answered my follow-up emails to them. The participants answered the questions, reporting their perceptions and experiences. Data was collected over a twenty-five month period. Then came the difficult task of attempting to understand the multiple realities of thirty dropout CBC adults.[8] I reviewed and analyzed each survey, identifying associations, regularities, variations, singularities, and exceptions and keeping track of the participants' focus and range of responses to each question. Cases were numbered. Demographics and other data were noted: city, church, gender, date of completion, etc. I listed in order which factors and questions were prioritized by the participants. I then made connections, identifying patterns and themes from the collective surveys by counting the number who indicated that each issue was a factor for him or her.[9] The data was organized chronologically, and a list of major factors emerged.

Dropout Participant Demographics

The average survey completion time was one to four months. Eleven of the respondents were female, and nineteen were male. The approximate ages

---

5. Oppenheim, "Problems of Survey Design," in *Questionnaire Design*, 1–23.

6. These issues are ethical considerations discussed by Creswell, *Research Design*, 165–66.

7. Oppenheim, *Questionnaire Design*, 24–48.

8. The attempt to understand included getting a sense of the whole and coding a list of factors. Creswell, *Research Design*, 155, 162–63.

9. I attempted to reconceptualize the data and see how the bits interconnected. Dey, "What Is Qualitative Analysis?," in *Qualitative Data Analysis*, 30.

of the respondents ranged from twenty to fifty-one, and the average age was about thirty. Each respondent had formerly been an adult member in an English congregation in a Chinese church either in Metro Vancouver or in Alberta. The respondents came from ten denominations,[10] but notably, all of the participants' churches were evangelical. The questionnaire also asked about current church attendance: eight no longer attend church. Two are attending a different English ministries congregation in a Chinese church. Ten are attending an intentionally multicultural church. Three are attending a second generation CBC English language congregation or church plant. Seven are attending a mainstream church (they did not declare the church model).

---

10. Included were: Baptist, Alliance, Evangelical Free, Mennonite Brethren, Christ Church of China, Lord's Grace Church (independent), Evangelical Chinese Bible Church (an independent church), Anglican, Pentecostal, and Lutheran.

Table 2. Dropout demographics

Case	Gender	Denomination	Baptized Member	Service / years	Age*	Transferred to a Chinese church	Attending a Multicultural Church	Attending a Mainstream church	Attending A CBC Church Plant	Left the church	Still has faith in God	Held office
1.	F	I–Pentecostal	Yes	Yes – 1	Late 20s					Yes	Yes	
2.	F	EF	Yes	Yes 15+	42+		Yes					Various leadership positions
3.	M	B	Not clear	Yes	U							
4.	F	A / MB	Yes	Yes 5+	U			Yes		Yes	Yes	Worship leader
5.	F	A / B	Yes	Yes 4+	32+			Yes				
6.	M	P	No	Yes 4+	51		Yes					
7.	M	B / A	Yes	Yes 5+	45+			Yes			Yes	Intern
8.	M	A / A	Yes	Yes 8+	35		Yes					Elder
9.	F	EFC / MB	Yes	Yes 10+	25				Yes			EM deacon
10.	M	L / MB	Yes	Yes	U			Yes				
11.	M	MB	Yes		32+		Yes					
12.	M	MB / A	Yes	Yes 10+	40+					Yes	No	Youth worker
13.	M	CCC / MB	Yes	Yes	29+	Yes						EM deacon
14.	F	MB	Yes	Yes		Yes						Worship leader

85

15.	M	A/MB	Yes	Yes	31					Yes	Yes	Intern
16.	M	I/I	Yes	Yes	32				Yes	Yes	Yes	Pastor
17.	M	MB	Yes	Yes	26							
18.	M	MB/MB	Yes	Yes	32		Yes					EM leader
19.	M	I/A			28		Yes					Leader
20.	F	A/I	Yes	Yes	30				Yes			Intern pastoral ministries
21.	F	A/?	Yes	?	29+		Yes			Yes		
22.	M	A/	Yes	Yes	27+					Yes	Not clear	
23.	M	MB	Yes	Yes	29					Yes	Yes	
24.	M	MB/A	Yes	?	31			Yes				
25.	F	MB/B	Yes	Yes	21			Yes				
26.	M	MB	Yes	Yes	31		Yes					
27.	F	EFC/Anglican	Yes	Yes	26					Yes	Yes	
28.	F	B/A/I	Yes	Yes	28		Yes					
29.	M	A/?	Yes	Yes	30		Yes					
30.	M	A/A	Yes	Yes	51			Yes				Board member
Total	**F=11 M=19**	**14**	**28**	**Majority**		**2**	**10**	**7**	**3**	**8**	**2 not clear**	**14 clear statements**

Findings from English-Speaking Dropouts from the Chinese Church

After the demographic information was taken, participants were asked to address eleven issues in seven sections. Section one of the survey was intended to clarify context. Of the thirty participants, nine said that they had been brought to the Chinese church since their birth.[1] Thirteen indicated that they had been brought to the Chinese church when they were children or between the ages of four and twelve. Five had been brought to the Chinese church between the ages of thirteen and sixteen. One had come to a Chinese church English congregation at age forty-nine. It would be a fair assessment to conclude that the majority of these participants were raised in the church and would have been expected to be emerging stakeholders in its future.

The denominational scope of the dropout participants was broader than that of the clergy surveyed; the dropouts came from fourteen different churches in ten denominational or independent streams.[2] Twenty-eight plainly stated that they had been baptized members.[3] One summary observation that could be made here is that this raises the bar on their level of understanding of the faith and their commitment to being a Christ follower and a contributing member of the faith community.

In describing the atmosphere of their churches, the majority spoke of them as being an English congregation in a Chinese traditional setting—Chinese in culture and practices, conservative, and a place of shared ideas

---

1. Participants indicated that twenty-one had been brought to the Chinese church by their parents. Six had had no parents in the church at the time. Three had had only one parent in the church. Seven had been introduced to the church either through friends or friends of the family. One had been introduced to the church through relatives, one had been introduced by an older sibling, and two had been introduced through a neighbor. One important observation here is that the majority had originally been brought to the church by a parent. Only four dropout survey participants said that their parents (or a parent) were not Christian. Six indicated that their parents did not attend the church they referred to in the survey with them. It is also important to note that attending generally meant that the parent attended the OBC service, not the English service with the children. The implications of missing a parental role model in worship warrants further commentary. Thirteen specifically noted their parents were no longer in the church that they had exited.

2. The additional denominations of the dropout participants included Anglican, Lutheran, and Pentecostal.

3. I mention baptism (which is often tied closely to membership) because in Chinese church contexts it is one of the gateways into fuller participation in the life of the church. One participant remembered refusing membership based on the perception that it was being used as a mechanism for social control. Two did not offer any information as to whether they had been baptized.

and beliefs.⁴ A summary observation here is that several participants noted cultural differences between the CBC English congregation and the OBC Chinese congregation. Several commented on the unequal division of power, with the board dominating the pastors. Several specifically noted that the church had no involvement with the community around it. A couple cited value issues between the CBC and Chinese language groups.

In section two, the dropout participants were asked to speak about the people and relationships they had encountered in the Chinese church. The experiences were varied. Although some participants had only known an English-speaking congregation made up of youth and young adults, church life for some others in the English congregation had extended into college and middle age. A key common factor of the participants' church life experience was that of being English-speaking like the majority of CBCs around them.⁵

---

4. One survey participant described the church setting as being predominantly made up of people who were university age and middle age. Two described their church as a busy place with lots of programs, strongly committed to Christian education and volunteerism. Six survey participants bluntly spoke of the atmosphere as fraught with division (conflict), heavily controlled by the board, or dominated by the OBC leadership and culture. Among the six, one cited tension around the different cultural views the CBCs experienced; one felt segregated and labeled the experience abusive; one labeled the experience authoritarian and xenophobic.

5. Some explicitly stated that "church was a big part of my life"—like another family they could rely on and a place they could meet friends. One contributor wrote that it was "nice to be around Chinese people . . . a real sense of community." Some spoke favorably of their teacher's character and efforts to make the sessions interesting. One survey participant made appreciative comments on the solid teaching on Christ that was received. Several recollected that the church was a positive, happy, strong community and recalled good memories of caring people. Several cited the fellowship and the meaningful relationships that were developed in the process of organizing meetings and events. Four participants commented on the busy programs and volume of planned activity. Reflecting on Chinese conservatism and church traditions, another participant noted, "I had many good and bad experiences at church." One survey participant had a lonely experience at a first Chinese church English ministry but later felt warmly embraced in a second Chinese church. Six surveys recalled a variety of negative experiences. One noted witnessing disturbing control issues. Another shared, "There was tension between the congregations, and it was felt more when it came to Sunday mornings." A different participant stated, "Growing up in [church name] was a study in living with constant tension between often competing cultural values and traditions . . . services were conservative following a fairly rigid format." One CBC mature adult referred to the unequal partnership, stating, "Our relationship with the Chinese congregation was one of tolerance . . . as long as we paid respect to our elders and saw the Chinese congregation as leading the congregation, everything would be fine and we could all get along happily." Speaking of the OBC leadership of another church, one participant commented it was "a place difficult to relate to; it was as though they were at another level." One survey succinctly stated, "The senior pastor and some board

Survey participants were also asked about their involvement or volunteerism. Twenty-seven out of thirty dropout participants indicated that they had been involved in multiple areas of service.[6] Sixteen survey participants cited being heavily involved in the upper levels of leadership in the English congregation, including serving as English elder, English track board member, English congregation representative, pastoral intern, congregational preacher, coordinator, counselor, mentor, chairperson of the college group, EM career adults leader, home group leader, small group leader, cell group leader, and youth worker. Over half of the survey participants (sixteen) commented that they had been teachers in the English congregation. Many spoke of being heavily involved in leadership in broad spectrum, ad hoc terms. A summary observation is: One cannot help but conclude that the loss of this leadership capital and these human resources must have had a cumulative negative impact on the growth and evangelistic momentum of the Chinese bicultural church.[7]

Dropout survey participants were also asked who their best friends and role models were. Only three could not answer the question; twelve participants focused on the quality of their peer friendships. Some remarked on the good times and valuable closeness experienced in the fellowship. One recalled knowing many people but not on a deep level. Another stated, "I didn't really fit in with the group." Six contributors referred to finding a role model in peer CBCs or older CBCs. One admired the quality of an older CBC who was "mission minded." One felt highly influenced by best friends who were more focused on God and by women who had a lot of grace. Another recollected, "A couple of people in the cohorts above me stood out as role models, sincere and thoughtful in their faith, passionate volunteers, [with] good character." One participant found role models in older mentors and worship leaders. Another wrote, "I looked up to all the older people in the church, they were great role models to me." In one such case, the participant found a role model in a couple who were very dedicated to God and

---

members did not really understand the needs of the English congregation. They would impose some of their Chinese values which are not necessarily applicable, nor biblically relevant onto the EM."

6. These included serving on music teams, as worship leader, in dramas and musicals, on committees, as a greeter or usher, as a fellowship leader (secretary-treasurer), as a sound tech or member of the tech team, and as a camp/retreat volunteer planner.

7. Although about half of the survey participants did not clearly indicate how long they had been in the Chinese church EM, those who did said their service ranged from two-and-a-half years to thirty years. One leadership aspect that is not captured in this section of the survey is English pastor turnover—or the exodus of English ministries pastors. There may be some correlation between English pastor turnover and the departure of other congregants.

helped set a standard for service. Two spoke of admiring teachers who tried hard to reach them. Four expressed disappointment in either not having role models or experiencing the exodus of role models. One put it this way, "To be honest, role models were lacking during my times at church." Two noted that initially older youth workers/leaders were role models but "later they mostly all left." Only four out of thirty indicated that they found a role model in their English ministries pastor (or young adult and family pastor); this lack of regard in emulating pastors is a surprising finding, given how clergy-centered and hierarchical many of these ministry contexts are. Given how busy the survey participants reported their church environments were, the appointed clergy may have seemed too distant to be role models. It's hard for people to identify with someone they are distant from.[8] Implied is a deficit in incarnational leadership.[9]

Survey participants were asked what their pleasant or unpleasant (memorable) experiences in church life were with people such as the pastoral staff, older generations, the Chinese-speaking congregation(s), and their contemporaries. Twelve participants cited both pleasant and unpleasant experiences. Eighteen commented on pleasant experiences.[10] Twenty-two commented on unpleasant experiences. Nine exclusively cited unpleasant experiences. The unpleasant experiences were associated with the Chinese OBC leadership, senior leadership, and a board dominated by OBC leaders. Six participants cited unpleasant experiences with members of the older OBC generation from the Chinese language congregation.[11]

---

8. However, only two participants spoke of people who behaved superficially or competitively. One indicated there were no role models due to negative politics. Three participants did not answer this aspect of section two.

9. Eugene Peterson's description of the unbusy pastor is helpful here: "To be a pastor who has the time to be with [congregants] leisurely, unhurried conversations so that I can understand and be a companion with you as you grow in Christ—your doubts and your difficulties, your desires and your delights." Paterson, *Memoir*, 278.

10. These included closeness in the community, social life with friends, fellowship and retreats, enjoyable leadership relationships, a close relationship with the pastor's wife, relationships with the EM pastors, the quality of Christian education and the level of volunteerism, good organizational structures, a good biblical and faith foundation, and opportunities to serve. One participant commented that pleasant experiences only happened during the teens; distance and disagreement with things began to surface during the college years. One survey from a participant who had left church completely stated, "Everything was pretty much pleasant; I don't think I had any unpleasant experiences."

11. In one case, the leadership had to be asked for permission to date. Another participant commented on the Chinese board banning drums in the church, stating, "The senior pastor seemed to always try to please the Chinese congregation because they were the predominant group . . . the English congregation seemed to be always the junior partner and considered less mature and spiritual—even though some of the members were young professionals . . . the church had difficulty keeping English adults

One single parent CBC man in his late forties who brought his biracial offspring to the English congregation commented on the absence of compassion in that church; he found the church inhospitable and the experience difficult, as his mixed-race son was stigmatized.[12]

On the topic of showing empathy, one common theme is summed up in the remark, "People from the Chinese side didn't share our feelings too much." Many comments were made regarding culture clashes. One person mentioned, "I didn't respect the senior leadership due to them not being willing to adapt to new methods to suit the new generation—I agree the gospel doesn't change, but the presentation must." Another CBC adult said, "The Chinese church used culture to sometimes mix in with preaching the Christian faith . . . cultural paranoia's [were] passed on." CBCs mentioned a variety of strains on intercultural relationships that included a high degree of formality, politics, and church rules being passed down as tradition.[13]

Two participants mentioned cultural clashes with older members of the Chinese congregation in the contexts of shared leadership or receiving teaching.[14] For example: "One thing that was persistently cited as a bother was the strongly conservative attitude of the older generation at the time in trying to manage [control] western raised [CBCs] using philosophies of older Asia." One noted that there were "certain rituals and games we all grew up having to observe in order to 'give face' to these people [Chinese leadership]. Later, when we began to get older, we regularly bumped heads with them, especially in terms of uses of money." Some participants indicated that the tension with the OBC Chinese leadership and congregation, including the senior pastor, turned sour as the English ministries congregation matured. One CBC public school teacher noted:

> The last few years certain pastors weren't supportive of the young adults' ministry [referring to power struggles and conflict] . . . A

---

due to the lack of opportunities to participate in the major decision making process and the CBCs not being listened to." Compounded with this was the "limited support and involvement from the Chinese congregation who used language barriers as excuse."

12. In reference to making some changes, his comment was, "Pastoral staff was bound, gagged and handcuffed by a controlling church board. It was horrible."

13. One woman, referring to the cultural gap, said one of her "not so fond memories with the older generation was being judged a lot for wearing make-up or clothes that [she] thought were cool." One young adult CBC said, "I did not connect with the pastors who did not express any weakness or failed to understand the generational and cultural gaps that existed in the church."

14. One participant noted, "They attended English adult Sunday school and brought with them viewpoints that seemed extremely prejudiced and judgmental." Another observed, "Board meetings were long and arduous; the people I came to find undesirable were those who complained or criticized about the quality of ministry of the English speaking congregation."

sizable group of career young adults departed over this. We all grew up in this church and were children of the [Chinese] leaders; this developed over time—there were many failed things and unforgiveness.

A patent observation is that breakdown in communication has been a factor in eclipsing shalom in a number of these communities.[15] There was a dearth of shalom leadership.

A concluding inquiry in section two was: "Were you ever comfortable bringing your outside church friends, including friends of another race, to the church?" Only thirteen of the dropouts indicated yes, that they might be comfortable in bringing outside church friends, including friends of another race. Three of those thirteen did have some concerns in inviting friends of another race but would be open to do it. Of the thirteen who said yes, one would only invite outsiders to fellowship events;[16] one would only invite a seeking, curious, and willing inquirer. Four of the thirteen cases had only brought other Asian friends (CBCs or Canadian-born Koreans or Japanese). Fifteen participants—half of the dropout group—indicated that they were uncomfortable with bringing outside church friends or friends of another race to their church. Some of these identified racial barriers as being an impediment.[17]

One CBC concluded, "The problem with ethnic churches is congregations can get too homogeneous . . . it is hard for them to accept people on the outside." Some of the survey participants discovered that "it was hard to bring non-Asians to this church." One participant stated: "I wanted to bring my friends and family to my church, but never felt comfortable doing that because I was aware of the 'Chinese-fied' environment." One CBC man commented, "Bringing my . . . school friends to church was something I wanted to do. But in the mid1970s, it was typical that I was the only Asian kid in the class and bringing a non-Chinese-speaking person to a Chinese church was something that never worked out."[18]

---

15. For example, see appendix F, remain-in cases 14 and 15. Second generation communication issues with first generation is also noted in Kasinitz et al., *Inheriting the City*, 18, 170.

16. Often fellowships hold activities offsite or in a room/location apart from the rest of the church.

17. One young man put it this way: "It is hard to bring non-Chinese friends to this church because it is a Chinese church." Another commented: "I didn't often invite friends to church because it felt like it was such a huge cultural hurdle to jump, especially for my Caucasian friends." Another said, "I brought friends from time to time, but not many were comfortable with the mono-racial bicultural atmosphere."

18. Another CBC felt that impediments to bringing people to his Chinese church

Another survey participant pondered whether a Caucasian would really feel comfortable or if there was a full welcome for friends of another race in his Chinese church: "Friends of another race were sort of welcome, although I think they felt more uncomfortable being there than we felt with them." Four of the fifteen participants who were hesitant to bring acquaintances or friends of another race expressed being "put off" by the religious culture or "churchiness"; this discomfort is perhaps indicative of a deeper issue. For one CBC, what began as "not [being] comfortable bringing friends of another race to church [evolved into not being comfortable] later on [in bringing] any friends." One CBC commented, "I was never comfortable bringing friends to church, regardless of race. I never felt that I could explain everything that went on." Another was "hesitant to bring any friends to the Chinese church and more hesitant to bring someone not of Chinese descent."

A basic summary observation from this survey section is that there is an impediment to pursuing intercultural missional initiatives when members are not convinced that the church they will invite people to will be an inclusive or caring "midwife." Another observation is that not one survey participant from the dropout group expressed a theology of reaching out to all nations and ethnicities.

In section three, survey participants were asked at what life stage they left the bicultural church. Participants generally left the bicultural church between the time they were in university (all dropout cases were over age twenty) and age fifty-one. Seven left between the ages of twenty-two and twenty-six. The majority—a total of seventeen—left between the ages of twenty-eight and thirty-two. One left at age thirty-five; three left in their forties, and two left at age fifty-one. A summary observation is that largest clusters of church transitions correlate with other common life stage transitions such as mobility in regard to employment and study, seeking a life mate, a change in marital status, and having children. When the dropout participants were asked how leaving the church happened, two specifically indicated that they felt they were being divinely called out. One couple left to be a part of a multicultural church plant: "We didn't feel we were growing enough and that people were not extending out; an opportunity came to work in a multicultural setting." Another CBC woman who left her Chinese church commented:

---

also included class issues: "I did bring friends to church on a couple of occasions (they were white) but usually felt uncomfortable about this. I was [also] reluctant to bring an open "seeking" friend to our church because . . . he was blue collar . . . the church was so professional. I figured he would feel out of place . . . I counseled university students to invite their white friends to Christian campus clubs."

> I did not feel called to be a part of the church's stage of growth where it was lacking in vision and conviction to be a faithful church. I became convicted to leave during a time when I was more established in the workplace and recognized the opportunity for marketplace ministry. Most of my colleagues are not Asian . . . I didn't feel comfortable bringing them to a Chinese church at all. I was evaluating the best use of my time . . . changes I deemed necessary to the health of the church were going to take a long time. Having made the case for change in the previous couple years and seeing very little movement, I wasn't prepared to wait to see if the changes would fully be adopted one day.[19]

Six participants responded that the leaving represented a life stage transition in which their needs were not being met in the Chinese church. One left to date someone outside the church and avoid criticism; he subsequently began attending a Caucasian church. Six left either during their marriage engagement or right after their wedding ceremony. Some of these were cross-cultural marriages. One CBC man shared, "I got married to a Korean wife and decided we needed to find a new church with people our age and stage of life." That man chose a multicultural church where he felt they could both fit in and raise a family. Another CBC woman shared that she married a Caucasian man and left to attend his multicultural church; she expressed feeling free from the former politics and activism. In two cases, getting married was a smoke screen for some of the deeper reasons the couples left. One CBC woman said the reason behind her leaving was the dismal treatment of her dad, who was a pastor, and the abuse of church power and politics. One married man with children also noted leaving over stage of life issues and concern for his children:

> We left this church in our mid 30s as we felt that we didn't have peers who were our age and at the same stage of life as we were losing the young adults. We wanted our children to be in a mainstream church to experience a balanced church life which focuses on biblical values and truth instead of cultural values.

The desire for spiritual health and a balanced church life was a key concern for many participants.

The primary factor in leaving for four other participants was mobility; they moved to another city to work or study.[20] Eight specifically noted that

---

19. Dropout case 9 in appendix D.

20. One CBC medical student commented: "I started thinking about leaving the church in my last years of . . . school. Most of my peers had left by then due to loss of faith. There weren't any programs suited to young adults. I stayed behind to serve in the

they left after experiencing conflict in the church with the Chinese leadership. In one case, a CBC left when the church went through a split. Another CBC woman spoke of leaving two separate Chinese bicultural churches over a risk management issue and feeling disconnected and unwelcome among peers (lack of belonging). Another CBC left after witnessing the disunity between ministry leaders. One CBC English ministries pastoral intern spoke of his struggle with church leadership while trying to advocate for egalitarian decision making for the English congregation:

> A political move and decision was made at the board level to administratively paralyze the English congregation signifying the desire of the church to remain a Chinese church with the Chinese congregation doing most of the decision making. I don't begrudge them for their Chinese-first philosophy. Another reason was that I felt we needed to move to a direction where we could begin to minister to these [silent exodus] "lost" people and provide an environment for them where so many of us could begin to heal from being "over-churched."

Testimony to the marginalization of the English ministries shows up in a couple of other CBC statements. One CBC elder noted, "Tension was building up between me (while serving as an elder) and the senior pastor; he was exercising unethical and unfair treatment on the English pastor . . . English ministry was being marginalized and not respected in the board." Another CBC woman in a Cantonese church stated:

> I left on account of the leadership style of the senior pastor that led to many altercations with people in the English ministries. Groups in the English congregation were being micromanaged. Our prayer group was shut down and people in the EM were being hurt; I felt unsafe within the church. Power struggles were happening between the board and pastors of the English and Mandarin tracks. It felt as though the elder board chose to protect the pastor over the congregation . . . it was taboo against speaking anything wrong with our leaders. Eventually I had to leave because I could no longer worship and felt that the church was a sham.

English ministries but over time started feeling dry spiritually. My parents encouraged me to go to a church where I could get fed instead of just serving. I started thinking about when would be a good time for leaving; upon being accepted into medical school I had to move . . . I saw this as a good time to leave my church without making others in the EM feel abandoned."

Two participants indicated they left with their whole families over church politics. A couple of participants left over a concern for the vision for English ministries and the church being Sino-centric. One said, "I left feeling very complacent in my faith and growth; I didn't want to serve . . . I didn't see a positive direction for the English ministries—it was like a sinking ship. There was a lack of a consistent English ministry pastor." Another CBC left when the Chinese leadership tried to integrate the English-speaking members into the Chinese congregation; he stated, "I could no longer bear the situation." One other CBC left the church because of ceasing to embrace the practice of faith in community. Another CBC left because of "a combination of busy work and study schedule. I had no family at that church, and I felt lonely at church." This statement is a reminder that congested schedules can choke out faith and people can feel lonely in a crowd (in church). One CBC case represented a desire to move beyond the practice of faith in a homogeneous unit. He said, "At about age 26 I began thinking the church ought to be involved in the community; I felt our church was very segregated. I want to be with a church that is involved in my neighborhood." This young man is currently in a neighborhood community church.

When the thirty dropout survey participants were asked if they decided to leave after a long process or more quickly, only one admitted to having left suddenly. Two participants said they made the decision over a six-month period. One mentioned it took one year. Three indicated it took them two years of struggling. In one of those cases, the person was struggling for change with the English deacons. Nineteen participants said that leaving was a long, slow process that took time. Some comments here were about gradually slipping out quietly with little fanfare. One noted how deeply painful this leaving was. Another CBC attributed the long process to God changing the participant from within. Two left with a whole group of young adults (not a silent exodus). One summary observation here is the depth, scope, and extended experience of internal dissonance these CBCs endured in making this profound transitional decision.[21]

All thirty participants were asked if any of the people at church cared about them after they left the church. Only fifteen (half of the participants) reported that friends, pastors, elders, peers, or family followed up.[22] All

---

21. One could expect that there would be an emotional dimension to leaving a Chinese faith community that has nurtured one's life, particularly one with a culture in which individuals see themselves as a part of the whole and a culture that stresses filial piety and deference to the elder generation, which in a majority of cases would include members of one's own family.

22. Six other participants expressed feeling that people didn't care or that a pastor seemed relieved when they left.

thirty participants were asked if the church they left understood why they were leaving, and only thirteen could say that it did understand.[23]

All of the participants were asked how leaving their Chinese bicultural churches affected them. Two noted that they stopped attending church; one of these has resumed a periodic attendance. Six noted that they struggled with guilt and sadness and missed the sense of community (family atmosphere) they had in the Chinese church. One CBC put it this way:

> I felt tremendously guilty for leaving, like I had failed. I felt like I was leaving a family, much like a divorce. However, I felt that if I stayed I would lose my faith altogether. I didn't trust the leadership, and my closest friends were gone or were leaving. I also felt that there wasn't anything more I could do to help the situation.

Nine participants refrained from answering this question. Eight spoke of this transition as launching them into valuable new discoveries. One CBC man put it this way:

> Since leaving I've had an opportunity to expand my horizons of meaning and understanding in life. Leaving the church I have learned to be less judgmental of groups that may have digressed from the popular current views of the church. I have had an opportunity to explore what spirituality and believing in God means in a more holistic view.

Another CBC said, "I have had time for healing and to gain a broader perspective and that's been a blessing. I live opened up to other opportunities." One CBC scientist reflected, "Looking back that was the best decision I ever made—I feel like I have grown so much since leaving the Chinese church; I am much more open-minded now." Three participants cited having positive growth experiences in their new multiethnic or mainstream churches.

All dropout participants were asked if they thought about the effect on other people and the church after they left. One reflected: "I had thought about the effect on that church, but nobody is irreplaceable, God's work goes on regardless." Another who had left with a sizable group of other career adults felt the action they had taken was a message to the church: "To be honest, at the time, leaving was my way of making a statement based on the belief that change will never happen. I actually had previously also seen an older English cohort—a decade older than me—majority leave; that group is just hitting their 40s now." One participant felt people were disappointed

---

23. One admitted giving the excuse "I just needed a break." Another stated, "I never told anyone why I was leaving." Sadly, one CBC commented, "Most only knew that I had abandoned my faith, while only a handful knew of my struggles leading up to this."

and sad. Another simply said, "I understand and see the effect of leaving a congregation." In another case, the English ministry congregation dissolved. Seven participants felt their leaving did not have any effect on people or the church; one of these felt it might have ignited thoughts in others to leave. Seventeen participants did not respond to this question.

The last query in section three asked the participants if they felt that they were accountable to the church or that the church was accountable to them. Only one felt somewhat accountable. Eight indicated that they had no accountability toward the church nor did the church have any accountability toward them. Twenty-one did not respond to this question. A summary observation here is that there is little mention of a covenant relationship in a faith family; one might conclude that it is the responsibility of church leadership to teach and model a theological understanding of how congregation members should honor and care for one another. These factors are the domain of incarnational and shalom leadership.[24]

Section four went straight to the reasons for and circumstances leading to leaving the church. The thirty participants could pick from eleven issues, or any combination thereof, as to why they had chosen to leave their church. These are elaborated in appendix B. The question was stated this way: "What was the main reason(s) that you decided to leave the bicultural church? There can be more than one reason; can you place them in some priority order and then we can proceed to talk about them one by one?" For the sake of brevity, I will list the issues here in a footnote,[25] but the reader will need to refer to the full definition of these issues and survey responses in appendix B.

One discovery from this survey was that, besides the direct answers to the questions asked, the survey can also reveal other information. In this case, I learned explanations for why CBC adults dropped out of their church other than the ones I had posed. I will now discuss my findings from the

24. Helping people during their difficulties and working toward reconciling people to God and the faith community.

25. Issue #1: Identity issue of being a CBC within a Chinese church
Issue #2: Life stage transition needs unfulfilled within a Chinese church
Issue #3: Intergenerational conflict (within church/family)
Issue #4: Shame culture: over-evaluation or rejection
Issue #5: Western postmodern values or worldviews at conflict with Chinese traditional values manifested in the bicultural church
Issue #6: Overemphasis on Chinese cultural identity and ethnocentrism
Issue #7: Personal choice of a secular lifestyle versus Christianity
Issue #8: Perceived problem with *church* beliefs, theology, or hypocrisy
Issue #9: Control issues with church power and politics
Issue #10: Church leadership, organizational structure, and program issues
Issue #11: Intellectual, rational, and pragmatic issues

survey questions, starting with the most frequent reasons reported. (Almost all dropouts listed more than one reason for leaving.)

Fourteen CBC dropouts listed as a reason for leaving Issue #2: their life stage transition needs were unfulfilled within a Chinese church. Thirteen CBC dropouts listed Issue #6: there was an overemphasis on Chinese cultural identity and ethnocentrism.[26] Thirteen CBC dropouts also listed Issue #10: church leadership, organizational structure, and program issues. Nine dropouts listed Issue #9: control issues church power struggles and politics (with the senior pastor and board). One summary remark here is that participants who cited Issues #9 and #10 were aiming their grievances toward the senior pastor and board.

Five participants listed Issue #7: personal choice of a secular lifestyle versus Christianity. Five listed Issue #8: perceived problem with church beliefs, theology, or hypocrisy. Three listed Issue #3: intergenerational conflict (within church/family). Three listed Issue #4: shame culture: overevaluation or rejection. Two listed Issue #1: identity issue of being a CBC within a Chinese church. Two listed Issue #5: Western postmodern values or worldviews at conflict with Chinese traditional values manifested in the bicultural church. Only one participant listed Issue #11: intellectual, rational, and pragmatic issues.

Further reasons for dropping out were discovered in the survey responses that had not been included in the construction of the survey questions. Eight (26 percent) participants mentioned leaving over loneliness and an attempt to seek friends, fellowship, and relationships. Belongingness appears to be the issue. Five were explicitly looking for spiritual growth, resources, and change. Four left for mobility reasons.[27] Three felt called to another church. Two questioned the validity and life application of the preaching. One lost confidence in the institution of the church. One left due to "burnout" from serving. Another left due to the xenophobia of the church. Another left over the church's focus on SES (wealth, social, and academic status). A final one left over personality clashes in the fellowship.

---

26. Some clergy participants predicted such a finding; Terry Woo won the Asian Canadian writer's award for his book *Banana Boys* (Cormorant, 2005), which highlighted the cultural and social limbo that Canadian-born Chinese can experience (alienation from both the mainstream Canadian and Chinese cultures) and how identity is something that has to be explored when in an in-between hybrid culture. A passing reference in this volume is made to the tension experienced by some CBCs specifically with the Chinese church cultural identity.

27. They moved to study or work elsewhere.

FINDINGS AND RESULTS

Table 3. Dropout findings ranking

Issue	No. of cases citing factor	Ranking
Issue #1	2	7a
Issue #2	14	1*
Issue #3	3	6a
Issue #4	3	6b
Issue #5	2	7b
Issue #6	13	2a*
Issue #7	5	5a
Issue #8	5	5b
Issue #9	9	3*
Issue #10	13	2b*
Issue #11	1	8
(New finding) loneliness, seeking friends, fellowship, and relationships	8	4*

The combined findings from the dropout surveys have uncovered that the top five reasons CBCs leave their Chinese bicultural churches are:

Issue #2: Their life stage transition needs were not being met within a Chinese church (14).

Issue #6: The overemphasis on Chinese cultural identity and ethnocentrism (13).

Issue #10: Issues with church leadership, organizational structure, and programs (13).

Issue #9: Control issues concerning church power and politics (9).

Discovered Issue: Loneliness and the attempt to seek friends, fellowship, and relationships (8).

Further summary statements and quotes can be found in appendix D, which records additional responses to questions in section five of the survey.[28]

28. If the bicultural church you left were a *car*, how would you describe it? If the bicultural church you left were a *household*, how would you describe it? If the bicultural church you left were a *person*, how would you describe it?

In section six, participants were asked to briefly describe what happened in their lives after they left the Chinese church.[29] (The participants had left their churches between 2.5 years and nine years previously.) The majority stated that they still believed in God (only two, 6 percent, said they did not). About half indicated they had reevaluated their concept of church and found a better way to integrate their spiritual beliefs and life. Twelve participants (40 percent) stated that they had grown because of the transition; nine participants (30 percent) indicated that they had to deal with their need for healing over pain and feeling wounded. Notably, more than one respondent indicated that the reflective experience of completing the survey brought back some unresolved painful memories. Three survey participants (10 percent) indicated they had left the church completely; five other participants (16 percent) noted that they infrequently attend a church. Only four survey participants indicated that they are again serving in the church; four other participants indicated they are not serving; one other participant indicated an inability to serve; twenty-one participants did not comment on serving. Some expressed an experience of coming to terms with their blended cultural background.

Questions in section seven were focused on gleaning constructive feedback.[30] Twenty percent of the group requested that there be more biblically based teaching on matters pertaining to ethnicity, mission, inclusiveness, and other practical life applications. They made an appeal for teaching the foundational truths of Scripture and cultivating a high view of God and his Word. Sixteen percent (five) of this group advised that the English congregation be given autonomy and that the Chinese congregation give up control in order to allow the English congregation to independently coexist side by side. Thirteen percent recommended that the Chinese congregation and leadership empower (give power to) the English congregation. Three percent recommended an English congregation church plant. Several participants cited their discovery that a multicultural (or primarily Western)

---

29. This section had a number of embedded related questions: How long ago has it been since you left the bicultural church you have discussed? What has been your life journey since you left that church? Have you found what you are looking for in another church, or are you still looking for something missing, or have you just given up on your faith? Do you still believe in God?

30. Hindsight can be 20/20. Looking back, if the situation(s) leading to your departure had not happened or had happened differently, would you see yourself still in that Chinese bicultural church now? In hindsight, what had to change or be changed in the bicultural bilingual Chinese church in order to provide CBCs like you (growing up and maturing) a real and fulfilling Christian life and service experience in church? If you were the bicultural Chinese church, what would you have done to prevent the younger generations from leaving?

church would be a more suitable environment in which to grow to maturity when there is not a sufficient degree of independence for the English congregation in a Chinese bicultural church. Several participants felt an exodus should not be prevented. Thirteen percent (four participants) recommended that the Chinese elders take a close look at hiring relevant leadership and reviewing leadership structures. Thirteen percent recommended that the Chinese church work on facilitating an environment where there is more connection, community, and authenticity for the English congregation. Thirteen percent requested more Christian character from the Chinese leadership. Discipleship should include modeling humility, giving genuine care, and showing more openness. Surprisingly, only ten percent expressed that the vision, direction, and goals of the English congregation needed to be addressed; the lack of interest in the EM direction might be less of a concern for those who had already left the bicultural church. Ten percent recommended that the EM have relevant mentors instead of being managed and "babysat." Ten percent recommended that the Chinese leadership be supportive of the EM and willing to listen. Ten percent recommended that the Chinese congregation be more accepting, less judgmental, and more graceful;[31] they encouraged the Chinese congregation to express Christian attitudes toward the members of the English congregation—welcome them, treat them like family, and be lovingly engaged in their lives. (The concern was with the *quality* of the community.)

---

31. This corresponds with the 2011 Angus Reid survey *Hemorrhaging Faith* regarding young adults leaving the church. That study concluded that "there are four primary toxins that keep young people from engaging with the church: hypocrisy, judgment, exclusivity, [and] failure." Penner, *Hemorrhaging Faith Report*.

Table 4. Dropout recommendations

	More connection, community, authenticity	Relevant mentors to EM	Listen, be Supportive, willing	EM direction vision, goals	Biblical teaching (e.g., ethnicity, application)	Relevant staff leadership, structures	Character, model humility, care, openness	Empower (give faith away)	★Give autonomy to EM (give up control)	More grace, acceptance	Church plant
1	N. R.										
2	N. R.										
3	N. R.										
4	✓	✓									
5	Too hurt										
6					✓						
7	N.R.										
8					✓						
9	N.R.										
10	✓										
11			✓								
12	✓			✓							
13					✓		✓				
14							✓				
15	Let them go										
16		✓			✓		✓	✓			

FINDINGS AND RESULTS

Age										
17									✓	
18		✓	✓	✓	✓					
19								✓		
20	✓							✓		✓
21		✓			✓					
22	N. R.									
23	Let them go									
24								✓	✓	
25						✓	✓			
26	Not sure									
27									✓	
28					✓	✓				
29		✓		✓	✓	✓		✓		
30							✓	✓		
	4	3	3	3	6	4	4	4	5	3	1

Remain-In Participant Demographics

Demographically, the remain-in survey participants, as a sample group, were similar to the dropout survey participants; most of them came from similar parish contexts. Eight of the respondents were female, and twenty-two were male. The approximate ages of the respondents ranged from twenty-one to forty-six. The average age was about twenty-eight. Nineteen participants were between the ages of twenty-one and twenty-nine; eleven participants were between the ages of thirty and forty-six. In comparison to the dropout group, there were slightly fewer females, and the age group was only slightly younger. The respondents came from nine denominations.[32] Notably, all of the participants' churches were evangelical.

---

32. Included were: Mennonite Brethren, Mennonite, Chinese Alliance, Lutheran, CCC, Anglican, Chinese Evangelical Free, and two separate independent Chinese churches.

Table 5. Remain-in demographics

Case number	Gender	Age	Denomination of (Chinese church)
1	M	22	MB
2	F	23?	MB
3	F	25	MB
4	M	Mid 30s	A
5	M	24	MB
6	F	Late 20s	MB / A
7	M	Mid 20s	A
8	M	Late 20s	MB
9	M	Late 30s	L
10	F	28	L / A
11	M	21	MB
12	M	30	L
13	M	45	CCC / A
14	M	32	EFC
15	M	30	MB
16	M	32	MB
17	M	33	MB
18	M	31	Anglican
19	F	23	Anglican
20	M	24	A / EFC
21	F	21	EFC
22	M	22	Independent
23	M	33	B / Independent
24	M	21	EFC
25	M	21?	M / MB
26	M	26	MB
27	F	27	CCC
28	F	24	MB
29	M	24	MB
30	F	46	A
Totals:	M = 22 F = 8	Average age = 28	Number = 9

Findings from English-Speaking Remain-In Adults from the Chinese Church

Thirty English-speaking adults were surveyed via email, telephone, and face-to-face interviews using the same seven sections and eleven issues as with the dropout group. Each was an *active* adult member in an English congregation in a Chinese church in Metro Vancouver or Alberta.[33] Forty-five questionnaires were sent out. Fifteen people dropped out with little or no explanation (33 percent). The purpose of surveying this group was to ascertain if they had an understanding of the factors for the CBC exodus and to see if they perceived the leadership needs for the retention of English-speaking adults in Chinese churches. I also looked for convergences, differences, and similarities between the remain-in group and the dropout group.

For the remain-in group, special focus was given to the responses to the eleven questions in section four and the responses to sections six and seven. Detailed data can be found in appendix F. Included here are summaries.

In section one, the majority reported being brought to church as a child. The majority were from Christian families and were baptized members in evangelical churches. In section two, the bulk spoke of their church experience as being family oriented, supportive, and warm, and said they were very involved in attendance and service. Eleven (36 percent) out of the thirty explicitly did not feel comfortable with bringing people of other races to church; an additional four did not feel comfortable bringing anyone. Five felt comfortable bringing other races.

In section three, twenty-eight (93 percent) of the participants acknowledged that the exodus of English-speaking adults from their churches was rampant. Only one said it was not common. When an explanation was given, the most commonly stated reason was related to life-stage needs not being met (seven participants); this finding was reinforced by the remain-in group's responses in section four. Next in rank were leadership problems (e.g., case 12) and conflict. Other explanations included cultural and language differences, faith struggles and choice for a secular lifestyle, study mobility, and opting for a different church. A list of other reasons included pastoral neglect of EM congregation needs/care, burnout, personal conflicts (related to breakups, dating non-Christians, work schedules), and the imposition of joint services.

Twenty-six participants (86 percent) observed that those who left did it after a slow buildup, a long process of careful consideration. A

---

33. Two remain-in participants, at the time of the survey, were in a Chinese church EM in the Toronto area, but both have history/backgrounds and a connection with Chinese church English ministries in BC and Alberta.

significant finding here is that in a number of cases there were prominent EM leaders who were observed leaving (deacons, EM committee members, and so forth). Many of the participants cited precipitating "red flags" they saw before the adults left; discerning reflective leadership should pay attention here.

Twenty-two participants (73 percent) noted that they were negatively affected by the exodus of English-speaking adults. Several remembered experiencing sadness and discouragement (especially because some CBCs completely abandoned the church), confusion, disappointment, and hurt. Several stated that when some adults left, more pressure from the Chinese side was put on EM volunteer leaders; in the aftermath of an exodus, a number of EM ministries were unsustainable. Some participants grieved the loss of role models. It was noted that when people leave, it can contribute to a "domino effect" (as other CBCs question why they should stay). Some noted that they constructively channeled their feelings into a call for improvement in the church toward the EM. Only four participants indicated they were not affected by CBC adults leaving. Nineteen participants (63 percent) reported they had thought of leaving the bicultural Chinese church; four of these stated that they were still thinking of leaving. Two of these nineteen have been thinking of leaving for another, healthier bicultural church. Only ten out of the thirty had not thought of leaving. The top reasons for wanting to leave included neglect of pastoral care for English ministries members' spiritual growth, marginalization of the EM, burnout in service, and concerns with irrelevant preaching; all of these reasons are related to deficits in spiritual leadership.[34] Additional reasons included: discouragement, the ignoring of poverty and social justice issues, the ignoring of neighbors, the church's distaste for ecumenism, the English congregation's lack of voice in decision making, the difficulty in inviting other races, and the imposition of Chinese culture on the EM. Clearly the findings in this section show that the remain-in's are also an at risk group;[35] if 63 percent of the members of EM congregations are concerned enough about their situation to consider leaving, why would the leadership ignore it? Where is the prophetic leadership speaking truth with love to power? If 73 percent of the English congregation members could be adversely affected by CBC adults leaving over deficits in a church's leadership initiatives, why would the leadership ignore it? "If one member [in the body of Christ] suffers, all suffer together" (1 Cor 12:26). The silent exodus represents profound hemorrhaging.

---

34. "Spiritual leadership is moving people on to God's agenda." Blackaby and Blackaby, *Spiritual Leadership*, 20.

35. For one example, see appendix F, case 8.

Seventeen out of the thirty remain-ins agreed that their identity of being a CBC within a Chinese church could be a factor in leaving.[36] Many indicated that the identity issue is accentuated by being locked into a reliance on the Chinese congregation's leadership and frequently not being given autonomy or a say in mission; some participants indicated that the Chinese church can make the CBC experience more difficult. Twenty-six out of the thirty (86 percent) felt life stage transition needs being unfulfilled within a Chinese church was an issue. The top reasons noted for why life stage transition needs are not being met included: the church not having a vision (not being prepared ahead of time to attend to the needs of a growing intergenerational [i.e., married with children] English congregation); lack of role models/mentors; insufficient resources to be relevant; and a lack of care or discipleship focus. It should be noted that these things are the domain of leadership—shepherding and allocating financial and human resources. Nineteen out of thirty participants (63 percent) considered intergenerational conflict (within the church/the family) to be an important issue. Notable comments were made regarding those in the English ministries not being treated as equal partners.

Fourteen out of thirty (46 percent) agreed that "shame culture" (over-evaluation or rejection) was an issue.[37] Some participants made reference to the EM experiencing a lack of respect and shame as a form of domination. Twelve out of thirty participants (40 percent) felt Western postmodern values or worldviews, in conflict with Chinese traditional values manifested in the bicultural church, were an issue. Fourteen out of thirty participants (46 percent) felt the overemphasis on Chinese cultural identity and ethnocentrism was an issue, but two of the fourteen felt it was only a minor issue; eleven did not feel it was an issue in their churches. A repeated comment was that the overemphasis on Chinese cultural identity was a factor in CBCs not bringing friends of other races to the Chinese church. Twenty-four out of thirty (80 percent) felt the personal choice for a secular lifestyle versus Christianity was an issue. Notably, of the twenty-four, four said they thought

---

36. The impression one gets is that the issue is not being Canadian-born and Chinese (having a CBC identity), but it is the problem of status and power inequality. Many CBCs feel they are in between—not fully finding their identity in either culture and experiencing cultural domination by the traditional Chinese congregation. Some theorists on biculturalism have seen a parallel to W.E.B. Du Bois's work, *Souls of Black Folk*, which describes those "caught between two cultures ('the ambivalence of in-betweeness')—the mainstream white culture and the culture of their ancestors." Dennis, *Biculturalism*, 79. See Kasinitz et al., *Inheriting the City*, 354: "torn . . . navigating between two cultural systems."

37. Notably, several participants felt that over-evaluation of the other cultural ministry was a two-way street.

it was a universal problem with all churches. A couple of participants felt it might be more a rejection of some elements of the Chinese church culture and a confusion of faith and culture (e.g., the segregated nature of some ethnic churches). Many felt leaving the church was the culmination of many disappointments, lack of support, lack of discipleship, and irrelevant ministry (caring) experienced by some English congregants. Of concern is the statement that many totally abandon the church. Eleven out of thirty participants (36 percent) expressed that a perceived problem with church beliefs, theology, or hypocrisy was an issue. Eighteen out of thirty participants (60 percent) indicated that control issues involving church power and politics was a concern; seven did not think it was an issue in their churches—two of the seven felt that it was just a perception stemming from CBC immaturity. Notably, participants commented on OBC leadership making decisions to control the English ministries congregation rather than empower it. Some participants suggested that the English ministry was being disabled by being put in an over dependent position; one participant indicated the members of the English congregation wanted to be treated as equals; another stated, "This issue has me on the verge of leaving." Twenty-one out of thirty participants (70 percent) felt church leadership, organizational structure, and programs were an issue in their church. Some participants acknowledged the high turnover rate among EM pastors (often because of pressure from the power brokers) and how that contributes to instability. Others highlighted the lack of relationship, funding, and support from a Chinese OBC board and leadership. A number of participants highlighted a concern over a lack of strategic vision and long-term goals for the EM that could lead to the beginning of an independent parallel ministry/congregation or possibly a church plant. Some indicated that independence for the English congregation was needed and that the EM should push for change.[38] One participant (case 29) was bold enough to say that "the EM will never flourish with a [OBC] ideology and vision."[39] Only nine out of thirty (30 percent) felt that intellectual, rational, and pragmatic matters were an issue; fifteen out of thirty did not. One notable comment was that leaving is more about relationships than intellectual differences.

---

38. E.g., see remain-in case 27 in appendix F.

39. In other words, a vision and mission statement by OBCs intended to reach only one ethnicity (homogeneous unit) is insufficient to sustain a healthy biblical future for a maturing multi-networked EM in a Canadian multicultural context.

Table 6. Remain-in findings ranking

Issue	Percentage	Ranking
Issue #1	30%	
Issue #2	86%	1
Issue #3	63%	4
Issue #4	46%	
Issue #5	40%	
Issue #6	46%	
Issue #7	80%	2
Issue #8	36%	
Issue #9	60%	5
Issue #10	70%	3
Issue #11	30%	

In section six, CBCs summarized their overall experiences and spiritual journeys in the Chinese church. Most participants used the key descriptive words *meaningful* and *fulfilling* to express their overall experiences in positive terms. Many commented on how appreciative they were of being given opportunities to serve and of finding an extended family and supportive community; participants were thankful for their spiritual growth and being helped to develop and mature in their relationships with God. One participant commented that church life had been both fulfilling and unfulfilling since some traditions and structures were holding people back from experiencing God (case 28). Participants gave a list of things they felt were lacking. These things included the need for a greater focus on listening and working with God; the need to focus on biblical training with relevant application; the need to focus on a process of transferring leadership power to the EM; the need to address segregation (case 30); and the need for more openness to new people with different lifestyles, ideas, and ways of doing things. Furthermore, there was a perceived need to equip the church to interact easily and comfortably with other races and a need to seek out more people who can bridge both cultures. There was an appeal to encourage more intercultural and intergenerational programs, encourage a multicultural vision, and support more interaction with other nationalities and mainstream society. Some saw a need to cultivate more mentorship and personal coaching and encourage more people to serve in their calling. CBCs in this group recognized that the impediments are a leadership issue; leadership needs to take responsibility to make change.

In section seven, the thirty remain-ins had an opportunity to offer some suggestions to prevent a further future exodus of English ministry adults from the Chinese church. The participants provided a list of preventative changes they would like to see in their churches. At the top of the list was the need to increase the quality of preaching and teaching (be relevant), so people could hear God more clearly.[40] Participants also saw a need to improve communication (reconciling relationships/shalom leadership) between the OBC and CBC congregations. They wanted both groups to be sensitive to one another when making decisions; to act like Christians; to share thoughts, to pray with each other, to ask and to give forgiveness; to serve and support each other; to be open and honest; to encourage mentorship, prayer partners and in-depth discussions; to invest in discipleship and accountability relationships; and to provide needed resources. Several summed up their perceptions as a need for proper respect to be given to the EM.[41] One participant advocated for respect for all people regardless of race or social status. Participants wanted their churches to be safe, welcoming places where people can find acceptance and friendship. A number of participants made recommendations about the leadership structure. Some were comfortable with the current associated dependent congregation model but called for improvements in intergenerational leadership, including ensuring that a good EM pastor was in place, one who is passionate about development. Other participants called for the Chinese leaders to empower and trust the EM to operate more independently and to have a more consistent clear vision for the EM. One participant felt that what was needed was "stronger leadership and a breakaway from the Chinese congregational governance."[42]

A significant finding with the remain-in group was their perception of how prevalent it is for CBCs to leave the Chinese church (93 percent). This group also had a cluster of concerns, similar to the dropouts regarding the health of English ministries. Because 63 percent of the remain-ins indicated they had either considered or were still considering leaving, I would conclude that, in some measure, they are also an at risk group to

40. Categorically, the quality of transformational leadership wanted in this domain of public ministry is prophetic. Notably with both the remain-in (case 12, appendix D) and the dropout (case 9, appendix F) groups, some concern was expressed regarding relevant teaching or guidance in addressing sexual and homosexual issues.

41. In 2011, Thom S. Rainer published some research project results in a volume titled *The Millennials: Connecting to America's Largest Generation*. He pointed out that the millennials are rejecting "particularly divisive and fighting churches." He noted that "for almost all of the millennials [in this study,] 97 percent to be precise, mutual respect was a critical issue in any relationship." Rainer, "Millennials Are Rejecting Fighting."

42. E.g., case 28.

leave. This conclusion is reinforced by the finding that both the dropouts and the remain-ins reported that the number one reason CBCs leave is that their life-stage transition needs are unfulfilled. This discovery is similar to To's smaller study in the year 2000.[43]

In 1996, Wong touched on meeting life stage needs in asking a key question of Canadian Chinese church leaders at a Regent College conference: "Will the Canadian Chinese church see its third and fourth generation going on with the Lord, growing up and taking up the leadership in its churches?" Wong said that "the numbers of CBCs will continue to grow in the churches, but if the spiritual, cultural and social needs (life stage needs) are not being met, we will see a great exodus from the church." It appears that Wong's words were prophetic.[44] Frequently, when remain-in participants were speaking of dropouts, the remain-in group showed a high personal affinity with the issues.[45] Several remain-in participants had left previous Chinese bicultural churches over a number of the same issues as those addressed in the survey questions. Both groups reported concern about there being limitations in doing outreach to non-Asians; in practice, the broader scope of the Great Commission is eclipsed.[46] One forty-six-year-old CBC put it this way: "I've spent 40 years in a bilingual church environment. The biggest regret is that I am contributing to the segregation of the body of Christ rather than the unifying of the body here in my city" (case 30).

What I find different about the remain-in group is that they have found reasons to stay based on having strong relationships. From that comes a hope in a positive future for English ministries congregations.[47]

43. To and To, "Exodus," 2. This three-month study was conducted with fourteen adults who left their Chinese churches.

44. Wong's predictive concern seems to be unfolding. In the second decade of this millennium, we see "a remnant remaining in the Chinese church; a [small] minority [have gone] to other Asian churches (e.g., pan-Asian, CBC), a minority have gone to community churches," and an uncalculated number have "joined the majority of CBCs [in] disillusionment with the church . . . . Those leaving the church represent 15–20 years of investment." Wayland Wong, "Towards a Mature English Ministry," 3.

45. Survey participants could write as much or little as they wanted in answering the questions; many of the remain-in survey statements were extensive—if length is a gauge—expressing their experiences seemed to be very cathartic and perhaps an indicator of their hope and desire to see change.

46. Assumptions within various bicultural churches regarding which ethnic groups to strategically target has had some effect on CBC personal initiatives in mission and outreach. The disposition in evangelism is predominantly toward Chinese.

47. Remain-ins tend to speak about being savvy about Chinese culture and language. Family factors are spoken of in positive terms. When answering section six in the survey, they tended to have a more positive outlook on the Chinese church and used the word "fulfilling" more often to express their experience. There do not seem to be

Like the dropouts, the remain-ins are also calling for the Chinese leadership and congregation (who hold the power) to empower the English congregation to cast vision and fulfill a mission relevant to CBC networks. All the issues of concern that the remain-in group identified are in the domain of leadership.

Comparative Results of All Three Groups

Table 7 shows how the three groups surveyed understand why CBCs drop out.

Table 7. Comparison of all three groups

Top Five Reasons for Silent Exodus Listed Ranked in Order		
Dropout Reporting	**Clergy Speculations**	**Remain-In Speculations**
Issue #2	Issue #6	Issue #2 (86%)
Issue #6	Issue #10	Issue #7 (80%)
Issue #10	Issue #9	Issue #10 (70%)
Issue #9	Issue #2	Issue #3 (63%)
Discovered issue: Loneliness/relationships	Issue #3	Issue #9 (60%)

Both dropouts and remain-ins see Issue #2 as the primary reason CBCs leave Chinese bicultural churches. Both dropouts and remain-ins also agree that Issue #10 is the third most important reason for leaving. Notably, the clergy failed to grasp the number one reason why CBCs drop out, although the clergy had a somewhat similar understanding of the third most important reason (Issue #10).[48] The differences in perception between clergy and dropouts/remain-ins is illustrated in figure 2.

---

huge differences in the theological understanding between dropouts and remain-ins. For lack of a better way of putting it, they seem to have a clearer sense of "calling" to be where they are. They haven't reached a breaking point that makes them want to leave—yet—and they want to make it work.

48. Why is it that the clergy ranked the most significant dropout factor in fourth place as a lesser issue? There are several plausible explanations. Perhaps the clergy have made an assumption, projecting the top challenging issue *they* deal with in bicultural settings (issue #6 the overemphasis on Chinese culture) onto why CBCs exit. Most likely further research with EM clergy could ferret this out. Most EM clergy intensely deal with mediating, advocating, and bridge-building between the two cultures—so

Figure 2. The main issues as seen by all three groups

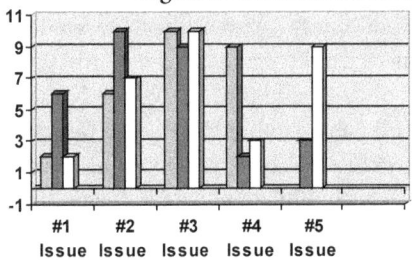
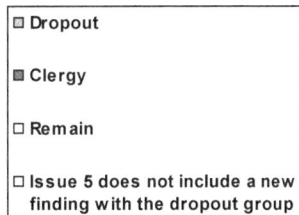

I also compared the findings of this study with the findings of Wang's 2003 survey of two Chinese churches, which asked participants for the primary reasons the second generation is leaving.[49] In Wang's research, the number one reason for CBCs leaving their church was a "lack of friendship and caring relationships."[50] In my research, CBCs ranked the lack of friendship and caring relationships as the fifth reason. However, in my survey this reason was an unexpected discovery; I would concede Wang's point that CBCs are "relationally oriented . . . where connectivity and individual social needs come first before cultural traditions."[51] Like third culture peoples who are growing up in two different cultures, bicultural CBCs put a high focus on "relationship rather than geography."[52] One finding in my survey that was identical with the research findings of Wang and Evans is that cultural rigidity (or overemphasis on Chinese culture)[53] is the significant *second* key reason CBCs leave their church.[54] This finding also matches the research of

---

culture likely has a high profile in their speculations. A second explanation may be that there is some relational distance between EM leadership and what CBCs are concerned about. This may be further supported by the fact that not many CBCs surveyed cited their clergy or board as role models—more often their role models were an older cohort, peers, or teachers. It begs the question as to whether the EM leadership is kept too busy to focus on the relational level. If so, this could be related to workload expectations and/or the high English pastor turnover that is so frequently cited in these surveys. This is an *incarnational leadership* deficit. No wonder the surveys reveal that a fifth reason CBCs exit is to seek meaningful relationships and be understood. Leaders cannot address this problem unless they get closer to those they serve—the relational distance must be bridged.

49. Paul C. Wang, "Study on Cross-Cultural Conflict," 149–52, 187–95.

50. Ibid., 151; also see 144–45.

51. Ibid., 151.

52. Pollock and Van Reken, "Rootlessness and Restlessness," in *Third Culture Kids*, 131.

53. Paul C. Wang, "Study on Cross-Cultural Conflict," 150.

54. This has been a frequently voiced concern for nearly three decades. In 1986, Dan Jue warned North American Chinese churches that they were facing both a danger and an opportunity in regards to next generation Chinese leaving over cultural baggage.

Ebaugh and Chafetz, who noted that "congregations that focus … strongly on recreating ethnic ambience of the old country are most likely to alienate" the next English-speaking generations.[55] Unlike Wang, I did not create survey questions addressing the silent exodus around the topic of conflict with parents, boredom, or a weak English ministry—although I think a weak EM might play into my question as to whether life stage transition needs were being met. I note that Wang surveyed both OBCs and CBCs. Perhaps one weakness of my survey research is that I did not survey a fourth category, OBCs, to obtain their comparative perceptions on the topic. Furthermore, I did not include questions on parental conflict, a factor that Wang found to be the third most important reason for CBCs' exodus.[56]

Description of my Experience during this Research and the Analysis of Dropout Findings

This research presented the challenge of thinking through the statement of the problem and the purpose of the study. Developing the list of questions required background reading, consultation, and feedback. One of the things that I tried to do was to keep the questions open-ended so that respondents didn't feel forced to answer what might be perceived as embarrassing questions. My hope was that the anonymity of the questionnaire would also help overcome this problem.[57] I was well aware of the fact that participants would perceive me to be asking sensitive cultural, familial, spiritual, and church family history questions. I felt that this fact could make recruiting and retaining participants more difficult. I tried to get around this problem by seeking referrals. I believe that what motivated participants to contribute was the "opportunity to give voice to their feelings and concerns. Many express[ed] the hope that their participation [might] make it easier in the future for others who have to cope with a situation similar to their own."[58] There were a couple of cases in which I did know of the participants' experi-

---

Jue predicted that if the Chinese churches did not "put priority in retaining" members, they would experience "great irretrievable loss." Jue, "Appeal to Sacrifice," 89, 85. James A. Evans saw ethnocentrism as the source of the problem, in that cultural preservation was prioritized over mission—there simply was "too much of an emphasis on Chinese identity and not enough on teaching and living out the Christian life." Evans, "Impending 'Silent Exodus,'" 175, 184.

55. Ebaugh and Chafetz, *Religion and the New Immigrants*, 119.

56. Paul C. Wang, "Study on Cross-Cultural Conflict," 151. It makes sense to also consider the role of the family in faith and social formation.

57. Oppenheim, "Question-Wording," in *Questionnaire Design*, 64.

58. Wahler, "Conducting Research on Sensitive Subjects," 25.

ence, and I believe the interviewees may have had reduced recall or told me what they thought I wanted to hear.[59] The data collection and analysis procedures took some time to establish. Once the key factors were identified, I attempted to match the outcome of the study with leadership theory, theological constructs, and a deeper literature review. The survey dispersion and follow-up was time-consuming and tedious. I had to send out weekly email reminders to many participants indicating I was waiting on them to forward their completed surveys.

Conclusion of the Survey Results on Dropouts

This survey has successfully identified some causative patterns and risk factors for CBCs leaving bicultural Chinese churches, which indicate where preventative kinds of leadership measures can be taken. For example, the research revealed that the life stage when the majority leave is young adulthood; that most CBCs deliberated for a lengthy period of time, assessing their options, before exiting; and that follow-up with them appears to have been minimal or nonexistent. The survey also revealed the top five reasons why dropouts leave, and all of these reasons are related to deficits in leadership. There is thus a need for a greater application of the qualities of transformational leadership: incarnational leadership, servant leadership, prophetic leadership, reflective leadership, shalom leadership, and calling-based leadership. I was surprised by a couple of factors (outliers)—not directly asked in the list of questions—that surfaced in dropout responses (i.e., cross-cultural marriage, mobility).

A Critique of the Project Including a Reflection on Theological Issues the Project Raised

In some survey cases, I was reluctant to report various "unrefined" remarks coming out of former conflict and obvious lingering hurt.[60] Reporting even

---

59. Inaccuracies or distorted responses from some participants are a probability with surveys. See Silverman, "Interview Data," in *Interpreting Qualitative Data*, 97; Yin, *Case Study Research*, 80. Ian Dey notes that "subjects perceive and define situations . . . according to their understanding of their own motivations and the contexts in which they act [and therefore one should] . . . allow for the usual mix of ignorance, self-deception, delusions and lies." Dey, *Qualitative Data Analysis*, 36.

60. Some of the conflict experiences reported were brutal. This disproves a Western stereotype of Asian leadership as having a gentle and sometimes effeminate quality—such as William P. Young's tender portrayal of Sarayu, the Holy Spirit, as an Asian in his book *The Shack* (Hodder & Stoughton, 2007). The atrocious reality for some next

some of the toned down comments doesn't mean I endorse the stated perceptions; the documentation represents how the participants understood their experiences with a Chinese church. A number of survey participants stated that completing the survey either caused some painful unresolved memories to surface or that the experience was therapeutic and cathartic.[61] Overall, a measure of love and appreciation for the Chinese church was clear. Though some participants ignored various questions, every participant was aware of the key issue of CBCs scattering from and leaving the Chinese church. When the motif of scattering, or being scattered, shows up in the canon, it is often theologically associated with relocating oppressed people back into alignment with God's purposes. Middleton and Walsh note such a correlation with Babel (Gen 11) in that the "community is fragmented and scattered. And while this scattering is in judgment upon an autonomous attempt at establishing unity, it also enforce[d] God's original intent that we multiply and fill the earth, thus diffusing an oppressive concentration of human power."[62]

I had a sense with some participants and some potential participants who dropped out of the survey (there was approximately a 60 percent return rate) that their contribution to this investigation might be dishonoring to their parents (telling on their parents or culture). This hesitancy touches on the theological tension between honoring parents (Matt 15:3–6) and prioritizing God's value on addressing systemic familial and institutional injustices (Mic 6:8; Matt 12:49–50). Prophetic leadership is needed to speak the truth with love to those who hold the power in broken systems. Certainly this project has refuted the flawed assumption that "if we just get CBC adults involved in ministries, they will stay in our church." Scripture does not put the emphasis for a sustainable faith community on works, duty, performance, or activism. A qualitative faith community needs to shift its emphasis to loving God (being theocentric) with heart, soul, mind and strength and loving each other (being relational) (Luke 10:27).[63] A healthy

---

generation CBCs is that they are slamming into powerful hierarchical, patriarchal, and paternalistic personalities and cultural barriers, often filtered through filial piety and Confucianism.

61. I am unsure if incomplete statements or unanswered questions in the survey are partly a reflection of this. I saw evidence of Wayne Wong's statement that "many Canadianized Chinese people who have left their churches without first reconciling . . . have not emotionally left." Wong, "Current Challenges," 40. There is a need for shalom leadership.

62. Middleton and Walsh, *Truth Is Stranger*, 189.

63. Eugene Peterson has lamented that activism and having people involved in programs has "developed into the dominant methodology of doing church . . . [the] problem here: a program is an abstraction and inherently nonpersonal. A program

faith community must express real Christian character (Gal 5:22–26) in relationships (Phil 2:4; 1 John 3:18).

Because the average age of the participants in my surveys was around thirty, which is more or less the "Asian age of adulthood," I have a sense that their survey participation represents the expressions of a group "coming of age" who are motivated to voice their experiences. Further reinforcing my belief that the participants were highly motivated (willing to talk about perceived negative experiences) is that almost all were referrals. I sense that the social roles and identities[64] of CBCs in bicultural churches (Chinese hierarchical cultures[65]) have a decisive effect in influencing their choices to leave. The theological issue here seems to be related to mentoring (2 Tim 2:2), discipleship, empowering, and launching a next generation into the fullness of leadership in the faith family (Eph 4:11–16). Although I can assert that love is what holds the bicultural church together, that love comes through a hierarchical cultural lens that needs to give way to a biblical picture of community (Matt 12:48–50; 1 Tim 5:1; 4:12; Luke 14:26). CBC adults in bicultural Chinese churches are a high risk group for a number of reasons identified in these surveys. First, 16 percent have either left the church altogether or infrequently attend. Second, about 30 percent specifically indicated they had been wounded and had been seeking healing elsewhere.[66] It's obvious from the self-reporting of the remain-in cluster that they are also an at risk group. Many are grappling with difficult contexts, and others are on the edge of considering an exit.

From a theological point of view (the doctrine of the body of Christ), the segregation of the Chinese bicultural church from the broader church has negatively affected a holistic understanding and experience for some survey participants. All Christians are a part of the same body of Christ (Eph 5:30; 1 Cor 12:27). It is an interesting observation that the majority of dropout survey participants who moved on to other churches have intentionally chosen multicultural or mainstream churches (56 percent). This choice may represent that they have done some theological reflection about

---

defines people in terms of what they do, not who they are." We should be understanding church in terms of "personal relationships and a personal God" not simply "getting things done." Peterson, *Memoir*, 254–55.

64. See Dey, "What Is Qualitative Analysis?," in *Qualitative Data Analysis*, 50.

65. For a historical discussion on the hierarchical nature of relationships in Chinese culture, see Shi, "Chinese Cultural Traditions," 19–22.

66. Two examples are dropout case 20 in appendix D and remain-in case 2 in appendix F. I also found documentation for this theme of CBCs leaving the Chinese church over being wounded in Evans's doctoral research. Evans, "Impending 'Silent Exodus,'" 176, 177.

who the church should comprise and how regressive persistent segregation can be (Ephs 2:13–17; 3:6; 4:15–16). Sometimes it helps people to know what they are supposed to be doing by seeing a vision of where they are going. Revelation 5:9–10 and 7:9 provide a picture of the whole family of God singing and worshiping before God—a multicultural, multiracial group drawn "from every tribe and language and people and nation."

Finally, I am left pondering why more males than females showed an interest in participating in this survey.[67] The outcome of this study might have been further enriched if the gender balance of respondents were more equal. I encountered more articulate responses from older contributors.[68] If I were to do this survey again, I would have included more questions on the churches attended. I would explore more deeply why the pervasive assumption about English ministries coming out of the CBC surveys is that they are oriented to CBCs and not pan-Asian or multicultural. I recognize that these surveys are a snapshot of static data; given some reported attachment of CBCs for their cultural group, I wonder how many might return later to another, more mature English congregation in a Chinese bicultural church.

Feedback from Leadership Focus Groups

This section represents an action-oriented step of convening three leadership focus groups with Chinese church leaders from three different parish models to obtain a response on the hypothesis and survey findings. A brief document containing the hypothesis and some survey findings was

---

67. Sixty-eight percent of the dropout and remain-in surveys were completed by males. What is interesting about this is that most church congregations generally have more women than men. There is a degree of motivation and intention required for one to complete a survey such as this; speculatively, these surveys might reflect that CBC men feel these issues more acutely. It may be that the CBC male experience in the Chinese bicultural church context has some connection with the findings of Ho and Wong's research on Chinese Canadian male identity development with immigrant men. The CBC male experience in the immigrant church is one where they are wedged in between Western and Eastern values on responsible male gender identity. Western society tends to extend a more egalitarian culture to younger adult males than the Eastern customs do in faith communities. CBC men are trying to make sense of their current experience (or limitations in role models) and future expectations by searching. Certainly there can be conflicting notions of when a male is recognized as a full-fledged adult in Chinese church communities; however CBC males seem intent on wanting to renegotiate and integrate Western values in the realm of permission to make their own decisions. Ho and Wong, "Searching for Manhood," 207–34.

68. The older the CBC reporting, the deeper and more articulate were the responses to the questions. This may be evidence of either mature reflection or theological integration with their lives.

communicated to these groups (see appendix G); the full reports of the focus groups are also included in appendix G. All leaders were either in a Chinese bicultural church or had left Chinese bicultural churches. The objective was to test the survey data and findings and obtain advice toward further improvements in addressing the silent exodus. Focus was given to the recommendations and counsel on the idea of giving permission to English congregations to have broader decision-making powers and what the focus groups might recommend toward an action plan. The following documentation represents a brief summary of their responses.

CBC Focus Group Feedback from a Multicultural Church Plant Model

The group (all had left a Chinese Church and were currently attending the same multi-ethnic church plant) resonated generally with the reasons[69] for the silent exodus except number #2 (see footnote 79). No one left their churches because of an over emphasis on Chinese culture and identity. More in the group identified with number #1 and #5 for their reasons for leaving (see footnote 79). One person in the group felt a "parallel associated independent EM congregation" could work if the expectations were clearly set out at the onset.[70] The others in the group were less optimistic. They felt the cause of the silent exodus is born out of differences and conflicts in core values and way-of-doing-things, and they ask, "How does this model eliminate these conflicts?" For example, in spite of the parallel independent structure, conflicts over use of facility are inevitable, especially if the CM feels they "built" the building. Furthermore, if children of the CM are "sent" to the EM, there will also be inevitable conflicts over "what" and "how" the kids are being taught. If these conflicts cannot be resolved, then history will repeat itself as the CM develops its own English ministry. Then conflict over schedules will emerge, and the EM will need to find its own facilities. One person pointed out that at issue is also the EM sense of "identity," and much like when a CBC marries, "leaving" may be necessary for them to develop

---

69 1. Their life stage transition needs were being unfulfilled within a Chinese church.
    2. The over emphasis on Chinese cultural identity and ethnocentrism.
    3. Issues with church leadership, organizational structure, and program issues.
    4. Control issues with church power and politics.
    5. Loneliness and the attempt to seek friends, fellowship, and relationships.

70. In a follow up dinner with this focus group I asked if any of them would go back to an arrangement where my recommended model was in effect with the Chinese church. Conditionally half the responses were affirmative.

an individual identity. Another person pointed out that for the kingdom, dispersing CBC disciples to the rest of society may not be bad for the gospel. It may be an act of God for evangelism; therefore the exodus is not a problem that needs solving.

CBC Focus Group Feedback from a Mature Dependent English Ministry Model

The representative pastor from this focus group reported back that the recommendation for Chinese Church leadership to allow English ministry congregations decision-making powers is one key track on the road to healthiness in CBC English ministries. The research was affirmed in correctly identifying key factors on why English speaking Chinese adults leave traditional Chinese churches. In their own communities this group of leaders has tried to deemphasize cultural exclusion. These leaders are part of a Chinese church that has moved to a multi-site and multi-congregational model. Each site and congregation has been given, since the inception of this model, a fair bit of autonomy and oversight through the leadership of a key "Congregational Pastor" with his own leadership team; thus, it is up to the CP to lead change and transform existing leadership. Key leadership traits of CPs are spiritual and emotional maturity, patience, a very strong cultural intelligence, wisdom in leadership, among others. The focus group point person stated,

> I agree that your submission of parallel associated independent English congregational models would be a good beginning. This though needs to be well supported and endorsed by senior leadership, senior pastor and any other supervisory pastors. I, for example, support our English ministries as a coordinator and also general Pastor of [office title the pastor holds currently]. All ministries need to be funded fairly and well, for example. You are preaching to the already converted in this case. I need to emphasize that not every pastor, be they from a Chinese, Western Caucasian, European, Singaporean, Korean, or other Asian background, by their very ethnicity, is able to be the change agent in transitioning English ministries to a healthy autonomy. Their cultural intelligence, spiritual and emotional maturity, character, chemistry with team and congregation, prayer life, people skills, and many other intangibles are a real key to changing the CULTURE of their own congregation as well as the whole church in general. To empower English congregations or any other congregation requires a general cultural shift for

the entire church. This said, there are many other factors that glue a community together. People will still come and go. Issues of relationship within a community, seeking life partners, healthy or unhealthy dating and marriage relationships, lack of wooden dogmatism . . . the willingness to accept, live with and receive various theological positions, sense of belonging, purpose, community, engaging one's spiritual gifts, preaching and teaching style and culture, sense of being loved and cared for, one's acceptance no matter where he/she is on the faith spectrum, etc. all have a bearing on one's connection with the local church community.

Focus Group Feedback from a Mature Dependent/ Interdependent English Ministry Model

The makeup of this focus group included second, third, and fourth generation CBCs in an age range from their twenties to late seventies (further details on group composition are in appendix G). One focus group spokesman stated,

> Having read your abstract and attached memo from [Lead pastor / focus group leader] . . . initial reaction to your study was that it seems that this is exactly what our church is going through. I just had drafted a business case for our [church] to review to present to the members of our Chinese Speaking Elders about the need to change our English name of the church, as in a sense it is self-limiting. We have crossed this road a few times in the past years and each time the members of the Chinese Congregation did not support the need to change from [Chinese church name] to a more community focus name like [gives an example of a community church name]. It seemed more important and significant to the Chinese speaking members to maintain our cultural identity . . . not sure if breaking away from the mother church, which is ethnocentric, is the best way of retaining CBC membership. I think it has to do more with how the leadership can work with both congregations and servicing their specific needs. At one time I would tend to agree with your recommendation but as I have grown in our church and watched people come and go, I think what is more important is not to think of our church as being limited to four walls, in fact our church may be the larger community of members who have moved on to other churches and still maintaining a sense of connectedness

with us. Even those members or adherents who have moved to other countries like Australia, Singapore or Hong Kong or United States still stay in touch with us and often ask how are church is managing . . . I think how we conduct our services including worship, and how well the ministers connect with our English congregational members *is more important in the sense of retention than having a separate parallel church within a church.* These are just some of my initial thoughts, although I know this is a very complex issue.

Another leader from this focus group felt it was important to communicate the factors for the reason her mature adult daughters' families exited and were no longer attending this English language congregation. The transcripts can be found in appendix G. In essence she was affirming some of my key factor findings as to why the silent exodus occurs.

Summary Conclusion on Feedback from Leadership Focus Groups

Based on the full feedback responses contained in appendix G, all three leadership focus groups responded with one or more of the following:

- a positive identification with some of this research's findings that explain the key factors for the silent exodus
- an affirmation that empowering the English ministry congregation is a sought-after solution
- an acknowledgment that the recommended associated independent model is, or has been, a desirable option for a healthier English ministry congregation

One observation from the two bicultural leadership focus groups is that they provided limited advice as how to further improve matters toward an action plan for an independent associated model; their solution to a healthier English ministry leans toward looking to skillful and mature executive and congregational leadership. The support and endorsement for greater autonomy remains in the hands of senior leadership, which is not surprising as my recommended independent associated model is both entrepreneurial and countercultural (it is not an intuitive model for a hierarchical cultural context).

7

Desired Outcomes

> The illiterate of the 21st century will not be those who cannot read and write, but those who cannot learn, unlearn, and relearn.
>
> —ALVIN TOFFLER

GAIL LAW HAS IDENTIFIED an important point relevant to this research in her Dynamic-Bicultural-Continuum Model.[1] She points out that that there are limitations to the ability of a parallel associated *dependent* model congregation to appeal to large numbers of Chinese who, after the first generation, acculturate faster and further along the continuum.[2] This doesn't mean they don't still embrace a mixture of Chinese values, but that the present associated dependent English ministry model of Chinese church becomes less attractive[3] given the degree of mainstream cultural integration that

---

1. Law, "Model for the American Ethnic Chinese Churches," 134–36.

2. Statistics Canada, "Immigration and Ethnocultural Diversity in Canada." Of the 6,264,800 members of visible minority groups in Canada, 26.7 percent of the ethnic Chinese were born in Canada (CBCs); the median age is 38.6. The question is: Who is reaching them?

3. It has been recognized that the vast majority of local-born Chinese adults are not in churches because of either not feeling comfortable or not feeling welcome. Also see Wayland Wong, "Reaching ABC's," 122. Jeung notes that "Asian Americans mark off 'non-religious' more than any other American." Russell Jeung, "Emerging Second Generation." Gail Law points out that "the [LBC] form one of the most unreached peoples" in North America, and that "the Chinese churches do not attract the total spectrum of the Chinese [because] there is a bicultural gap between the Chinese churches and the [LBC] whom the church leaders want to keep." Law, "Model," 131, 137. D. J. Chuang's

they have in their familial,[4] work,[5] and community[6] networks; that is to say, the associated dependent English ministry model in a Chinese bicultural church has limitations to its ability to do mission with the "marginal [and] alienated ethnic."[7] Furthermore, LBC adults' bicultural capacity for multiethnic ministry and racial reconciliation is further evidence of their broader mission capacity. They have a handle on the dominant culture[8] and therefore an ability to bridge reconciliation with their primary cultural experience.[9] I resonate with Rah's prophetic assessment of the phenomenal missional capacity of the second generation: "Multiracial individuals, the Third Culture kids, the growing number of individuals who seek and experience a multicultural identity will be able to lead with confidence, knowing

---

2007 survey of Asian American churches found that the majority who participated had English language services (95 percent), but the untapped opportunity for the English language congregation is in the realm of outreach. Chuang, *Asian American Churches*, 13, 9. Wayland Wong notes that 98 percent of the CBCs are "outside of the church of Jesus Christ" and that "the Chinese church essentially has little impact on the CBCs [though] many have been raised in the churches." Wayland Wong, "Towards a Mature English Ministry," 4, 2.

4. For example, based on the 2006 census, Statistics Canada reported that "mixed unions are higher for Canadian-born than foreign-born visible minority groups." In particular, 53.7 percent of Chinese-born in Canada were in mixed unions. Statistics Canada, "Persons in Mixed Unions." Gail Law would say that LBCs have a "larger bicultural capacity [to] function over a wider range along the bicultural continuum." Law, "Model," 139. Kenneth Fong's data shows that by the third generation over 60 percent are in interracial marriages; he notes that interracial dating and marriage are indicators of moving "away from an immigrant outlook" and that LBCs have a concern for the future of their own children in a "multilingual, immigrant-oriented church." Fong, *Pursuing the Pearl*, 226, 45–46, 195. Soong-Cha Rah notes the increase of intercultural and interracial marriages. Rah, *Next Evangelicalism*, 184. Amy Chua anecdotally notes that LBC women "often marry a white person." Chua, *Battle Hymn of the Tiger Mother*, 21. The "high out-marriage rate among Chinese women" is also noted in Kasinitz et al., *Inheriting the City*, 234.

5. Jeung, *Faithful Generations*, 79, 151.

6. Rah, "Multicultural Worldview," in *Next Evangelism*, 192: "Many second-generations have experienced a social economic uplift that means they are able to move into middle and upper middle-class neighborhoods."

7. Fong, *Pursuing the Pearl*, 10. Fong also argues that many marginal ethnics are not willing to be more ethnic and so they leave the "immigrant-focused churches" (13); "they dropped out or will not come because what some of our churches are about and how we go about [doing church] is a poor fit with who they are or who they have become" (173).

8. Rah, "Multicultural Worldview," in *Next Evangelicalism*, 186.

9. Ibid., 192–93.

that their unique identity is truly a gift from God and a gift for the next evangelicalism."[10]

Given LBCs' cultural orientation, they should be empowered to expand into new, accommodating models. God has given the next generations

> opportunities to further God's redemptive and reconciling work in our increasingly diverse society. God will forge new models . . . that will advance [his] eternal purposes beyond this generation's aspirations and dreams. Our work as agents of change and transformation begins with embracing God's heart for the world and being open to participate with God however God leads.[11]

CBC adults want to move beyond being semi-autonomous, beyond the current limitations on doing outreach to other ethnicities, beyond language and cultural tensions with the OBC leadership, and beyond the experience of feeling like a second-class congregation.[12] It's important to say that a church model should serve the church's mission to the demographic reality around the church; an antiquated model should not determine the mission. Incarnational leadership recognizes that there must be a "willingness to enter into another culture [and] learn" and to overcome our "cultural blindness"; this willingness stems from a "holy desire to make people of a different culture our family and friends" for the sake of the Good News.[13]

If, as church growth statistics are showing,[14] Chinese churches are some of the fastest growing churches in Western Canada, then it is an anomaly that the English ministries—under an associated *dependent* con-

---

10. Ibid., 193. Rah says, "If given the chance, the second-generation . . . have the great potential to lead the next evangelicalism" (197).

11. Jonathan Wu, "Trusting Households," 119.

12. Jeung, "Emerging Second Generation."

13. Wing H. Mak, "Embracing the English-Speaking Ministry," 8–9. Mak cites examples of incarnational ministry in Luke 10:8–11 ("Eat what is set before you") and 1 Cor 9:22 ("Become all things to all men").

14. Fueled by ongoing Asian immigration, Asian church growth is the most prolific in the country, especially in centers such as Toronto and Vancouver. "Greater Vancouver in BC is one of the most Asian metropolitan areas in continental North America." DeVries et al., *Asian Religions*, 6, 2. Li Yu has commented on "the rapid growth of Christianity among the Chinese in British Columbia [where 2001 census data] found that Chinese Christians . . . totaled 24 percent of the total Chinese population, making Christianity the largest religion in the community." Li noted that in 2006 the "Greater Vancouver area [had] 110 Chinese Protestant churches" and that this number was based on an incomplete list. Yu, "Christianity as a Chinese Belief," 234; see also 278. Soong-Chan Rah notes a parallel phenomenon in the United States, where the immigrant churches are the fastest growing in the country. Rah, *Next Evangelicalism*, 12, 191.

gregation model—are stifled in their evangelism (mission)[15] and vision and impaired (in too many cases) by the long-term dominance of the OBC hierarchy.[16] Therefore, I want to recommend a model that holds the possibility of alleviating these factors. When an adult English language congregation is kept financially, operationally, missionally, and structurally dependent and denied a legitimate voice in leadership or in the unfolding future of its own ministries, then it is time to consider renegotiating the association model. It is time for a paradigm shift to an associated *independent* model.[17] In this model, the English ministries congregation would be registered legally with the denomination as a self-governing congregation. This model would empower the English ministries congregation to develop its distinct (hybrid) vision and mission[18] focus. One CBC adult expressed it this way:

> I really feel that being bicultural is not a crutch but an advantage, there are so many parents that feel better in a Chinese church because of language and culture, the problem lies in their children to be able to coexist in the parallel English ministry. Maybe the answer is breaking down the English ministry to model after

---

15. It has been noted that when the "core mission is reaching Chinese, it [can be] difficult [to] create space for second-generation leaders to expand beyond that mission." Tsang and Rah, "Disillusioned Generation," 54. Furthermore, cross-cultural mission can be hindered by certain emphases grounded in Asian cultural values, such as hierarchy, conformity, deference, and respect for tradition and elders (filial piety), and by certain cultural challenges either rooted in Confucian-based perspectives or the inability to resolve conflict. Cha et al., *Growing Healthy Asian American Churches*, 32, 61–62, 66–67.

16. They are not free to grow, not free to develop their own styles of leadership and worship, not free to reach the unchurched and unreached from other racial and ethnic backgrounds, and they are viewed as a potential threat to Chinese church cultural practices. It is noted that a dilemma is often created for a minority cultural group in a majority cultural group where adaptation becomes one-sided and unequal. The structures in which decisions are made for the minority cultural/language group can be closed, limiting, and restrictive. When two cultures are sharing a common context, "the relationship between the two entities [will have to address] power and conflict relations." Dennis, *Biculturalism*, 15, 25.

17. Kuhn highlighted that in any given era practitioners can be operating within accepted models and paradigms; however, every now and again the suppressed elements reveal an inadequacy to incorporate a new understanding of reality. Some assumptions in a traditional paradigm require change. A change requires a conceptual shift, reeducation, and a transformed vision to enable incorporating what has not been incorporated and to see things in a new way. The application here is that when a church model is not working and things don't fit, it is time for a shift, time to change what has not been working to a framework that better matches the emerging reality. Kuhn, "Revolutions," 111–35.

18. After all, "the goal of the Christian mission . . . is the transformation of life." Gladys Lee Tsang, "Churches in Ethnic Transition," 67.

non bicultural churches but keeping [EM] under the same roof, like two churches sharing a building.[19]

This recommendation is for those churches where the mature parallel dependent or interdependent model is not working. It is *not* necessarily for churches whose English ministries are flourishing, are seen as full partners, are given autonomy, and can fully carry out their mission/vision with other ethnics.[20] I want to state at the outset that the model I am presenting is an *option* for bicultural churches where there is an absence of mutual partnership, where there is a stifling experience of cultural hegemony, and where other positive mature models—such as the healthy interdependent associated congregational model—are unachievable and beyond reach. On the positive side, there can be an amicable recognition that the two congregations have different missions and visions while still recognizing that there are some things that they can do in association; they can be legally independent without completely severing the relationship. Hence the recommendation here is not for the unthinking, hasty importation of a model just because conflict exists and a solution is needed. White wisely stated: "Even very good ideas, if they are done without the partnership, insight and ownership of the residents, will likely be done in a way that is not appropriate for the context or sustainable over the long haul. An imposed blessing is rarely a blessing at all."[21]

Certainly one doesn't start to initiate a new structural model by "pulling a rabbit out of the hat." There needs to be a healthy process of discussion (see the recommendations for a course of action in chapter 8) and a clear understanding that "the normal we are in is not the normal God wants."[22] What is needed is to introduce a "virus" into the system that will begin to do its work even if it doesn't take effect for a lengthy period of time. I acknowledge that before structural independence can be negotiated, the English

---

19. Quote from dropout survey participant case 12 in appendix D.

20. For example, I came across a discussion of a second generation congregation which "began to move toward organizational autonomy." The leadership jointly "took specific steps to reverse this movement" and put a higher premium on intergenerational relationships. Cha et al., *Growing Healthy Asian American Churches*, 152–62. Note: If the EM is culturally leaning toward Chinese culture (because of factors such as demographics or living in a Chinese concentrated area such as Richmond, BC) and its board truly embraces an egalitarian interdependent relationship, then likely a shift to an associated independent model and structure may not be necessary.

21. White, *Encounter God in the City*, 146.

22. White noted that the goal is to convince everyone involved that "this will make our system better, not worse." White, "Debriefing."

ministry congregation must have reached a threshold of mature[23] ministry independence.[24] Perhaps an assessment tool or process needs to be created to assess the tipping point of when a model change might be warranted. This book does not explore in detail the process needed to commence the recommended associated independent model but concedes that a respectful and vigorous process is necessary to get there.[25] Transformational leaders who embark on this road should be prepared to put together a realistic action plan and present it to the executive leadership and governing board of the bicultural church.[26] Advice from the denomination also needs to be sought. The transformational leader needs to be prepared to address objections that

---

23. In light of Eph 4:11–15, the leadership should have been investing in the EM to build it up to maturity so that it can serve God's mission. Maturity is a reference to things such as attitude, character, the ability to handle pressure, a commitment to stable doctrine (2 Tim 3:16–17), growth in grace and the knowledge of Christ (2 Pet 3:18), the ability to control carnal desires (1 Cor 3:2–3), and obedient living in following Christ (John 15:14). Malphurs, "Making Mature Disciples," in *Advanced Strategic Planning*, 195–210.

24. Independence in itself is not what makes a healthy English congregation.

25. In this regard, I want to note an October 29, 2013, discussion with Dr. Timothy Quek of Scarborough Community Alliance Church in Ontario who, at the time of our dialogue, indicated that his congregation was in the fourth year of being an "autonomous interdependent English language Chinese church" (a model somewhere between a parent/child structure and a church plant); this church uses a separate facility on the same site as the Chinese-language congregation. Rev. Quek came to Canada at age twenty-one and is trilingual. He noted that the English congregation spent eleven to twelve years meandering in a parent/child dependent English ministry model and then moved toward gradual autonomy. He needed to be a very intentional and focused leader to transform the traditional model. He began by strengthening ministry independence (training, discipleship, investing in leadership development, nurturing through small group structures, etc) and then moved to structural independence. (This included registering as a separate church, financial independence, being released to do independent hiring of staff, having deacons appointed by the EM, having a separate constitution, redefining the biblical role of elders, and so forth.) This English congregation is fifteen years old and has been four years in this new model, which has been instrumental in nourishing church growth and allowing leadership to flourish. This is the closest structure I am aware of that resembles the model that I am recommending in this research.

26. I do not want the reader to assume that I am skipping over this very pivotal step. Anytime a person wants to change the model and governance of some aspect of the church, the transformational leader should be prepared to be misunderstood by people who fear for the unity of the church. Steven Chin's story of transitioning the EM from one model into a different model holds some valuable principles to negotiating into an associated independent model. In negotiating the new model, Chin focused on clear (inoffensive) communication, a slow approach to gaining unanimity rather than fighting and splitting the church, demonstrating maturity and responsibility (165), and prayer to melt opposition and affirm trust in the sovereignty of God. Chin, "God's Double Blessing," 161–66.

may come from these various circles.[27] It will require vision and foresight for the English ministry to incrementally be granted full associated independence. This task will require the transformational leader to gather a group of like-minded leaders around him or her. It requires the transformational leader to be exceptionally focused on being a part of the transition over the long term and to start educating, cultivating, and planting the vision of a new model into the congregation.[28] Accomplishing such a transformation will take tenacious intentionality and plenty of work. The transformational leader needs to seek and trust God's guidance for the progress of the unfolding vision.

An associated independent[29] parallel English ministry congregation[30] comes with the self-determining option to later church plant[31] a parallel independent church (on the same site or a different site) or to choose other models that accommodate its evolving mission potential. This kind of adaptable model follows "the inevitable flow of the generations [and] acculturation."[32] The reason I am not advocating a sudden break church plant is because of the recognition of the culturally deep linkages between the CBC and OBC congregations. This approach is born out of the acknowledgment that religion is complex, personal, and social—where the "past and present are . . . intertwined."[33] Bakke encourages "ethnic Christians

---

27. For example: the source of an OBC board or congregation's objections may be concern over losing control of the church or the perception that such a shift is an attack on the unity of the church. The transformational leader needs to be able to address the "patriarchs of the church family" who may be invested in the Chinese traditional point of view that "Father knows best."

28. How inclusive will this new church be? How diverse will the leadership be? What location will it choose to worship in? Has thought been put into how adaptable the new church is going to be to the new ideas, practices, etc. that new people might propose?

29. The independent relationship (legally, constitutionally, operationally, financially, ministerially, missionally) would parallel that of launching a Mandarin ministry church plant or renting to another ethnic group (e.g., Korean or Filipino).

30. Associated means that the association is completely volitional. Independent means that the congregation is operationally, financially, and ministerially independent and registered as a separate entity with the denomination and government bodies. It is an English-speaking ministry in that this is the language used for all public ministries.

31. Several participants in the surveys for this book also had a strong disposition toward a church plant; e.g., dropout cases 19 and 20 in appendix D and remain-in case 13 in appendix F.

32. Fong, "Pursuing the Pearl through the Flow of Generations," in *Pursuing the Pearl*, 23.

33. Bramadat and Seljak, "Toward a New Story about Religion and Ethnicity," in *Religion and Ethnicity*, 222. Baker and DeVries point out that "by the third generation, hyphenated Canadians are usually no longer fluent in the language of their forbears, and

to . . . identify [their] spiritual map and celebrate God's sovereign movement in [their] past"—the unfolding transition the English congregation seeks is part of the predetermined seamless work of the Holy Spirit within its ethnic church.[34] Cha aptly points out that the church models Christians choose to belong to "also communicate how they relate to their own ethnic identities and to their cultures and communities"; furthermore, one must not forget that "immigrant churches [are also part of] the body of Christ [and a] gift from God."[35] There needs to be a recognition that bicultural CBCs identify with different aspects of Chinese culture and mainstream Canadian culture that are not found in the same way in a mainstream church. One of the parallels that bicultural adults have with third culture peoples is "not wholly identifying with [the immigrant culture] or mainstream culture."[36] CBCs often "live in two cultural worlds . . . [and] believe themselves to be culturally and socially enriched by the . . . customs and social networks made available [and] see themselves as having the right to lay claim to both identities."[37] Almost all the survey respondents in this study expressed a commitment to their cultural identities and heritages.[38] This commitment is another reason why an *associated* independent model makes more sense than a complete church plant split—the benefits can outweigh the liabilities. The reasons to remain associated while becoming independent can include linkages such as marriage, intergenerational associations (family solidarity, interpersonal relationships), outreach to families, cultural exchanges, intercultural ministry referrals, educational partnerships, opportunities for intercultural celebrations, and a way of keeping in touch with a dual heritage. An associated

---

family dynamics tend to become Canadianized over time but . . . religion survive[s]." DeVries et al., *Asian Religions*, 2.

34. Bakke, "Ethnicity in the Church," 175–76.

35. Cha, "Finding a Church Home," 148–49.

36. Pollock and Van Reken, *Third Culture Kids*, xiii, 123. Also see: Rah, "Multicultural Worldview," in *Next Evangelicalism*, 185: The third culture person "experiences being an outsider insider" and is a person with a dual identity.

37. Dennis, "Towards a Theory of Biculturalism," in *Biculturalism*, 16–17. Research by Philip Kasinitz et al. "underscores the importance of a distinctive second generation advantage: its location between two different social systems allows for creative and selective combinations of the two that can be highly conducive to success." Kasinitz et al., *Inheriting the City*, 354.

38. Samuel Ling has noted the "residue of resiliency of Chinese culture among local born Chinese [up to the] 4th and 5th generation" of EM adults; he recognizes that LBC adults are "on the move" in the bicultural continuum" of Western acculturation, Ling, "Beyond the Chinese Way," 61, 62.

independent English bicultural congregation "represents an unfreezing of cultures and recognition of the cultural validity of another group."[39]

The term *associated* implies that initiatives of shalom leadership will be needed to produce the fruit of a reconciled relationship. Everyone involved needs to come to agreement that the calling for the adult English congregation has some differences from the calling for the immigrant congregation, which requires autonomy and empowerment. Also needed is a mutual understanding that no one has the right to exclude other races from the body of Christ, and a more holistic "missional ecclesiology challenges the church [to] reflect the full social mix of the communities they serve."[40] An associated independent model requires shalom leadership to mitigate the transition, so there is no confusion that this represents a move that dishonors all that has been bequeathed/given/sacrificed by the elders of the church to date. Shalom leadership communicates that the EM does not want to break fellowship but wants to expand mission. The basis for this is the theological foundation that God is "not willing that any should perish, but that all should come to repentance" (2 Pet 3:9). Everyone needs to understand that the reason for the change of model is to expand mission to reach other ethnicities and be able to fully incorporate them into the church; to be able to retain CBCs and bring back CBCs who have left the church; and to be able to reach "unchurched Canadianized Chinese [who] are perhaps the most difficult of all subgroups for the . . . church to minister to."[41] A proof of the EM's desire to honor the past is the desire to remain associated and to seek the whole church's blessing on this transition to a new paradigm/model.

Remaining an independent associated English congregation does not contradict the well-being of the church; it opens the way to healthy cultural syncretism/pluralism. It can be beneficial also for OBC families, many of whose members may be in the process of redefining cultural boundaries and will find it helpful to have accessible examples of others who have made the transition. Remaining in an *associated* independent relationship requires spiritual character. My knowledge of many CBC church plants in British Columbia is that they have been born out of a painful break from the Chinese church (like a divorce), or they were begun by those who left the Chinese church and then reconvened to start such a ministry. I would agree with Sugikawa and Park that

---

39. Ibid., 28.

40. Guder, *Missional Church*, 70.

41. Wayne Wong, "Current Challenges," 41, quote taken from Huang, "Chinese American Christianity," 3.

without an outlet for the fulfillment of their own visions and passions, many second and third generation leaders leave their immigrant communities, joining or planting English-speaking . . . and multiethnic congregations. The experience and spiritual maturity of older generations are lost, and these young leaders are often left to develop on their own. Their longing for parental affirmation and blessing in their calling and mission remain unmet.[42]

My advice to anyone contemplating starting an independent church is if it is possible to avoid creating a church plant out of appalling conflict, then do it. If it is possible to gain a good neighbor with an associated model shift, then do it. If mature adult CBCs want to do church in accordance with their hybrid culture, then why should they be hindered? If CBCs feel a need to integratively identify with the society they live in, why can't it be understood as "related to [their] social responsibility, which in turn is related to [the] cultural mandate."[43] If Canada is the CBC homeland and future, then why shouldn't CBCs be permitted to move into an *independent* model that still retains family ties and gives them more freedom in governance and mission/vision? An in-between *associated independent* English ministry congregation model is desirable, not only because it retains a relationship with the mother church, but also because it potentially is granted a *blessing* on its calling.[44] Kim and Lee explore the matrix of blessing and theologically argue that "God designed his blessing to be passed on from one generation to the other";[45] furthermore, "it is the biblical imperative and privilege for each generation to commission the next generation to go forth into the world to be fruitful and multiply. God infuses this commission with a blessing that is passed from one generation to the next."[46]

42. Sugikawa and Park, "Formation of Servants," 125.

43. Hsu, "Question of Identity," 23.

44. Mitchell Kim and David Lee note that "while the EM might flourish by striking out on its own, could such a move at that time miss out on an aspect of God's blessing in such a situation? How does God desire to release the blessing of the parents' generation to multiply and extend the next generation and accomplish the work of God's kingdom?" Furthermore, each generation has a responsibility to the next generation that comes after it; "it is a biblical imperative and privilege for each generation to commission the next generation to go forth into the world to be fruitful and multiply." Kim and Lee, "Intergenerational Ministry," 22, 29.

45. Ibid., 24. Texts that demonstrate the blessing passed on to the next generation include Gen 49:1–28; 9:26–27. The authors argue that "no generation can fully develop its sense of identity when divorced from its parent generation" (30) and that delegating authority is a "necessary aspect of the process of maturation" (28).

46. Ibid., 29.

Smalley and Trent have highlighted the fact that receiving "the blessing" includes being valued, sharing in a picture of a special future, and experiencing a supportive posture from the older generation.[47] Receiving the blessing is something each generation longs for.[48] Affirming an associated independent relationship says, "We care and value being near you." The OBC governing board can help in completing this transition, in part, by giving the blessing to the new shape of the expanding church family.[49] Just as in families, marriage and the move to living independently doesn't have to mean the end of an association. Who doesn't try to retain a relationship with grandchildren, aunts, uncles, and cousins? Retaining a relationship with a mother church is a spiritual parallel. An associated independent model is likely an easier step for both OBCs and CBCs for several reasons. I will cite just two here. First, it invites a collaborative spirit whereby OBCs are invited to participate in helping make the new arrangement happen by giving away power. Second, staying in geographical proximity (i.e., on the same premises or site) can be less complicated for CBCs than leasing or buying a building in some other geographic area.[50] Most importantly, I would agree with Guder that "a tangible form" of a church understanding its identity as a servant and messenger of the reign of God "is a willingness to change its

---

47. Smalley and Trent, "Blessing: Yesterday and Today," in *The Blessing*, 27.

48. Ibid., 11, 17–21. I was very encouraged to read Russell Jeung's comment that "leaders of immigrant churches . . . have blessed [LBC] ministers in starting multiethnic churches"; it reinforces my sense that this is a very positive ingredient in this transition. Jeung, *Faithful Generations*, 150.

49. Evans describes what receiving the blessing from the OBC board and leadership might look like: it would include the English ministry being prayed for in its new ministry formation, being treated as an equal, and being empowered "to move ahead and organize itself as an autonomous body." Evans, "Impending 'Silent Exodus,'" 160, 159. Although Evans briefly suggests a separate location for a CBC church plant option (160, 184), he really focuses more on a model for a "newly empowered CBC congregation" (163, 173). Structurally, it is still in a parallel mature *dependent or interdependent* model (163). Evans is advocating for "a major structural change [so that] a CBC congregation [can have] a voice [and] ownership in the church" (184). I would argue that Evans's "new idea" of "allow[ing] for the formation of an *autonomous* congregation parallel with the OBC congregation, but with its own leadership team, pastor, budget, and authority," is *not* a legally associated *independent* EM model; it is either an associated parallel mature *dependent* or *interdependent* model, and therefore still under the supremacy of the OBC board. This means that its autonomy can be clawed back anytime in the future when there are transitions in the central leadership or when there comes "a new king, to whom Joseph['s]" leadership means nothing (Acts 7:18). I am advocating an independent model between Evans's two options.

50. Using existing churches is a form of good financial stewardship: Fong, *Pursuing the Pearl*, 219.

visible structures in order to become more faithful to its mission."[51] This willingness requires the quality of servant leadership from all the elders that deliberate on such a transition.

In John 13:1–17, Jesus demonstrated a servant leader's love in practical terms. Servant leaders are to follow Jesus' example by practicing true shepherding rather than lording over people (1 Pet 5:1–5). Further, servant leaders should not be insecure with change but understand that it is God's purposes they are ultimately supposed to be serving.[52] Servant leadership is not about self-preservation but about self-denial through obedience, following Christ's example of unselfish, sacrificial service (Mark 8:34–36). One relevant application is that "the call to sacrifice extends to the cultural issues of . . . ethnic tradition"; the apostle Paul understood this call when he set aside culture to move forward in mission (Phil 3:2–11).[53] The servant leadership that is needed to accomplish a transition to an independent EM model is a

> shift . . . away from traditional autocratic and hierarchical modes of leadership toward a model based on teamwork and community; one that seeks to involve others in decision making; one that is strongly based in ethical and caring behavior; and one that is attempting to enhance the [people's] personal growth while at the same time improving the caring and quality of our . . . institutions.[54]

A servant leader may need to rebuild the culture of the bicultural church so that it willingly agrees to serve in order to do mission.[55] A servant leader would not want to minimize people's future, but rather expand it. When an EM is perpetually dependent, unhealthy, ingrown, obstructed, impeded, dominated, and restrained, the question for both the OBC and the CBC leadership to reflect on is "Do those served grow as persons; do they, while being served, become healthier, wiser, freer, more autonomous, more likely themselves to become servants?"[56] Conversely, are EM congregants—like many dropouts—hurt by their leaders' actions either directly or indirectly?[57]

---

51. Guder, *Missional Church*, 102, 125, 231.
52. Blackaby and Blackaby, "Leader's Influence," in *Spiritual Leadership*, 166–68.
53. Sugikawa and Park, "Formation of Servants," 127.
54. Greenleaf, *Power of Servant Leadership*, 2.
55. Ibid., 122.
56. Ibid., 1, 4, 43, 123.
57. Ibid., 43.

Cultural diversity, generational differences, assimilation, and mission potential are loaded issues. Given that the prevalent Chinese church model has all too often been reported as suppressive of the English ministry, the gesture of the EM proposing an associated independent parallel English ministries model represents good will toward remaining in reconciled relationship while pursuing authenticity and holistic mission. Associated reconciliation is better than disassociation, which metaphorically is the equivalent of a divorce. An associated independent English ministry model is one shift ahead of a mature associated dependent EM and one shift behind an unassociated church plant.

The advantages of an associated *independent* EM model can include:

- It removes the EM from the risk of an arbitrary philosophy of ministry being imposed by the OBC congregation based on the default to cultural hierarchical leadership approaches—particularly when there is a change of executive pastor or a change in the church board.[58]
- It legally establishes the EM as a separate registered entity with the denomination and the government in constitutional, operational, financial, and ministry matters. This formal separation safeguards the EM in case the Chinese congregation defaults to hierarchical duress.
- It cuts away the EM's financial dependency. The old saying is that "he who pays the piper calls the tune." Financial dependency on the Chinese OBC congregation means a loss of independence for the EM.

The EM should choose association not out of insecurity, a need for money, a need for manpower, or the like; it should choose association out of an affinity, relationship, consanguine or lineal ties, shared history, heritage, and out of a desire to voluntarily collaborate in joint ministry initiatives. Some may allege that what I am suggesting sounds like a call for less stewardship regarding the mission of English ministries. On the contrary, it is a call for better stewardship and a healthier theology of the institution of the Chinese bicultural church. I am calling for the leadership of Canadian Chinese churches to reflect on several principles.

The first principle is that the Canadian Chinese church should be an inclusive faith community. As a *Canadian* church—in a country whose

---

58. I have experienced several Chinese executive lead pastor changes. I have seen a "new ruler who didn't know Joseph" come in with a heavy-handed philosophy of leadership totally different from that of the previous executive Chinese lead pastor, who had valued a partnership. It was regressive and suppressive for the EM but happened because of the dependent model.

official policy has embraced multiculturalism since 1971[59]—shouldn't the Chinese church reflect on whether it is an inclusive and welcoming community toward acculturating CBCs and people of other cultures who come to its English services? Survey participants who reported on their silent exodus indicated that this attitude has not permeated very deeply in various Chinese churches.

The second principal is that there should be a biblical theology for the institution of the Chinese church. In other words, it is important to have "a theology of place." The Chinese bicultural church matters because true churches belong to God. Could it be that Providence is behind the establishment of the Chinese bicultural church—and also its transitions? Since God has determined the places where people should live out their lives (Acts 17:26), these become contexts where transformation should be collaboratively achieved. I am suggesting that the Chinese church needs to ask: Why does the church exist? The right answer is that it exists to do mission, not to preserve culture.[60]

The third principal is that the Chinese church leadership should work toward building an improved relationship of trust with the EM leadership. This principal is based on the attitude advocated in Philippians 4:8.

I am advocating the retention of English-speaking adults from Chinese Canadian churches through associated parallel independent English congregation models, which I see as recognizing a linkage in the process of acculturation and the imperative to leverage mission. I acknowledge that this recommended model is not for every Chinese church EM, but I do believe that those who opt for it will find a structure that aids the transition to empowerment; furthermore, it is a model open to further augmentations.[61] It can help facilitate a renewed theological vision, congregational identity, and missional strategy. This model is for places where there must be a more generous kingdom-minded paradigm for subsequent generations of the bicultural Chinese church. It requires a collaborative attitude born out of sensitivity, humility, and understanding. To move toward this model re-

---

59. DeVries et al., *Asian Religions*, 12. Given this "official policy and state ideology," "ethnic minorities [are encouraged] to preserve and celebrate their cultural heritages." Wing Chung Ng, *Chinese in Vancouver*, 105, 3.

60. Enoch Wan points out that there is a need to teach a theology and missiology of diaspora churches and recognize the sovereignty of God in the movement of people and the placement of diaspora churches (Acts 17:26–27). Throughout Scripture, migration and relocation (gathering and scattering) served God's purpose for cross-cultural mission. Christian diaspora are called to be a blessing to the nations. Wan, *Diaspora Missiology*, 62, 74, 94, 186–94.

61. E.g., church plants, an English-language mixed generation model, or collapsing back into an interdependent model.

quires embodying the principles of peace, justice, and brotherhood. It is an abandonment of ethnocentrism and a move toward embracing a culturally heterogeneous conception of the faith and the principles of intercultural cooperation and mutual respect.

This book challenges the assumption that most bicultural Chinese faith communities are navigating the leadership processes of transition, acculturation, and adjustment in an optimal, healthy manner. These faith communities are socio-cultural microcosms of how the broader Chinese community is adjusting, integrating, and assimilating, over time, into the Canadian cultural context. Therefore, this research also has possible implications for advocates of Canadian social policy regarding the need to be more sensitive to the needs of immigrant communities. The Canadian ideal of pluralism includes the objective of advocating for harmonious intergenerational and intercultural living; the recommendations could also affirm progress toward a healthier, respectful community praxis and piety.

8

Summary and Conclusion

> There is no passion to be found in playing small—settling for a life that is less than the one you are capable of living.
>
> —NELSON MANDELA

AT THIS POINT, I would like to draw some conclusions and summarize what has been accomplished up to this point. Based on anecdotal reporting of a silent exodus of CBC adults from Chinese churches, the purpose of this book was to propose transformational leadership strategies *toward* longitudinal retention of these adults; it is my intent to help leaders strategize toward community transformation and lasting congregations that maximize missional capacity. From the literature review, I explored former models and proposed solutions that have been historically used in Chinese churches to retain their English-speaking congregants. Mindful of some of the deficiencies of such models with an aging and acculturating EM demographic, I investigated texts on leading change and transformational leadership. I have been able to understand how the EM was bequeathed an associated dependent model. More importantly, I have explored a theological basis for empowerment and why there is a necessity for a paradigm shift to facilitate an expanded mission and remove the constraints on CBC growth and leadership capacity. Core qualitative research design and fieldwork execution required two years of gathering information and then processing and analyzing it. The qualitative research conducted with participants from diverse Chinese church affiliations established the key factors for CBC adults' exodus:

Issue #2: Their life stage transition needs not being fulfilled within a Chinese church.

Issue #6: The overemphasis on Chinese cultural identity and ethnocentrism.

Issue #10: Issues with Church leadership, organizational structure, and programs.

Issue #9: Control issues involving use of church power and politics.

Discovered Issue: Loneliness and the attempt to seek friends, fellowship, and relationships.

The qualitative research identified patterns and common dynamics with Chinese bicultural churches that have contributed to a silent exodus and risk factors for further departures. Based on the examination of the research findings, CBC adult recommendations,[1] theological reflection, transformational leadership studies, and the sociological need for cultural integration, one strategy toward the retention of English-speaking adults in Chinese Canadian churches could be establishing associated parallel *independent* English congregational models. This strategy recognizes a link between the process of acculturation and the imperative to authentically leverage mission. The recommendation requires a courageous negotiation with the Chinese church leadership to give power away to the English ministry leadership/congregation, so an alternative associated model can be established. It is anticipated that this approach would create a governance framework for strategizing, reducing the exodus, and permitting transformational leadership practices that contribute to shalom. This research included an action-oriented step of convening leadership focus groups with a number of Chinese church leaders to obtain feedback on the hypothesis and survey findings. The aim of this research has been to contribute useful information and recommendations to stakeholders to avert the silent exodus from repeating itself through transformational leadership praxis. The proposal will help leaders strategize toward addressing the spiritual life stage needs of CBCs, and capitalize mission/vision potential.

1. For example: many adult CBC survey participants were calling for an independent model (e.g., dropout cases 24, 25, 25 in appendix D, and remain-in case 28), the empowerment of the EM (e.g., dropout cases 16, 20, 30 in appendix D, and remain-in cases 1, 2, 13, 15, 17), and a change of vision for the English language congregation (e.g., dropout case 18 in appendix D and remain-in cases 3, 18, 29).

Concluding Recommendations

Quinn's exploration of the process of transformation demonstrates that leaders and organizations can lose focus on their mission and subsequently undergo atrophy and decline. He states that "we must continually choose between deep change or slow death."[2] With the Chinese church EM, the choice ranges along a continuum from rigid cultural preservation to obedience to the expansion of Christ's mission. Intentional and transformational leaders are needed. Such leaders must be willing to address deep change from an adult CBC's point of view as it biblically relates to the church's mission and purpose and then bring that understanding to the Chinese hierarchy. Ley is correct that "new circumstances require institutional re-visioning."[3] Based on this research and reflection on the literature, this study advocates the retention of English-speaking adults in Chinese Canadian churches through associated parallel *independent* English congregational models, which recognizes a linkage between the process of acculturation and the imperative to authentically leverage mission.

There are a number of steps[4] needed in order for this new paradigm/model to be developed in Canada. I believe that most Canadian Chinese churches are only at step one. However, the research presented here provides a foundation for those who might want to pursue a timetable of two to five years to fully achieve launching this model. This book merely starts a process that would require the following next steps.

Transformational Leaders Must Know Their Gifts and Calling

Now is a good time for leaders to consult[5] and do some soul searching. Any leaders undertaking this challenge must be journey oriented. They

---

2. Quinn, *Deep Change*, xiii.

3. Ley, "Immigrant Church," 2070.

4. Jonathan Wu outlines seven steps to consider regarding making significant change; these include initiation, identification, inquiry, invitation, information, implementation, and influencing: Wu, "Trusting Households," 120–21.

5. In my own denomination, a leader refocusing opportunity has been offered to pastors discerning significant next steps. Preparatory consultation should include networking with experienced leaders who have helped an EM congregation through a change of church model. It should include discussions with denomination officials. It should include peer feedback and evaluation, and it could include doing some leadership testing such as the Myers-Briggs Type indicator or a psychometric leadership inventory such as the EQ-I Leadership Report. This report helps the leader understand his/her emotional intelligence capabilities in four key dimensions of leadership: authenticity, coaching, insight, and innovation. It is a ministry fitness check.

must have confidence that God has called them to lead change in the bicultural church. They must be committed to the future ministry of LBCs who are seeking to broaden mission, reach their neighborhoods, be more inclusive, and experience growth. As change agents, these leaders should consider that they are representing Christ.[6] These leaders need to abide in their calling and dream of what their English congregations can be.[7] These leaders need to be praying, asking God to miraculously transform cultural conventions to bring a renewal to Christ's mission. Change leaders also need to shore up their inner life by being deeply rooted in practicing spiritual disciplines[8] so that they will be able to go the distance. "Transformation is essential but . . . will only occur when leaders commit to personal transformation."[9]

Transformational Leaders Must Engage in Vision Dreaming

Transformational leaders need to reflect and pray about how a new paradigm model can retain EM adults, expand mission (in alignment with Matt 28:19–20), and "create a compelling picture of the future."[10] Envisioning

6. Murren, "Leader as Change Agent," 199.

7. Guinness, *The Call*, 172–82. Kim and Lee argue that going independent needs to be calling-based. Kim and Lee, "Intergenerational Ministry," 31.

8. I recommend Foster's list of inward disciplines (meditation, prayer, fasting, study); outward disciplines (simplicity, solitude, submission, service); and corporate disciplines (confession, worship, guidance, celebration). Foster, *Celebration of Discipline*. Before planning to lead a congregation through changing its model, leaders would be wise to take a realistic look at the spirituality they are bringing to the table from their own lives. Things to consider include knowledge of the kind of church model they intend to grow, their relationship with God, their emotional health, their marriage and family relationships, their ability to do the work of an evangelist (2 Tim 4:5), their depth of faith, their leadership skills and abilities, their relational abilities, their personal integrity, their vision and philosophy of ministry, their ability to be an entrepreneurial organizer, their ability to preach relevantly through such a process, their ability to disciple others through the process, and their ability to maintain enthusiasm and productivity throughout the process. Kim and Lee also make the point that there should be evidence of spiritual health and maturity on the part of the congregation to accompany a move toward independence—the first generation should not be blamed for all the challenges. Kim and Lee, "Intergenerational Ministry," 30–31.

9. Herrington et al., *Leading Congregational Change*, xiii. The "spiritual and relational vitality of the leader(s) drives transformation" (159) and "is foundational to the change journey" (10). The leader needs to make personal preparation on several levels (e.g., logistics, fiduciary capabilities, revisiting mission), but most importantly by being in spiritual alignment through spiritual disciplines to hear God (29–31).

10. Lewis, *Transformational Leadership*, 235. This resonates with Rom 12:2: "Do not conform to the pattern of this world, but be transformed by the renewing of your

involves asking questions such as Who are we? Where are we going? Why are we going there? What can it look like?[11] Remarkably, "change comes from dissatisfaction [e.g., with the present situation] . . . takes energy [and] requires insight."[12] At the end of the day, transformational leaders will be leading with a new vision and picture[13] of what their particular faith community could look like and could potentially achieve for the kingdom. "Transformational leadership . . . helps followers embrace a vision of a preferred future."[14]

Transformational Leaders Must Cast Vision

Transformational leaders should seek a like-minded base, a group of EM adults who resonate with a desire to move into the new paradigm/model of an associated independent EM congregation and the vision that inspires it.[15] They should dream together, keeping in mind the statistics regarding the silent exodus, the unreached "marginal and alienated"[16] LBCs, and the unreached neighborhood and friendship networks within their reach. Though the English ministry needs to change to a new model, being honest about the risks may not be easy. The like-minded base should support the transformational leader in addressing the Chinese church board and asking for a change.

---

mind. Then you will be able to test and approve what God's will is—his good, pleasing and perfect will."

11. Malphurs, *Advanced Strategic Planning*, 26.

12. Murren, "Leader as Change Agent," 204–5.

13. Malphurs urges creating a "mental model" so that people are enabled to embrace change. Herrington et al., "Discipline Two: Harnessing the Power of Mental Models," in *Leading Congregational Change*, 117.

14. Herrington et al., "Disciplines of Transformational Leadership," in *Leading Congregational Change*, 9.

15. Herrington et al., "Establishing the Vision Community," in *Leading Congregational Change*, 41.

16. Fong, *Pursuing the Pearl*, 10. There needs to be a renewed understanding of Christ's mission in order to discern vision and outline a vision path. The leader needs to have a good understanding of the differences between mission, vision, and vision path. Herrington et al., "Discerning and Communicating the Vision," in *Leading Congregational Change*, 49, 50.

Transformational Leaders Must Be Prepared to Talk to the OBC Leadership

Transformational leaders must talk to the OBC leadership about how the process of acculturation, shift in mission, and desire for self-governance are central to seeking a new model. It is a known fact that the OBC leadership has "the power [and] . . . the ability to empower the CBC congregation"; the challenge for prophetic leadership is to "persuade the power-holding group to share some of its power."[17] The request to change the model is an appeal to grace-based governance, servant leadership, and a process of listening, understanding, and discerning change. The church is supposed to have an "alternative understanding of power" and how it should be used.[18] Transformational EM leaders should state that they are seeking to address "change in a healthy manner [and that they want to] anchor this process in a strong trust in . . . what God is doing."[19] Such leaders need to be resolute on the current reality: why the church is losing CBC adults; why CBC adults are the most unreached mission field; why a Chinese church *dependent* model may hinder mission to other ethnicities. I would recommend leaders utilize some of the material from Ken Fong's *Pursuing the Pearl* to help with this presentation such as the degrees of assimilation figure,[20] the flow of generations model,[21] and a tailored version of the "open letter to the 1.0 generation"[22] to present to the church board and executive pastor (written and translated into Chinese if necessary).

Transformational Leaders Need to Prepare an Initial Action Plan

Transitional leaders need to prepare an initial action plan outlining what, why, who, when, where, and how.[23]

---

17. Evans, "Impending 'Silent Exodus,'" 151.
18. Guder, *Missional Church*, 120, 123.
19. Jonathan Wu, "Trusting Households," 109.
20. Fong, *Pursuing the Pearl*, 10.
21. Ibid., 216.
22. Ibid., 193–95.

23. Lewis discusses the value of spending time on strategic implementation and thinking in terms of actions needed to be taken to make change happen. For example: (1) examine the internal . . . forces that require change (2) diagnose the reasons for change (3) determine an appropriate intervention to introduce change (4) examine the constraints and limitations that may inhibit change (5) identify the performance objectives and outcomes (6) apply methods to implement change (7) provide means for evaluating the effectiveness of implementation and feedback mechanisms to correct

What: The transformational leader needs to define every word of the new paradigm model.

Why: The leader should explain the EM's concerns with acculturation, mission,[24] governance, and different cultural needs.

Who: The leader should explain that this proposal pertains to the EM congregation only.

When: The leader should set out a timetable, of perhaps two to five years, to achieve full *independent association*.

Where: The leader should explain the rationale for remaining *associated*.

How: The leader should be ready to explain the measurable and achievable steps in the plan to reach this goal.

The plan should be doable, and everyone should know what to expect and what is expected. "Transformation occurs through intentional processes"[25] and "leaders engaging in strategic planning."[26] To aid in this very crucial area of planning, I recommend that the leader build in SMART goals that help make the plan Specific, Measurable, Attainable, Realistic, and Tangible.[27]

Transformational Leaders Should Be Prepared to Address Objections

Evans is correct that when approaching the OBC board, transformational leaders should make their requests in a respectful manner to those in church office because "in Chinese culture respect is the equivalent of love."[28] Consultation is advised here. Proverbs 15:22 says, "Plans fail for lack of counsel, but with many advisers they succeed." Transformational leaders should operate out of a "non-anxious assertiveness,"[29] humbly entering into discus-

---

the implementation if required. Lewis, "Strategic Implementation," in *Transformational Leadership*, 159–60.

24. "The question [of going independent] is missional, not logistical or organizational." Kim and Lee, "Intergenerational Ministry," 31.

25. Herrington et al., "Art of Transformational Leadership," in *Leading Congregational Change*, 159.

26. Lewis, *Transformational Leadership*, 232.

27. Lewis, *Transformational Leadership*, 95–96. Also see Top Achievement, "Creating S.M.A.R.T. Goals."

28. Evans, "Impending 'Silent Exodus,'" 180.

29. Herrrington et al., "Art of Transformational Leadership," in *Leading*

sion with the Chinese church executive and board leadership and knowing they will most likely encounter a polarized point of view. "Transformational leaders plan communication[30] paths that lead to understanding . . . put in a 'lay person's language.'"[31] It is in this context that leaders need to continue to insist on why there is a need for change and be ready to engage in "life-giving conflict."[32] Leaders should know how to diffuse unnecessary disagreement and remain focused even in the context of conflict.[33] At the end of the discussion process, everyone may not be in agreement (they may be only able to agree to disagree), but even if a change to an associated *independent* model may not be achieved, there may be a positive secondary outcome of an OBC recommitment to work toward improvement and the creation of an ideal interdependent model. Transformational leaders should expect that, whatever happens, the net effect can be a constructive collaborative change that will make a God-honoring difference.

Transformational Leaders Should Plan to Meet with Denominational Leaders

Transformational leaders should seek the wisdom of the regional/conference headquarters leaders on the proposal. They may be able to offer both the leader and the church resources to work through the transition. Ultimately, the new paradigm model requires the denomination's blessing to register the EM as a separate entity.

Congregational Change, 161.

30. Kim and Lee, "Intergenerational Ministry," 33. The authors' experience in pursuing an independent model required a commitment to healthy communication with the first generation leadership. They did not want to pursue the independent model at the expense of the relationship; they wanted to pursue the biblical template of seeking the blessing.

31. Lewis, *Transformational Leadership*, 237.

32. Herrington et al., "Learning to Lead Change," in *Leading Congregational Change*, 9. The leader should expect that "the change process . . . creates conflict"; however, "deeper understanding and commitment [can] grow out of a significant disagreement." Consider Acts 6:1–7.

33. Perkins et al. recommend some very resourceful principles to use in a highly conflicted board context in "Resolving Conflicts."

Transformational Leaders Should Plan to Do Some Deeper, Detailed, Strategic Planning

One of the better resources to help leaders do advanced strategic planning is written by Aubrey Malphurs.[34] Transformational leaders must review, make strategic evaluations, measure progress, and take corrective actions as necessary.[35] Advanced strategic planning includes reestablishing core values,[36] developing mission, creating vision, introducing a ministry strategy, building a ministry team, and establishing assessment procedures.

Transformational Leaders Should Educate, Train, and Develop the EM Congregation

Transformational leaders should plan to educate, train, and develop the EM congregation toward accepting the full responsibility and the opportunities to flourish in the new paradigm model. This process involves cultivating, enabling, and empowering the EM leadership and aligning their gifts and the strategizing steps toward the vision.[37]

Transformational Leaders Should Plan to Stay Focused

It is important for transformational leaders to be attentive in strategizing the next steps and navigating the challenges (Luke 9:62). Being an incarnational leader means reorienting oneself[38] to the present and future needs of the EM and what it will take to expand mission initiatives. It means helping the EM and Chinese leadership pace through (cf. John 1:14: "lived for a while among us") the changes in an attitude of humility and servant leadership (Phil 2:5–11; 1 Cor 9:22–23). It means imitating the loving nature of God despite the growing pains (Eph 5:1–2), and it means leaders must share their

---

34. Malphurs, *Advanced Strategic Planning*.

35. Lewis, *Transformational Leadership*, 185. Lewis calls this "initiatory leadership," in which there is a willingness to begin and follow through (51–58).

36. On this point, I resonate with Fong that values and issues "carried over from the mother church" need to be addressed and brought into alignment with the new model. The church's self-understanding, handling of visitors, decision-making process, distribution of power, and method of leadership all need to be aligned. Fong, *Pursuing the Pearl*, 189, 183, 184.

37. Herrrington et al., "Achieving and Maintaining Widespread Impact," in *Leading Congregational Change*, 69–85.

38. Lingenfelter and Mayers, *Ministering Cross-Culturally*, 23.

hearts and lives with those they are coaching and remaining with through the long process of change (1 Thess 2:7–8).

Yew sums up the point that ultimately Christians must recognize that they are all a part of the body of Christ and need to release each other to effectively do mission: "There is only so much the "head" can tell the "tail" that he is different before he realizes they belong to the same coin . . . now shall we move on . . . the world is still waiting for us to bring the Good News. Shall we get on with it?"[39]

One observation I have gleaned from David Aikman[40] is that all things structurally religious may likely be controlled (e.g., the church) but the omnipotent and omnipresent activity of God's progressive work cannot be restrained because the Holy Spirit exists. Therefore I am "confident of this that he who began a good work . . . will carry it on to completion until the day of Christ Jesus" (Phil 1:6 NIV).

Nunc dimittis.

---

39. Yew, "Postscript," 174.
40. Aikman, *Jesus in Beijing.*

Appendices

Surveys, Survey Data

Appendix A

A Synopsis of the Silent Exodus Research Design

Specific Issue, Specific Objective

HELEN LEE[1] FIRST COINED the term "silent exodus" over a concern with the high dropout rate of second generation Asian adult English-speaking Christians from Asian North American churches.[2] She noted there are multiple pressure points that Asian second generation Christians have to grapple with in the bicultural setting that contributes to the exodus.[3] My survey focus is the attrition and retention of English-speaking Canadian born Chinese (CBC) adults. The target audience is English-speaking CBC adults who have exited English language congregations in Chinese Canadian churches in Metro Vancouver, BC, and in Alberta. The specific question I am asking is: *Why do CBC adults in bicultural Chinese churches depart?*[4]

---

1. Helen Lee, "Silent Exodus," 50–53.

2. This section is written using the S.M.A.R.T. goals and strategic plan format and is a statement of the problem, naming of the context, background and research method that will be used. Top Achievement, "Creating S.M.A.R.T. Goals."

3. These pressure points can include: "intense attention paid to native language, ethnic discrimination . . . immigration needs . . . demands for leadership equality, the role of ethnic identity in the church, and the importance of spiritual development." Peter Ong's Asian American ministry website indicates that Helen Lee's foundational article "still echoes today." See Ong, "Silent Exodus," http://peterong.wordpress.com/2006/08/29/silent-exodus.

4. This is my one-line statement of the specific problem in the practice of ministry, putting the problem as a question.

If certain factors cause people to leave, my big picture concern is: What preventative measures can be recommended?

Measurable Outcomes

The core of this research on the silent exodus is a qualitative study based on sixty[5] in-depth open-ended emailed questionnaires[6] of former church dropouts and remain-ins selected from a wide spectrum of circumstances and bilingual church affiliations. The questionnaires were designed to identify and establish certain common patterns and risk factors (i.e., cultural, organizational, spiritual, and personal) that may contribute to the occurrence of a silent exodus. It is recognized that there will likely be multiple "causes" or factors; each church may have its own unique circumstances due to its own history and cultural practices. However, the measurable outcome for this proposed project is: (1) the successful attempt to identify and articulate patterns and common dynamics pertinent to the Chinese bicultural churches that are contributing to a silent exodus, and (2) the formulation of a list of potential risk factors.

Attainable Result with Added Support

The research design, methodology, and analytical procedures will meet accepted practices and standards in the professional and academic research community. It will produce the expected outcomes in a truthful manner according to data collected from the intended sources.

Realistic Concerns, Realistic Solutions

The ultimate ideal goal of learning from past unfavorable experiences is to prevent history from repeating and to go forward with healthy transformational leadership insights into the future. The intended outcomes of producing a self-diagnostic checklist of potential risk factors for churches

---

5. I began with surveying thirty English ministry pastors. The CBC adult contacts were randomly recruited by referral. Beyond twenty surveys, the law of diminishing returns applies whereby insights generated by respondents might no longer be new.

6. Throughout the questionnaire I have sequenced and funneled the questions, paying attention to questionnaire flow and length, avoiding double-barreled, ambiguous, and leading questions. The open questions allow respondents to be free to respond as they like; where the answers to the open questions are more likely to reflect a person's own thinking and to be more valid.

to use are: some healthy leadership recommendations for change and the potential articulation of alternative Chinese bicultural church models based on research.

Time-Defined Project Schedule on Deliverables

This includes the conception of the research topic and the solicitation and collection of observations. The core is the qualitative research design and fieldwork execution that involves gathering, processing, and analysis. The two-year collection of surveys was completed at the time of transfer into the BGU program. The time frame for completion of this project spans about thirteen months.

Appendix B

Sample Research Survey Form and Questions for Dropouts
(Adhering to ethical imperatives in research)[1]

Email Self-Administered Interviewing Form—Silent Exodus Research for Interviewee Use in Answering the Questions[2]

Introduction and Consent

THANK YOU FOR RESPONDING and showing interest in this research project. Before you start responding to my interview questions, it is important to emphasize *your participation is entirely voluntary*. This means that *you have the right* to not answer any question you do not feel comfortable answering. You also have the *option not to continue* at any point if you so choose.

I am Matthew Todd, and currently a doctoral student. This research project is of *my own initiative* with the intention to have the completed results and analysis published. The *purpose of this research* is to seek a more complete understanding of the factors leading to the attrition of Canadian born Chinese adults from the bicultural Chinese church. Based on that data, positive preventative measures and transformational leadership initiatives

---

1. Booth et al., "Ethics of Research," 285–88. Creswell, "Qualitative Procedure," in *Research Design*, 148.

2. Note: the face-to-face interviewing form is the same; slight variations of this form were made to accommodate interviewing remain-in and exodused CBC adults.

will be recommended to help build healthier adult English language congregations in the bicultural church.

The reason why you have been contacted is that I have previously communicated with you on the subject or you have been referred to me in confidence by someone we know mutually.

I am here to listen and to learn from your experience with an open mind. I will give you *guarantees of complete anonymity and privacy.* This means your participation in this research will be completely confidential. All the information that you offer me in this interview will also be preserved in *strict confidentiality* and *security.* Information will only be collected and used pertaining to the purpose of this research and subsequent research on a related topic. I guarantee that I will be *truthful and accurate* in the interpretation, analysis, and reporting of all the data collected in this research. No personal information or the identity of any individual in this research will be released or reported. If it is necessary to use any "quotes" to illustrate a salient point in my eventual publication, it will only be done with absolute care.

If you are comfortable with these guarantees and arrangement that I have stated to you, please proceed with the "Instruction to Interviewee" on the next page. However, I will ask you *not to circulate or redistribute* this research interviewing form or any of the questions out of respect for the integrity and intellectual properties of my research. By virtue of your participation in this interview, you have agreed that you are informed of and have consented to the terms above.

I thank you again for your cooperation and participation.

Instruction to Interviewee

This self-administered interviewing form is sent to you by means of an email attachment. It is just a simple *Microsoft Word 97-2003* document with groups of related questions typed up on top and then some space provided below for you to type in your answers. Please feel free to expand the space as required in answering the questions.

This in-depth interview may require *20 to 60 minutes* of your time, depending on the length and details of your answers. Because we are not able to conduct the interview in a face-to-face format, I will rely on you to provide me with *written answers, with as much detail as possible,* to the questions that I have for you in this simple electronic form.

There is an ordered sequence in the design of the questions. Please follow this order from the beginning to the end. I ask you to provide a truthful response to all the questions with as much detail as you can. There is no right or wrong answer; just genuine feelings, responses, and honest opinions.

It is perfectly fine if you do not have the time to complete answering all the questions in a single sitting. You can save the document and come back later to continue where you have left off until you finish. I would like you to return the completed document to me as an email attachment within seven days. However, if you need more time, or have questions, just email me at boomdrum.45@gmail.com. As mentioned, this document was created using *Microsoft Word 97-2003*. If you are using a higher version of Microsoft Word, please save a copy of the completed document to version 2003 or lower when you return it to me.

After I have received your completed document, I may make a follow-up phone call or email to you later on if I have the need to seek further clarification on specific information you gave me.

1. Start with the context

In your recollection, when did you start going to the bicultural Chinese church that you left? What brought you (circumstance), or who (people) took you to that church: your friends or your family? What church was that (the denomination, beliefs, etc.)? Were you baptized (a church member) there? Briefly describe what the church was like. (Not the physical building but the congregations, the church culture, values, beliefs, practices, etc.) Are your parents/family Christian? Did they attend the same church with you? Are they still in the same church?

2. Talk about the people and relationships

Briefly describe what it was like growing up there, in the bicultural Chinese church that you left. What did you do most of the time in church? What level of involvement, in what capacity? How long had you been there? Who were your best friends or role models and who were the not so desirable people? Why did you think so? Can you talk about both the pleasant and not so pleasant (memorable) experiences in church life, relationships with other people—such as, with the pastoral staff, with the older generations, with the Chinese-speaking congregation(s), with your contemporaries at church, with parents, and with friends outside church (while you were attending the church). Were you ever comfortable bringing your outside church friends, including friends of another race, to the church?

SAMPLE RESEARCH SURVEY FORM AND QUESTIONS

3. Let's talk about your decision to leave

At what stage of your life did you leave that bicultural church? How did it happen? Was it a decision after a long process or a short-term decision? Did any of the people at church care that you left the church? Did they know or understand why you were leaving? How has leaving that church affected you? Have you thought about the effect on them (other people and the church)? Whether leaving or staying, did you feel accountable to the church or that the church conveyed it was accountable for you?

4. State the reasons and circumstances leading to leaving the church

a) Talk about the most important personal reasons first.

What was the main reason(s) that you decided to leave the bicultural church? There can be more than one reason; can you place them in some priority order and then we can proceed to talk about them one by one? Please give me as many personal reasons as you see relevant by using the space provided below.

Your main reason(s) for leaving:

1. _____
2. _____
3. _____

Please answer the following questions based on each *of your given reasons above:*

What made you feel so uncomfortable or strongly about the situation (or this kind of church practice)? Why did you think the situation (or the church practice) was like that? Or why did you feel that way? And how was it affecting you? Were you the only one affected by the situation, or how did other contemporaries feel about it?

Was this the only factor that caused you to leave the church? Or how important was this issue in affecting your decision to leave? Were there other young people at the time leaving because of the situation?

Before moving on to the next section:

b) Are there any other reasons that you can think of that may have led to your departure from the church?

c) Let's talk about others' reason for leaving.

Opening question:

In other research, including some of my other interviews with pastors and some CBCs who have left the bicultural Chinese church, respondents said various factors (refer to list below of issues one by one) were major reasons for their departure. Some of these factors may or may not be the same as yours. But I would like to seek your opinion on each of them.

Issue #1: Identity issue of being a CBC within a Chinese church

Some people say that the identity issue of being a CBC in a predominantly Chinese church is one of the factors in their leaving the church. In all honesty, have you ever encountered such a thing in the church that you attended? Do you think that the identity issue would be an important factor at all for CBCs in general to leave their bicultural Christian church? Why do you think such a factor is important or not important?

Issue #2: Life stage transition needs unfulfilled within a Chinese church

Another factor in why some people claimed they were leaving the bicultural Chinese church was that they could not fulfill their life stage transition needs (trying to meet fellowship or spiritual growth needs while transitioning to university, career, marriage, or family). What do you think and how do you feel about this? Did you ever face such a challenge in the church? Do you think that life stage transitions are an important issue at all for CBCs in general to leave their bicultural Christian church? Why do you think such a factor is important or not important?

Issue #3: Intergenerational conflict (within church/family)

Some people cited that they left the bicultural Chinese church because of issues arising from inter-generational conflicts within the Chinese church/family. In many cases this was a result of: entrenched attitudes and traditional values; self-righteousness; hypocrisy; reluctance to listen and reconcile; lack of respect and recognition of emerging leadership and differences in church practices and expressions of faith in worship and services. Have you ever encountered any such situations in the church that you attended? What do you think and how do you feel about this? Do you think that any such situations would be an important issue at all for CBCs in general to leave their bicultural Christian church? Why you think such a factor is important or not important?

Issue #4: Shame culture: over-evaluation or rejection

Some young adults left their bicultural Chinese church saying that they were being judged, criticized, put down, or rejected most of the time in whatever they did or tried to do in the church. They did not feel comfortable sharing their real thoughts or feelings without being judged. Have you ever encountered such a thing in the church that you attended? What do you think and how do you feel about this? Do you think that such a factor would be an important issue at all for CBCs in general to leave their bicultural Christian church? Why do you think such a factor is important or not important?

Issue #5: Western postmodern values or worldviews at conflict with Chinese traditional values manifested in the bicultural church

Some CBC young adults said that they left over the issue of a conflict between their individualistic worldview and spiritual belief and the traditional cultural practices of the bicultural Chinese church. Some felt that their spirituality should be more of an individual pilgrimage, and less accountable to hierarchical institutions like the church. What do you think and how do you feel about this? Has this ever been an issue in your decision to leave the church? Do you think that postmodern values would be an important element at all for CBCs in general to leave their b-cultural Christian church? Why you think such a factor is important or not important?

Issue #6: Overemphasis on Chinese cultural identity and ethnocentrism

Some CBCs said they left the Chinese church in a rejection of the preaching of a "Chinese gospel" as well as overemphasis on Chinese cultural identity and ethnocentrism. Some felt alienated instead of being embraced. What do you think and how do you feel about this? Was this ever an issue in your leaving? Do you think that ethnocentrism would be an important issue at all for CBCs in general to leave their bicultural Christian church? Why do you think such a factor is important or not important?

Issue #7: Personal choice of a secular lifestyle versus Christianity

Some people left the Chinese church because of a conscious (or unconscious) choice, under the influence of secularism and self-absorbed lifestyles, which led to the abandonment of the practice of Christian faith. What do you think and how do you feel about this? Do you have any idea why CBCs in a church would choose a secular lifestyle over a Christian lifestyle? Do you think that choosing a secular lifestyle would be an important issue at all for CBCs in general to leave their bicultural Christian church? Why do you think such a factor is important or not important?

Issue #8: Perceived problem with church beliefs, theology, or hypocrisy

Some people left as they perceived a problem with church beliefs and theology or hypocrisy. Was this ever a problem you perceived in your church or family? What do you think and how do you feel about this? Do you think that perceiving such a problem would be an important issue at all for CBCs in general to leave their bicultural Christian church? Why do you think such a factor is important or not important?

Issue #9: Control issues with church power and politics

Some young adults left as a protest towards their Chinese church over issues related to power, autonomy, patriarchy, paternal control, lack of decision-making or empowerment, repulsion over legalism, or disillusionment. What do you think and how do you feel about this? Were power and politics an issue in your leaving? Do you think that control issues would be an important issue at all for CBCs in general to leave their bicultural Christian church? Why do you think such a factor is important or not important?

Issue #10: Church leadership, organizational structure, and program issues

Some young people left the Chinese church due to: a frustration with inadequate leadership or representation of the English ministry or inadequate programs and structure, and lack of purpose or vision. English ministry was expediently confined primarily to a youth ministry babysat by the church. What do you think and how do you feel about this? Was this ever an issue in your leaving? Do you think that these elements would be an important issue at all for CBCs in general to leave their bicultural Christian church? Why do you think such a factor is important or not important?

5. Briefly describe what has happened in your life after you left the church.

How long ago has it been since you left the bicultural church you have discussed? In brief, what has your life journey been since you left that church? Have you found what you are looking for in another church, or are you still looking for something missing, or have you just given up on your faith? Do you still believe in God?

6. Hindsight can be 20/20

Looking back, if the situation(s) leading to your departure had not happened or had happened differently, would you see yourself still in that Chinese bicultural church now? In hindsight, what had to be changed, in the bicultural bilingual Chinese church in order for CBCs like you (growing up and maturing) to find a real and fulfilling Christian life and service experience in church? If you were the bicultural Chinese church, what would you have done to prevent the younger generations from leaving?

Appendix C

Clergy Data

Table 1. Clergy data

Clergy Survey	Associate	Lead	Years Pastoral experience	Age	Denomination
		✓	20	50+	A
	✓		3	40	MB
	✓		6	30+	MB
		✓	10+	60+	EFC
	✓		?	30+	MB
	✓		10+	40	A
	✓		15+	35+	I
	✓		10+	50+	A
	✓		8+	40+	A
	✓		5+	40+	CCC
		✓	15	35+	R
	✓		10+	35+	A
	✓		10+	40	MB
	✓		?	40	A
		✓	20	71	MB
	✓		5	28+	B
		✓	20+	50+	P
	✓		15	40+	A
	✓		15+	60+	MB
	✓		12+	45+	MB
		✓	20+	55+	MB
	✓		5+	35+	I
	✓		25+	50+	A
	✓		20+	50+	B
	✓		30+	60+	EFC

	✓			2+	35+	MB
	✓			9+	45+	MB
	✓			21+	45+	A
			✓	24+	55+	P
			✓	24+	55+	I

Denomination Acronyms:

Baptist = B
Alliance = A
Mennonite Brethren = MB
Independent = I
Christ Church of China = CCC
Reformed = R
Presbyterian = P
Evangelical Free = EFC

Appendix D

Dropout Data

1. Start with the context

Started in the Chinese church:

1. ?
2. from birth
3. from birth
4. from a child
5. age 12
6. First went to a Caucasian church, then at age 49 went to a Chinese church
7. age 12
8. age 14
9. age 7
10. from birth
11. age 8
12. from a youth
13. age 4
14. age 9
15. from a child
16. from a child
17. age 15
18. from birth
19. from birth
20. from junior high
21. from a youth
22. age 6
23. from birth
24. from birth
25. age 4
26. age 16
27. from birth
28. age 13
29. from birth
30. age 21

Summary: Nine were born (or brought as a baby) in the Chinese church. Thirteen were brought to the church as a child or between the ages of 4 and

12. Five were brought between the ages of 13 and 16. One came to a Chinese church at age 49.

What brought you to the church?

1. friend	16. parents
2. parents	17. fellowship friends
3. parents	18. parents
4. Mom's friends & Mom	19. parents
5. parents	20. friend
6. neighbors	21. parents
7. parents	22. Dad & neighbor
8. older brother	23. parents
9. Mom's relatives	24. parents
10. parents	25. parents
11. friends of the family & Mom	26. friend
12. not clear	27. parents
13. parents	28. parents
14. parents	29. parents
15. parents	30. acquaintance

Summary: Twenty-one were brought by parents to the Chinese church. Six had no parents in the church. Three had only one parent in the church. The decision was made for the majority in *originally being brought* to the church.

Denomination:

1. I—Pentecostal	10. L
2. EFC	11. MB
3. B	12. MB / A
4. A / MB	13. CCC / MB
5. B / A	14. MB
6. A / A	15. A / ?
7. B / EFC	16. I / I
8. A	17. MB
9. EFC / MB	18. MB / MB

19. I	25. MB / B
20. A	26. MB
21. A / ?	27. EFC / Anglican
22. A	28. A
23. MB	29. A / ?
24. MB / A	30. A

Summary: Ten different denominational or independent churches are represented among these adult CBCs.

Baptized / member

1. Y	16. Y
2. Y	17. Y
3. N	18. Y
4. Y (but refusing membership)	19. Y
5. Y	20. Y
6. N	21. Y
7. Y	22. Y
8. Y	23. Y
9. Y	24. Y
10. Y	25. Y
11. Y	26. Y
12. Y	27. Y
13. Y	28. Y
14. Y	29. Y
15. Y	30. Y

Summary: All were baptized church members.

Church atmosphere:

1. university & middle age	3. church division (conflict)
2. busy & committed to Christian ed / strong volunteerism	4. liberal?
	5. tricultural / lots of programs

6. Chinese traditional
7. Chinese traditional
8. conservative / ethnic Chinese
9. Chinese traditional
10. Chinese in culture & practices
11. Chinese traditional (Hakka)[1]
12. Chinese traditional
13. Chinese traditional
14. shared similar ideas and beliefs
15. Chinese traditional
16. Chinese traditional
17. English cong in Chinese traditional
18. traditional Chinese—conservative
19. traditional Chinese
20. traditional Chinese (abusive / segregated
21. traditional—conservative—heavily controlled by board
22. traditional
23. traditional—CBC EM had different cultural views
24. traditional—authoritarian, xenophobic
25. traditional
26. traditional
27. traditional
28. traditional
29. traditional
30. traditional (dominated by Chinese / Cantonese culture)

Summary: Three noted CBC differences from the Chinese congregation. Three commented on the unequal power (division) of the board over pastors. Three specifically noted the church had no involvement with the community around it. Two cited value issues between the CBC and Chinese groups.

Are your parents Christian?

1. Y
2. Y
3. Y
4. Mom only
5. Y
6. N
7. Y
8. Y
9. Mom
10. Y
11. Mom only
12. not clear
13. Y
14. Y

1. *Definitions.net*, s.v. "Hakka people," www.definitions.net/definition/hakka%20people.

DROPOUT DATA 169

15. Y	23. Y
16. Y	24. Y
17. N	25. Y
18. Y	26. Mom
19. Y	27. Y
20. Mom	28. Y
21. Y	29. Y
22. Dad	30. Mom

Summary: Only four commented that a parent was not Christian or were unclear on this.

Did your parents attend church with you (in the OBC service)?

1. N	16. Y
2. Y	17. N
3. Y	18. Y
4. Y	19. Y
5. Y	20. N
6. N	21. Y
7. Y	22. N
8. Y	23. Y
9. N (different Chinese church)	24. Y
10. Y	25. Y
11. Y (Mom)	26. Y
12. not clear	27. Y
13. Y	28. Y
14. Y	29. Y
15. Y	30. Mom

Summary: Six indicated that their parents did not attend this church with them. Also note that attending generally means that the parent attended the OBC service not the English service sitting beside the family. The implications of missing a parental role model in worship warrants further commentary.

Are your parents still in the same church?

1. N/A[2]	16. N
2. Y	17. N
3. N	18. Y
4. Y	19. not clear
5. Y	20. Y (Mom only)
6. N	21. N
7. Y	22. not clear
8. Y	23. Y
9. Y	24. N
10. N	25. Y
11. Y (Mom)	26. N
12. not clear	27. not clear
13. N	28. N
14. N	29. Y
15. N	30. N

Summary: thirteen specifically commented that their parents were no longer in the church that they had exited.

2. Talk about the people and relationships

What was church life like?
1. English-speaking only—college and middle aged (majority CBC)
2. "Church was a big part of my life"
3. spent in fellowship or church organized meetings / events
4. enjoyed some teachers
5. programs

---

2. From this point forward, N/A = response not applicable to the question.

DROPOUT DATA

6. disturbing control issues witnessed
7. positive
8. like a family, positive
9. 1st church (lonely). 2nd church (warmly embraced)
10. "The SS teachers did their best to make SS interesting."
11. Like another family you can rely on; you could meet more friends.
12. "Nice to be around Chinese people . . . a real sense of community."
13. happy
14. busy
15. busy
16. "Our relationship with the Chinese congregation was one of tolerance. As long as we paid respect to our elders and saw the Chinese congregation as leading the congregation, everything would be fine and we could all get along happily."
17. fellowship most meaningful
18. "Looking back, it was a very good experience."
19. lots of activity
20. "There was tension between the congregations and it was felt more when it came to Sunday mornings."
21. strong sense of community, felt like a family
22. A place difficult to relate too; "it was as though they were at another level." (speaking of the Chinese side)
23. "I had many good and bad experiences at church."
24. "Growing up in _____ was a study in living with constant tension between often competing cultural values and traditions . . . services were conservative following a fairly rigid format."
25. "I definitely have very good memories"—people caring
26. solid teaching on Christ
27. Chinese conservatism and church traditions
28. not clear
29. not clear
30. The senior pastor and some board members did not really understand the needs of the English congregation. They would impose some of

their Chinese values which are not necessary applicable, nor biblically relevant onto the EM."

What was your involvement like?

1. served in a few areas
2. very active in activities—overwhelming time spent in committees
3. music
4. music, greeter, dramas, musicals (extensive)
5. volunteered in VBS, camps, Sunday school
6. sound tech, music & worship
7. served in fellowship & tech team (fairly involved)
8. elder, teacher, preacher
9. served in various capacities (e.g., board member)
10. served in worship team, misc helps.
11. minimal
12. "heavily involved in leadership."
13. not clear
14. extensive (music, planning, many serving positions)
15. very involved (teacher, leader, musician, intern, etc.)
16. vast and varied (leadership, pastoral intern, preacher, worship leader, counselor)
17. minimal
18. very involved (teacher, counselor, worship leader)
19. leader, chairperson of college group, EM career adults leader, home group leader
20. leader, coordinator, counselor, mentor, etc.
21. "I was quite involved and served in a variety of areas"
22. worship team, ushering, "just a participant in activities"
23. music, youth worker
24. extensive: fellowship secretary-treasurer, children's ministries leader
25. very involved; Sunday school, children & youth worship leader, planned summer camps & retreats
26. youth counselor

27. actively involved—small group leader, worship team, etc.
28. very involved in fellowships, worship team, taught Sunday school, cell group leader, etc.
29. not clear
30. English congregation representative, teacher

How long had you been there?

1. not clear
2. not clear (about 15 years?)
3. not clear (about 10 years?)
4. 11 years
5. 16 years
6. 2.5 years
7. not clear
8. 8 years
9. not clear
10. 23 years
11. 12 years
12. not clear (many years)
13. not clear (many years)
14. not clear (many years)
15. not clear (many years)
16. over 19 years
17. 5 years
18. over 30 years
19. over 23 years
20. 14 years
21. 8 years
22. over 10 years
23. 27 years
24. not clear (many years)
25. not clear (many years)
26. not clear
27. not clear
28. not clear
29. not clear
30. not clear

Who were your best friends; who were your role models; who were the undesirables (why?)

1. friends—college age group
2. friends—girls my age
3. friends—church peers
4. friends—the boys, not the girls (this is a female)
5. knew many people but not on a deep level
6. negative—politics
7. many good times and made some very good friends
8. friends—other leaders. Role model—EM pastor
9. role model—wife of EM pastor

10. "I didn't really fit in with the group"
11. friends—"don't really have best friends, just friends of same age;" role models—"not really."
12. role models—"I looked up to all the older people in the church; they were great role models to me."
13. friends—"had many . . . close friends" especially in the fellowship.
14. role model—older youth workers. Later "I didn't really have a role model in my church."
15. role models—"A couple of people in the cohorts above me stand out as role models, sincere and thoughtful in their faith, passionate volunteers, and good character."
16. friends—"had three really good friends"
17. friends—peers in fellowship were best friends.
18. role models—other CBCs
19. role models—young adult & family pastor, EM pastor
20. role models—older CBCs, people who were mission minded.
21. best friends—"whose priorities were more focused on God; role models—"women who had a lot of grace;" undesirables—"the ones who seemed more interested in keeping up with the Jones"
22. friends, admired SS teacher who tried hard to reach him
23. friends ("people I grew up with"). role models—"some group leaders at times but they mostly left the church."
24. role models—several teachers, older peers, EM youth pastor
25. "some very valuable friendships;" role model—one couple, dedicated & committed to God set a standard for me in my own service"
26. not clear
27. "To be honest, role models were lacking during my times at church:"
28. role models—older mentors and worship leaders; undesirables—superficial peers
29. not clear
30. not clear

What were the pleasant or unpleasant (memorable) experiences in church life with people like the pastoral staff, older generations, the Chinese-speaking congregation(s), and your contemporaries?

1. close group—but leadership had to be asked permission to date
2. Pleasant (quality of CE & volunteerism). Unpleasant (politics & high degree of formality)
3. close group
4. did not enjoy all the Sunday school teachers
5. Pleasant (enjoyed teen years). Unpleasant (college years difficult—not close to others, busy), disagreed with some things
6. Unpleasant (compassion was missing there); "Pastoral staff was bound, gagged, and handcuffed by a controlling church board. It was horrible." Found it inhospitable & difficult for his mixed race son being stigmatized.
7. Pleasant (fellowship, retreats). Unpleasant ("I didn't respect the senior leadership due to them not willing to adapt to new methods to suit the new generation—I agree the gospel doesn't change, but the presentation must.")
8. Pleasant (various leadership relationships). Unpleasant ("things turned sour with the senior pastor")
9. Pleasant (close with pastor's wife). Unpleasant (board meetings were long and arduous; "the people I came to find undesirable were those who complained or criticized the quality of ministry of the English-speaking congregation.")
10. (did not comment)
11. "Everything was pretty much pleasant; I don't think I had any unpleasant experiences." (Note: this survey participant left the church).
12. Pleasant (diligent in Scripture, learned a good foundation of my faith). Unpleasant ("the Chinese church used culture to sometimes mix in with preaching the Christian faith . . . cultural paranoia's [were] passed on.")
13. Pleasant (fellowship)
14. Pleasant (tight-knit fellowship group). Unpleasant ("not so fond memories with the older generation—I remember being judged a lot for

wearing make-up or clothes that I thought were cool.")—referring to a cultural gap.

15. not clear

16. Pleasant (friendships). Unpleasant ("Certain rituals and games we all grew up having to observe in order to 'give face' to these people [Chinese leadership]. Later, when we began to get older, we regularly bumped heads with them, especially in terms of uses of money.")

17. Pleasant (fellowship). Unpleasant ("never anything unpleasant). (Note: this case left the church for good.)

18. Pleasant (overall). Unpleasant ("People from the Chinese side didn't share their feelings too much.")

19. Unpleasant ("The last few years certain pastors weren't supportive of the young adults' ministry [power struggles, conflict]. "A sizable group of career young adults departed over this. We all grew up in this church and were children of the leaders; this developed over time—many failed things (unforgiveness)."

20. Unpleasant ("I did not connect with the pastors who did not express any weakness or failed to understand the generational and cultural gaps that existed in the church.")

21. Pleasant (social life with friends, good relationships with EM and youth pastors).

22. Unpleasant (a Chinese side person turning out the sanctuary lights while he and his friends were still inside; "I ran out to say, there's still people there. The guy just looked at me and walked out the door without saying sorry or bothering to turn the lights on.")

23. Unpleasant ("One thing that was persistently a bother was the strongly conservative attitude of the older generation at the time in trying to manage Western raised children using philosophies of older Asia.")

24. Unpleasant (cultural clashes with members of the Chinese congregation—who represented the older generation—when they attended English Adult SS and brought with them viewpoints that seemed extremely prejudiced and judgmental.")

25. Pleasant (many good experiences). Unpleasant (conflict—"some of my unhappiest moments in church include the big split that happened . . . attacking each other . . . heated arguments . . . half the people left our church including the pastor. To this day many of the main people involved in the conflict have not reconciled.")

26. not clear
27. Unpleasant ("There were tension between the Chinese and English-speaking youths . . . the Chinese-speaking people did not seem approachable by the English-speaking people, and vice versa:" communication issues.)
28. Pleasant (in fellowship, on the worship team).
29. Pleasant (the sense of community—more opportunities to serve; organized, good structure & Bible teaching). Unpleasant (the church itself had its own rules passed down from tradition; there weren't a lot of spiritual experiences.)
30. Unpleasant (board banned drums. "The senior pastor seemed to always try to please the Chinese congregation because they were the predominant group . . ." "The English congregation seemed to be always the junior partner and considered less mature and spiritual—although some of the members were young professionals." "The church had difficulty keeping English adults—due to the lack of opportunities to participate in the major decision-making process and the CBCs were not being listened too." "Limited support and involvement from the Chinese congregation—using language barrier as excuse.")

Were you ever comfortable bringing your outside church friends, including friends of another race, to the church?

1. occasionally
2. not clear
3. Y
4. Y / N
5. not clear
6. N
7. Y but only the fellowship—not services
8. Y—then later N because "it was hard to bring non-Asians to this church."
9. N—"I wanted to bring my friends and family to my church, but never felt comfortable doing that because I was aware of the 'Chinese-fied' [sic] environment." (Participant commented on the church signage.)
10. Y—"if they were willing, seeking, curious"
11. Y—"I was fine bringing people in."

12. Y—"I mostly brought Asian friends."
13. N—"Bringing my ... school friends to church was something I wanted to do. But in the mid 70s, it was typical that I was the only Asian kid in the class and bringing a non-Chinese-speaking person to a Chinese church was something that never worked out."
14. Y—"The majority of them were also not of Asian ethnicity. However, as we all began our years in college and university, most of them started leaving as they started questioning the church's doctrines and ultimately the validity of the Bible . . . I felt like there were some inadequacies for seekers and I stopped bringing friends."
15. N—"I did bring friends to church on a couple of occasions (they were white) but usually felt uncomfortable about this. I was [also] reluctant to bring an open "seeking" friend to our church because . . . he was blue collar . . . the church was so professional. I figured he would feel out of place . . . I counseled university students to invite their white friends to Christian campus clubs."
16. Y/N—"Friends of another race were sort of welcome, although I think they felt more uncomfortable being there than we felt with them."
17. Y—"I brought a couple of friends a few times."
18. Y—"Most of my friends were CBC; some were Korean & Japanese that I brought to the service. Still felt comfortable bringing Caucasians."
19. not clear
20. N—"I didn't often invite friends to church because it felt like it was such a huge cultural hurdle to jump, especially for my Caucasian friends."
21. N—"I was not comfortable bringing friends of another race to church, and later on any friends."
22. N—"I was never comfortable bringing friends to church, regardless of race. I never felt that I could explain everything that went on . . ."
23. N—"I brought friends from time to time but not many were comfortable with the mono-racial bicultural atmosphere."
24. not clear or stated
25. N—"the problem with ethnic churches . . . congregations can get too homogeneous . . . it is hard for them to accept people on the outside."
26. Y—"I was comfortable in bringing my friends to [church A] but not to [church B] because I felt that the youth ministry was too young to bring them."

27. Y—"Yes, I would feel comfortable to bring friends from various cultures to this church if I had the opportunity."
28. Y / N—"I brought some Chinese friends of mine from school a few times to special events—other than that I didn't really bring them, I was worried that it would be too "churchy."
29. N—hesitant to bring any friends to the Chinese church; more hesitant to bring someone not of Chinese descent."
30. N—"It is hard to bring non-Chinese friend to this church because it is a Chinese church . . ."

3. Let's talk about your decision to leave

At what stage of your life did you leave that bicultural church?

1. late 20s
2. age 40
3. early 20s
4. early to mid 20s
5. early 30s
6. 51
7. mid 40s
8. early 30s
9. mid 30s
10. 25
11. 22
12. early 30s
13. early 40s
14. 29
15. 31
16. 32
17. 26
18. 32
19. 28
20. 30
21. late 20s
22. late 20s
23. 29
24. 31
25. 23
26. 31
27. 26
28. 28
29. 30
30. 51

How did it happen?
1. The church did not serve my needs (life stage); people were too cliquey (conformity expected); seemed as though leadership favored only certain people.

2. Marriage to a Caucasian man—left to attend his multicultural church, but felt free from the politics and activism

3. Church split—then I left the church completely.

4. (spoke of leaving experiences in two separate churches) Church #1 left in a two-week period over a children's safety and justice issue. Church #2 left after a longer time—felt criticized by older people, felt disconnected & unwelcome from peers.

5. "I didn't agree with the way the senior pastor handled some stuff... his beliefs, his treatment of people (he was a very insecure person). I decided to leave because I knew deep down that something was wrong. I could not explain it, but I could not sit and listen to another sermon without wondering if it was God's Word or personal propaganda. So I left.

6. I left when it was too hard to bear. One day I just stopped going to church because I was seeing no future, hope or power at that church. Totally no compassion and it was Chinese centered not Christ centered.

7. Concerns with traditional leadership, board decision making, and sermon applications.

8. Tension was building up between me (while serving as an elder) and the senior pastor; he was exercising unethical and unfair treatment on the English pastor; furthermore he was manipulating congregations through his preaching. English ministry was marginalized and not respected in the board.

9. I did not feel called to be a part of the church's stage of growth where it was lacking in vision and conviction to be a faithful church. "I became convicted to leave during a time when I was more established in the workplace and recognized the opportunity for marketplace ministry. Most of my colleagues are not Asian... I didn't feel comfortable bringing them to a Chinese church at all. I was evaluating the best use of my time... changes I deemed necessary to the health of the church were going to take a long time. Having made the case for change in the previous couple years and seeing very little movement, I wasn't prepared to wait to see if the changes would fully be adopted one day.

10. My parents left because they did not feel they fit in; and I went with my family.

11. I just decided not to go, it just didn't seem right.

12. Got married to a Korean wife and decided we needed to find a new church with people our age and stage of life.

13. The Chinese leadership tried to integrate the English-speaking into the Chinese congregation; I could no longer bear the situation.

14. I began dating a non Christian—pastoral leadership was judgmental—so I left to attend a Caucasian church.

15. At about age 26 I began thinking the church ought to be involved in the community; I felt our church was very segregated. I want to be with a church that is involved in my neighborhood.

16. A political move and decision was made at the board level to administratively paralyze the English congregation signifying the desire of the church to remain a Chinese church with the Chinese congregation doing most of the decision making. "I don't begrudge them for their Chinese-first philosophy." Another reason was that I felt we needed to move to a direction where we could begin to minister to these [silent exodus] lost people and provide an environment for them where so many of us could begin to heal from being "over-churched."

17. A combination of busy schedule with work and study, no family at that church, and I felt lonely at church.

18. Left to be part of a church plant; we didn't feel we were growing enough and that people were not extending out; an opportunity came to work in a multicultural setting.

19. Over witnessing the disunity between ministry leaders

20. Left on account of the leadership style of the senior pastor that led to many altercations with people in the English ministries. Groups in the English congregation were being micromanaged. Our prayer group was shut down and people in the EM were being hurt; I felt unsafe within the church. Power struggles were happening between the board and pastors of the EM and MM tracks. It felt as though the elder board chose to protect the pastor over the congregation . . . it was taboo against speaking anything wrong with our leaders. Eventually I had to leave because I could no longer worship and felt that the church was a sham.

21. (Mobility) I left the church because I moved to another city and started going to a multicultural church.

22. I left right before I got married, about two years after graduating from university. My fiancé convinced me to leave.

23. While in university I stopped attending; I no longer related to the church.
24. On account of church politics, I finally left when my parents left, which was in my early twenties.
25. (mobility—moved closer to med school) I started thinking about leaving the church in my last years of high school. Most of my peers had left by then due to loss of faith. There weren't any programs suited to young adults. I stayed behind to serve in the English ministries but over time started feeling dry spiritually. My parents encouraged me to go to a church where I could get fed instead of just serving. I started thinking about when would be a good time for leaving; upon being accepted into medical school I had to move . . . I saw this as a good time to leave my church without making others in the EM feel abandoned.
26. Left the Chinese church over life stage needs and got married.
27. Left the church over a combination of doubt (there is a great quote in this case), church hypocrisy, and moving elsewhere to study (mobility).
28. I left shortly after I was engaged to be married and I was in my last year of grad school. The key reason was because of the ungodly mistreatment of my father by the board and senior pastor. I felt I couldn't stay at the church knowing the hypocrisy and yucky background dealings that had been going on. (Key issue here: power and politics).
29. I left feeling very complacent in my faith and growth; I didn't want to serve; I wasn't feeling welcomed anymore; I didn't see a positive direction for the EM—it was like a sinking ship. There was a lack of consistent English ministry pastor.
30. We left this church in our mid 30s as we felt that we didn't have peers who are our age and at the same *stage of life* as we were losing the young adults. We wanted *our children* to be in a mainstream church to experience a balanced church life which focuses on biblical values and truth instead of cultural values (key concern for spiritual health and balanced church life).

Was it a decision after a long process or just an instant determination?

1. took two years of intermittent attendance
2. no comment
3. sudden
4. no comment
5. reads like it took a period of time

6. reads like it took a period of time.
7. a long process
8. two years
9. about a year
10. had been thinking about leaving for quite a while
11. It took some time for me to actually make this decision.
12. no comment
13. a long process
14. a process
15. I gradually slipped out and started going to neighborhood churches.
16. I left after almost two years of struggling by the English deacons for change.
17. slow process
18. six months
19. after a long process
20. I left quietly and with little fanfare. It was deeply painful.
21. no comment
22. long process
23. long decision.
24. made over a period of six months.
25. long process.
26. It was a long process of God changing me from within.
27. The decision was a long bubbling process.
28. It was a decision that took a long time to make.
29. My leaving was after a long process.
30. long process

Did any of the people at church care about your leaving or after you left the church?

1. no remaining friendship contacts
2. no comment
3. no comment
4. no remaining friends
5. I was phoned by some of the elders and the senior pastor.
6. No one even noticed . . .
7. The people at the church didn't care for the most part.
8. Many members were surprised.
9. Yes, the assistant pastors cared about my reasons for leaving.
10. yes
11. yes
12. yes
13. yes
14. "For a while the pastor chased after me . . . I just avoided him at all costs." "Most of the friends I had there never really called or followed up on me after I left."

15. There wasn't much relationship there.
16. no comment
17. yes, friends from the fellowship and the English pastor
18. yes
19. I wouldn't say anybody reached out . . . one pastor seemed relieved; there was conversation by parents and deacons (many of us were their children).
20. no comment
21. no comment
22. Yes, we still have friends there.
23. Yes, some did.
24. I suspect many people did care that we had left, but they respected our decision.
25. no comment
26. no comment
27. some close friends, peers, and family friends knew and noticed
28. no comment
29. People did not try to follow up with me, only people close to me, not acquaintances.
30. no comment

Did they know or understand why you were leaving?
1. not clear
2. no comment
3. seems so
4. no comment
5. "I told them I just needed a break" (a smokescreen)
6. no comment
7. no
8. yes—lack of spiritual nourishment and church direction
9. yes but disagreed
10. yes

11. yes
12. yes
13. yes, they understood I needed fellowship and hearing sermons in English
14. no comment
15. no comment
16. yes
17. I never told anyone why I was leaving.
18. yes
19. the pastors understood why
20. no comment
21. no comment
22. no
23. Some did—I definitely understood why I left.
24. no comment
25. yes, to go to medical school
26. no comment
27. Most only knew that I had abandoned my faith, while a handful knew of my struggles leading up to this.
28. I think people had an idea of why I left since my father and the English pastor had left shortly before me.
29. no comment
30. no comment

How has leaving that church affected you?
1. no comment
2. no comment
3. left the church
4. For a while I did *not* attend church.
5. I felt guilty for leaving but I have tried not to think about it much. I'm glad I got out of there.

6. Leaving that church has showed me that even though I'm Chinese I don't fit into their world.//
7. I am learning more in a multicultural church but have fewer friends.
8. no comment
9. I still feel pangs of guilt.
10. Still not receiving much of God's word every Sunday; I am at a Caucasian church.
11. "As of this moment, nothing I guess."
12. no comment
13. positively
14. no comment
15. no comment
16. I am more comfortable in a multi-ethnic environment.
17. Sometimes I don't feel enlightened or fulfilled; I miss the family atmosphere at the service and fellowships.
18. leaving has allowed me to grow
19. I don't look back with regret; but looking back I can see mistakes on both sides. I have had time for healing and to gain a broader perspective and that's been a blessing. The leave opened up other opportunities.
20. I felt tremendously guilty for leaving, like I had failed. I felt like I was leaving a family, much like a divorce. However I felt that if I stayed that I would lose my faith altogether. I didn't trust the leadership and my closest friends were gone or were leaving. I also felt that there wasn't anything more I could do to help the situation.
21. Looking back that was the best decision I ever made—I feel like I have grown so much since leaving the Chinese church—I am so much more open-minded now.
22. When I left I felt like a grunt worker. They'll be able to find someone else to sing and usher. I felt I was non-essential.
23. Since leaving I've had an opportunity to expand my horizons of meaning and understanding in life. Leaving the church I have learned to be less judgmental of groups that may have digressed from the popular current views of the church. I have had an opportunity to explore what spirituality and believing in God means in a more holistic view.
24. I don't regret the subsequent experience of attending other churches.

25. positively
26. no comment
27. I am not sure if leaving the church has affected me much . . . my rediscovery has been valuable to me.
28. I still really miss the sense of community I had in the Chinese church and often feel sad about leaving.
29. no comment
30. no comment

Have you thought about the effect on them (other people and the church)?
1. "I don't believe that my leaving had any effect on the church."
2. no comment
3. no comment
4. "I do not feel like my leaving had any effect."
5. no comment
6. no comment
7. not sure
8. The English ministry dissolved.
9. people were disappointed and sad
10. no comment
11. no effect on others (actually *un*true—I knew his mom and English deacons felt concerned; I did pastoral visits)
12. no comment
13. no comment
14. "I don't think my leaving really affected most people in any way, excepting maybe igniting thoughts for them to leave as well."
15. no comment
16. no comment
17. no comment
18. no comment
19. To be honest, at the time, leaving was my way of making a statement based on the belief that change will never happen. I actually had

previously also seen an older English cohort—a decade older than me—majority leave; that group is just hitting their 40s now.

20. no comment
21. I don't really think about the effect on the people and the church as I don't keep in touch with people from that church; because I've grown so much I don't feel like I have much in common with them anymore.
22. I felt my leaving had little effect on the group or leadership. Only one person wanted me to come back. I declined the offer and no one has asked me since.
23. I understand and see the effect of leaving a church on a congregation.
24. I had thought about the effect on that church but nobody is irreplaceable, God's work goes on regardless.
25. no comment
26. no comment
27. I don't believe my departure had any impact.
28. no comment
29. no comment
30. no comment

Whether leaving or staying, did you feel accountable to the church or that the church was accountable to you?

1. no comment
2. no comment
3. no comment
4. no comment
5. no comment
6. The church was not accountable; leadership failed me because the pastoral authority was not impartial.
7. I didn't feel accountable to the church and I didn't feel the church was accountable to me.
8. I felt somewhat accountable for what had happened because I was one of the elders in the church.
9. no comment
10. no

11. no
12. no comment
13. no comment
14. no comment
15. no comment
16. no comment
17. I didn't feel accountable to the church but it was accountable to me.
18. no comment
19. I didn't feel there was much to be accountable to; there wasn't much effort on the pastors' part to keep us together.
20. no comment
21. no comment
22. no comment
23. No, I do not feel accountable to the church group nor do I expect them to be accountable to me.
24. no comment
25. no comment
26. no comment
27. To be honest there was no accountability in the first place. As much as I wish that there were it wasn't the case.
28. no comment
29. no comment
30. no comment

4. State the reasons and circumstances leading to leaving the church

The thirty case participants could pick from eleven categories of issues, or combination thereof as to why *they* chose to depart from their church. These are elaborated on in appendix B. The dropout participants were asked to talk about the most important personal reasons for leaving their church: "What was the main reason(s) that you decided to leave the bi-cultural church? There can be more than one reason; can you place them in some priority order and then we can proceed to talk about them one by one?" Almost all participants could provide a short list of reasons why they dropped out of their bicultural church. For the sake of brevity I will list the issues here but the reader will need to refer to the full definition of these issues in appendix B.

Issue #1: Identity Issue of being a CBC within a Chinese church

Issue #2: Life stage transition needs unfulfilled within a Chinese church

Issue #3: Intergenerational conflict (within church/family)

Issue #4: Shame culture: over-evaluation or rejection

Issue #5: Western postmodern values or worldviews at conflict with Chinese traditional values manifested in the bicultural church

Issue #6: Overemphasis on Chinese cultural identity and ethnocentrism

Issue #7: Personal choice of a secular lifestyle versus Christianity

Issue #8: Perceived problem with church beliefs, theology, or hypocrisy

Issue #9: Control issues with church power and politics

Issue #10: Church leadership, organizational structure, and program issues

Issue #11: Intellectual, rational, and pragmatic issues

Table 2. Reasons CBCs dropped out of their Chinese bicultural church

Cases	Issue / Reason / Category										
	1 (2)	2 (14)	3 (3)	4 (3)	5 (2)	6 (13)	7 (5)	8 (5)	9 (9)	10 (13)	11 (1)
1						✓	✓				
2		✓									
3			✓						✓	✓	
4		✓		✓						✓	
5		✓							✓	✓	
6						✓			✓		
7										✓	
8						✓		✓	✓		
9										✓	
10		✓									
11							✓				
12		✓	✓								
13	✓					✓					
14				✓		✓				✓	✓
15						✓					
16						✓				✓	
17	✓	✓		✓	✓	✓					
18		✓				✓				✓	
19		✓								✓	
20		✓							✓	✓	
21		✓									
22			✓				✓	✓			
23						✓			✓		
24				✓		✓			✓		
25		✓				✓					
26		✓									
27							✓	✓			
28						✓		✓	✓	✓	
29		✓				✓				✓	
30		✓				✓			✓	✓	

a) Talk about the most important personal reasons first

Respondents were asked: "What was the main reason(s) that *you* decided to leave the bicultural church? There can be more than one reason; can you place them in priority order then we can proceed to talk about them one by one? Please give as many personal reasons as you see relevant by using the space provided below." Your main reason(s) for leaving:

The case participants' responses are all logged in table #1 in this appendix D. Most of the reasons and circumstances leading to leaving the church fell within the parameters of my survey questions, but a few did not; for example, here is a case that expressed concern for social justice issues:

Case 9: "I felt the church was more interested in upholding Chinese values rather than pursuing biblical values . . . the church lacked vision and discipled leaders in the Chinese-speaking congregation gave in to poor decisions that negatively affected the congregation. I disliked how certain leaders canvassed support for a particular party because of its stand on homosexuality. I didn't feel I could bring my gay friends to church for fear of their being judged or hearing something disrespectful. I felt there was no interest in *social justice issues* except for where overseas Chinese people were concerned . . . Preoccupation with the upholding of Chinese values led to poor uses of resources and unfaithful decisions, such as choosing to pay pastors low, unlivable salaries in spite of surpluses from the last five years. I couldn't in good conscience participate in a church that continued to choose paying inequitable salaries . . . Also I felt that the English-speaking congregation was paying the price for bad decisions made, suppressing growth in the next generation . . . I was very angry about poor stewardship [not taking care of workers and] hoarding of resources not blessing people who need them . . . I felt uncomfortable because the other parts of my social life were diverse and my faith community didn't reflect that . . . [Serving] expectations were unrealistic and ill-informed. Other peers who served also felt tired, discouraged and unappreciated . . ."

DROPOUT DATA 193

B) Are there any other reasons that you can think of that may have led to your departure from the church?

Note: This section of questions was asked *only* of the dropout group.

C) Let's talk about others' reason for leaving

In this section the dropouts speculated as to why other CBCs exited from their Chinese bicultural church. In particular, they were asked to comment on a list of possible issues that may have led to the departures.

Issue #1: Identity Issue of being a CBC within a Chinese Church

1. no response
2. not that large of a problem. "On occasion, when issues arose between the two congregations, the CSC having the 'heavy weights,' (being older) get the final say but I personally didn't get too bothered by this."
3. "I would say it is an important factor . . . It is difficult for a person . . . to be comfortable in an environment with people that do not share many of the same cultural beliefs and practices."
4. this perhaps could be an issue.
5. "Identity? Do you mean that CBCs don't want to be identified as Chinese, that they want to be seen as different? To be honest, that is not an issue for me; I can see it being an issue, like the way a country wants to be autonomous . . . no comment."
6. (Note: this CBC older adult participant was bitter.) "Being a CBC also brings diversity and open mindedness . . . it's hard for a child who is mixed like mine to even be considered as a part of their church let alone culture. After all, if you aren't pure in race, you are a second class citizen. To be a child in a single parent home . . . well that just moved you 10 notches down the totem pole. Well, you can't mix with my pure child, your rebellious influence (obviously you are in a single parent home) like your father's will taint our rank and file teachings to our kids . . . The identity and level of acceptance amongst the pure Chinese is quite a factor for some." (The participant spoke extensively of a quiz passed around by some CBCs titled, "How much of a Honger are you?") . . . "What is sad is that some CBCs want to be more 'Hong

Kong' to fit in. The little cliques are so Hong Kong that it doesn't have room for the CBC kid."

7. no response.

8. "This factor does not have much effect on me. I cannot speak for others."

9. "Given my own experience, I'm inclined to think the identity has to do with being raised with Western values alongside Chinese ones. It's the Westernized thinking and education that is an integral part of the identity causing conflict."

10. "No . . . I don't know, I try to learn about my Chinese roots, that's me, I can't speak for other CBCs."

11. "It shouldn't matter . . . aren't we all God's children?"

12. "I liked the culture identity issue, I love being a Chinese and being with other Chinese people, but when a church is defined by its culture, then you are closing the door on other people and it seems a bit racist . . . I just didn't like it when these cultural forces superseded the religion and the Bible . . . when we confuse children by saying God first except . . . wanting our kids to become lawyers and doctors, and marry within the same race, I find that ignorant."

13. "Personally I do think (OBCs) know CBCs are different in how we think and feel. The point of friction comes from not recognizing that we have anything valid to contribute to the growth and direction of the church. They often fear the input of CBCs particularly at the deacon and elder level. There might be one or two token representatives on the board but it is not uncommon that CBCs hit that 'glass ceiling' when it comes to church leadership. We are considered to be their perpetual children and in Chinese culture parents do not share authority with their children . . . I believe CBCs leave because their identity frequently precludes them from key leadership roles and their input into church affairs are considered to be potentially destabilizing. After five years . . . my wife and I decided we had enough of Chinese churches and began to experiment with Canadian churches . . . [after four years] we felt like we did not truly belong . . . now . . . a husband and a father to three children. Something deep within me was calling me to stop running and denying the Chinese component of my identity. God . . . has shaped me to view the world through the lens of two cultures. (Note: this family transferred back into the Chinese church 10 years ago.)

14. "Growing up, I've been confused about identity . . . I was a chameleon in church—I would meld into the Chinese culture if I needed to . . . everyone wants to be accepted."

15. "The faith is supposed to be a global faith for all cultures. I found that once you are no longer going to an ethnic church with your family, there is no longer a reason to be there. You can worship in mainstream churches . . . (however) cultural segregation is still a reality . . . still lingering in Metro Vancouver . . . One thing your study should consider seriously, is the self-perpetuating nature of the exodus. I wouldn't have left the church for a lot of the reasons you list . . . I want to be where the other young adults are. And when there's a demographic hole in the middle in a bicultural church, I'd rather go to a mega church . . . just because I can hang out with more people there . . ."

16. "Yes, I encountered this. My relative inability to speak and understand Chinese led to some awkward moments. Although I completely understood the culture and how to operate within it, I was mostly seen as 'a good boy,' if a little 'dim' for not really knowing the language . . ."

17. "This is one of the reasons why I kind of disappeared; others were a little more in the church because their families were there . . . as time progressed I felt like I was on my own."

18. "Yes, some of the people attending [church name] did have some issues in relating to the Chinese congregation . . . being able to identify would be a factor . . ."

19. "Yes . . . there are very distinct differences . . . at a young age I was critical . . . They are too Chinese for me; there is a big difference between my parents' generation and mine . . ."

20. "This was an issue . . . CBC identity . . . it would have helped to identify the core issues between the congregations and leadership styles. Many English leaders felt constrained and bound by tradition and that we had to sacrifice our identity for the sake of church unity. Church unity was a HUGE value or ethos."

21. "A very important factor—growing up as a CBC is very confusing and you feel torn between the two cultures . . . the fact that there is a cultural as well as a generational gap makes it very difficult for the older and younger generations to co-exist harmoniously in the same church."

22. "I had no issues. I was the lucky one who felt like I could belong to either side."

23. "I think calling a church a 'Chinese church' for one in today's culture in Vancouver is a deterrent and misnomer . . . I view that as racially discriminating."

24. "Absolutely . . . CBCs I believe constitute a new ethnic minority, a mulatto or Métis sort of group, which is culturally related to, but distinct from both parent cultures (Chinese and Western). We often even have our own Creole language, effortlessly mixing Chinese and English. Our cultural value system, while influenced by our Chinese heritage (e.g., in regard to thriftiness and familial responsibility) is often dominated by our Canadian heritage (especially regarding our interactions with other ethnicities and cultures, our valuation of such Canadian ideals as tolerance and freedom of speech). Seeing the older generation in our church consistently evince prejudicial and often xenophobic views towards other cultures or practices, even among other similar doctrinal background churches, did not inspire confidence in their ability to foster a loving attitude toward all people, as we are called to in Christ."

25. "I've never experienced an identity crisis like many fellow CBCs . . . however some of my friends felt stifled by Chinese churches and their conservative beliefs. Some friends are also annoyed at constantly being judged and assessed by the 'uncles and aunties' who have watched them grow up at church. They don't like being compared to the other church kids in academics, jobs, accomplishments, etc. . . . this is very annoying . . . I personally try to minimize my interactions with adults that I am not close to at church."

26. "I have never encountered an identity issue for myself going to a Chinese church—but maybe that's because I did not grow up going to church."

27. "This could be a factor but I don't believe this is the ultimate cause . . ."

28. "I don't think I saw it as a problem in the church I attended . . . The English congregation was quite strong . . ."

29. "For me this was not that big a deal; I have a close tie to my Chinese heritage. At times the CM swayed decisions that were not made with the EM included; I felt like we were a voice not being heard. Either you are Chinese or more Western, there's always a conflict between this."

30. "My wife and my children were commented on in a negative way because they did not know much Chinese. It seemed very important to the Chinese congregation that the CBCs learn Chinese and be able to communicate with the Chinese-speaking group. [I perceived that] the

CBCs were sometimes being seen as rebellious to the culture and may one day become 'white' and forsake their Chinese culture. I am okay of being a part of the mainstream culture and retain some of my Chinese virtues and values."

Issue #2: Life stage transition needs
unfulfilled within a Chinese church

1. no response
2. "There were fellowships to meet various life stages . . . more than what I have seen at many similar-sized non-bicultural churches."
3. "I do not think this is such an important factor because this can be an issue in any church . . ."
4. "A problem of resources . . . or perhaps the church not catering to their needs. I have found a lot of Chinese churches that are by universities to really cater to university students and they have a good set-up for them. I really enjoyed them . . ."
5. "The church I went to tried its best to have many different ministries geared towards different age groups and demographics . . . I think the main problem was people did not feel safe to share their ugly problems with each other. Maybe they weren't able to be vulnerable to each other."
6. (participant ranted but did not answer the question)
7. no response
8. "Having attended several Chinese churches, I risk painting with a very broad brush; there is a general lack of good biblical teaching/preaching in these churches. Local Chinese churches are at least ten years behind in their theological thinking when compared to their parent churches in, say for example, Hong Kong, and at least 20-30 years behind the better Western churches . . . How can God's people find fulfillment when God's word is not being expounded?"
9. "I never thought about my life stage transitions being supported or not until I started feeling tired but pegged to continue supporting youth ministry. When I realized I spent an inordinate amount of time serving the church, I started to see how imbalanced my life was in terms of my relationships outside of the church. I was having rather superficial contact with family and friends outside of my faith community . . . I

felt that the middle-agers pegged the entire English-speaking congregation as children and youthful even though we had full-time jobs, owned property, were married, and had children of our own. They seemed to forget that we were growing older as well and just as busy as themselves with adult responsibilities. I didn't feel that life stage transition needs were supported in the long term by the church as a whole because no real understanding of our growing needs were shown (except by the English-speaking pastor)."

10. "Life stage was a big issue for my parents—not me." (participant followed his parents out of the church)

11. "It shouldn't be a factor . . . people do jump churches . . . it's a 50/50 factor . . ."

12. "Yes, for over 10 years . . ."

13. "I think this is an issue with the leadership not being familiar with the distinct challenges faced by people growing up in Canada. I found that I had to look elsewhere (to other churches) for support in these matters."

14. "The transition between high school and university was significant at this old church I attended. Most of the core college group left after feeling unsatisfied and unanswered. I think the Chinese who grow up in Canada have it especially difficult—because the influence outside your home is so drastically different from what's inside the home that you've grown up confused . . . After college you generate your own ideas and I think a Chinese church would definitely sometimes conflict with that—especially if it's a social circle who have never really ventured out of their culture comfort zones to explore their Canadian surroundings."

15. "I wouldn't have pegged that for me, but I have seen this with cohorts my age . . . some 2-3 years ahead of me that helped mentor my age group . . ."

16. "There is an element of truth to this, since many of the people who left [former church] with us wanted to go to a place where their families could be supported and their children could grow as free from "cultural obligations" as possible outside of the culture of the kingdom of God . . ."

17. ". . . another factor . . . loneliness is felt; work, school consumes you and then church?"

18. "I don't think this is an important factor, within the fellowship structure it would have addressed life stage needs . . ."

19. "Yes . . . I asked the English pastor 'Where is our church going with the young adults?' It felt like an uphill battle, us initiating things and then having to prove ourselves."

20. "We lost a number of students after the college fellowship. Many drifted once that support network was gone, or when the Christian bubble burst. It's also difficult for singles when their peers are coupled off and married. Some moved away and used that as an excuse to try a different church because they were tired of Chinese churches."

21. "Once [CBCs] become more independent (i.e., go to university, start a career), they start making choices based on what they want vs. what their parents want. Sometimes those choices include deciding what church to go to. So some people may leave the Chinese church as a way of separating from their parents and not necessarily because they have issues with the Chinese church per se (although most people I've talked to who have left the Chinese church had more issues than just separating from their parents)."

22. no response

23. "To a generation of CBCs who grew up in the church for most of childhood and adolescence the decision to go to church is cultural or by choice of family/friends. Views growing up are thus shaped by that environment only. When people grow up, meet people from other walks of life and expand their knowledge base in culture, science, religion, politics, history, etc. their views may and most likely will vary from that of their church upbringing. It is a reasonable and understandable point in a person's life when a church will 'lose' attendance."

24. "I think this is certainly a very relevant issue with respect to bicultural Chinese churches . . . definitely barriers to participation in church ministries involving the wider church body."

25. "My church did not have the resources/manpower to create a youth group that could help my age group transition into the next stage of life . . ."

26. "I agree with this issue because it relates directly . . . I left [church name] because I was beginning a new stage in life within marriage . . . I served at [church name] for seven years without a break. Now that I am older, I feel that I can only focus on [participant refers to his job as a school teacher at a Christian school]."

27. "I am not sure about this one . . ."
28. (No) "I didn't feel that these needs were not met at the church I was at. I transitioned to university and career in the church quite comfortably . . ." (Participant noted being very involved and integrated in the church.)
29. "This was an issue for me—a sense that you didn't achieve accordingly. The fellowship was great but some resources were missing. When getting into the career fellowship something was trying to be established but it wasn't meeting my needs; there weren't small groups offered—I was needing a small group or men's group—I came to a point of just going to church on Sundays and went to other churches to seek meeting my needs."
30. "It is important for us to have peers to transition [with] through the different stages of life."

Issue #3: Intergenerational conflict (within church/family)

1. no response
2. "In my particular situation, the conflict was within the ESC where there was an older counselor/mentor that I feel was overtly strict and often critical of those who didn't line up with his 'desert experience' Christianity."
3. "This would be an important factor in causing a CBC to consider leaving the church because it would impede their spiritual growth or make them uncomfortable in the church . . . I have not had any issues relating to this factor."
4. "I did notice it in [a] second church . . . I felt like they were critical of me and not compassionate . . ."
5. "Yes this is a problem. Our church has been run the same way for as long as I can remember. I wouldn't use the word 'conflict' as Chinese people avoid conflict at all costs. It is definite 'frustration.' [We experience] the younger yielding to the older because they know better . . . and feeling powerless and unable to change things."
6. "Until pride and the issue of 'loss of face' is removed . . . the Lord is not Lord of all . . . The important point to consider here is that it's rude and disrespectful to challenge the Chinese elders in their leadership practice, but the problem remains that the older guys are stuck in won

ton molds and haven't considered sushi. I have been speaking to some of the CBC kids . . . move forward. We don't use rickshaws anymore; we've traded in for Hondas."

7. no response
8. "This is very important as for my reasons for leaving. Traditional Chinese society is paternalistic, in the sense that those who are in authority tend to be older, which in turn means they can rule with an authoritarian style, for they are like the parents in a household. Parents are (almost) always right. One cannot question the parents without being disrespectful."
9. "I encountered this often. Issues stemming from intergenerational conflict may seem petty but in the long run I think they become symbolic of something bigger."
10. no
11. yes
12. "The conflicts arose when the deacon board (which is primarily older generation) treats you like a kid instead of really listening to what you have to say . . . I really felt that no one listened except [the English pastor] . . . at some point, the whole list of things mentioned above, I have experienced . . . in little spurts . . ."
13. no response
14. "I agree that there are entrenched attitudes and traditional values . . ."
15. "The older generation of Chinese OBCs is very diverse; some have a lot of pride and don't realize what's going on around them so that they can be supportive in real terms with the emerging English congregation leadership . . . I have seen others being criticized in the English congregation for things that seemed trivial . . ."
16. "Intergenerational conflicts played a major role in the schism of our church. All of the attitudes mentioned above were factors in our departure, but the greatest difference lay in the lack of respect and recognition of emerging leadership. [Name of church] tended not to be an empowering environment for people to be equipped and explore their kingdom calling . . . it seemed inordinately focused on maintaining programs and traditions . . ."
17. "I didn't experience anything on this point directly but if there was a conflict it seemed to be around the money issue . . ."

18. "Yes this is important; the open expression of love and outward expressions of emotions in a Chinese church isn't a cultural value."

19. "We saw something erupt later, our departure was quite sudden; I heard it happened again after us."

20. "A huge factor for those in leadership and especially looking towards pastoral ministry. One needs to ask why there are *so few* CBC pastors . . . I think many leave because they have little support or mentorship and are tired of fighting an uphill battle . . ."

21. "I think Chinese churches, because of their cultural bias, tend towards a 'works based' faith . . . it plays a big role in why I would never go back . . . I think in some situations there is borderline spiritual abuse happening, where the elder tries to accuse the youth of being disobedient to God when really it's about the youth being disobedient to what the elder wants to happen."

22. no response

23. "Yes . . . but in terms of intergenerational conflict both sides need to accommodate and grow up . . ."

24. "I have encountered all of these issues within the church I attended . . . I do believe this to be a very important factor . . . if not the most important factor." (Participant notes moving and being recommended to attend a new Chinese church in the new city, the recommendation being based on its higher socio-economic status.) ". . . recommended based on classism . . . I am a physician myself, but I was certainly not looking for a church environment where respect was garnered by occupation. This sort of attitude was prevalent in the church I left. Most of the older generation seemed very self-righteous in the way they judged others and in how they would not tolerate anyone culturally different than themselves (often exhibiting hypocritical racism)" (Participant spoke of a church full of gossip, short on forgiveness.) "Many of us viewed the traditional Chinese approach of extreme outward stoicism and apparent decorum, coupled with inward critical attitudes and gossip, to be incompatible with a Christian lifestyle . . ."

25. "I think these are issues all churches . . . struggle with . . ."

26. "I cannot relate to issue #3."

27. "Yes, I have experienced situations like this at the church that I've attended . . ."

28. "A big YES for encountering this issue—all of the above were observed . . . it is impossible to have a real relationship with God and [others] when you believe that hypocrisy and lack of respect are rampant. It is impossible to be genuine in your worship and walk with God if you are hindered by these things."

29. "I saw certain times when there were conflicts in the service . . . I have seen there was a pride issue; holding yourself in high regard; they [the older Chinese congregation] would not readily admit wrong or seek reconciliation; because of that CBCs became disheartened and frustrated. You could see change wouldn't happen because the Chinese side was set in its ways."

30. "I think this is one of the main reasons why the Chinese church cannot keep the young English-speaking adults, as they want to have their needs met and be recognized as people who can lead and serve. The CBCs seemed to constantly struggle to be heard and recognized. The church board is still dominated by the older generation with very different cultural values and views."

Issue #4: Shame culture: Over-evaluation or Rejection

1. no response

2. "Overall, I feel I was respected in that church and seen as a Christian who was serious about her faith."

3. "I would say this would be the most important factor . . . being judged, criticized, put down or rejected are all factors that affect anyone at a personal level . . . I have seen some of this going on in my previous church, but I was probably not directly involved as I had no 'say' . . ."

4. "I think it is important because growing up in Canada we are taught to be more open and more accepting. It seems like there is no room for discussion and dialogue . . . people do not want to just be sheep blindly led or forced to be led into somewhere they do not want to go. If there is a better church suited for their needs, then why not go to that one?"

5. "Yes this had happened. The children are always the children . . ."

6. "The biggest one that I heard about was this girl who dyed her hair blonde. [She was told] . . . you look too white, you're not Chinese anymore, it's shameful. You'll attract rock and roll drug addicts . . . Chinese taboos being infiltrated into the church and used as judgment material, not the Bible."

7. no response

8. "This is part and parcel of a paternalistic culture."
9. ". . . important factor . . . judgment, criticism, and rejection raises fear . . . I have encountered this in the church and it can cause much anger, bitterness, distrust . . . healing is required . . ."
10. no
11. no "[However,] the older generation will always win."
12. spoken by a CBC youth worker: "The last exodus of mine, I was told through the grapevine that many parents blamed us for how their kids turned out, or blamed us for leaving and not continuing to take care of their kids, which points out that Chinese parents rely too heavily sometimes on the church to raise their children or take care of their children . . ."
13. "I believe part of my eagerness to leave the church I grew up in was because I wanted to be free of my parents."
14. "I never felt that way. I've always felt appreciated by others and was encouraged . . ."
15. no response
16. "We felt this many times . . . this was more of an issue for those in leadership . . ."
17. "Yeah I encountered that—this was a big issue for me being looked down upon—I didn't grow up in the church; I felt that because I didn't have any family support I didn't know who to talk too; I did feel kind of intimidated . . . I was more independent—didn't feel I had the support because of that."
18. no response
19. "Yes I witnessed this with our advisers; it was hard to open up about things (e.g., clubbing, sexuality, etc.). This is why I feel more comfortable in a multicultural context; in a Chinese church there are a lot of expectations and a very conservative view; wanted more opportunities to experience things . . . [there was] a lot of judgment about things related to life choices (career) and lifestyle—a lot of comparison and competition."
20. ". . . not a huge factor . . . you learn to navigate between cultures . . ."
21. ". . . seems to be a lack of grace within the Chinese church around anything that is viewed as wrong. I have a cousin who struggled with homosexual feelings and talked to his pastor about it—the pastor reacted

very badly to it, and as a result my cousin has completely rejected the church, Christianity and God. I myself struggled with some issues that I never would have felt safe or comfortable sharing in a Chinese church—I have since attended a healing program in a multicultural church where I felt safer sharing about my issues . . . fear of being judged . . ."

22. no response

23. "I don't think this is restricted to the bicultural church. That would be a cop out in my mind. The issue lies in the lap of organizational religion in general . . . its human nature to try to shape others into the views and accordance of a particular cultural-ethnical group setting. It's the same dilemma faced by adolescents growing up. People are shaped to believe what the group feels or desires together. I don't see it as bad or unusual, it's the way people are. It's just when people are under the delusion that they don't do it or are not part of it because the doctrine of their religion says it's not so. That's a bit odd."

24. "Closed mindedness was definitely a big factor for leaving the church . . . Academic achievement was over-valued by many of the older generation and often served as the basis of their criticism . . ." (Participant further expressed not being able to be themselves.)

25. "Hmmm . . . I think the young people at my church are more embarrassed and judgmental of what their parents and the older generation are doing than the other way around. In general the adults seem to be quite impressed and proud of our youth group. Many . . . have amazing accomplishments."

26. "I cannot relate to issue #4."

27. "Yes . . . this was partially the reason that I left—the fact that I could not express myself freely and when I did, I felt that my peers or some leaders were looking the other way . . ."

28. (Yes) "I would agree that this is important as well and did encounter this at the church I attended. There is an expectation for how Chinese Christians should behave . . . right and wrong is very black and white, even if it doesn't have biblical basis (participant expressed the fear of being judged or losing a position of service) . . . people cannot be honest in their worship or walk with God if they feel they are constantly being watched or judged."

29. "There wasn't a lot of opportunity to voice opinions . . ." (The majority view was adhered to.)

30. "The English-speaking congregation was judged and criticized because they are not as Chinese as the older generation; [things dissolved] because they are powerless."

Issue #5: Western postmodern values or worldviews at conflict with Chinese traditional values manifested in the bicultural church

1. no response
2. "Like me, many of my peers grew up in the church, so being accountable to the church was not an issue. We were quite comfortable with each other and did not mind others looking out for us."
3. "In general this is probably an important factor . . ."
4. no problem here
5. not an issue
6. (ranting, didn't answer the question.)
7. no response
8. "This has not been an issue for me. Many Chinese churches are quite individualistic already."
9. "I disagree . . ."
10. no
11. (participant didn't answer the question)
12. "Not an issue with me."
13. "In this one area . . . Postmodern Christianity certainly appeals to those who want to retain sovereignty of their lives . . . I have a real problem with that. In the end it is just another form of rebellion."
14. "I strongly disagree with this point . . . the bigger problem is that as people try to keep others accountable; they might abuse that position and instead try to push their own values or morals without any biblical basis on others."
15. (participant didn't answer the question.)
16. "I can see this being an important issue for a lot of CBCs, but this was never my particular issue since I believe that if tradition is handled rightly it can be a source of great life for the church . . . However, the ethnic church we left was not equipped to understand postmodernism. This was in part because they were operating in a protectionist

immigrant paradigm that sought to keep tradition alive for its own sake, not to engage and address worldviews as they should have done . . ."

17. "I had a lot of questions to ask but didn't know who to turn to; without support it can eat you up." (Note: Darwinist view challenged him, wanted someone's take on it.) "Conflicting worldviews can determine if you go to church."

18. "Not for myself . . ."

19. "From my experience I really feel a freedom to select things like what church I attend, ministries I get involved in, dress in church . . . in terms of worship, I felt trapped before; now I have more choices."

20. "A communal way of doing church is one of the plus sides of Chinese culture . . . I see this more as a generational issue . . ."

21. "In a Chinese church there's more of a tendency to point fingers and blame and criticize, because that's how mistakes are pointed out in Chinese culture."

22. no response

23. (participant didn't answer the question.)

24. "While the Chinese church I was in did have a strong focus on . . . being family . . . the older generation often stressed what seemed like very individualistic, materialistic, and selfish goals for the younger generation (e.g., emphasis on career choice and financial gain) . . . paradoxically . . . where family was important . . . the individual was taught to be selfish . . ."

25. (participant concludes no.)

26. "Maybe the Chinese church should not think that their upcoming leaders will always stay for a long time or want to serve for a long period of time. Those upcoming leaders may feel called to other ministries locally or globally."

27. "This is not exactly the reason why I left . . . I understand that a good number of my peers left for this reason . . . they explained to me that they do not believe that attending church is necessary—nor is it symbolic of their faith. They believe they are very much Christians and the only hierarchical figure they are accountable to is God. Other than that, the institutionalized format of church and Christianity has caused more damage than good." (The participant expressed that postmodern

values are permeating CBCs on account of their North American educational experiences.)

28. (yes) "Since I left the Chinese church I have started to see that my own spirituality has taken more of an individual view as opposed to following everything the church said . . ." (Participant expressed concerns over rules and not allowing women to be ordained or elders.)

29. "Not a huge factor for me when I left the church."

30. "If you don't fit into the Chinese brand of spirituality you will be seen as not spiritual and not fit to serve in the church. The CBCs are judged according to a set of values that may not be shared by them and this becomes very discouraging."

Issue #6: Over emphasis on Chinese
cultural identity and ethnocentrism

1. no response

2. rating of 1 (participant was unclear with how they were using their number rating.)

3. yes

4. no response

5. "Yes, this is a big thing. It seems that sometimes Jesus is Chinese. But he isn't. I would say, 'Forget about saving face! Confess your sins, cry together, and take risks! Make mistakes!'"

6. "'Chinese gospel' is the most accurate description I've heard yet. It alienates, politicizes, criticizes, and marginalizes the essence of Christianity. Until they see that it's a relationship with Christ and not a performance of an 'x' number of good ideas, it will continue to push hungry seekers away."

7. no response

8. "Ethnocentricity is one of the hallmarks of the Chinese tradition. This may tick off people more than anything . . . by itself it is an important factor for leaving . . ."

9. "I only heard 'the Chinese gospel' about four times a year due to joint services . . . I felt annoyed by it rather than pushed to the point of leaving . . . The Chinese gospel to someone educated in Western tradition is often not relevant to the struggles of CBCs . . . heard in terms of 'a

gospel of works'; . . . I think ethnocentrism [is] an important issue as CBCs become adults and figure out what life looks like. If they come to connect with many non-Chinese then it becomes especially important to consider leaving because a bicultural church (while it says they welcome non-Chinese) does not in action fully embrace non-Chinese. If CBCs want to pursue the calling of 'making disciples of all nations,' then the issue of ethnocentrism cannot be ignored."

10. "I haven't experienced that . . ."
11. "I don't know."
12. "I did not have a problem . . ."
13. "Someone once said that Sunday school should be taught in Chinese. Sentiments like this come from cultural pride. As I think back, what I typically remember hearing in sermons in the Chinese congregation is an incomplete gospel . . . Any time Christ crucified is not at the center of the gospel it is a gospel that Paul describes as being 'another.'"
14. "I didn't feel this so much in the church since I felt that the Chinese and English congregations were separated and the pastor leading the English congregation was Caucasian . . . however . . . there were slight concerns about what was being preached from some of the Asian parents. For example future jobs and aspirations was something that would conflict with Chinese interests. While the pastor seemed to encourage people to find their passions . . . most parents of the 'attendees' of the English congregation would encourage studying tediously (even if it meant skipping church or youth group) to be able to get into a good school later and get a good job. That seemed to be God's plan for everyone. I do think this can be a problem . . . Christian doctrine becomes muddied with cultural values and morals . . ."
15. "Wasn't an issue for me . . ."
16. "[Name of church] was relatively free of this, though I have heard it multiple times from a number of friends from other Chinese churches . . ."
17. "This has not personally affected me. The central message was there."
18. "Where the Chinese congregation comes in is where they want to see a certain direction or the operational side of the English congregation."
19. "Yes . . . teaching and preaching . . . used Chinese values and experiences in the messages; the issues and topics being preached were

reflective of a different place, period, and time that didn't speak to us (CBCs)."

20. "I do think this is an important factor when it comes to missional living. I don't see how this is fruitful when living in a pluralistic and multi-ethnic society. How can we bring our non-Chinese friends into a Chinese church and expect them to simply adapt not just to the Christian subculture but also to an ethnic one . . . It makes it very difficult for congregants to live out the gospel with integrity."

21. "The danger of a cultural church . . . is that its so homogeneous: in a Chinese church the vast majority of the congregation is upper middle class working professionals, and when you're in that bubble too long, you start thinking that all Christians are upper middle class working professionals and anyone who isn't, isn't a Christian . . ."

22. (the participant touched on this.)

23. "It was in the past when there were fewer Asians in Vancouver."

24. "I think that ethnocentrism was definitely a prevalent attitude in the church . . . even having a vocal minority who professed their belief in Chinese cultural superiority was enough to make the environment very unpalatable to a CBC raised in a multicultural society . . . There was such a hostility toward what were perceived as 'inferior' cultures that very few individuals from other cultures, even other South East Asian cultures, ever felt welcome in the church I left."

25. "One thing I really like about my new church is its multiculturalism. I think when a church is too homogeneous it is hard for them to accept outsiders. A multicultural church has more practice in accepting others and loving people despite awkward differences." (Participant's answer: yes.)

26. "I cannot relate to issue #6."

27. "I am not too sure what this means . . . I fail to understand how emphasis on Chinese cultural identity for a CBC could cause one to leave . . ."

28. (no and yes) "There was definitely a Chinese gospel type of twist on everything, and it was very strange for me to see other churches and their cultures once I had left. I could see that this may be important because Chinese culture often clashes with biblical teachings. So in Chinese churches, there is sometimes a reinterpretation of things according to traditional Chinese ways."

29. "This was an issue for me in leaving the church; I felt alienated in the preaching of a Chinese gospel..."
30. "I feel strongly about this Chinese brand of spirituality and the 'Chinese gospel.' I don't want my children to grow up under such an environment."

Issue #7: Personal choice of a secular lifestyle versus Christianity

1. no response
2. rating of 1
3. (participant felt it was important because faith and choosing to live a life guided by the Bible are correlated with church attendance.)
4. "If God is not in their life, it's like there are no differences to them to take either lifestyles so they might as well take the one that is easier or the one they want to take."
5. "I think in this case they missed the point. The grace of God was not embraced/preached/shown/displayed or accepted in its entirety. They think of Christianity as legalistic narrow mindedness."
6. "Secularism ironically is where most of the CBCs who rebel turn to. That happens to be in the clubbing world of night life . . . Drinking [and practices] . . . a subculture same as the world. These are happening to a lot of Chinese Christian CBCs . . ."
7. no response
8. "This factor . . . I do not think it will function any differently in Chinese churches vs. non-ethnic ones."
9. no response
10. no
11. yes. "If they see themselves as someone else, they can't live the devoted life of a Christian."
12. "From grade 12 [graduation] and through the first year of university is when the secular lifestyle calls out and rips so many Christian youth away from the church, the key is having ministries on campus . . . incorporate university freedoms and church into one . . ."

13. "Balance . . . with the fact that if a church neglects to teach and disciple her children, then they will be vulnerable to Satan's devices. The leaders will have to someday give account for their negligence."
14. "I've seen friends leave the church because of this reason. It was heartbreaking at the time . . ."
15. "There may be something to this; a lot of people just stop going to church."
16. (participant expressed this reflects a lifestyle choice.) "A number also leave because of the perception of the Chinese church as stodgy and concerned with comfort and wealth—and they'd be partially right."
17. "This was a big one for me . . . environment . . . my parents were atheists. Everything around me was secular, there are so many temptations out there to live a secular lifestyle (nothing supporting a Christian lifestyle) . . ."
18. "Yes . . . materialism . . . they are convinced something outside of the church is easier to live a secular lifestyle (than by strict oppressive guidelines) this would be a form of rebellion against their culture rather than the church . . ."
19. "I think that because of some of the judgment on some of my peers it has contributed to a more secular direction and rejection of the church in their life."
20. "I know a number . . . I feel this may have resulted from the lack of real and intentional discipleship and the emphasis on programs and formulas. A few left because of relationships with non-believers, and others left because they didn't fit into the Christian culture; they felt excluded and misunderstood. Many felt, as I had, that they couldn't voice their questions about life and God in church. And since church wasn't available or unable to give the answers they needed, they left."
21. "I could see people leaving the Chinese church to pursue a secular lifestyle because they felt so judged and because their experience of Christianity in a Chinese church led them to believe that Christianity wasn't for them because they couldn't live up to the high expectations and couldn't stand the hypocrisy."
22. no response
23. "People grow up and expand their horizons. Children grow up and have different views from their older generations, only to return to the

core values at a later point in life. I don't think this had much to do with the church in itself."

24. "I would definitely agree that many CBCs do end up becoming enculturated in a secular or postmodern lifestyle and leave the church as a result of that . . ."

25. "I think some of my friends have lost their faith as a result of too long of a period of spiritual dryness . . . they spent too much time without support and in an environment that wasn't very passionate contributing to their later loss of faith . . ." (Participant noted the challenges of CBCs relating to the older generation who have a different set of values.)

26. "I cannot relate to issue #7."

27. "I don't know . . . If one simply abandons one's faith, then I think it is one's decision based on their course of life to leave the church."

28. (yes) "A Chinese church may feel very restrictive with its rules and guidelines, and so CBCs may become turned off Christianity entirely because of [such] experiences . . . Now that I am no longer in a Chinese church, I certainly see how narrow a worldview it is, and feel that it would have been difficult to make friends with anyone outside that worldview if I had stayed."

29. "Not an issue for me . . ."

30. "If church life becomes irrelevant . . . people will seek other means [for] their spiritual and social needs . . ."

Issue #8: Perceived problem with church beliefs, theology, or hypocrisy

1. no response

2. rating of 1

3. (felt this was an important issue in generic terms)

4. "I think it is an important issue . . . if some CBCs have some close friends that are gay perhaps they will not like the stances from the church that looks like hate . . ."

5. "Yes . . . this is a valid reason to leave . . ."

6. "My last church was so full of hypocrisy. One set of rules for those who are the big donors and money bags, and then another set for those who struggle. They don't help much. Only those who are not traditional

Chinese have a heart to help. They stand in awe of those who have money. Their theology is that: The Love of money is NOT the root of all evil; it's the LACK of money."

7. no response
8. "This is an important factor for me and some of my friends."
9. no response
10. no
11. "Yeah, I've seen it, I've heard it, but to me I've seen people live double lives; they do have faith but don't leave it up to God; they leave it up in the air; whatever happens happens."
12. ". . . most Chinese churches are strong in theology . . ."
13. "I do not think this is particularly a cultural issue. I saw more hypocrisy, etc. than I care to recall. In Chinese culture you do not correct those who are older even if they are flat out wrong."
14. ". . . I did feel this way sometimes about some things that were said in church—but they would be minor doctrinal details and not major interpretation flaws that would be considered heresy . . ."
15. "Not doctrine . . ."
16. ". . . I doubt that this really is the issue for most people to leave the ethnic church . . ." (Participant expressed this factor could be a universal problem with many churches).
17. not a problem
18. no response
19. "As I look back, theology was not the problem, but the problem was what the church chose to emphasize (e.g., "We just don't do that here.")
20. "Hypocrisy is an issue . . ."
21. no response
22. (yes, the participant seems to touch on this)
23. "Not an issue to leave a "bicultural church" but just a reason to leave a particular organization bicultural or not."
24. "The stated church beliefs and theology (as described in the denominational manual) I felt were mostly sound . . . beliefs of individuals varied greatly . . . I would say that the biggest problem was institutionalized hypocrisy . . . customs such as false humility were abundant

while pride lay beneath the surface . . . duplicity . . . is a big reason for CBCs leaving bicultural churches."

25. (participant referred to bad character—gossip and conflict—as affecting some of her CBC friends and disappointing her). ". . . I try not to let the actions of others affect my impression of God . . ."
26. (participant noted that the belief that leaders should stay a long time is a problem belief).
27. ". . . could be a problem . . ."
28. ". . . church hypocrisy was a major reason for my leaving the church . . ."
29. "Not an issue for me . . ."
30. ". . . may be one of the reasons why the CBCs left the bicultural church . . . negative church experience."

Issue #9: Control issues with church power and politics

1. no response
2. rating of 1
3. "Power and politics was an issue in leaving my church."
4. "Power and politics . . . has been an issue for some of my Christian friends (who are not particularly Chinese). I think it is important to have a balance of power, let the pastor lead the sheep but hold him accountable to the Bible. I think the most important factors in this issue are stability of the church, accountability and whether the decisions were biblically based or felt that it was a godly thing to do (like God wants this to happen, not man)."
5. "This is the main reason I left and the reason why many people I know left."
6. "Control issues are the main reasons for my leaving. A certain leader in the board has more imprints of peoples lips on his [bitter case participant referred to the posterior] than the drinking glasses in a bar. (This case referred to politics)."
7. no response
8. "This is a *very* important factor for me and my friends."
9. no response

10. no

11. "Yeah . . . I think people would rather have democracy, rights; and rather not be controlled one way . . ."

12. ". . . the English congregation sometimes does not have the time to devote ourselves to church committees and deacon boards, and then we complain that we are not heard but it's mostly a time issue and the issue of power within a church is always going to be an issue . . ."

13. ". . . I have seen and heard of churches losing their entire English congregation because of power or politics. Either that or no one stays past age of 25."

14. ". . . an unavoidable issue . . . it is an important factor . . ."

15. ". . . I saw more OBCs leaving . . . in protest to the power and politics going on . . ."

16. ". . . this is one of the primary reasons I chose to leave, and why most of the leaders in our church chose to leave as well . . . people never considered themselves humbly and only saw us (English ministries) as enemies instead of people who were just as concerned as they were for the life of the church and the growth of its people . . . this was more of a leadership issue that trickled down in different ways to congregational life (e.g., opposition to style of worship) . . . this led to people leaving."

17. ". . . it didn't affect me . . ."

18. "I believe that it is . . . the grown-up children were of the mind-set that they are more spiritually connected to other members in the CBC congregation and were more spiritually connected with God. Because the parents were some of the teachers; the Chinese side would make decisions for the English side—approving or not approving things like missions or how money is spent (English budget matters).

19. ". . . There was a part of me at a certain point of time where there was need for greater autonomy . . . either another service . . . or a church plant . . . this was supported by some . . . and shot down by other leaders. Power and politics led to this whole group leaving."

20. "Yes . . ."

21. "Power and politics weren't an issue in my leaving, but it was the cause of my parents and many others (old and young) leaving that particular church."

22. (yes the participant seems to touch on this area)

23. "... It does not necessarily pertain to CBC or not. It's seen in the present professional world. The baby boomers were a large flux of people who established a system. There is a large gap in ages between which could fulfill roles taken by baby boomers. Same goes in the church . . . the first generation of immigrated parents helped establish the church. The greatest expansion of the church at the time would be through friends of common age. As such there is a noticeable gap in all bicultural churches. In all churches, when people are in their 20's they find the need to expand and venture out to see where life takes them. But chances are and I'm willing to bet many will return when they're older or have children of their own. The parable of the prodigal son is in my mind . . . that speaks to this . . ."

24. "... the control by oligarchy ... certainly constituted a major point of disillusionment for young adults who had a vision for changing the church for the better. We realized that despite being ostensibly democratic, our church was functionally a tyranny ... most of the CBCs I knew definitely found that the very strict, authoritarian views of the church leadership often stifled innovations in ministries. Power and politics were the primary reason for my family leaving the church.

25. "Yes this was a problem at my church that left me quite disappointed at times . . ."

26. "I cannot relate to issue #9."

27. "I don't really know how to answer this question . . ."

28. "Yes power and politics was the main reason I left . . . I think many people left after me because of issues with the power and politics."

29. "This was a factor for me (repulsion over legalism); felt there was a lack of power and autonomy; there was a lot of politics going on, it made me more bitter."

30. "Yes, I was on the board and I know the frustration of voicing for the needs of the CBCs and being rejected due to the power and control issues. I felt tired of always fighting for the needs of the English congregation. The establishment did not see the need for change. They need to keep the CBCs in check for the sake of unity." [/NL 1-30]

Issue #10: Church leadership, organizational structure and program issues

1. no response
2. rating of 1
3. "... any unnecessary or inappropriate hurdle that may impede an individual's spiritual growth may give them enough reason to leave the church."
4. (yes) "I think a lack of an English ministry is an issue. At this age I am interested in about the vision and the passion of the church that I attend... I think inadequate leadership does show [itself to] the church attendee in that those in leadership are burnt out and the needs of the congregation are not met..."
5. "Yes, the English ministry did not seem as important as the Chinese. But then again, the involvement of the English was not as strong. They did not speak up at General meetings or even attend. Perhaps they did care, but didn't think it would make a difference?"
6. "Frustration and inadequate leadership, programs for the English ministry was confined by a baby sat attitude for the youth."
7. no response
8. "That is generally the case... There were only two leaders out of ten who represented the English ministry in my church; me and the English deacon, whereas the ratio in population is three to one.
9. no response
10. "There might be an inadequate degree of programs for a bi-cultural church."
11. yes and no
12. "This was definitely a hot topic, and everything you mentioned above is at least perceived to be true if not guilty of being absolutely true in a Chinese church..."
13. no response
14. "I felt this about my old church at times..."
15. "I think there was lip service generated to cultivate leadership in the English congregation, but I don't think they knew what we really needed..." cultivate leadership" in the English congregation? I'm sure they didn't know..."

16. "Yes this is often how English ministry was perceived in our old church. It was frustrating because we were often infantilized when we should have been given opportunities and mentorship into leadership—which didn't happen. This culture of empowerment was one of the reasons I left, and again, in a trickle-down effect, led to the leaving of non-serving peers who then would perceive the church as being simply content to be left to its own devices and traditions without being sensitive to the needs of the community and the way God is leading the church."

17. ". . . it wasn't a determining factor for me . . ."

18. "Absolutely I agree with all these points."

19. "Yes lack of vision for this generation . . . I like to see that when the church moves forward that I can see myself in that."

20. "Our church was a bit older and the English ministry more autonomous than most. However there were still strong traditional ties between congregations which made it difficult for the English ministry to feel empowered."

21. no response

22. no response

23. ". . . Age gap. No role models that were in their 20's when we were in our teens. Most leaders were in their 30's and mostly above."

24. ". . . I know that with friends who come from smaller Chinese churches the English ministry does often become a token ministry for a small minority which can cause that minority to feel marginalized."

25. (participant evaluated and decided—yes) "I think that for many years my church did not recognize the importance of bridging the gap from the Chinese adult congregation and the growing English speaking young congregation . . ." (Participant noted that change happened when more resources were given to the EM).

26. "I cannot relate to issue #10."

27. (participant described the opposite positive outcome) "I have also seen the opposite happening—where the growing CBC began to take on more leadership roles, and eventually teaching and guiding the blooming young ministry to "establish" their own programs and structure . . ."

28. (no) ". . . our English congregation was very strong, so I don't think this would necessarily be a problem in our specific church . . ."

29. "This was a factor for me; inadequate leadership (taking such a long time to get an EM pastor); there was a lack of vision—not knowing where this EM was going. Without strong leadership there is no direction that can relate to our generation. There was too much emphasis on programs rather than unity and personal growth—that was a turn off for me."

30. "Being a representative for the English congregation on the board, I felt that I am fighting a losing battle because we cannot retain the young adults . . . After 20-30 years a lot of Chinese bicultural churches English congregations are still teenagers."

Issue #11: Intellectual, rational and pragmatic issues

1. no response
2. rating of 1
3. "This is one of the most important reasons an individual may leave a church."
4. no response
5. "No, not really. Our church was very intellectual and encouraged the asking of questions."
6. ". . . the doubts and lack of faith and disbelief come from poor leadership, poor coaching and you don't see Christ in their lives. You see a neatly dressed business person running a Christian corporation . . ."
7. no response
8. "This factor may or may not be important. But I do not think it will function any differently in Chinese churches vs. non-ethnic ones."
9. no response
10. no
11. "This is not an issue for me, my sense of need for God and belief in God is two different things."
12. "I did not leave under these circumstances . . ."
13. no response.
14. "This was fairly common. In fact the ones that have very openly left the church announced that this was the reason . . . This was also an issue for me—in fact I'm still struggling with this right now. The doubt,

lack of faith and disbelief can come from a lot (participant noted "bad experiences in serving").

15. "... this could be more of a problem in the Chinese church ... because the English congregation is told how they will do church in a Chinese church ... (paternalism) does not have autonomy, it is run by the Chinese congregation and its elders."

16. "I don't think this was a major issue for most of my peers ..."

17. (participant affirmed this was an issue for him).

18. "It happens. If I were to assign a speculated percentage I'd say one third leave because of this ... it is not talked about very much (not much follow up). A little bit of that culture, "don't ask," it's a tough thing."

19. "I didn't sense that there was very much room for the practicing towards things like healing, prophecy, tongues etc. (matters pertaining to the Holy Spirit); a message on "Dry Bones" was met with objections. Some people left because there wasn't openness to the charismata ..."

20. "In my case, the church I was in was highly rational and conservative ... [there was] a thirst for the miraculous and supernatural ..."

21. no response

22. no response

23. no response

24. "... I would say that rejection of Christian values and beliefs among CBCs is no higher than in any other demographic ..."

25. "For my brother this was a really important issue ... He was tired with a focus on theology but a lack of actions (in community and world). This was an important issue for me as well ... I was able to satisfy my curiosity by reading books on my own."

26. "I cannot relate to issue #11."

27. "This is the biggest reason that I have for leaving the church ... because I think that many Christians including the church that I grew up in, rejected and refused too quickly, for any possible answers and interpretations and quickly dismissed them as wrong and sinful (Participant gave an example of questioning a six-day 24 hour creation), (participant expressed struggling with doubt and unbelief) ..." I think sometimes church members also rely severely on the resident pastor's sermons that we end up relying on interpretations instead of exploring history, development of theology, and piece them together with

current knowledge. In that case, I can only speak for me and a few of my friends who left the church."

28. no

29. "Not an issue for me . . ."

30. "Not an issue for me . . ."

5. Tying it up

If the bi-cultural church you left were a car, how would you describe it?

1. no response
2. "It would look like someone who had an arm he did not have complete control over. This hand would frequently no move in harmony/rhythm with the rest of the body. The arm could be seen directing him where to go. Even when the individual was in relaxation mode, his one arm may be moving about with determination. If he had an itch, the arm/hand may scratch so aggressively to the point of extreme discomfort or even pain (I am relating my experience of one board member/counselor who seemed overbearing and in 'overdrive.' Compassion / empathy were not a quality we saw very often but rather a critical spirit)."
3. "It would be one with an engine that ran with wheels, but did not go anywhere or went very slowly."
4. "A nice decent car that others would drive but wasn't for me because there were something that I didn't agree with about it (i.e., too expensive, or had a stick shift).
5. "A bus or a limo—big Chinese elders in front, English brats at the back."
6. "A write off. No gas, no power, 55 horse power engine fueled with expired cooking wine. Four flat tires going nowhere. Scratched and fogged tinted windows because you can't see inside. Nice paint job and shine, but empty and void. Steering wheel missing, doors stuck closed so that no one could get inside to see what is really going on.
7. "An Oldsmobile (Old)"
8. "It is an old, unreliable American car that doesn't start right most of the time. It makes a lot of noise when it runs and tends to pollute the air. It can only go up to 50km/h before some parts will fall off and

you'll have to start all over again. At a certain stage in life you may need it to go from A to B. But once you have reached your next stage, it becomes a liability. And yet you still love the people with whom you have traveled along in this car. The car speaks to a common journey and experience."

9. no response
10. "It would just be running, maybe not efficiently."
11. "It was fun while it lasted."
12. "A Ferrari on the German autobahn going 40 km/h with a big N sticker on it—so much potential to do great things but held back for many reasons."
13. no response
14. "Very comfortable. All the passengers love each other and are like family. It's not the newest, nicest, fastest or the most high tech. It probably won't appeal to the mass public of pop culture, but its cozy, warm and you're always comfortable in it. You also would probably love every little detail there."
15. "the interior has a musty smell because nobody bothers to clean it up; it won't break down but you wish it did so you could replace it; it's functioning but not comfortable. People who have a mentality to tough it out will and won't complain about the car."
16. "Chinese perception: A motorcycle with a sidecar, with the side car being English ministries (harsh, I know, but this is what I perceived of their attitude to us sometimes)."
17. "it was a new car with a few defects (small congregation starting to grow—a few things stuck)
18. "It would be a car that is very minimal—not much is spent on the vehicle and the people itself (no amenities, no air conditioning) and you have to do what the driver (who is usually not the CBC) says all the time."
19. "it has all the bells, whistles and features (beautiful on the outside) but it was lacking at the quality of relationship; there were certain things we couldn't get over. A vision for the church would be a hybrid car . . ."
20. "It would be a car with different steering wheels, each at a different side."
21. no response

22. no response
23. "Early 90's car. Still runs but needs to be updated. Not sustainable or integrated."
24. "An antiquated vehicle they never let most people drive."
25. "A functional car but in need of maintenance and upgrade (revival)"
26. "Do not know."
27. "It is basically a car with too many functions and features that hinders a driver from operating it for what its main purpose is. It is probably sitting at the garage for maintenance at the moment."
28. "Relatively nice and good-looking on the outside, but pretty much broken and nonfunctional on the inside."
29. "Felt like it constantly needed maintenance; looked nice on the outside but was less pleasant on the inside."
30. "It is stuck in second gear and hard to move forward."

If the bi-cultural church you left were a household, how would you describe it?

1. no response
2. no response
3. "Close but many sub-groups of people."
4. "Lots of different types of people that didn't interact much except on a superficial level."
5. "The big father and little children. The family was very respectable . . . but deep down the children are troubled and messed up because they cannot find solutions to their problems. They cannot mess up because they don't want to look bad . . . and so they grow up and move far far away. They know how to work, how to look good, what to say, how to think, how to act . . . but they don't know how to be human . . . how to deal with dirt and problems . . . they want a quick and easy formula for everything . . . they are uncomfortable with being weak and broken."
6. "Dysfunctional lacks sensible parents and a breeding ground for more."

7. "The parents making all the decisions for the child, using value and trends of their childhood while not listening to the children's needs."

8. "Like a typical Chinese household, you feel ambivalent about it. It is often dysfunctional, with the father figure always trying to rule with an iron fist. No one can question or challenge his authority. He is dragging the whole family through the mud. But it also is a place where you once belonged. It gave you shelter, the companions and the basic skills to survive before you could move out on to the next destination."

9. no response

10. "Somewhat stable"

11. no response

12. "A slightly dysfunctional family works most of the time but there are times of turmoil and conflict."

13. no response

14. "Similar to the car—warm, cozy, small, always filled with good company. There are lots of fuzzy warm stories by the fireplace, but not so much intellectual conversations around the table where everyone can agree."

15. "It's an extended family living in a big house; everybody has rational reasons for living together but nobody is actually happy because they have to put up with what everybody is doing. Not even grandma or the teens are happy about things. When the kids move out it will be a happier place for the mom and dad as they can do what they want."

16. "Parents in denial over the distance of their children and the quality of relationship they have with them. Children in denial of wisdom of parents."

17. "It would be like a cohesive unit, but with one or two who don't want to follow the rules."

18. "Within your own room, it was nice and warm—you would have your family/friends; if you stepped out of your room you would have a lot of awkward moments—yet at the same time it was a family."

19. "I want to say dysfunctional at times, but somehow it stays together somehow; there was genuine love but a lack of communication or a bent to give either way."

20. "I see it as a household with several families that share common spaces, but they want to use it for different purposes. However only one

family gets to have their name on the front door, while the rest come through the back door."

21. "The bi-cultural church is very much like a typical household that a CBC grows up in, not only is there the generational gap, but also the cultural gap—there area a lot of cultural expectations placed that the younger generation may or may not want to fulfill, and if the older generation is not willing to try to understand the younger generations point of view and compromise a little then the younger generation feels their only option is to leave."

22. no response

23. "Same as any CBC first generation home. It's what we all had to deal with growing up. Its okay, we still love the family. But we're charting new territory now to integrate with this society; it will take time and a couple of generations."

24. "Generationally strained."

25. "A family that needs each other but not completely happy with each other."

26. "Do not know."

27. "A very typical Chinese household . . . who hold very different opinions. The parents who are leaders and older generation of the church, are loud spoken and overly enthusiastic, but slowly learning what their children need. During the process probably some children receive more attention than others, but they are in the midst to realize that some children are neglected—and are slowly adjusting to fostering them."

28. "Many separations and issues between family members, competition between siblings."

29. "Dysfunctional"

30. "The children are always dependents and not allowed to grow up."

If the bi-cultural church you left were a person, how would you describe it?

1. no response

2. no response

3. no response

4. "One that was occasionally sick and introverted."
5. no response.
6. "Lost, insensitive, in much need of a Savior. The persona and their witness: if it was poison, it wouldn't kill, if it was medicine, it couldn't cure."
7. "Good, nice, traditional but loyal, but not one that I would be a close friend with."
8. "Not sure. But two sayings with the motherly figure come to mind: "No one can have God as Father who does not have the church as mother;" and "the church is a whore but she is still my mother.""
9. no response
10. "A person who hangs around with cliques "to itself""
11. "It was nice meeting you"
12. "It would be a mixed person, perhaps, mom is Caucasian, dad is Asian, possess the qualities of both cultures but not totally realizing what they can do with this skill set."
13. no response
14. "It's a Eurasian person, who grew up in Asia. There are some white elements to him/her, but he/she is mostly Chinese. He/she understand Chinese values, has been exposed to some North American values, but mostly prefers Chinese company and thinks and lives like a Chinese person does. There are bits and pieces of him/her that are confused about his/her identity—but she/he is still able to function as a normal person. He/she is warm, caring, very comfortable to be with, always has a friendly countenance—but he/she wouldn't be someone you'd find in a philosophy tutorial having stimulating conversations and attracting people to his/her amazing intellect."
15. "The person has drives and wants to do a lot of different things; but the part that is in control causing him/her to only be effective in one area."
16. "Schizophrenic, with good days and bad days—sometimes delusional, sometimes lucid, always needing help."
17. "A very happy fulfilled person wanting to learn but also judged people and had different opinions."
18. "It was a good person; a lot of church / history and I appreciate the history; someone you would have gone to war for . . ."

19. "Like a multiple personality, with different faces; we have the good and bad (even bipolar . . . extreme at times, extremely loving and even cruel). We still have this underlying love for each other in that situation."
20. "Messed up and conflicted."
21. "Friendly and welcoming; narrow-minded, having a works-based faith, unwilling to listen, lack of grace, not very concerned with social justice issues."
22. no response
23. "Like our parents who first immigrated to a new country . . . give it time. Force something and it'll go the wrong way."
24. "Conflicted."
25. Well meaning but perhaps a bit lost in terms of direction of what they want to do with their life. Somewhat frustrated and tired with the work they have to do, not being able to enjoy very much fruit."
26. "Do not know."
27. "They would be a very confident yet helpful person on the façade while quieting dealing with their emerging inadequacies. They intend well, but sometimes the results beg to differ. However they are receptive to change and are in the process of dealing with their inner conflicts."
28. "Someone who speaks well and seems like an upright successful person, but has a very low self-esteem and is an over-achiever in order to compensate for the issues s/he has with others and his or her own self worth."
29. "Selfish, less giving."
30. no response

6. Briefly describe what happened in your life after you left the church.

1. left 5 years ago; on occasion visit a local church; "I still firmly believe in God and haven't given up my faith. However I am extremely critical and cynical of the church and am unlikely to take a very active role in the church if I ever decide to go back."
2. (participant is married with children in a mainstream church).
3. "Its been 6 or 7 years since I left my church . . . I believe my faith has grown exponentially from the experiences outside the church since

I left . . . Though I have not, on a regular basis, attended church, my faith and trust in the Lord will never fade as my life is shaped and constantly guided by "what would Jesus do?" and his compassion and just teachings constantly allows me to evaluate myself to reveal if my life is what God would like it to be. Presently I have not been looking for a church but I have friends who have invited me to church activities. I would like to start attending church (again) on a regular basis because I would like to bring others to God and inspire others through my own experiences with God and his way of doing things through the proper channels and times."

4. "I've left the church about 5-6 years ago now (commented on visiting many other churches); . . . I now attend a Chinese church in Toronto. I do feel that I will serve in a Chinese church. I want to improve my Chinese so I can communicate with others in the church and area about God. I would say I have grown a lot spiritually . . . I find that churches that cater to university students are friendlier and reach out to them more."

5. "I left [two years ago]. Since then I have attended mostly Caucasian churches. I feel that there is less pressure to perform and I don't have 5,000 pairs of eyes watching me and knowing that I am so-and-so's daughter . . . I am trying to just focus on God."

6. "It's been nearly 3 years since I've left . . . The wounds and pains that left me disillusioned for a long time needed the Holy Spirit to do spiritual surgery to remove. Even doing this survey pulled up painful memories. I've consciously forgiven them, the residue of the filth will take time to come out and heal . . . I have found a church home for now and they are very supportive. I find there's power in [this new] church. Strong leadership and depth in biblical teaching. It's not a perfect church but I'm getting fed not fed-up. I believe that God took me through this wilderness so that I can find Him the pillar of fire. I want to dream again, prepare my heart to risk again. I found that is not the race or color of the person, it's their belief system that is flawed."

7. "I believe in God" (participant is attending a mainstream church at present and engaged to a non-Christian who infrequently attends church)

8. "It's been almost a year since I left my church (shares about visiting different churches); I am happy that [I've] found a church that majors on the majors . . . I now find the sermons challenging, the worship

enriching. I feel that I am growing spiritually again . . . Of course nothing is perfect . . . joined a small group and it's been going well."

9. no response

10. (left 2-3 years ago); "I've become more serious in following Christ in wanting to follow that lifestyle; that is because of maturity." (has not found a church) . . ." Not yet, I'm content where I am at for the moment; I believe in God."

11. (left almost 2 years ago); "I haven't given up on my faith, I just stopped going to church; I still believe in God to a certain extent."

12. "We are now at [a multicultural church], where we are surrounded by friends our own age and families in the same walk of life and its been good . . . this is definitely a church where I have no reservations in inviting peers for work or life to come . . . there is a freedom not worrying they will be comfortable."

13. ". . . I have accepted the fact that I come from a blended cultural background. I try to embrace the strengths of both culture and depend on God's Word to discern what the things I should reject are. I no longer chase after the idea that church is about what fits me. My faith today is stronger than it has ever been . . ."

14. "I left the church about four years ago now (spent a year in China and HK) . . . I haven't gone to church for almost 7-8 months now and I admit that I've given up on my faith. I'm agnostic—I don't know if God is there; he could be, he couldn't be. I don't know if this God loves me—of course I know all the cliché bible school answers . . . I know answers from theology books too, but I just don't know if any of it is true. Life experience has proven the opposite from some of the things I've learned. I wouldn't say I'm really searching anymore either—I'm drifting and floating through life."

15. "Left the previous church 2.5 years ago. I have not settled into another church yet; still looking for a church that has other career CBCs . . . still a believer in God.

16. (participant is now an associate pastor with a CBC/multicultural church plant) ". . . there are encouraging signs . . . I feel sad for the church we left, even though there are noises of change and repentance there—which are good things. However I feel we are in a good place right now with our current church (primarily composed of 2nd generation Chinese Canadians) and that we are doing what we are called to do. I see God moving in new ways . . . He's led a lot of people into

areas of healing and growth, something I'm sure would not have happened if we had stayed at [former church] and kept on maintaining tradition for tradition's sake . . ."

17. (participant left the church 5 years ago); "I've grown as an adult; spiritually I've stagnated and somewhat grown in my Christian views (looked back on my older Christian views); the maturity is in age perspective. I have not found another church; I am still looking—whether I go back to church I don't know; I absolutely still believe in God."

18. (participant went to a multicultural church with his wife and indicated that he hasn't found yet what he is looking for) ". . . I have found I can still grow, but having found accountability relationships." (Still believes in God).

19. (participant left former church four years ago). "One thing I miss is the community I had at [church name]. In terms of other areas of my life I was able to grow; spiritually I have been able to move away from 'identity being in my works (serving);" I was able to step back and develop my relationship with Christ. I have been able to heal and come to peace."

20. (participant left former church four years ago); ". . . Through that process I had to reevaluate what church is and why we bother to meet. God has brought me through much healing and has redeemed much of the hurt and pain that was caused. I'm thankful for coming out of that church because I have an entirely different perspective on ministry . . . I didn't lose my love for God . . . came out of all this more passionate to see authentic Christian living. The church I went to next became a place of healing . . . I've been tremendously blessed by this group! I felt the call to ministry . . . I have found a new home [at a second generation church plant] . . . I am so thankful to God . . ."

21. "It's been seven years since I left . . . my faith has grown a lot . . . I'm currently in a multicultural church that is very seeker friendly and I love that I can invite friends there."

22. no response

23. "I still believe in God and have found more experiences in life that bring me back to God. I have found a better way to integrate my spiritual beliefs and my life. There is not church life and the real life anymore, they are one and the same."

24. "It has been about nine years since I left the bicultural church . . . I now attend a smaller Western church of the same denomination . . . the relative lack of cultural clashes is refreshing. I still believe in God."

25. "I started going to my new church for a year and so far have really enjoyed the refreshing sermons and the very different dynamics of the church. I hope to be more involved this year . . . I definitely believe in God but hope that my faith can get back to where it was when I was a child."

26. "It has been two years since I have left [church name]. I currently attend [a multicultural church]; I have found that at [church name] there are people around me the same age as me and some there for the same reason. I believe in God—there's no doubt He is real to me."

27. (participant is not committed to a church) "It has already been eight to nine years since I left my old home church. My life journey has been interesting—growing from someone who was living in the dark when I left church, nearly ran away from home, moved away to study, became an atheist, an agnostic, into being interested in Buddhism, and finally to being a Christian again. Although admittedly the agnostic part of me has never completely departed as I am still somewhat like a "doubting Thomas." I still truly believe in God and His words. I have not found what I have been looking for in another church . . . I still feel that I don't want to be closely associated with other Christians to avoid controversy . . ." carrying a bad name" for other Christians. Fortunately I still stay in touch with certain Christians and pastors whom I trust in order to share and verify the things that I have discovered about Christianity."

28. It's been more than over four years since I left that church. I have gotten married . . . I haven't quiet found what I'm looking for in another church—we do call another church our home church, but it doesn't feel like "home" the same way our old church did. I miss the community of that church, and I am not involved in service at church anymore. I do still believe in God . . . but I am actively aware of being too "churchy"—I have made more friends outside of the Christian faith now and aim to show them that Christians don't have to be the stereotype they expect."

29. (participant did not answer the question)

30. "It's been 12 years since we left the bicultural church; I and my family are still going to church together (two adult children). We are involved

in serving in various ministries. I am very happy with my current church life and growing in my faith and Christian walk." [/NL 1-30]

7. Hind sight can be 20/20

1. no response
2. no response
3. "[this is] difficult to answer . . . I believe the issues can never fully be resolved because of the diversity of people that go to church and probably no solution can be universal to all the issues, including cultural ones which may arise in the church."
4. (feeling connected was a problem) "I would say if the English congregation was older and there were more English speaking adults (not just 3-5 families), and if Sunday schools were more challenging, and we had more mentors that we could relate to, that might be better. A lot of our mentors were from the Chinese side and not fully involved with the younger ones on Sundays."
5. "No . . . I would not see myself there, even if that whole fiasco with the senior pastor had not happened. I think we just needed to pray. Stop everything . . . stop trying to fix things . . . just stop and listen and seek God. It was run like a business."
6. "My solution to all of this . . . stop imposing tradition onto all the people. Choose whether you are going to live Chinese or live Christian . . ."
7. no response.
8. "I wouldn't have moved if not for the reasons listed . . . but I am glad that I did move. God's world is much bigger than the four walls of a church . . . I question the notion of ethnic churches. Perhaps a church should have various languages to serve the first generation immigrants. But why just Chinese? I think we somehow need to work toward the picture of the church described in Ephesians 2. Rather than to set up barriers, we should try to break the barriers instead."
9. no response
10. (participant would still be there) "if my parents were still there, if I blended in better, if I was still involved in a [serving] position . . ."

11. (if things had been different this CBC might still see themself still in the church). The participant recommended "Try to fill [CBCs] needs; see what they really need instead of just teaching them; as they mature ask them for opinions (e.g., what problems do you encounter?") from year to year as they grow up . . ."
12. "I thought I was going to raise my kids at [the former Chinese church] . . . it came down to community and direction of the church."
13. "There are just too many variables to take into account . . . What I do recognize is that God in his mercy preserved me so that today I am still faithful to him . . . What I do now is love the next generation by being engaged with their lives. Teach them foundational truths of Scripture. Cultivate in them a high view of God and his word, to think theologically. To sum up what I would do to prevent an exit under my watch; I would lead them humbly to love the lord their God with all their heart mind and strength."
14. "Yes, I possibly would still have been in that church . . . I think its important for Chinese churches to understand that their next generation is being affected by a different environment and perhaps they need to hire staff that would be able to understand the situation or possibly have a similar background so that they would be able to help the CBCs that are really struggling."
15. This participant imagined that he would still be in his past family Chinese church if he hadn't moved, but he feels happier now. He felt that trying to retain the English congregation peoples was questionable: "I'm not sure this should be a goal; maybe it's a goal for the larger Chinese church leaders; right now I don't see a downside for CBCs going away from the Chinese English ministries and on to other mainstream or multicultural churches."
16. ". . . the problem seems to be one of confusing personal and cultural biases with kingdom prerogatives. The first thing that comes to mind is empowerment. If the bicultural church had thought to empower and mentor its children earlier instead of managing and babysitting them—in other words, to "give their faith away"—there might not have been such a large departure . . . The second thing that comes to mind is one of a ruthless practicality whereby the church gave into reducing the good news to good advice, something that can be found anywhere with any way of life . . . a reduction of the gospel and failure to preach it wholly led to people seeing "any way as a good way" . . . the third thing is that there was a failure of certain church to disciple/

discipline its members such that love and truth were both given for the health of it s people . . . what can be done better . . . modeling of humility, genuine care, genuine openness."

17. the participant indicated that he would still be in church if (a) he had "a more Christian environment at home" and (b) "If I didn't feel I was being judged . . ." The participant recommended "really encourage the Christian lifestyle in that environment; welcome them with open arms, treat them like family; definitely don't judge; be there for their questions; encourage them to ask questions about their beliefs; be engaged in their lives . . ."

18. "In hindsight I don't know if there is anything that can be done (discussed the idea of leaving the nest) . . . really look at the leadership and set vision and goals for the English congregation; breaking from the mold that we only service people of Chinese descent; breaking prejudice. The leadership of the Chinese congregation needs to support the leadership of the English congregation, not just find someone that baby-sits the CBCs (people were brought in just to baby-sit); [name of church] has catered to those who are happy where they are."

19. "I don't think so; something inside me yearned . . . (what had to change?) "It works for the older generation; to change it might not work . . . I don't have a clear cut answer. (Preventing young generations from leaving) "We have grown up in a generation that is about us; the church doesn't necessarily exist to serve us; if I was to step back into that situation, I know it shouldn't be about me. The younger generation is seeking out opportunities . . . but they do need to be inspired by those slightly above them to be an influence on what church can be."

20. "If that didn't happen, I would have likely stayed . . . in order for Chinese churches to prevent their young people from leaving, I believe the solution is to empower and support them to fulfill God's call on their lives. The ideal solution is for the Chinese speaking side to church plant a second-generation-led-church and allow the Chinese identity to fade in order to be accessible to everyone. Our generation and younger are starving for authenticity. They also desire a safe place where they can be heard and loved."

21. ". . . I'm glad that I left . . . I think if I had stayed in that church it would have hindered my spiritual growth and I would not have been aware of it. I think to prevent the younger generations from leaving the bi-cultural Chinese church needs to be more open-minded and more willing to let God direct the spiritual growth of the younger generation instead

of dictating what they think should happen. More willing to acknowledge that God works in many different ways, more than any of us with our cultural blinders can understand, more able to celebrate cultural and generational differences instead of viewing them as a problem."[1]

22. no response

23. "I don't think they need to be prevented. Otherwise there is no realization of what their faith is all about! There would be no growing up or maturing. That would be the single worst thing a church could hope to do to raise a healthy congregation. Salmon return home after four years at sea in the furthest reaches of the Earth, the ones that return are the strongest of the ones that left so that they can pass on their genes to make a stronger next generation."

24. ". . . I think that for many CBCs a multicultural or even primarily Western church would be a more suitable environment in which to grow up and come to maturity. The only way I could see a bicultural, bilingual Chinese church fulfilling this role would be to have sufficient independence of the English and Chinese congregations to allow the separate cultural groups to co-exist. I still believe there are many prevalent spiritual traps that exist in Chinese cultural churches, including legalism, traditionalism, and judgmentalism, which would need to be excised prior to the environment being conducive for CBCs."

25. "I am very thankful to my church and the people in it for nurturing me and bringing me to God . . . I however that bicultural churches need to be more prepared to transition from Chinese to officially bilingual in the future. Young people, in order to stay at the church, need to have programs and roles they can grow into. Churches need to supply the resources to find people to relate to and teach these young people. The church also needs to be ready to pass on the torch to these people eventually as they mature into leaders and adults. The church and the older generation need to give the guidance and freedom young people need to build a sister church from the one they grew up in. One that perhaps doesn't share the same language of preaching or all the same ideas, but can still worship God side by side." (Participant is giving reference to an independent associated congregation).

26. "I am not sure—I guess if I was still single I may have stayed to help out . . . there are different priorities in life now and there is only so much time." (Participant is referring to stage of life needs after marriage).

1. I believe this case resonates with David Park's article, "'Silent Exodus' Leads to Freedom." Park reflects that "Exodus in the biblical sense meant freedom . . . and a journey—so it begs the question as to why [an exodus] would be a bad thing."(1).

27. "Sometimes I wonder if I have the courage or calling to return to church. (Participant wished they could be able to "encourage CBC youths to speak out truthfully and to go through the spiritual journey with them.") ". . . I would remind them . . . there is never the concept of "no return" . . . I notice that Chinese in general often focus on the "Do Not" and "mistakes committed" without solutions. Similarly, bilingual Chinese churches seem to appear the same way. However, it would be nice if churches can also address the part that comes after "Do Not"—which for someone like me, would be incredibly helpful." (Participant is calling for a greater focus on grace). "What comes after "Do Not" is essentially the "I have broken all the Do Not's, now what?" If Chinese bilingual churches are willing to address the "Now what?" Without blind judgment, perhaps [CBCs would be] more inclined to want to stay or return."

28. (participant expressed that if the character of the senior pastor had been different and if her father had not been mistreated she would have stayed) . . ." the issues with the leadership structure and rigid rules led to my leaving . . . I think that being open to changes in the structure of leadership would be a huge issues. Also being able to talk openly about things that were normally "taboo" in a Chinese church would be important. And having a more accepting view of everyone instead of having veiled judgmental attitudes about things like separation, divorce, etc. would be important."

29. (participant spoke of discipleship being crucial and hoped that the Chinese side would give autonomy to the EM as that is how the EM will grow; more vision and leadership as a separate entity is needed). ". . . the big issue is to put emphasis into begin a follow of Christ—it's not about programs and numbers, but to save people and release their gifts. The bible needs to be relevantly applied to the next generation's situation so that they can relate to it. Moving away from traditional practices and helping them grow through mentorship, discipleship and strong pastoral leadership."

30. "It [was just] a matter of time [before] I would leave the bicultural church because I found it did not meet my needs, including cultural needs. I find some Chinese churches are stuck in a culture time-warp. The Chinese churches need to allow the CBCs to be their own being and be an equal partner in the church life. They need to give up control and not be threatened by the younger generation and make church life meaningful and relevant to CBCs."

Table 10. Dropout data

Drop out Case	Gender	denomination	Baptized Member	Service / years	Age*	Transferred to a Chin. Ch.	Attending Multicultural Ch.	Attending Mainstream Ch.	Attending A CBC Church Plant	Left the church	Still has faith in God	Held office
1	F	I – Pentecostal	yes	Yes - 1	Late 20's					yes	yes	
2	F	EFC	yes	Yes 15+	42+		Yes					Various leadership positions
3	M	B	Not clear	Yes	U							
4	F	A / MB	Yes	Yes 5+	U			Yes		yes	yes	Worship leader
5	F	A / B	Yes		32+			Yes			yes	
6	M	P	No	Yes 4+	51		Yes					
7	M	B / A	Yes	Yes 5+	45+			Yes				Intern
8	M	A / A	Yes	Yes 8+	35		Yes					Elder
9	F	EFC / MB	Yes	Yes 10+	25				Yes			EM Deacon
10	M	L / MB	Yes	Yes	U			Yes				
11	M	MB	Yes		32+		Yes			yes	No	Youth worker
12	M	MB / A	Yes	Yes 10+	40+							
13	M	CCC / MB	Yes	Yes		Yes						EM Deacon

	Sex	Ethnicity			Age							Role
14	F	MB	Yes	Yes	29+	Yes						Worship leader
15	M	A / MB	Yes	Yes	31					yes	yes	Intern
16	M	I / I	Yes	Yes	32			Yes		yes	yes	Pastor
17	M	MB	Yes		26							
18	M	MB / MB	Yes	Yes	32		Yes					EM leader
19	M	I / A			28		Yes					leader
20	F	A / I	Yes	Yes	30			Yes				Intern pastoral ministries
21	F	A / ?	Yes	?	29+		Yes					
22	M	A /	Yes	Yes	27+					yes	un-clear	
23	M	MB	Yes	Yes	29					yes	Yes	
24	M	MB / A	Yes	?	31				Yes			
25	F	MB / B	Yes	Yes	21				Yes			
26	M	MB	Yes	Yes	31		yes					
27	F	EF / ACC	Yes	Yes	26					yes	yes	
28	F	B / A / I	Yes	Yes	28		Yes					
29	M	A / ?	Yes	yes	30		Yes					
30.	M	A / A	Yes	Yes	51				Yes			Board member

* Age = at the time of interview (interviews were completed between Dec 2007–Aug 2010; the analysis of this data is 2013; they are all about 6 to 6.5 years older currently).

U= university age
I = Independent church
P = Pentecostal
EFC = Evangelical missionary fellowship of Canada
L = Lutheran
A = Alliance
B = Baptist
CCC = Christ Church of China
P = Presbyterian
ACC = Anglican

Note on case #15—infrequently church-hopping
Note on case #27—only infrequently attending Anglican
Note on years of service—I cited the number when indicated, but my sense was that most of the cases had many years of service in the English ministries

Top five reasons CBCs Self-reported why they left their Chinese bicultural churches:

1. Issue #2: Their life stage transition needs were being unfulfilled within a Chinese church (14).

2. Issue #6: The over emphasis on Chinese cultural identity and ethnocentrism (13).

3. Issue #10: Issues with Church leadership, organizational structure and program issues (13).

4. Issue #9: Control issues with church power and politics (9).

5. Discovered Issue: Loneliness and the attempt to seek friends, fellowship and relationships (8).

Table 11. Self-reported CBC dropout findings Issue	Percentage	Ranking
Issue #1	30%	
Issue #2	86%	1
Issue #3	63%	4
Issue #4	46%	
Issue #5	40%	
Issue #6	46%	
Issue #7	80%	2
Issue #8	36%	
Issue #9	60%	5
Issue #10	70%	3
Issue #11	30%	

Appendix E

Sample Research Survey Form and Questions for Remain-Ins

The remain-ins represent a group who stayed—why do they stay? The adjustments in this survey are intended to glean ancedotal perceptions as to why CBC adults leave (silent exodus). This sample is included in the appendix because there is some variation in the wording and questions that were asked of English speaking adults who remained in their Chinese churches.

Email Self-Administered Interviewing Form—Silent Exodus Research for Remain-in-Church Interviewee Use in Answering the Questions

Introduction and Consent

Thank you for responding and showing interest in this research project. Before you start responding to my interview questions, it is important to emphasize that *your participation is entirely voluntary*. This means that *you have the right* to not answer any question that you do not feel comfortable answering. You also have the *option not to continue* at any point if you so choose.

My name is Matthew Todd. This research project is of *my own initiative* with the intention to have the completed results and analysis published in an academic or professional journal. The *purpose of this research* is to seek a more complete and in-depth understanding of the factors leading to the attrition and retention of Canadian born Chinese (CBC) young adults from the bicultural Chinese church.

The reason why you have been contacted is that we have previously communicated on the subject or you have been referred to me in confidence by someone we know mutually.

I am here to listen and to learn from your experience with an open mind. I will give you *guarantees of complete anonymity and privacy*. This means your participation in this research will be kept completely confidential. All the information that you offer me in this interview will also be preserved in *strict confidentiality* and *security*. Information will only be collected and used pertaining to the purpose of this research and subsequent research on a related topic. All records of the information that you have given me will be *physically destroyed* upon completion of this research project. I guarantee that I will be *truthful and accurate* in the interpretation, analysis, and reporting of all the data collected in this research. No personal information or the identity of any individual in this research will be released or reported. If it is necessary to use any "quotes" to illustrate a salient point in my eventual publication, it will only be done with absolute anonymity and with prior request for your approval.

If you are comfortable with these guarantees and arrangement that I have stated to you, please proceed with the "Instruction to Interviewee" on the next page. However, I will ask you *not to circulate or redistribute* this research interviewing form or any of the questions out of respect for the integrity and intellectual properties of my research. By virtue of your participation in this interview, you have agreed that you are informed of and have consented to the terms above.

I thank you again for your cooperation and participation.

Matthew Todd

Instruction to Interviewee

This self-administered interviewing form is sent to you by means of an email attachment. It is just a simple *Microsoft Word 97-2003* document with groups of related questions typed up on top and then some space provided below for you to type in your answers. Please feel free to expand the space as required in answering the questions.

This in-depth interview may require *an hour and a half to two hours* of your time, depending on the length and details of your answers. Because we are not able to conduct the interview in a face-to-face format, I will rely on you to provide me with *written answers, with as much detail as possible,* to the questions that I have for you in this simple electronic form.

There is an ordered sequence in the design of the questions. Please follow this order from the beginning to the end. We ask you to provide a truthful response to all the questions with as much detail as you can. There is no right or wrong answer; just genuine feelings, responses, and honest opinions.

It is perfectly fine if you do not have the time to complete answering all the questions in a single sitting. You can save the document and come back later to continue where you have left off until you finish. I would like you to return the completed document to me as an email attachment *within seven days*. However, if you need more time or have questions, just email me at boomdrum.45@gmail.com. As mentioned, this document was created using *Microsoft Word 97-2003*. If you are using a higher version of Microsoft Word, please save a copy of the completed document to version 2003 or lower when you return it to me.

After I have received your completed document, I may make a follow-up phone call or email to you later on if I have the need to seek further clarification on specific information you gave me.

You can now proceed to answering the interview questions on the next page.

1. Start with the context

For this interview, I am interested in talking with Canadian born Chinese (CBC) young adults who started going to a bilingual Chinese church at a young age and have remained in that same church till today. If you have left your original bilingual Chinese church not due to any unpleasant or negative experience and have remained continuously in the Christian faith within a bicultural Chinese church environment till today, I would also be interested in talking to you. The focus of the interview will then be on the Chinese church environments that you grew up and /or spent a majority of the time attending.

If you currently have ceased attending any church of the Christian faith or have left the bicultural Chinese church because of any unpleasant experience or incidents, or are attending a non-Chinese church, this interviewing form is *not* for you. Please contact me, Matthew Todd, at boomdrum.45@gmail.com immediately, and I will provide you with a different form.

Let's start with the first set of questions:

In your recollection, when did you start going to the bicultural Chinese church that you grew up or spent a majority of the time attending? What brought you (circumstance) or who (people) took you to that church:

your friends or your family? What church was that (the denomination, beliefs, etc.)? Were you baptized (a church member) there? Describe what the church was like? (Not the physical building but the congregations, the church culture, values, beliefs, practices etc.) Are your parents/family Christian? Did they attend the same church with you? Are they still in the same church?

2. Talk about the people and relationships

Describe what was it like growing up there, in the bicultural Chinese church that you attended for a majority of time? What did you do most of the time in that church? What kind and level of involvement, at what capacity in church service, etc.? How long had you been there? Who were the best friends or role models, and who were the not so desirable people? Why did you think so? Can you talk about both the pleasant and not so pleasant (memorable) experiences in church life, relations with other people—such as, with the pastoral staff, with the older generations, with the Chinese-speaking congregation(s), with your contemporaries at church, with parents, and with friends outside church (while you were attending the church). Were you ever comfortable bringing your outside church friends, including friends of another race, to the church?

3. Let's talk about yours and your contemporaries' attendance experience of the bicultural Chinese church

Quite a few pastors told me that CBCs attending the bicultural Chinese church come and go for various reasons and at different stages of their lives. There are natural reasons as well as negative experiences. In the whole time that you have been with your bilingual Chinese church, did you observe any of your contemporaries leaving the church? How prevalent or not prevalent was this situation? Were there more or less CBCs leaving the church than young CBC adults staying with the same bilingual Chinese church that you attended for a majority of the time? Did you have any idea why or how these departures happened?

In your observation, was the leaving of these young CBC adults often a decision after a long process or just an instant determination? Did any of the Chinese people at church care about these young adults leaving or after they left the church? Did the people at church know or understand why these young adults were leaving?

Did seeing your contemporaries leaving the bicultural Chinese church affect you? If it did, in what way has the situation affected you? What about the general effect of the departures of these young adults on other people in the church? Do you know or are you aware of what happened to those young adults after they left the bilingual Chinese church?

Has the possibility of leaving the bilingual Chinese church ever crossed your mind at any one time in your whole time there? If the thought of leaving the church ever existed, can you tell me specifically what issues or challenges had caused you to enter into the thought of leaving? How did you resolve that eventually? Whether leaving or staying, did you feel accountable to the church and the church accountable to you? Unlike your contemporaries who chose to leave, what has kept you remaining in the bilingual Chinese church this whole time?

4. State the reasons and circumstances leading to leaving the church

Opening question:
In other research, including some of my other interviews with pastors and CBCs who have left the bicultural Chinese church, respondents said various factors (refer to the list of issues below one by one) were major reasons for their departure. Some of these factors may or may not be the same as you have observed. But I would like to seek your opinion on each of them.

Issue #1: Identity Issue of being a CBC within a Chinese church

Some people say that the identity issue of being a CBC in a predominantly Chinese church is one of the factors in their leaving the church. In all honesty, have you ever encountered such a thing in the church that you attended? Do you think that the identity issue would be an important factor at all for CBCs in general to leave their bicultural Christian church? Why do you think such a factor is important or not important?

Issue #2: Life stage transition needs unfulfilled within a Chinese church

Another factor in why some people claimed they were leaving the bicultural Chinese church was that they could not fulfill their life stage transition needs (trying to meet fellowship or spiritual growth needs while transitioning to university, career, marriage, or family). What do you think and how do you feel about this? Did you ever face such a challenge in the church? Do you think that life stage transitions would be an important issue at all for CBCs in general to leave their bicultural Christian church? Why do you think such a factor is important or not important?

Issue #3: Intergenerational conflict (within church/family)

Some people cited that they left the bicultural Chinese church because of issues arising from inter-generational conflicts within the Chinese church/family. In many cases this was a result of: entrenched attitudes and traditional values; self-righteousness; hypocrisy; reluctance to listen and reconcile; lack of respect and recognition of emerging leadership and differences in church practices and expressions of faith in worship and services. Have you ever encountered any such situations in the church that you attended? What do you think and how do you feel about this? Do you think that such situations would be an important issue at all for CBCs in general to leave their bicultural Christian church? Why do you think such a factor is important or not important?

Issue #4: Shame culture: over-evaluation or rejection

Some young adults left their bicultural Chinese church saying that they were being judged, criticized, put down, or rejected most of the time in whatever they did or tried to do in the church. They did not feel comfortable sharing their real thoughts or feelings without being judged. Have you ever encountered such a thing in the church that you attended? What do you think and how do you feel about this? Do you think that such a factor would be an important issue at all for CBCs in general to leave their bicultural Christian church? Why do you think such a factor is important or not important?

Issue #5: Western postmodern values or worldviews at conflict with Chinese traditional values manifested in the bicultural church

Some CBC young adults said that they left over the issue of a conflict between their individualistic worldview and spiritual belief and the traditional cultural practices of the bicultural Chinese church. Some felt that their spirituality should be more of an individual pilgrimage, and less accountable to hierarchical institutions like the church. What do you think and how do you feel about this? Has this ever been an issue for you in the bicultural Chinese church you attended? Do you think that postmodern values would be an important element at all for CBCs in general to leave their bicultural Christian church? Why do you think such a factor is important or not important?

Issue #6: Overemphasis on Chinese cultural identity and ethnocentrism

Some CBCs said they left the Chinese church in a rejection of the preaching of a "Chinese gospel" as well as overemphasis on Chinese cultural identity and ethnocentrism. Some felt alienated instead of being embraced. What do you think and how do you feel about this? Was this ever been an issue in the bicultural Chinese church you attended? Do you think that ethnocentrism would be an important issue at all for CBCs in general to leave their bicultural Christian church? Why do you think such a factor is important or not important?

Issue #7: Personal choice of a secular lifestyle versus Christianity

Some people left the Chinese church because of a conscious (or unconscious) choice, under the influence of secularism and postmodern lifestyles, which led to the abandonment of the practice of Christian faith. What do you think and how do you feel about this? Do you have any idea why CBCs in a church would choose a secular lifestyle over a Christian lifestyle? Do you think that choosing a secular lifestyle would be an important issue at all for CBCs in general to leave their bicultural Christian church? Why do you think such a factor is important or not important?

Issue #8: Perceived problem with church beliefs, theology, or hypocrisy

Some people left as they perceived a problem with church beliefs and theology or hypocrisy. Was this ever a problem you perceived in your church or family? What do you think and how do you feel about this? Do you think that perceiving such a problem would be an important issue at all for CBCs in general to leave their bicultural Christian church? Why do you think such a factor is important or not important?

Issue #9: Control issues with church power and politics

Some young adults left as a protest towards their Chinese church over issues related to power, autonomy, patriarchy, paternal control, lack of decision-making or empowerment, repulsion over legalism, or disillusionment. What do you think and how do you feel about this? Were power and politics ever an issue in the bicultural Chinese church you attended? Do you think that control issues would be an important issue at all for CBCs in general to leave their bicultural Christian church? Why do you think such a factor is important or not important?

Issue #10: Church leadership, organizational structure, and program issues

Some young people left the Chinese church due to: a frustration with inadequate leadership or representation of the English ministry, or inadequate programs and structure, and lack of purpose or vision. English ministry was expediently confined primarily to a youth ministry babysat by the church. What do you think and how do you feel about this? Was this ever an issue in the bicultural Chinese church you attended? Do you think that these elements would be an important issue at all for CBCs in general to leave their bicultural Christian church? Why do you think such a factor is important or not important?

Issue #11: Intellectual, rational, and pragmatic issues

Some people left the Chinese church because of philosophical conclusions that led to doubt about the Christian belief and the inability to reconcile it with philosophical ideas (e.g., evolution, materialism). Christian values and beliefs (e.g., acting in faith, miracles, etc.) were discarded in exchange for a full embrace of rationalism (faith in reason.) How common was this among CBCs who left the Chinese bicultural church? Has this ever been an issue for you? Do you have any idea why the doubts, lack of faith, and disbelief arose?

5. Tying it up

If the bicultural Chinese church you have been attending for a majority of the time were a car, how would you describe it?

If the bicultural Chinese church you have been attending for a majority of the time were a household, how would you describe it?

If the bicultural Chinese church you have been attending for a majority of the time were a person, how would you describe it?

6. Let's talk about your overall experience and spiritual journey within a bicultural Chinese church environment

How many years now you have remained in a bicultural Chinese church environment? In your spiritual journey, what has been your overall or conclusive experience for the whole time you were growing up and maturing in a bicultural Chinese church environment? Has the bicultural Chinese church experience been fulfilling? In what way has it been fulfilling and in what ways has it not been? From the perspective of a CBC, what has given you particular meaning in a bicultural Chinese church? On the other hand, is there anything you have found missing or lacking in the bicultural Chinese church environment? What is your outlook or hope for the bicultural Chinese church in the future?

7. Hindsight can be 20/20

Looking back, if the situation(s) leading to the departure of your contemporaries had not happened or had happened differently, would you see them still being in the church now? In hindsight, what had to change or to be changed in the bicultural bilingual Chinese church in order for young CBCs like you to grow up and mature and find a real and fulfilling Christian life and service experience in church? If you were the bicultural Chinese church, what you would have done to prevent the younger generations from leaving?

8. Thank you

Do you think there is anyone I should talk to on the same subject, whether s/he is like you in having remained in the bicultural Chinese Christian church till today or unlike you and has left the church? I would appreciate your referral.

Appendix F

Remain-In Data

1. Start with the Context

1. started going to church around seven years old with the whole family . . . a Baptist church . . . Chinese sermons translated into English simultaneously . . . everyone seemed to know each other . . . celebrations . . . variety shows . . . many programs . . . My family is Christian and attended the same church as I at that time. My parents no longer attend that church.

2. ". . . My parents took me to church . . . Evangelical . . . I was baptized. The Chinese congregation was always considered the 'parent' congregation. The English congregation was always viewed as the 'child' congregation. Decisions focus and direction always came from the Chinese side . . ."

3. I started attending [church name] at the age of 17; a close school friend invited me to this church to join their new youth group. After attending three years I was baptized . . . culture of the church is predominantly Chinese. The English congregation . . . majority under age 25 . . . mainly the children of parents from the Chinese congregation whom have grown up in the faith. My parent's family are not Christians.

4. ". . . born and raised in a conservative, non-denominational Chinese church . . . my grandfather was an elder, my father a deacon and elder, my mother a choir director . . . I was baptized and confirmed there.

God has blessed me with a Christian heritage five generations deep on my father's side; six on my mother's side . . . (Participant spoke of growing up in a second/next generation English congregation). The . . . English service and congregation was not without its trials, including a significant turnover rate of English pastors . . . (Participant spoke of this being a commuter church).

5. Started attending at eight; family brought me to church; church affiliated with the Mennonite Brethren; still a baptized church member there; Church description: English congregation primarily younger, high school age; Chinese congregation, primarily older; beliefs and practices placed emphasis on tradition but open to exploring new ideas; parents family partially Christian; grandma attends same church.

6. "I started church when I was five; my mother took me . . . to a Mennonite Brethren Chinese church . . . My mother has just gone through a divorce . . . the pastor's wife helped my mom take care of me." (Participant was a baptized church member and describes the fellowship as being friendly and tight; parent's family was not Christian).

7. "I have attended this church for 13 years; I started attending with my entire family. My church is part of the Alliance denomination. I am a baptized member. My whole family is Christian and attends the same church. In my church there are three congregations; Cantonese [mother congregation], English and Mandarin."

8. (participant started in his church in grade 11 brought by a friend); ". . . I made a confession of faith during a youth rally that year. It is [church name] Alliance . . . I was baptized there . . . the English side was (and arguably still is) treated like "children" because they are younger, and only now are there adults and couples and a fully functional congregation. Aside from that, it was often treated like a babysitting service. (Participant indicated his parents do not attend church).

9. (participant noted he began to go to a Chinese Lutheran church in 1990, was baptized; his parents are Christian and in the same church; the church was conservative; the older generation have the Chinese value and merged it with Christian perspectives).

10. (participant has attended several Chinese Lutheran churches and currently attends an Alliance church; baptized and confirmed by age 15).

11. (participant noted being brought to the Alliance church in grade one, later he was baptized).

12. "I started attending [church name] when I was ten years old. My family took me to church . . . I was confirmed at that church during my teenage years . . . The people were predominantly Christian Hakka Chinese. The church was the only church in North America that conducted its Chinese services in the Hakka dialect . . . Values and practices at church were mostly conservative. Beliefs are closely affiliated with the Lutheran faith. Practices and procedures are more like the Basel Christian church of Malaysia as the senior pastor was from that part of the world . . . My mom's siblings were the founding members of the church . . ."

13. (participant indicated his family brought him as a child to a CCC Chinese church in Vancouver BC. Later he transferred to a Chinese alliance church and became a baptized member; his parents were deeply involved in the church leadership and he got to know all the church families intimately in this small congregation) . . . I developed a larger understanding of the church as intergenerational . . . not perfect . . . By the time I reached university I felt that involvement in church, leadership, mentoring and being mentored were as natural as breathing . . . my father now teaches at the Alliance bible seminary in Hong Kong . . . I now live in Calgary (Participant notes the name of a missions ministry he is involved in) . . ."

14. (participant indicated he grew up in a Tri-cultural Chinese Evangelical free church, where he was baptized and met his wife). "It is a congregational church meaning . . . the pastors serve the congregants and the lay leaders do have more authority . . ." (Participant described the church as being a family to him, a place of friendships and where his parents also attend).

15. (participant started attending a Chinese MB church in 1997 when a high school friend brought him; he was baptized in 2000; EM was 30 members, CM 150; his parents are not Christian yet).

16. (participant started to attend a Chinese MB church at age 19. He did formerly attend a mainstream church. He was baptized in the bicultural church and has watched it grow over the last 13 years into a growing English congregation with a career group.)

17. (participant grew up in a second generation Christian family in a Chinese Baptist church where he was baptized.)

18. (participant came to his Chinese Anglican church twenty years ago; his parents go to the Chinese service. He was baptized in Hong Kong

and later confirmed in his present parish). "It's a big family community . . . its grown to become like a home to me over the years."

19. (participant noted that her father is the senior minister at this church); I came almost 20 years ago; I was baptized in Hong Kong as a baby and confirmed in my present church. My whole family attends this church. It feels like a family atmosphere having lots of aunts and uncles.

20. (participant was brought as a baby to a Chinese Alliance church; he was baptized as a teen; his parent's entire immediate family are active Christians). ". . . the English congregation was well taken care of. My church seems to be known for its excellent quality of preaching and Sunday school . . . my church tends to produce very intellectually sound Christians (. . . provides a good environment for such Christians). It is a rather contemplative church—an environment that tends to produce quiet people who chose their words carefully . . . (Participant notes that only one sibling left to attend a multicultural church because an adult fellowship was lacking to meet her needs).

21. "I was born in a Christian family so I have always been brought to church (Evangelical Free) . . . My mother led me to Christ when I was 6 years old at home and I was baptized at the church when I was about 16. My parents and I still attend the same church . . . the church is about 50% Cantonese, 40% English, and 10% Mandarin. There is not much communication or interaction between congregations . . . many in the English congregation do not speak Cantonese or Mandarin fluently. The only time there is interaction between all congregations is during Christmas and Easter, where there are joint services . . ."

22. (the participant noted he was born into a Christian family and brought to church by his parents). ". . . the congregation was more lopsided towards the Chinese culture . . ."

23. (participant was born in Canada and came to the church at age 14). I was baptized in [church name] in 1991 . . . (participant was married in this Baptist church in Vancouver). ". . . my parents are not Christians (they consider themselves Buddhists and follow ancestral worship); they allowed me to go to church because they believed that having religious belief was good for a person."

24. (participant grew up a Chinese Evangelical Free church from a baby; level of involvement was sparse until high school after which he helped lead a small group and joined the worship team. A big factor in remaining in the church was his dad becoming a pastor in the church. His best friends were at church. One of his non-Christian friends came

to the church; he was not really comfortable in reaching out to bring his outside friends to church).

25. (participant noted growing up in a bicultural Mennonite church and that his father was a pastor of; he was a baptized member. This church was made up of extremely poor members from various parts of Asia who spoke Cantonese). ". . . There was a huge gape between the ages of 20-35; we didn't have anyone that age. Most of the people were ages 55+ . . ." (Participant then spoke of his next Chinese church). I currently work at a MB church, have been here for seven months . . . an English ministry position . . . the EM is still is still quite traditional because of the way these kids were raised . . . there was no training or mentorship. We are still in the developmental stage because it was run so long by the Chinese senior pastor and parents from the Chinese congregation, much of the traditional stuff remains but we are transitioning . . ."

26. (participant started going to his church at age 14 with his mother; the church had a clear focus on the Great commandment, Great commission, core values, and a vision "to build and grow a caring and adventurous community of believers enriched by multiple generations and cultures, deepening their love for Christ and teaming together with passion to reach and serve others.")

27. "I started going to this bicultural Chinese church when I was five . . . My uncle and his family were Christians and brought us . . . I was baptized around 18 years old . . . My parents and most of my family here in Canada are Christians. Most of them attended and are still attending the same church . . . My cousin is a pastor, uncle a deacon board member, and various aunts and uncles are involved in choir."

28. (participant was brought into a Chinese MB church since she was age six and baptized; her family is all in the same family oriented church.)

29. (participant's family was brought to a Chinese MB church by his aunt when he was eight years old; he is a baptized church member; he was born into a Christian family that still attends the same church).

30. (this participant has attended three Chinese churches since 1969 when at age five her parents brought her to church in Chinatown Vancouver; she is married and currently in a Chinese Alliance church; she remembers an exodus of young English speaking couples that decided to go and form the first CBC church called Corner Stone. Almost all the youth group left; her parents were very involved in leadership on the Chinese side of the church).

Summary on this section: The majority were brought to church as a child except three who came as teens. The majority are from Christian families; the majority (if not all) are baptized members in evangelical churches.

2. TALK ABOUT THE PEOPLE AND RELATIONSHIPS

1. "I was well nurtured during my time in the church I grew up in. I had the support of my family, my peers, and the adults . . . youth I grew up with in the church became my close friends . . . I . . . participated in some of the church [programs] . . . I made some of the older youth my role models, as I was fond of their experiences and the way they served with skill and maturity. The pastor never really played a role in my life growing up at that church, mainly because they were brought in for the adults in a more Chinese-cultured environment . . . I felt very comfortable with everyone in the church . . ."

2. (Participant described following her parents to church, attending fellowship, then serving as a bible study leader, worship leader, worship coordinator etc.). ". . . I don't think I had any best friends in church . . . the church became more a workplace for me . . . I never felt comfortable bringing others to the church because I always felt that it seemed like I was bringing a 'prize' to church to show others that I was 'converting' my friends . . ."

3. ". . . involved at the youth fellowship level. I served [in the] committee . . . in worship leading, Sunday school teaching and small groups. I have been there seven years . . . my best friends . . . from fellowship group. Our congregation is fairly young and there aren't many older role models. However there was always a pastor or youth worker whom I could approach if I had any issues. I remember back in the earlier days when our fellowship was just forming there were constant struggles with the older generation. It felt as though we were under scrutiny and disapproval. We'd come back fully charged from a youth conference, with new ideas, but somehow our ideas would be discouraged. I felt that the church was more a place of pointing fingers and criticizing others under performances rather than embracing others hurts, pain and shame."

4. (participant spoke of being very involved in the teen and university years in various serving capacities; role models were best friends and a youth group counselor). ". . . I never had a problem with bringing non-Chinese friends to church, but I didn't consider much whether

they'd feel at-home or not at a Chinese church. Church was and still is extended family to me, so bringing a friend to church was just like bringing a friend to meet my family, culture and all. I have no doubt that within that church there were cultural tensions between the immigrant generation and the local born generation . . . However, I did not experience much of that tension personally due to the genuinely godly example of reconciliation and love within our family. We had no double-standard in our family, or the traditional Chinese dictatorial father: "You eat my rice, and you live under my roof—so you do what I say!" Our whole family knew that we were all under God's authority and God's rules—and that those rules were for our benefit and for an abundant life. The intergenerational and cross cultural peace experienced in our family then spilled outward to the church family."

5. Growing up in the church: many programs, enjoyable time with friends. (Participant noted being involved in many programs and in various areas of service ranging from music, leading fellowship, to leading bible studies). Been in the church approximately fifteen years. Best friends were people I grew up with, people that appreciated Scripture and spiritual growth; people less desirable were the opposite. I value spiritual growth. Pleasant experiences [included] working with the leadership, serving in Sunday worship music team, teaching bible studies, planning summer camps and other events; no significant memorable unpleasant experiences; interactions with pastoral staff were good, older generations were generally good, Chinese speaking congregations generally good, contemporaries good, parents good, outside church good. Yes I was comfortable bringing friends (of another race) to church.

6. (participant describes a close relationship with the fellowship group and active in the church's programs; participant served in the music and fellowship; a span of time covering some 20 years. Best friends were similar people in the fellowship; role models included a high school counselor and competent peers. Participant indicated that she had pleasant experiences with certain pastoral staff who would offer opportunities to lead or take on more responsibility. Unpleasant experiences included having a parent try to parent you . . . [and] "decisions being continually resolved with the reasoning "that's how its traditionally done in the Chinese church—by the Chinese congregation and you don't have a say because you're younger and therefore less experienced (This was a type of reasoning that was used for quite some time in my current church!) I did bring two high school friends

to church—but strictly in a very social manner . . . About bringing friends of another race --- no. I never contemplated this . . . I was never very comfortable just hanging with friends of another race; throughout university and high school . . . I really stayed inside a Chinese-Canadian circle, much to my detriment."

7. "Growing up in the bicultural church is somewhat a challenge at times, but I believe it is what God intended . . . to learn about [others] of different cultural backgrounds. The challenge lies in the differences in culture and the belief that unique cultural ways of worship and ministry are better . . . Having served many years . . . in the English ministry, I have learned that cultural differences are inevitable and there is no more right way [in preferences] if both sticks to the doctrine of the bible. (Participant expressed the challenge in requesting a worship ministry budget and encountering lots of questions if the focus was not too much on performance) . . . One of the most difficult things growing up . . . older adult/leaders of the church sometimes look down on myself and others [new ideas] as if we are still kids . . . this to me is contrary to what is shown in the bible as God uses young people a lot in big ways! . . . sometimes there is more criticism to what we do than encouragement even when God allowed us to do his work to a great result with his power. While I generally have a great personal relationship with my pastoral staff/elders . . . I know that [they have a] "young kid" mentality [about me] and sometimes I have to be wise and diligent in my ways to convince them to give us a chance in doing certain things. In terms of friends to bring to church, my church is supposedly a multicultural English congregation, and it is represented partially in our Sunday attendance. However, the attendees in my youth group are all English speaking Asians . . . it is difficult for me to invite a friend of a different culture to fit in comfortably if they're completely new . . . so far I am only successful in inviting . . . English speaking Asians to join my group; but if there is a chance/choice, I would love to see my group diversify to what it is supposed to be, multicultural."

8. "I was somewhat involved [noting helping and assisting with AV team]. But as time went on, and I began to desire to serve in ministry and studied religious studies/philosophy/classical studies in undergrad, I was given more opportunities to lead . . . I had very few role models in the church . . . the pastors (English congregation) were very busy and although enthusiastic about my desire to learn were not able to properly mentor me . . . the Chinese side didn't notice me since my parents weren't on [there] . . . its like I had no voice, no presence. It was

very annoying and discouraging at times . . . I did not think of THIS church as my primary community of friends. And I would not bring them unless we were having some sort of night where I was taking part like presenting or speaking—I invited them to my baptism, that that is all."

9. "Like a family church; the older generation would treat the younger generation like family. To start [I was] not very involved. 1990—2008 (18 years), then left the church for five years in his twenty's. Role models—in Sunday school, someone older. Some of the older generation was not very friendly—it's more status. Yes [I] brought outside friends."

10. (participant described the church as a family and being very involved as a youth and teen; English Sunday worship was started when she was age 18. She became very heavily involved in leading worship and preaching—later becoming a youth worker. Her role model was a youth worker and a male worship leader) . . . "During two years working as youth worker I attended regular council meetings held in Chinese language. I usually just do my reporting and did not say much because those meetings are always very long . . . And I saw the more political side of how ministry gets decided behind the curtains. It was an eye-opening experience. As a CBC I began to appreciate some of the older people and how much effort they put in church ministry and their heart for service, but I also dislike some of the old traditional ways of doing ministry. I always felt there was not enough prayer and the leading of the Spirit."

11. "Growing up in [church name] was a very pleasant time. (Participant noted significant involvement in programs, volunteering, interchurch sports league, and fellowship; over the years he observed a number of his church friends involvement decline) . . . I was comfortable bringing other friends into my church through sports events or rally nights, but as I grew up my invitations to others declined."

12. ". . . I was quite involved in church life over the years . . . committee . . . chairperson of the fellowship. Today I'm the youth advisor . . . I was also elected into the church council . . . the last four years I'm the chairperson for the English ministry at church. Most of my friends and role models were also from the church. I grew up with my best friends there. I also met my wife at church. My experiences with the church were mostly positive except for a few hiccups . . . [for] the most part, I got along with pastors from both the Chinese and English sides

over the years. They helped me grow spiritually and gave me good teachings and advice. Another struggle was as a leader of the youths, was dealing with their Chinese parents. Some were not very open minded . . . On the positive end, I enjoyed participating in the many programs . . . conducted by the church. I had the advantage of knowing the Hakka, Cantonese and Mandarin dialects. I was not lost in translation as most of the English speaking youths and adults would be. As such I was able to connect with the majority of the people at church from both the Chinese and English side . . . I was well connected with the pastors, adults, youths and kids. The seniors also knew me. Our church welcomes everyone from all walks of life and those of another race. However, I would have to say that our church was more suited for Chinese people and specifically those from East Malaysia. (Participant notes the English ministries growing) . . . I had no problem inviting people with Chinese background to our church. I don't think I would feel comfortable today encouraging someone of another race to our church given the culture there. It would be hard for them to connect with the rest of the congregation."

13. (participant notes being very involved in various programs and ministries of his church; he grew close to older youths and his Sunday school teachers) . . ." Speaking Chinese in my own home . . . made me a bridge between the generations . . . served me well as a Sunday school teacher of kids who could not understand their parents culturally and whose parents could not understand them. I did bring school friends to church but only those who were of Chinese descent. I was never comfortable introducing non-Chinese into this setting. There was too much 'baggage' involved and it was way beyond me to reconcile so much that I did not and could not understand at that stage in my life."

14. "Growing up in [church name] was similar to an extension of my family . . . much of the connection took place outside of the church as the families were close . . . I respected the pastoral staff [and] older generations . . . maybe a result of the fact that my parents did not serve on any church board or get involved in any church politics. This resulted in very little negative feelings or impressions trickling down to me . . . most of the friends that I brought along to the church were Chinese/Asian due to my network of friends being more Asian . . ."

15. (participant noted the separate nature of the two language congregations with some joint services and events). "My serving included: deacon, worship leader, Sunday chair person, teacher, fellowship

counselor, fellowship executive. No bad experiences. [I was] okay in bringing Chinese friends, but not other races."

16. "Prior to joining this church, I rejected Chinese culture. As a CBC at this church, I learned to embrace the Chinese culture and language. I also felt accepted by all members at this church . . . was given many opportunities to serve . . . (fellowship committee member, camp planning committee, worship chair) . . . I was very enthusiastic to serve and regularly spending time reading the bible, in prayer, sharing the gospel . . . (Participant went to the US to study for three years). When I returned from the studies in the US . . . many of those that were attending this church before I left were no longer there including my younger brother, cousins and cousin-in-law. This was perhaps the most painful memory I have in my time at this church. I really felt their departure was due in large part to the church leadership's neglect of the English congregation . . ."

17. (participant transferred to a Chinese MB church where he has been for 15 years; his best friends are also Christian—a few moved on to other churches) ". . . My role model is definitely the youth pastor . . . he lost a battle to cancer about 10 years ago but his influence is still deeply rooted in me. The most unpleasant experience was with our ex-senior pastor as he has different opinions than the youth pastor which is my role model . . . it was a taste of church politics . . . my friends outside church . . . are all of Chinese descent . . . I have not brought any friends of different race to church."

18. "The general feeling was comfortable and natural; I had become a helper, teacher, involved in the fellowship committee [and] later got involved in the church board, subsequently a trustee with the board. My best friends were found in the Sunday school and fellowship. I was comfortable bringing friends from high school—but when university started it was tougher to bring friends into the church. I don't recall any negative experiences."

19. "I was the pastor's kid—I feel like the example people think of representing the youth. I was involved in all the things my age group was—I went to Sunday school, fellowship, and served as a platform worship leader (various involvements). My closest friends were from both church and school. I did feel comfortable bringing Chinese friends" (participant lives in East Vancouver, so the Chinese demographic is high).

20. (participant noted attending the children and teens programs). "... I think from a pastoral management perspective it was excellently run. I think I did lack individual attention though—mentors... right now I'm headed for pastoral ministry myself... I continued to go to church service and fellowship—pretty much every event, till I finished university... I got very involved in whatever planning committees and leadership positions there were available in fellowships and then I got involved in Para-church stuff... very involved... My best friends were guys I grew up with; role models were my pastors, a couple of Sunday school teachers and my older brother who was a Sunday school teacher and very involved in ministry activities. (Participant noted a not so desirable person as being two contentious and argumentative Sunday school teachers; one was described as being "very rigid [with] little understanding of grace"). I was never comfortable bringing friends to church—people would say the crowd was a little cliquey. I could see myself bringing someone to fellowship, but not to church service... As for friends of a different race, it was fairly comfortable. We were fairly westernized in our culture and I often forgot I was Chinese."

21. (participant described parents being heavily involved in the church and also being fairly involved and enjoying leadership roles; she found a respected role model in her fellowship counselor). "The pastoral staff has always been very kind and nurturing, always available..." (participant described her needs in sermons changing once in university).

22. (participant described himself growing up and being part of the various children and youth programs). "... My best friends were my classmates in Sunday school... I didn't have any role models... I have few memorable moments with people older than me. One of the memories is an older single man who knew I loved his cartoon drawings and he'd always draw me pictures on scrap pieces of paper or napkins. (The participant described being a difficult kid); "... always getting into trouble doing whatever I wanted—always receiving punishment during or after Sunday school. I never thought of bringing anyone else to church at this time."

23. (participant had no family or elders in the church). "... I spent almost all of my time in the English congregation attending the worship service and the student fellowships... I served on the committee of the college fellowship during my university studies. The people whom I served with during that time still remain very close friends (most of us attended SFU together). My contact with church leadership was

limited . . . Money was usually a sensitive subject especially when it came to discussing pay raises for church staff. For a while the impression I had of the Cantonese congregation was that they had most of the power to make decisions in the church and often said "no" to requests from the English congregation when it wanted to do something that would benefit the English congregation but was not "Chinese" (for example I remember the disagreements about whether or not to allow drums and guitars for the worship band). I rarely brought friends to church because my school friends were either not interested in Christianity or I was too shy to invite them."

24. "During my time growing up none of my friends left; people who left were people who didn't attend often. A few of my friends have now left the church since finishing high school—most have stayed; whether they were thriving is a good question. Why some left—doubt—a lot of unanswered questions; also because of school friends and secular (party life) lifestyle."

25. "Growing up, it was a lonely place . . . I normally helped out my dad . . . My best friends were my brother and sister; I didn't have a role model. However there was this really nice old lady who would cook so we always looked forward to potlucks. She was pretty cool because she was always cheerful and loved the kids. There was one not so desirable old Chinese guy who didn't like our family . . . I would never bring friends of another race to my church because there was only Cantonese and Mandarin, no English service. It was a very difficult place to be in because it tailored to Chinese people. (Participant now speaks about his current Chinese church); "There have been a lot of tensions between the EM and parents. Teenagers think the parents are here to take over. However fro me, I feel the ability to bridge these generations . . ."

26. (participant did not complete this question, leaving it incoherent).

27. (participant described being very involved in Sunday service, Sunday school and fellowships. Also serving in Sunday school and ushering). ". . . My best friend was a girl that I had grown up with . . . family friends. My role models mostly came from fellowship and Sunday school leaders. A pleasant memory would be having a joint luncheon with the Chinese and Mandarin congregations. It was nice to see everyone and the Chinese parents making food. Unpleasant memories would include conflicts regarding dress code, use of nontraditional forms of worship (i.e., drums should not be used in worship because they are

too loud). I've brought Chinese friends once or twice but never a non-Chinese friend, they would most likely have felt uncomfortable."

28. (participant was actively involved in church, her role models were "the older, wiser brothers and sisters;" her pleasant experiences were with her senior pastor and unpleasant experiences with leadership that liked to maintain tradition. She commented on "church leaders who weren't too happy with questioning why things were the way they were, or proposing things that were risky." She cited examples of both positive and negative experiences with the Chinese congregation members.) ". . . I was never comfortable bringing friends of a different race to come to our church. I saw way too many people who brought their loved ones to church who were of different races and they never felt fully accepted . . ."

29. (participant described church life as exciting; he has served in various capacities since he was a teenager; currently he is serving as a Sunday school teacher, Sunday service chair person, and an executive for the career fellowship. His best friends and role models were found in this church. He described the not so desirable people as being "people who left the church for dumb reasons;" his parents also actively serve in the Chinese side). ". . . sometimes conflict will arise between the two congregations because the Chinese side would like to control the English congregations direction of ministry. Some of us think our parents still treat us like kids when it comes to decision making for the English congregation. We had a forum . . . to speak out on what we want and dislike about the Chinese congregation. They took it very offensively . . . however I am a firm believer that wars are won through battles, so conflict must be there in order for a better future. I have never brought any friends that are from different races."

30. participant explained at length the rebuilding of the English ministries after a large English exodus. She describes some of her perception of interacting with the Chinese side and the process of coming to maturity in the faith. She expressed feeling that her and her English peers "were always marginalized and treated as kids . . ." After her family changed to another Chinese church she was baptized; she expressed the experience of listening to translated sermons every Sunday with a focus on learning Chinese and the needs in China. She noted, "I did not feel comfortable bringing any other friends to our church."

Summary on this section: The majority speak of their church experience as being family oriented, supportive, warm, and one where they were very involved in attendance and service. Eleven (36 percent) explicitly did not feel comfortable in bringing people of other races; an additional four did not feel comfortable bringing anyone. Five felt comfortable bringing other races; ten did not comment on interracial outreach.

3. Let's talk about yours and your contemporaries' attendance experience of the bicultural Chinese church

1. "During the time I was with my first bilingual Chinese church, I observed some youth leave the church around me, but most of them were in the older age bracket of youth. I was less associated with those youth and did not pay too close attention . . . and it was I who left the church later on. There were more young CBC adults leaving the church, for our church couldn't find a way to provide for their Christian needs as their sizes were the lowest out of all the other age brackets in the church."

2. (the participant described a church plant that was "a thinly veiled church split . . ." The individuals leaving the church were from the English congregation . . . due to some fundamental differences between the deacons and the pastor . . . [To] see my contemporaries leaving has caused me to grieve over the loss and also feeling the hurt that they experienced. Currently I am feeling angry at the situation and my reaction is to become emotionally detached from the church so that I can stop feeling the hurt. The general effect of the departure has created a bit of instability in the church . . . Leadership in the English congregation is struggling to help the congregation move through this time of grieving and hurt. These individuals have gone to attend a different church . . . as far as I know the majority of them that left are attending a different church."

3. "Our congregation is young, so I didn't observe many contemporaries leaving the church."

4. ". . . I moved . . . and in the process have been involved with other Chinese churches large and small . . . [in] my hometown church . . . I perceived a sudden and overwhelming trend of young adults . . . leaving that church at a particular point in time . . . Most left for another church . . . Many of them went to one of a few new upstart "multicultural" churches composed predominantly of young single professionals . . . [at] my hometown church . . . there are almost none of my

youth group cohort left . . . [speculating on] contributing factors to the mass exodus . . . significant problems in our leadership . . . a leadership vacuum . . . I think a lot of my cohort saw the problems in the leadership, got fed up with waiting for them to sort things out, and struck out on their own."

5. "Yes, experienced contemporaries leaving church. A quite prevalent experience. Approximately the same number of CBCs leaving the church as staying. I had a good idea why or how departures took place."

6. "Yes . . . the age group which left were the new parents with young toddlers. I think all of them left for either a larger church with better kid-friendly sites, or for other reasons of which I'm unsure. I think it also depends if your pastor is able to cater to/ mentor/address needs and challenges of your age group."

7. "Since some CBCs did leave the church mainly based on the fact that they cannot grow very well under the influence of the Chinese culture of their parents generation . . . within the Chinese culture, it is very seldom that the kids will get encouragements from their parents when they're attempting to do something spiritual. When they do run into a slight bit of a problem due to the lack of guidance and experience . . . they will get highly discouraged." (Participant indicated this eclipses their growth in faith, interest, and passion; it contributes to them leaving; it is linked to not dealing with reconciliation).

8. "My CBC friends . . . [leaving] is not very prevalent. However, I am aware of this situation . . ."

9. "Yes I observed contemporaries leaving; "I think it is more the cultural background (e.g., dialect, someone might feel left out). I think it is the culture and differences. A lot of our members are Canadian born with their roots in Hakka. Those not Hakka who stayed did so because they focused on the gospel. Those who left did not see the bigger picture of the family of God, they had a more worldly perspective" (the culture in the church became an obstacle).

10. ". . . I did see a fair number of people who were slightly younger than me leaving the church or not interested in the church. I think the reason being was that there was a period of time when we had no youth worker taking care of this group . . ."

11. "Yes I did think about leaving the church during my high school years because I wanted a different setting. I wanted to go into a church where I could learn the foundations of the faith again and confirm

my beliefs ... There were definitely more people who left the church than stayed, but [the church I am in has] been on the receiving end of this trend. Many ... came from different churches [to] our church as a group with a large young adult program. Speaking from my experience, people leave the church mainly because they went through a tough time and felt that God was not by their side. Either this or the fact that their entry into college or university made them think critically of faith and religion ... facts of the bible may seem fictitious to some ... we say that it's a miracle or that some things we cannot explain. But to concrete thinkers they are not satisfied with [such] answers and feel that Christians explain [bible] events that they cannot explain by always answering with "it's an act of God."

12. "Yes over the years many of our youths and young CBC adults left for various reasons. Some of the major reasons are: breakups, work schedules, dating non-Christians, not meeting their spiritual needs, inadequate programs to deal with sexual orientation and brokenness; language transition issues—sometimes English speaking people felt neglected; pursuing career or schooling in other places, the parents leaving due to negative experiences. In general a majority who grew up and have families at the church remained with the church until today."

13. "Many of my contemporaries left the church (participant attributes this to poor leadership attention given to emerging maturing fellowships) ... some/many left their faith completely and have never gone back to church. In the past 20 years since high school some have now found their way to non-bicultural churches and other bicultural churches while a very small few have found their way back to [church name]. Most left because they grew frustrated with the highly culturally slanted, guilt-based faith they saw their parents pushed on them. Being free of church actually took a load of guilt away "You should do this ... you shouldn't do that"). Some came to feel the potent mixture of immature faith and the baggage of Chinese culture their parents clung on to simply could not translate into addressing the daily challenges they faced in a western world with completely different sensibilities and values. Those who kept their faith often sought other avenues to live out their faith whether at other bicultural churches which they felt could better address their spiritual needs or non bicultural churches at which they could simply leave behind the specter of their parent's Chinese culture ... To varying degrees all of us who have come out of that context have stories of varying success in reconciling three cultures: Chinese, western and the church ..."

14. "Yes I did notice some of my contemporaries leaving the church. However I think part of that has to do with the language barriers (Participant refers to communication deficit). For those who had a stronger grasp of Chinese, they were more inclined to stay. Their language ability allowed them to better navigate the relationships with those who spoke Chinese. For many of the CBCs who left my church, it was more often a case where they didn't have the family connection within the Chinese congregation context" (Participant refers to relationship deficit).

15. "It seems that many of my Christian friends have left to attend more western churches such as Tenth Avenue alliance church because the sermons are more relatable and there is a mix of races and cultures. I would say that once my friends were twenty-five plus years old they would leave the bilingual churches."

16. "Yes I observed contemporaries leaving. Those that left were predominantly CBC adults . . . some felt overworked and unsupported. Others felt they were being pushed too quickly into a position of leadership without any real leaders to support or train them. Many left because they felt unnourished spiritually at this church. Many left during a period of two to two-and-a-half years when the English congregation was without a pastor and relying on guest speakers each Sunday and on two occasions there was no speaker. It was clear a good majority left because they felt the English congregations' needs were being ignored by the leadership."

17. ". . . Yes I have seen some of my contemporaries leave this church (and church in general). It is an occurrence that happens in the church . . . If you were to ask me how many CBCs from 15 years ago still attend our church I would say it is about thirty percent . . . my feeling is that there are more CBCs that leave the church than those that stay. Based on my friends . . . they left because of personal conflicts with others in the church (both Chinese and English ministry); they have found a more fitting church in terms of worship; or they have relocated . . ."

18. "Most of my [adult] peers are still in the church—those that did move were because of work or study mobility. (Yes) There were those about 5-6 years older than me that went with a church plant—some unpleasantries seem to have happened and I heard they left."

19. "There was a group of people who disapproved and they stopped coming—it wasn't a priority in their life. There were a few who went to other churches; others I think switched churches but I don't really know

why. I do have a friend who switched churches because she couldn't reach out to her friends . . . Most of the people who left did so during the university years."

20. "Yes I think roughly half of my contemporaries came and went . . . The core group has remained to this day, but I think this group is exceptional because it took leadership positions in the fellowships . . . I don't know why these departures happened."

21. "I saw quite a few older young adults leave the church (mid to late 20's). I think they left because they were dissatisfied with what the church could offer them in terms of programs and fellowship. But they were also the type of people to not put any effort into making things happen. For example if they wanted a year end BBQ for fellowship, and no one planned one, they would complain about it but not step in themselves to help plan and make it happen. There were more CBCs that stayed than left."

22. "I noticed only a few contemporaries leave the church and it wasn't too noticeable . . . Most of the adults from my church were not CBCs. However there was some sort of conflict within the elders/pastors of the church and it came to be that most of the congregation left the church."

23. "The exodus of my peers in the English congregation took place in two phases: graduation from high school and then completion of post-secondary education (usually university or college). Almost all of the people who were the same age as me who also attended the high school fellowship left [church name] and to my knowledge did not attend another church. I think many of these people left . . . because they were no longer under their parents influence to attend church functions. If their friends were not at church then there was very little attraction to stay. If these people did not have good relationships with their parents then there was even less incentive to stay. I think that most people leave the church because the faith that they inherited is from their parents (with the Hong Kong Cantonese cultural influence) and did not have deep roots. Church was never going to be as fun as the outside world . . ."

24. "After a long process, one thing after another that builds up; I think people cared but I don't think there was any formal follow up. Between our friends we understand, the reasons are close to home."

25. (participant first speaks of the church he grew up in) "Let me first clarify that bilingual to my church refers to Mandarin and Cantonese . . . I

know a lot of older teens left the church because they weren't Christians. Their parents weren't solid Christians either . . . All the CBC's left when they were in their mid/late teens because they found church a waste of time . . . there were zero remaining CBC Chinese left. (Participant then speaks of the Chinese church he serves in the EM). ". . . College CBCs were far and few between, from what I hear many of them left because there was no one to take care of them once they graduated high school. At that time no one cared because they saw EM as youth ministry and did not have the capacity to run college ministry. Now we pay for that mistake. We have remaining a handful of college age CBCs who show up half the time. The rest are gone, either to study abroad or left the church completely."

26. no response

27. ". . . I've noticed many people leaving too. Our congregation is getting smaller. Some of these departures were from conflicts with the pastoral staff." (Participant noted people leaving over conflict, finding another church, quitting church, being too busy with work on Sunday, or stopping because their partner did not attend).

28. "This situation was very prevalent . . . the same amount of people that leave is the same amount of people that are new . . . People rarely talk about how these departures happen (but it's odd that we celebrate it when people join the family!) These departures happen when people don't feel as if they're growing, or feel as if the church structure doesn't permit them to grow." (Participant notes the impact of peers leaving). "There are fewer and fewer people their age in church they can relate too." (Participant also cited practical reasons like no children's program for the children of CBC parents, too many joint Chinese-English services, study mobility, etc.).

29. "Yes I have witnessed a few members leaving . . . a few major reasons people leave are a) Guy/girl relationships . . . b) Dating non-Christians . . . c) lame excuses . . . resources to accommodate our needs" . . . d) lame excuses like I cannot grow spiritually in this church . . ."

30. "Most of my peers whose parents also attended church stayed in bilingual Chinese churches . . . one close friend [did not feel comfortable] has attended multicultural churches. Her parents are not church goers. People stay in churches for community and that only happens more strongly when there's family. (Yes) In my present church [church name] young adults leave and attend more multicultural churches or

churches with stronger teaching and preaching. Those who stay, stay because of ministry opportunity and/or parents."

Summary on this section: Twenty-eight (93 percent) of the participants acknowledged that the exodus of English speaking adults from their churches was prevalent. Only one said it was not common, and one participant didn't indicate either way. When an explanation was given, the most commonly stated reason was related to life stage needs not being met (7). Next in rank were leadership problems and conflict. Other explanations ranged from cultural and language differences, faith struggles and choice for a secular lifestyle, study mobility, and opting for a different church. A lesser list of other reasons ranged from; pastoral neglect of the EM congregation needs/care, burnout, personal conflicts (related to break ups, dating non-Christians, work schedules), and the imposition of joint services.

In your observation, was the leaving of these young CBC adults often a decision after a long process or just an instant determination? Did any of the Chinese people at church care about these young adults leaving or after they left the church? Did the people at church know or understand why these young adults were leaving?

1. "I believe the leaving of these young CBC adults was after careful consideration and persistence to find a reason for them to remain. These young people played significant roles in serving the youth at the church and therefore were sadly missed by the congregation. I think the people at the church did know and understand why the young adults were leaving."

2. "... after a long process..."

3. no response

4. "... many ... who left also themselves had difficulty communicating with their own OBC parents ... But the coordinated timing of the exodus seems to me to indicate some precipitating event, like perhaps the problems in leadership ..."

5. "Most CBC young adults decide over a long period of time. Older generation showed some concern. People at church likely did not have a good understanding of why people were leaving."

6. "I think for the few I did see leave, it was a slow process, not just an instantaneous decision ... I believe the people who left suddenly lost a whole social group! Some young adults left without explaining why ... and did not want a confrontation ..."

7. "... a decision based on a slow build-up of resentment through years of growing up in the church..."
8. "... they decide 'I don't belong.'... It is rare that the rest of the church hears or gets to hear from the leavers the reasons for their decisions."
9. One intercultural marriage (Caucasian spouse), he could not fit in; he stayed a couple of years but seemed to have not been able to see the spiritual aspect of God. People who were CBC who left seem to have left of their own interests, whether they were getting their needs met (church shopping). The council has been talking about the cultural background of those raised in the second generation western culture.
10. "I think the reason for those who left the church has something to do with their age. Once they are old enough and cannot be forced anymore by parents, they don't come. I also observed that parents played a big role. The parents who are very traditional in their Chinese ways often criticize and expect lots... the kids from these families most often turned rebellious and see through the hypocrisy of their parents who are supposed to be Christian but not practicing it at home. It seems some Chinese parents cared more about "face, honor, Confucianism" than being a Christian parent who teaches by God's principles. The parents cared more about school work and face than the kid's feelings (which is a more western concept to them)... The older generation do care about losing the youths and think that the next generation is important, that's why they hired the youth worker and often have discussion about youth ministries... but it seems that their solution is all laid on the shoulders of the hired youth worker or pastor rather than on themselves as a whole congregation..."
11. "The decision to leave or attend a different church is usually a long process because one would not want to rebel against the parents. It sometimes feels like you're causing drama by leaving your home church because it seems like you're leaving something behind..."
12. "... some left after all options were exhausted. Others left based on instant determination... usually negative experiences with the church... some of the Chinese people somewhat involved with the young CBC adults did care about their departure but on the most part, not many of them knew or understood why they left." (Participant notes it was up to the English pastor or fellowship committee to follow up).
13. "It's never an instant determination. Even if there was a defining moment, it was the culmination of months if not years of internal angst... most couldn't stand how they felt or were made to feel at

church (parents cared) . . . Most could never understand or were willing to try to understand the deeper reasons for the departure of the young people . . . many of the OBCs had no framework of understanding to grasp or for some, even the ability to move toward an acceptance of the differences of their children. Most remain resigned to the lack of connection as if there is an unbridgeable gap."

14. (participant gave reference to a large group from the English congregation who left after a "fall-out;" there were attempts made to reach those who left [letters written]. Those who left still kept in touch (weddings, funerals, special events). They made it explicit why they left (Note: this wasn't made clear in this interview); some left due to their spouse."

15. "I would say it happens over a span of time in making their decision. Chinese congregation members were not overly concerned except maybe the deacon board. People at church often assume that personal conflicts are the reason for leaving."

16. "The majority left after a lengthy process. Much time was spent pondering the potential negative impact of their departure. There was no attempt by the Chinese people at church to contact those that left. There really was no expectation either since they had been feeling abandoned and overworked by the church and especially the leadership for quite some time. Aside from the sense of abandonment, they also left because they felt their growth was limited at this church—the English congregation was without a pastor for a period of about three years . . . Apparently there were suitable candidates that were not chosen based solely on the fact they could not communicate with the Chinese side."

17. "The majority of the time this decision is after a long process of deliberation. They consider a lot of factors, including change in friends, life style, worship style, etc. before they make their decision. People from the Chinese ministry mainly care for those who are currently serving and have an impact in the church . . . they do not know why [some] people leave most of the time."

18. "Those who left for work or study did have a long process; the impact was significant because there were not many of us—it was significant to me and at the leadership level."

19. ". . . they sometimes disappeared quite abruptly; in other cases after a long process. A factor in leaving seems to be low participation (not coming to fellowship after high school). There was nothing keeping them there any more so they just left. The leaders over EM did care

about people leaving. There were efforts put out to try to reach these people."

20. "The young CBC adults seemed to leave after a long process of drifting. Their peers cared (at least in my group) but the people leaving had other priorities in mind, like pursuing careers."

21. "I don't know what caused the decision to leave in many people . . . better sermons . . . they weren't being fed at the church. I think the Chinese people did care but they didn't bother trying to understand why they left. They kind of classified them as young, rebellious and unwilling to contribute to the church as their reasons for leaving. I don't think they ever tried talking to the people who left to find out the real reason why and I think that's something prevalent in Chinese culture . . ."

22. "I believe it wasn't too long a process when the congregation dispersed—the majority of my church was mid-to-older folk so there weren't too many young adults to begin with."

23. "Most people simply left over a period of time . . . I do not think that the church leadership or members understood why these young people left . . . I am not sure they would know how to make the adjustments to church."

24. "Yes for sure it affected me; it makes me think what path I could have chosen; sad thing to see. I think it affects the church quite drastically."

25. (Participant speaks of his first church) "The leaving of the CBCs was a result of no English service as well as their parents not being committed Christians. They had no reason to stay. The rest of the people at church could care less. What's a bunch of 55+ refugee immigrants going to do with 18 year old CBCs anyways? The culture gap is too big . . ." (Participant then speaks of his second church). No one cared before, but now we panic because we realize we need them . . . I don't think anyone realized what was going on because everyone was too worried about youth ministry and not looking that far into the future."

26. no response

27. "From the people that I've spoken with, it appears that they have thought quite a bit about their decision. It's always hard to leave when you've grown up with the church and have established so many relationships with people. For some other people it wasn't really an active decision it just sort of happens, for instance when people get busy with school, boyfriends, work, etc.—church just fades into the background and you see that their attendance becomes less and less frequent. I'm

not sure if everyone leaving was cared for . . . people have an idea/opinion of why people leave . . . when I stopped attending our Chinese church to go to a more multicultural and less conservative church, I definitely felt a little misunderstood even by one of my closest church friends." (Note: Participant currently has been alternating between attending her Chinese church and a multicultural church for the past two years to the date of completing this survey).

28. "It seems there's a long thought process behind these decisions, these were prominent leaders that left . . . deacons or on the English ministry committee. They were my role models. They had much invested into this church . . . leaving was not an easy decision for them. Few people seemed to care that these people left . . ."

29. "Most of them are a long process . . . I think some of them got frustrated with the way the Chinese congregation does things . . . I sometimes feel this myself. Instead of staying here and fight it out, they decide to leave the church to find a better place . . . the Chinese side say they care but they do not do anything about it . . ." (Participant cited other reasons for leaving such as career moves, friends gone).

30. "Yes but as long as they are going to another church, it is seen to be sad but okay."

Summary on this section: Twenty-six (86 percent) cases observed that those who left did it after a slow buildup, a long process of careful consideration. Only one case noted that sometimes the leaving has been abrupt. Three cases were not clear. A significant finding here is that in a number of cases there were prominent EM leaders who were observed leaving (deacons, EM committee, and so forth). Many of these cases cited precipitating red-flags they saw before adults left; discerning leadership should pay attention to these.

Did seeing your contemporaries leaving the bi-cultural Chinese church affect you? If it did, in what way the situation has affected you? What about the general effect of the departures of these young adults on other people in the church? Do you know or aware of what happened to those young adults after they left the bi-lingual Chinese church?

1. "Seeing those young adults leave around me did have an effect because I held most of them as role-models and had always looked forward to my interaction with them . . ."

2. "Seeing my contemporaries leaving caused me to grieve over the loss and also feel the hurt that they experienced. Currently I am feeling

angry at the situation and my reaction is to become emotionally detached from the church so that I can stop feeling the hurt. The general effect of the departure has created a bit of instability for the church . . . Leadership in the English congregation is struggling to help the congregation move through this time of grieving and hurt. These individuals have gone to attend a different church . . . as far as I know the majority of them that left are attending a different church."

3. no response

4. "I am a bit saddened by the departure of that cohort . . . my friends who I grew up with. But I know that almost all of them are serving God and continuing to grow, and I am glad for that . . . Many of them truly have lost most of their Chinese culture and so they really do fit in better at a Caucasian or multi-cultural church than in a Chinese church . . ."

5. "Seeing contemporaries leaving the church did affect me. [It] helped me gain a different perspective on certain issues in life as well as church politics. The general effect is discouragement to other young adults in the church. [I was] typically aware of what happened after they left the church."

6. "The only significant exodus I've seen is the one of young parents; when a few leading couples left, everyone else followed suit. I don't know what happened to them; I was only in university at the time."

7. "It affected me somewhat as I am a leader . . . the parents will blame me or other leaders in the same area for running our programs poorly. Many parents will start comparing between the English and Chinese youth ministries and it is not a good feeling hearing people belittle the hard work that we constantly try with our limited resources. Usually when a person leaves it might tend to shake the faith of those who are not as strong in their beliefs . . ." (Participant noted seeing some church-hop or lose passion for service).

8. "More than my contemporaries leaving the church, the attitude of the church has affected my view of it. I just feel that in its current form and iteration the Chinese church is dying a slow death, and I feel it deserves this fate—given the trajectory and the unwillingness to change that we are locked into. General effect is a loss of morale, confusion and questioning of identity of the church . . . A few friends I keep in touch with, and they enjoy their locations. Some leave the church altogether and feel that their faith cannot be upheld due to their past experiences."

9. "Yes—affected; a lot of the leaders strive to find out what is the main reason for leaving; is there any way the church can improve."
10. "Seeing some contemporaries leave does affect me somewhat . . ."
11. "My thoughts about leaving did have a negative effect on my attendance and attitude towards my home church because I would always think of the reasons I did not want to be in this church rather than being involved and help out around my home church. The general affect of people leaving is that the group that is even younger than us look at it as something they might contemplate when they reach the older age group. This may set a negative trend or cycle." (Participant refers to negative role modeling); ". . . I do not stay in touch with young adults who left the church, but I assume that they either relax on Sundays or found another church."
12. "It's always hard seeing people leave the church. Being a leader of the church we are always striving for ways to keep people and grow the church. It prompts me to think what the church may be doing wrong or how we can improve the situation. The departure of certain people will also trigger other ones to consider leaving . . . some of the young adults either ended up attending other churches or stopped attending church."
13. "I did begrudge those who decided to move away from the bicultural church. After all the goal of a Christian is to find community and be in relationships that endeavor to be Christ-like . . . I think those left behind are poorer for the loss, especially if they do not learn and grow from it. Many I know who have left the bicultural church (but not their faith) have flourished in the process."
14. "It was challenging. It did because these were friends I grew up with and some were leaders of different ministries. Our church had difficulties in sustaining the ministries after they left; it took time for a new younger group to serve. [I was] aware of where they went—they either went to Tenth Avenue Alliance or formed their own church; some went to Willingdon."
15. ". . . it absolutely affected me because part of coming to church is fellowshipping with my contemporaries. It also affects younger members (high school, college) because they wonder what is wrong with our church. Interestingly enough, I find that once my friends leave their service in the church fades away as well."

16. "At first I resented their departures and felt betrayed . . . As I learned more of the politics of the church I began to feel like they did the right thing from the perspective of being good stewards of the time God gave them. Some of the CBCs remaining at the church were influenced to leave as well, and they later did in fact go. Some that left have joined up with other churches that only have English speaking congregations. Many stopped going altogether."

17. ". . . their departure certainly affected me . . . I get discouraged as it seems they do not see the same things/goals that I do. It also forces me to question the way we do things to see whether anything we do is excluding others—even if it is done [unintentionally]. I am aware of what happened to the majority of these people after they leave . . . Most of them stopped going to church while some have attended other bicultural churches. There are only a handful of those whom I know of who is attending other non bicultural churches."

18. "Yes. We still kept in contact."

19. "Disappointing; feeling like we're missing something because these people are feeling like they don't belong."

20. "It did not affect me . . . it did not shake my faith. Perhaps it was because the ones that left all tended to be newer Christians . . . [I was not inclined] to learn their way of seeing things . . . and conclude that the person leaving has made a mistake which is not to be followed. These young adults continued to be friends, to be welcomed back to the community if they ever came back."

21. ". . . it only affected me in that their departure made me wonder why they left . . ."

22. (the impact of conflict amongst OBCs and its effect on a CBC). "It definitely affected me, because I didn't understand what was going on—and actually it wasn't until recently that I found out why a pastor and most of the congregation left that church. I was confused."

23. "I felt sad to see so many people leaving. The effect on the English congregation is that it continues to remain young (in age and spiritual maturity) and in atmosphere. There is a shortage of role models and mentors for young people. Most of my friends from the college fellowship have moved on to multicultural churches."

24. "Yes for sure it affected me; it makes me think of what path I could have chosen; it's a sad thing to see. I think it affects the church quite drastically."

25. (participant speaks of his first church). "It did not affect me at all because I lived the life my parents did . . . it was a parenting issue and because their parents were either single, uneducated and immigrants, they had little knowledge about CBC culture or Canadian culture . . . parent could barely speak English. These young adults do not go to any church, they have become CBC non-Christians. (Participant speaks of his second church). Those who left either went to study abroad, or to a different church, or don't go to church at all. It didn't affect me because I work for the church."

26. no response

27. "I'm usually curious as to why people leave. Some people that left for another church seem to be doing really well . . . [and] quite passionate in serving. When I ask them why they left, some of the things I hear are church politics [or] a need for change because they were not growing. Sometimes this makes me think if I would be better at another church. Do I also need this change or should I just stick with the church I've grown up with."

28. "Yeah, seeing them leave also affected me. There are fewer people for me to look up to (participant noted fewer spiritual guides in her church home) . . . My pastor works in a church setting and I don't feel as if I can speak with him about working in secular jobs . . ."

29. "It did not really affect me spiritually . . . it affected the church because people who left were capable people who can serve as teachers, deacons, etc." (Participant laments that they have abdicated the possibility of making change and helping serve).

30. "I have not allowed my peers in general to affect me much in my walk with God and my ministry."

Summary on this section: Twenty-two (73 percent) cases noted that they were negatively affected by the exodus of English speaking adults. Some expressed experiencing sadness and discouragement (especially because some completely leave the church), confusion, disappointment, and hurt in grieving the losses. Some expressed that when some adults left more pressure from the Chinese side was put on EM volunteer leaders; in the aftermath some EM ministries were unsustainable. Some grieved the loss of role models. It was noted that when people leave it can contribute to a "domino effect" (people question why they should stay). Some noted that they constructively channel their feelings into a call for improvement in the church towards the EM. Only four cases indicated they were not affected by CBC adults leaving; four other cases did not respond to the question.

Has the possibility of leaving the bilingual Chinese church ever crossed your mind at any one time in your whole time there? If the thought of leaving the church ever existed, can you tell me specifically what issues or challenges that had caused you to enter into the thought of leaving? How did you resolve that eventually? Whether leaving or staying, did you feel accountable to the Church and the church accountable to you? Unlike your other contemporaries who chose to leave, what has kept you remaining in the bi-lingual Chinese church this whole time?

1. "The thought of leaving my old church never crossed my mind . . . In regards to accountability . . . I had always felt I was a valued member of that church and that I am accountable to the church through attendance and in the relationships between my peers . . . What kept me in the bilingual Chinese church I attended were the relationships I developed. Nowadays . . . it's the youth and the next wave of believers growing up in their parents' Chinese churches that keeps me there. I feel I can make an impact in their lives . . . so that . . . they will continue to have a sense of belonging and purpose in their churches which they have grown up in."

2. "The possibility of leaving . . . has crossed my mind . . . in the past when I was burnt out. I considered going to a different church so that I can recuperate . . . currently I am considering another church so that I can go somewhere that I feel I can worship . . . but the fact that I am comfortable at my present church (even though tired) has kept me at church and also because I know people at my church . . . my sense of responsibility is motivating me to remain . . . I do feel accountable to the church . . . I don't really feel the church is accountable to me. I . . . [also] want to support the associate pastor who has this heavy burden dumped on him."

3. "Yes the thought has crossed my mind. I feel that often our culture hinders us from fully embracing God's people and His true intent for the Church. Our cultured doesn't allow for failures or brokenness. There is a constant need to prove oneself as credible or as righteous "enough" to serve. As a church, for example, we would get caught up in legal concerns rather than reaching out to our less fortunate and homeless neighbors. What has kept me remaining at this church are the changes that have been made and the slow delegation of responsibility and trust to the second generation. In addition, the authentic and open relationships with my close brothers and sisters have kept me there."

4. "I have never in my life considered leaving the Chinese Christian community. It is my extended family, a deep part of my identity . . . it's . . . about who we are in Christ. We are Christians; we are Chinese; we live in North America—and we are going to leverage every aspect of our identity in order to bring whoever we can to Christ. Now, having said that let me add that identity in the Chinese Christian community and identity in a particular Chinese church are two separate issues . . ."

5. "Leaving the bilingual Chinese church has crossed my mind. Issues or challenges that got me thinking: a concern about the heavy emphasis on tradition versus sound biblical training; lack of (or poor) nourishment available to meet the demands of people (e.g., fellowships, bible studies, door-to-door evangelism, mission trips). [Resolved by] realizing that spiritual growth needs to be proactive: refocusing my whole time at church on Jesus and pondering over the purpose of each event and program. Felt accountable to the church and the church accountable to me. Understood that perseverance is something that needs to be developed and that running from the problem doesn't solve it."

6. "No . . . I've been lucky enough to attend churches when they were still growing, not dying. I have witnessed a church dying slowly, but did not live in the city any longer to watch any "full death . . ." (Participant noted that friendships and solid preaching help staying).

7. "Others including my parents have suggested I try another church to expand my growth in faith. I have decided to stay in my home church . . . I have learned [its good and bad]. I view going to and serving my home church like a family relationship . . . I should [not] give up on others . . . it means there are many ways we can improve . . . I stayed because I see the potential for change . . . it takes time. It also takes the humble effort for those who serve to continue to strive for the best for God . . ."

8. "Yes I have thought about leaving the Chinese church. One reason is their approach to ecumenism and distaste for it. Another is their approach towards poverty and social justice—or lack of it. Another is a very strong condemning and judgmental character that's pervasive and destructive. Another is a focus on the building and the four walls of the church as the limit of God's kingdom on earth . . . I feel that essentially their theology is far too influenced by their Chinese ways and they refuse to look at the world outside their local community and essentially create a ghetto-walled structure. I have not resolved this,

but for the love of Christ, the grace and love that he shows me, who is guilty of some of those things at times. A deep love for the church universal, of ALL denominations. I feel that I am accountable to the church . . . those who know and support me. I feel that the church ought to be more accountable to its congregations, those who put their faith and trust in the church to be an instrument of God—but not to shirk responsibility, which is far too often the case in Chinese churches."

9. (yes this participant left the Chinese church for five years and then returned); reasons: related to cultural factors. "I basically didn't feel I needed church; probably because the way the gospel was being presented; I did not connect with the whole gospel; did not come to a broken point . . . past was only focused on a certain thing."

10. "I definitely thought about leaving during university age. One big reason would be that I [was not] receiving spiritual food from sermons and worship time when others [were] leading and preaching, also because I [was] serving almost every week . . ." But why did I stay? I found my role and identity as a leader in the English congregation . . . helped me see the needs of the church and not think selfishly only of my own needs. Amazingly I received spiritually through serving others as a leader. As I prepared for worship time and sermons I received directly from Scripture and God's intimacy. So for my own spiritual feeding I find other conferences or church services that do not coincide with my own church schedule . . . What kept me in church is the sense of identity as a servant leader and love for the congregation and younger generation. I saw the needs of others before my own needs [and felt] belonging to people who are the same as me . . . if I left our church I don't think I would of grown so much . . ."

11. yes.

12. "The thought of leaving has not crossed my mind yet. I strongly feel that I should stick with church during both the good and bad times. I feel God is giving me lots of opportunities to serve at [church name]. I feel connected . . . language is not an issue . . ."

13. "After getting married in 1994, my wife (CBC but not raised in church) and I went to her non-bicultural church [church name] for two years. I kept feeling the draw to return to [former Chinese bicultural church name] because I felt my role as a bridge was important there. Indeed with each visit back I was asked by parents who felt they were losing their children to return and become that bridge once again. After

two years away I returned and resumed my role in that community in teaching Sunday school, being a deacon for missions and being a part of a men's home group. I did not feel accountable to the church but God, who I wanted to serve with the resources he had given to me with personal experience and past service. I feel a deep sense of rootedness in the bicultural church because I feel I have come to reconcile the different forces at play and can "step outside" of the pressures to become an agent of change ... toward a God-centered spirituality, understanding but not dictated by our cultural baggage."

14. (participant has thought of going to visit another bilingual church); "language is no issue for me ... [I am] sustained by a larger social network. [I have] the ability to understand the cultural context and don't worry about the cultural expectations." (The participant did question the multi-ethnic model for the English ministries and now feels it would be more of a challenge).

15. "I am currently strongly considering leaving [church name]. I find that everything has become routine and coming on Sunday is not uplifting—sermons [are] not inspiring. I'm praying to God that he would resolve this issue because I do not want to make an irrational decision, so I continue to ponder the options. I also stay because I'm needed to be here in a leadership role (I'm sure this is a common reason among CBCs!!!)."

16. "I was tempted to leave several times in my 13 years as a member. When I was studying in the United States I attended an English speaking only church and served ... My experience there opened my eyes to the strength of having one language, one culture. The main reasons for entertaining the thought of leaving had to do with my doubts that the English congregation was ever going to grow. I felt we were held back by the church leadership which was almost entirely composed of the Chinese speaking members but more so by the senior pastor. (Participant noted how members from the English congregation were often recruited by the Chinese side often burning them out and creating resentment) ... I also feel there is a lack of respect for the English congregation as well (Participant cites several examples). The Chinese side seems to only care about the mere existence of the English congregation but not at all concerned with whether it thrives spiritually ... The leadership structure was also a huge problem (Participant is speaking of a Chinese MB church context). In the deacon board, the senior pastor and Chinese pastor were permitted to vote on all church matters. The English pastor was not, not even matters concerning the

English congregation. Being one of the longest standing members of the English congregation and my history of service, I knew I had influence. My single greatest concern was the youth feeling abandoned and the older members feeling discouraged. I absolutely felt accountable to the church and vice versa."

17. "Yes it has . . . the current state . . . I am going to get married and I have to make a decision as to whether this is the best place of growth for my wife (a new Christian . . .) . . . It will likely be another bicultural church . . . (Participant cited another reason why he considered leaving on account of a conflict with a person in the EM) . . . I certainly feel accountable to the church . . . I don't know whether I feel the church is accountable to me since I am simply a part of the church . . . what kept me here is the sense of responsibility that I have for those I serve—and the fact that I really have nothing against this church. I have continued to learn and grow."

18. "I never considered leaving; my entire family is here. I do feel quite accountable to the church. The family connection is a strong tie."

19. "I've had my share of frustrations with EM but that's as far as it went. At some point a while ago I felt God convicting me that I am here at my church for a reason. I have been involved in [positive] Para-church involvements that I have wanted to bring into my church. The one time I considered leaving was to go to UFT's grad school (mobility), but then I got into a UBC program instead. A tipping point was to stay in my church here—I already had a calling here."

20. "I have never really considered myself locked into bilingual Chinese churches and I don't particularly support them more than other churches. It just so happens though that my first church was a bilingual Chinese church . . . when I moved . . . the church I could best identify best was a bilingual Chinese church . . . if I ever became a pastor, I would be fine not serving in a bilingual Chinese church. (Participant describes a crisis of faith during his university years in struggling with doubt; he described how he worked through that and stayed in the faith). ". . . I am indebted to the theologians and philosophers mentioned in Case for Christ for being my inspiration for a rationally solid faith . . . In my time of questioning, I felt support from the Christian community that I emailed frequently to update them in my crisis of faith. I attend a Chinese bicultural church because it works for me . . . My contemporaries who have left the church generally left for lack of faith rather than dissatisfaction with the church."

21. "Yes I've considered leaving it. In a sense I already have, since I attend a Caucasian church when I'm away at university . . . I've considered leaving my home church because of the level of preaching . . . I don't feel like the pastoral staff is going as deep into the Word as they could . . ."

22. "I did . . . I know for me I wasn't being spiritually fed, although I was in fact serving at the time. I also couldn't stand how the Chinese culture got "in-the-way" of being a Christian; how it affected the adults of the church, what practices were accepted that shouldn't have been and the general 'fakeness' of many people. The problems were never really solved—I had a talk with the pastoral staff and left the church to find another. I felt accountable to the church—the church was not accountable to me."

23. "I wanted to leave many times but I did not want to leave simply because I was unhappy or felt my needs were not being met. I did not want to end up drifting from one Chinese church to another never settling down, besides God never told me that it was time to leave. It was safe to remain in this Chinese Canadian Christian circle. The lack of a permanent English pastor left a void in church leadership, congregational care and a voice in decision-making. My theological questions and "faith seeking understanding" led me to begin a long journey of studies at Regent College where I found many caring and mature Christians who helped to nurture me . . ."

24. "Yes—thought of leaving. Why—there is a certain feel to Chinese churches in general, sometimes it can be a really great feeling and sometimes it can be more harmful than helpful. (Participant spoke of feeling anxiety in inviting people of another race it comes from this area; "Why don't I feel comfortable in bringing a non-Chinese person—everyone will be asking questions;" if the Chinese church could welcome other races in its church it would be a beautiful thing. What has kept me remaining? Culture and heritage; similarities—CBCs friend connection—I can't connect as well with OBCs. The CBC is similar to me; I don't know where else I could connect with people like me."

25. "No I have never thought about leaving. Maybe because my family ran the church and I knew I had to help out . . . we were a family and we stick together . . . its loyalty, maybe its hidden pressures, but we did not even think about leaving . . ."

26. no response

27. "The issue was not being able to get anything from the sermons . . . I ended up leaving for a while but I felt bad about it. So many people were leaving. The fellowships were getting smaller. People were needed to serve. A few people asked why and they respected my decision. Sometimes I go back (currently I alternate months) because it just feels safe and familiar. Maybe I can give it another try." (Note: this participant is actually an in-between category of a drop-out and remain-in).

28. "Oh I have definitely thought of leaving! . . . I'm just looking for the right time to leave . . . right now I don't feel as if I am in the best conditions to grow, to be challenged in my understanding and appreciation of God . . . I'm desperate for something more . . . My ties to my family are probably the biggest factors that keep me at this church . . ." (Participant shared how the parents have tried to pressure this CBC adult to attend the same church as them).

29. "Fortunately I have not thought about leaving this church because I can see great things are being done here. However I am not so sure in the future when I have a family. Since a lot of people who formed a family here left, maybe I would do the same too . . ." (Note: this participant has presented a No for the present but possibly a Yes for the future; categorically it fits with '*Yes I have been thinking about leaving in the future*').

30. "I personally would like to attend a multicultural church but because my husband is more Chinese speaking, he feels more comfortable in a bilingual church. For a while when I was young I really resented how the English speaking congregation was marginalized by the leadership but now many churches have a truly English speaking pastor for the English speaking congregation and no longer do we need to listen to translation. We are also more involved in the leadership of the church . . . [we] do not believe in church hoping or that there is greener grass somewhere else. I believe in being committed to the body of Christ that He has put me in unless there is strong indication from God that I should do otherwise. My son is happy at our church . . . but we are seriously talking about and searching for ways to become a truly multicultural church. I'm all for it and am willing to contribute in any way."

Summary on this section: Nineteen participants (63 percent), out of thirty, have thought of leaving the bicultural Chinese church; four of these are still thinking of leaving. Two of these nineteen have been thinking of leaving for another, healthier, bicultural church. Ten out of thirty have not thought of leaving. One participant did not respond to the question. The top reasons for wanting to leave included: neglect of pastoral care for EM spiritual growth, marginalization of the EM, burnout in service, and concerns with the preaching. Additional reasons included: discouragement, ignoring poverty & social justice issues, ignoring neighbors, the church's distaste for ecumenism, the English congregation's lack of voice in decision making, the difficulty in inviting other races, and the imposition of Chinese culture on the EM. Clearly the findings in this section show that the Remain-In's are also an at risk group; if 63 percent of our congregations had a concern on their minds, why would the leadership ignore it?

4. Straight to the Reasons and Circumstances Leading to Leaving the Church

Issue #1: Identity Issue of being a CBC within a Chinese Church

1. "... I don't see it as an important factor..."
2. "I think that identity plays a big role . . . the Chinese congregation's perspective of the English congregation is one of a young child . . . they can only do those things that are allowed by the Chinese congregation and are not given any autonomy . . . this perspective is locked in place and is unchanging . . . as a result, the members in the English congregation, as they grow older and are wanting to make more decisions for themselves are prevented from doing so . . . we are not allowed to change to evolve or grow—we are locked into a relationship that forever is defined by our reliance on the Chinese congregation's (Chinese deacons) leadership. Even though there is an emphasis on bringing leaders into the deacons' board to help make decisions, often the reality is that these English individuals do not get their say and are not given license to help make changes. The frustration in not being allowed to change stifles growth and people leave because they are not allowed to be more responsible or are not empowered to step up to help the congregation grow . . . growth may take the congregation out of the realms that the Chinese leadership is comfortable with . . . I believe it is because they don't want to lose control that they confine the role of the leaders and the identity of the English congregation."
3. "Yes the CBC identity within the church is an important factor. I believe that the CBC generation has a distinctive way in relating to one

another, to our community, and to non-believers. How we define these relationships affects the methods in which we do church—different styles of worship, different outreach activities, different preaching messages."

4. "This is the central issue . . . It's not really about the church; it's about one's own identity. But the church certainly has been shirking its responsibility to teach and exhibit a proper self-identity in Christ, just like the traditional Chinese church has long shirked its responsibility to teach a biblical sexual identity, or approach to dating. If it is any consolation, the bicultural CBC identity issue is not new; another name for it is mestizo."

5. "Identification as a CBC was not in general problematic. Identification shouldn't be an issue. It isn't important because most youths have a relatively easy time interacting with others that are not CBCs (i.e., culture is not one of the main concerns of the youth)."

6. no response

7. no response

8. "I think identity is an important factor, and the recognition that we are in an identity crisis as CBCs, not fully accepted by either the Canadians (non-Asians) and certainly not by our Asian parents, unless we conform and lose an aspect of our heritage. I think it is important to embrace both sides . . . I think many CBCs who leave Chinese churches may feel that they need to give up their Chinese side in order to pursue greater faithfulness and growth."

9. "I do come across some members that have talked about that (a minority do feel ashamed of being a part of a Chinese congregation; I don't understand that) . . . people do leave the church because of the Chinese side emphasizing the English ministry must reach out to the Hakka people—it hurt the English side of what church is about (giving a second class feeling)." (Note: this case recognizes the problem—a Yes).

10. "Yes I think this is a very important issue for CBCs . . . I can fit in both sides (Chinese and English) but I do identify more with the CBC side . . . Freedom of expression and ways to do ministry must be given to the next generation and expecting them to have separate council meetings, and even given the freedom they might start their own church in the future. If the Chinese congregation can have that mind set, then I think the identity of being CBC should not affect them as much."

11. "This shouldn't be too big of an issue because there are plenty of people in the same situation, therefore the group can create their own identity together. If a person is lost in their identity of being a CBC they can seek others for guidance and there is a group of CBCs in every church I know."

12. "... I don't think this is an issue in our church..."

13. "Identity is something to be understood not run away from. But as a young person trying desperately to understand identity, it often seems much easier to reduce the challenges, especially that which causes difficulty with the prevailing culture. That is why my wife, who is a CBC who did not grow up in church, rebelled against all things she perceived as "Chinese," including speaking Chinese and doing family activities within the larger Chinese community. As her outlook on life has matured she has learned to be more comfortable, literally, within her skin. Her initial contact with church was in a bicultural church but over time has come to be much more comfortable in a non bicultural church. I grew up within the bicultural church but attended public school where there were very few Asians, chose an undergrad major that had few Asians (geography) and a graduate degree also with few Asians (architecture). I am therefore quite comfortable in either setting, within church and outside of it. I cannot forget that I bring my Asian features into any setting I find myself, but usually act as if it is irrelevant and expect others to accept me simply for who I am. In missions I work in a multicultural setting, leading multi-ethnic teams into Africa, Asia and the Americas. I typically forget I am Asian until some child asks me, "Are you Jackie Chan?" (Note: I placed this participant as a No).

14. "I think it is a factor . . . The two groups approach decision making differently (educational upbringing—hierarchical versus egalitarian ways of decision making [and] processing; CBCs question each other [but] the Chinese don't question hierarchy); this plays a role with language—coexistence can be complicated over language difficulties."

15. "This is true when the deacon board, who are the vast majority Chinese members, make decisions assuming the English department is fine with those decisions. English department should be more autonomous and less influenced by the Chinese department."

16. "Yes I did feel at times disconnected. Once a month the church used to have a joint English-Chinese service. By all accounts . . . these were not popular. There were later reduced to six per year and are poorly

attended by the English speaking members . . . much can be and often is lost in sermons that require translation."

17. ". . . identity is an important factor as one must be comfortable enough to outreach to others and bring them to church. If you don't know who you are, there is no sense of belonging."

18. "I think it's an issue; I do know people who don't come to our fellowship, they go to Willingdon or to a CBC small group."

19. "The issue of evangelism—of being CBC—and having non-Chinese friends who would feel the Chinese culture in the church; it kind of ties into an identity issue. Some people thing it's important in terms of getting in the way of outreach.

20. ". . . a small factor, but unimportant."

21. "I'm not entirely sure what is meant by identity."

22. "Cultural identity wasn't really a problem for me—the language barrier was."

23. "Yes I would agree. What does it mean for a person to be ethnically Chinese (with varying degrees of knowledge and experience of Chinese culture and language) living in a western country? Where do I fit into this society? What am I? Who am I? The people from Hong Kong do not really accept me because I am too westernized and do not understand Chinese culture or speak much of the language. The 'white people' do not understand the tensions of living in two or more worlds and expect me to act like a western person. How does a Chinese church help such people in this process? Or has it made the experience even more difficult?"

24. "Yes this is definitely an issue. In my church there is a nice cultural split (E.M./C.M.). When I was growing up everyone in our EM was up to early university, I felt really comfortable because we were all young. This might have played into the equation; my friend left and now goes to a Caucasian church."

25. (participant speaks of his first church). "In my church I think it was a huge factor in leaving because we offered no English service. They had no reason to be there so they left. (Participant speaks of his second church). ". . . The identity factor is important because CBCs take a lot longer to figure out who they are. Not 100% Chinese, but no 100% Canadian, but a mixture of the two . . ."

26. "I have only encountered a case where the person planning to leave was based on the perception that our church is currently too gospel-centered and another case where the person claimed to have felt that they did not belong to their fellowship group. So I do not think I have enough empirical information to answer this question . . ."

27. "Our Chinese church is full of CBCs and so is the multicultural church that I also attend . . . identity-wise I feel comfortable in both places."

28. "One of my main reasons to leave is because most of my friends aren't Chinese. I have a mix of friends from different races and haven't been comfortable inviting them to my church. I have felt guilty about this, but have seen case after case where they weren't truly welcomed . . . the predominant goal of the church was to reach out to Chinese and the English congregation has no say in this. They weren't given a say. The non-Chinese leaders in the English congregation saw that the buck stopped there where the original vision of the church was Chinese outreach . . . there wasn't anything they could do to contribute to that vision. They probably felt . . . [they] could contribute more to the kingdom elsewhere. I grew up in Vancouver where we were taught in school that everyone is equal regardless of the color of skin or heritage. I don't understand why the Chinese church doesn't get that. It's okay if the leaders in the Chinese churches have a specific target; however they need to understand that we a young folks that were born in Canada really want to be useful in advancing God's kingdom too and that we were shaped to reach a broader group of people."

29. no response

30. "Yes definitely. It really bothers me how Chinese churches are navel gazers and do not sincerely care about the Canadian society at large. This is a major difference in perspective. But I see changes in some churches. It really depends on the pastor."

Summary on issue #1: Seventeen out of thirty cases (30 percent) agreed that this was a factor in leaving; nine disagreed that it was a factor in leaving; one participant did not understand the question; three participants did not respond to the question. Many indicated that the identity issue is accentuated by being locked into a reliance on the Chinese congregation's leadership (a form of hegemony) and not given autonomy or a say in mission; for some, the Chinese church makes the CBC experience more difficult.

Issue #2: Life stage transition needs unfulfilled within a Chinese Church

1. "Although I think that this is a leading issue in the reasons of departure from any church, I don't see it as being any more or less evident for a bicultural Chinese church . . . During transitional periods people tend to be more self-centered . . . therefore making time for church and serving may be difficult when there is difficulty taking care of themselves."

2. ". . . in my church . . . we had fellowships . . . where we could go to belong . . . those groups worked, but eventually as the leadership started getting burned out, there was no one to step in . . . as a group we tried to take leadership, but it was difficult to try to lead ourselves and a result our university/career group disbanded. I think that as a church, trying to look ahead to the needs of a growing (in age) congregation is important . . . failure to anticipate and put tools in place to help people move through these stages will cause people to feel that their needs are not being met, and as a result, will go shopping elsewhere." (Participant refers to the need for vision).

3. "Yes I believe that some bicultural churches aren't fully equipped with resources for the spiritual growth of today's young adults. Again, there is that cultural and communication barrier with the older Chinese generation (many whom are our own parents, or respected "aunties" and "uncles"). Therefore there is a lack of older role models who can open their lives to invest, share, counsel, relate and impart wisdom to younger generations."

4. ". . . this is not an issue specific to Chinese churches . . ."

5. "This concern is very valid; in general, in my experience, there are insufficient resources to deal with the different aspects of life. I faced a similar challenge. This factor is very important because the church needs to be relevant to people at different stages in life and care for their people based on their needs."

6. "Perhaps not just CBCs, but anyone in general would find this a challenge."

7. no response

8. "Yes. If the English/CBC side is always run as a babysitting service, there will be no growth. No focus on discipleship, no care and love for others outside the four walls of the building . . . I do feel that

challenge... I think it is a reason that people leave. They feel that their current life stage is not being cared for. [This] leads us to create small groups that target a specific age and I feel that is the wrong answer. I think it's important because life stage can also translate into spiritual life stage."

9. "For our church it's more like a generation gap; there is a missing age (stage of life); English speaking from age 40 and up is missing. Ninety five percent of the English congregation is from grade 10 to age 33; mentors are missing to provide life stage transition needs and support."

10. "Yes I agree with this. But it really depends on how big the church is... the bigger and longer history of the church, the more experience and available helpers... I think looking ahead is very important... newer smaller churches need to prepare ahead of time for this group before its too late..."

11. "I would agree with this issue because I do see a weakness in the English department catering to the marriage/career transition. This is an important stage in everyone's lives and they look for a bigger network and may move to a better established church with a big group of couples or adults in that age group."

12. "This is a major one for our church... This is an important issue that bicultural Chinese churches should address. The church sometimes lacks the experience to initiate programs that are geared towards the needs of the CBCs. Many of them focus on youth ministry only. There are lesser programs for those who are married and those with children as well."

13. (participant notes this depends on the resources of a church) "For university students, if their own church is lacking in support... there are campus groups. (Participant served with the UBC Chinese Christian Outreach for English)... the bulk of our attendance was students from smaller churches although the majority of leaders were from larger churches. I assumed that the larger churches were more adept at leadership development while the smaller churches produced more students who needed spiritual/relational support than their church could offer. This has always been one of the strengths of campus ministries. Pastors of smaller churches should recognize this... often they are concerned with larger churches stealing their young folk. If they build a community with strong spiritual and relational development this should not be an issue... For young families [life stage transition

needs] may become an apparent challenge. But if the ongoing teaching and nurturing of the pastor is always toward an appreciation and maturing of an intergenerational environment, people with families should be nurtured by older mentors while taking their place in mentoring the younger generation. If church is to be a true community, it ought to be . . . multigenerational. Anything else is gimmicky and bound to eventual failure. A church was founded in Vancouver by the leaders of a youth group in a bicultural church. They had split because they wanted to reach the younger generation and leave behind the cultural baggage of a bicultural church. Soon the young wanted to bring their parents to church and suddenly the English speakers needed to plant a Chinese-speaking congregation. Sounds ironic but should have been anticipated. That was thirty years ago and that church [name given] remains fully bicultural to this day."

14. "This is definitely an issue that becomes more of an issue in the late twenties and early thirties if CBCs are not married (and wonder if they'll ever get married); that's where some CBCs will want to leave to a larger church or they may stay. This is a challenge."

15. "This is the number one reason at our church. I can't put a finger on the exact issues, but it seems that career CBCs lose interest to a lack of life transition help."

16. ". . . my wife and I are going through this problem . . . the English side has no members beyond the age of 35. The older members of the English side are concerned about the lack of mentorship and resources available to them in terms of members with more life experience to share."

17. "I have not faced this challenge myself . . . this problem could exist in any church . . . I believe as we have more and more CBCs this factor becomes less important. I can remember while I was a teenager there was always one or two older (late 30s) CBCs who would not 'fit-in' when they joined us, but it is no longer the issue in most cases."

18. "It is a factor because we have a small CBC group in each life stage."

19. "I think it's not an issue—it's an issue of church ministry of whether you have support for that transition."

20. "I think this is a major one for lots of people . . . (Participant described a problem of people not belonging to a church because they can't find a quality fellowship; he did not get spiritual needs met in Para-church organizations). ". . . I think the question doesn't have much to do with

the ethnicity of the church as much as the health and general function of the church."

21. "So far my church has been able to meet my life stage transitions quite well . . ."

22. "I agree with this and I did face challenges like this at my previous churches. It is a factor because if there is nobody to lead or organize that generation there is a feeling of being lost or not having a place along with the fact you probably do not have much spiritual growth."

23. (participant did not answer the question)

24. "Yes . . . for one friend."

25. (participant speaks of his first church). "In my church people left because they weren't Christians." (Participant speaks of his second church). ". . . Life stage transformation needs were definitely unfulfilled . . . there was no effort in college age group which was a huge mistake. That is why many college people left. Life transition issues were huge . . . many also go away for university . . . they leave the country . . . it is difficult to offer something to those who stay due to the lack of resources. So they leave."

26. "I would argue that the generational and cultural gap between CBC's and their Chinese parents would impede them from transitioning into different life stages together as a family . . . CBC's . . . might often turn to their peers . . . or other social groups for advice, guidance and encouragement during their transitions . . . I see a need for CBC's and their Chinese parents to use effective ways to close this gap and go through these transitions together."

27. (Note: this participant attends two churches at the same time). "I think this was the biggest factor for my leaving. I felt like I wasn't growing. The sermons threw a lot of bible knowledge onto me but the connection to my life just wasn't there. Life stage transition is an important factor because that's usually when people leave. It's the time when people evaluate what to keep in their life and what to change."

28. (participant described being in the workplace and seeking out a spouse; her church may not be able to accommodate her needs at this life stage). ". . . the church where I am at is stagnant in growth . . . yes life stage is an important issue for CBCs . . ."

29. (participant notes that the older CBCs seem to have left the church).

30. "Yes (Participant noted leaving one church) . . . I felt frustrated with complacency among my peers who only cared about careers and having a good life. I could not find fellowship there anymore. I know many who come to our church because of the children and youth ministries so this is a life stage decision."

Summary on issue #2: Twenty-six out of thirty (86 percent) felt this was an issue; two did not; two did not respond to the question. Four out of the twenty-six also felt this is not an issue specific to Chinese churches. Top reasons noted for why life stage transition needs are not met range from: the church not having a vision (prepared ahead to attending to the needs of a growing intergenerational (i.e., married with children) English congregation; lack of role models/mentors; insufficient resources to be relevant; and a lack of care or discipleship focus. Note: these things are the domain of leadership, shepherding, and how, or to whom the board allocates its financial or human resources.

Issue #3: Intergenerational conflict (within church / family)

1. "I have encountered almost all those situations that were listed above, and I feel as though this issues arises more in a bicultural Chinese church. I think a lot of young people follow their parents to church at the beginning and when they are old enough to make their own decisions, they notice how their parents and other adults approach their Christianity and usually its more rigid, closed minded, and even stubborn at times than the way those young people have developed in western society. Often when these young people reach an age where they have a freedom in where they want to worship, they choose to go elsewhere because the adults appear to have a hard time letting go of the "parent-child" guidance, when all the younger generation wants is for the older generation to treat them as equals. Sometimes this may be unavoidable unless they leave their church in which they were growing up in because their own parents may still attend the church who continue to impose a parental rule over their children, who when they leave aren't children anymore. I believe this is a very important factor."

2. "I think all of the items listed above are important . . . they are the same issues that arise in the Chinese family growing up in western culture . . . as the children grow and adopt the expectations of western culture, the Chinese traditional parents are placing Chinese

expectations on their children ... when the expectations clash, neither side is willing to give up on their beliefs ... as conflicts arise, both parties become more and more entrenched in what they believe is right or is for the best ..."

3. "Yes for me the hypocrisy and differences in church practices and expression of faith in worship are important factors. Certain "traditional" practices and attitudes are entrenched in the church without a true explanation of its purpose—leaving many younger generations questioning why we do these certain rituals/practices at church. This often leads CBCs to develop their own expression of faith in worship and services ... This can present friction and misunderstanding between the generations and the uphill battle can discourage CBCs to leave to a place where their expression of faith is accepted."

4. "Oh yes, I've encountered every single one of those problems in every church! ... Its not limited to the bicultural church and its not necessarily a good reason to leave the church ... conflicts within the nuclear families spill outward to the church family. We in our church ministries need to be building up the families rather than segregating them ..."

5. "Yes, faced intergenerational conflicts. The difference in opinion between generations is valid, but again, the church needs to appeal to the needs of the people. These situations are critical to people deciding to leave ... because the people need to have their needs met and not feel like they are coming to church to be molded into the ways that an older generation 'does things;' they need to be able to be creative in their worship and have the opportunity to express themselves."

6. "Yes all of the above ... All the deacons for the English congregation are about my age or older, but even the older deacons are all English speaking or have English as their first language, so its less painful to come to any decisions or argue any points. There's less cultural issues to sort through." (Participant suggests being in a very westernized Chinese church).

7. no response

8. "YES. I think it is a big source of frustration and anger and a stumbling block. Answer? Increased COMMUNICATION [sic]. It is very important and can lead to not only leaving the Christian church but leaving their Asian heritage because of the bad baggage it can carry."

9. "At the moment we don't have this kind of conflict; we try to resolve it. We do feel that the English side needs are so different we actually fear the two sides will drift apart; we try to find activities to build up the relationship and build up understanding."

10. no response

11. "I have not sensed this in my church, but that may be because I haven't been talking to the older generations much about our issues. I have heard from other church young adult leaders that there a lot of church politics at hand, and the funding of young adults is very conservative. I would have to be more involved in the church to answer this question fully."

12. "Yes we have encountered many situations like this at [church name]. (Participant noted some who put more focus on growing the Chinese congregation and the use of the Chinese language). There were instances of the older generation looking down on emerging leadership and not listening to opinions offered by the CBCs. The older generation is very resistant to change at times. Differences in worship format and expression of faith can sometimes be challenging issues to reconcile . . . I feel we should strike a balance and decide on what is good for the church as a whole . . . This can be an important issue to address in order to keep the CBCs. CBCs are more open minded and independent. Their needs and feelings need to be addressed and heard. If nothing is done to reconcile the conflicts at hand, they will have negative experiences with the church and ultimately decide to leave."

13. "All of this is real and I have seen it from the day I began church as a child 40 years ago in Vancouver. The burning question is, "If an issue comes down to doing something the way God would have it (grace, love, patience) versus the "Chinese way" (saving face, arrogant, self-righteous), which should prevail in church?" This is a stupid question but one which is all but ignored "because we are Chinese." Really? Chinese before Christ? As a leader in the English congregation in a bicultural church, I have learned to "work the system." I understand the inevitable baggage and have learned how to push the boundaries, practically to bursting. But I relate to the OBC at their level, with proper deference and respect. Sounds crazy? I have been able to keep many of the CBCs in church (bicultural or not) and my largest financial support base is from the Chinese speaking portion of my bicultural church. I return each year and share with them in my simple Cantonese but they appreciate the effort and respect I show. But when I share I

push their Chinese sensibilities and espouse grace and love. I am willing to lose face to achieve goals for the gospel. I perfectly understand that many are fed up with this are simply burned out and tired. So they leave the bicultural church. Many cling to the bicultural church because they belong in the "in-between" of cultures. Everybody handles it differently, but the intergenerational gap is definitely there."

14. "It really depends on the church and the leadership that you have and if the CBCs have children growing up in the Canadian culture. It is a conflict if the leaders of the church bring their family expectations into their role inside the church. Some leaders are very open; others are very conservative and mandated. Depending on the leaders there goes the church."

15. "I think [church name] has come a long way to emerge out of this conflict, [the lead pastor] and some key deacon board members have tried very hard to alleviate the issues and in my opinion have been very successful in the past couple of years."

16. (participant noted that the Chinese side had some difficulty in ordaining a female pastor).

17. "... There is certainly a difference in traditional values and there are times when the Chinese ministry does things that would offend some members of the English ministry. I can see how some CBCs may leave their church because of these conflicts . . . conflicts exist in all churches . . . the question is how the bicultural congregation sensitively handles the other side's concerns. Is there enough respect and communication (in-between peace makers) to open up so that they can resolve the situation? I do think this is an important factor as this is the kind of conflict which is hardest to resolve . . . different ways of doing things . . ."

18. "I haven't encountered any conflict because of cultural differences; if it's intergenerational, it's just between age groups."

19. "I haven't had any of this personally; I have this vague impression of differences at the leadership level."

20. "... Traditional Chinese culture and values do find its way into the Chinese church—like perhaps a greater emphasis on hierarchical leadership and on education and I think this can cause problems sometimes . . . but I don't think ethnicity is a factor . . . I think sharing ethnicity helps people get along better (which is probably why ethnic

churches are formed in the first place), and there are less cultural misunderstandings and conflicts."

21. "Yes I think all those conflicts have happened at my church. I think its part of Chinese culture to think that tradition is always best and to leave tradition behind is a bit like betrayal. It also has to do with comfort. The older people in the church are usually comfortable and dislike newer worship practices such as newer worship songs instead of hymns, and the addition of noisy instruments like drums and electric guitars. The younger people get frustrated by the lack of willingness to try newer methods of worship and so the conflict ensues with the younger ones finding the old methods too boring and the older ones finding the new methods too radical. Our church did go through a period of time when some of the young adults left church due to this conflict, but now things have evened out and we've come to a fair balance, incorporating both old and newer worship practices . . ."

22. "I have encountered some of these issues. I had felt I had done all that I could have at the present time, voiced my opinions—I believe initially I wasn't heard, but after visiting a few times a few years later, I can start to see some of these issues starting to be addressed—however the issues are still at large and I know of contemporaries that still leave this church. For myself, it was important for me to leave because I felt God's calling for something more and I'm glad I listened. However running away or leaving isn't always the right answer."

23. "Yes I do believe that many people end up leaving Chinese churches because conflicts at home end up being played out at church as well. I think of Friedman's classic book on family systems, *Generation to Generation*. He explains that unresolved issues in your biological family will affect your relationships with your church family." (Participant indicated that he felt it is a common phenomenon for next generation CBCs to leave their Chinese church over family conflicts).

24. "I can't really think of any issue in our church."

25. (participant speaks of his first church) "There were not very many noticeable intergenerational conflicts because the church was small . . . my dad ran the church and that was that. (Participant speaks of his second church). Intergenerational conflict is almost as common as peanut butter and jelly . . . as common as rice. You can't escape it because its there. Every single issue you've listed can be seen because Chinese culture is so complicated . . ."

26. (participant has *not* seen open conflict in his particular church, just differences) ". . . The differences in values and perspective . . . are evident in [CBC] perceptions of the other generation and culture during fellowships . . . I have encountered direct conflicts in tradition, values, and perspectives as a volunteer member leading intergenerational workshops in other Chinese churches."

27. ". . . minimal . . . the older generation didn't really like the loud/rock style of praise and worship . . . no one leaves solely because of these problems . . ."

28. "This is too much of a loaded question for me. All the issues that you mentioned are true. We're Chinese, so we've been taught not to talk back to our elders. I think the higher the number of issues one deals with contributes to the higher the likelihood of him/her leaving the church. Most of all I think CBCs would see that church people don't quite understand what really happens "in the real world" and would want to find a church that is truly making an impact in their immediate neighborhood or city."

29. no response

30. "Yes but again this depends on the pastor(s) and the leadership. Unfortunately many churches and church goers are more interested in community than discipleship. Hence such bickering."

Summary on issue #3: Nineteen out of thirty participants (63 percent) considered this to be an important issue; eight did not think it was important. Three did not respond to the question. Notable commentary here was the English ministries not being treated as equal partners.

Issue #4: Shame culture: over evaluation or rejection

1. "I think the Chinese culture does have a tendency to judge others in a very black and white manner, or in a polarizing way. I believe the older Chinese generation struggles with pride, and are quick to point fingers when something (or someone) is not right in the church . . . Its always the young people having to meet up to the standards and expectations of the deacons and people who have authority . . . this may be an important factor . . ."

2. "I think that plays a role . . . in my church there were incidents where members of the English congregation who were serving in the deacons

board—when discussing issues [experienced being] verbally abused and put down by the more senior members . . . comments were made which were of a personal nature . . . as a result, those people who served (almost all those who served on the deacons board) resigned and left the church."

3. "Yes a church who does not embrace people's authentic feelings and thoughts is not effective. When church becomes a place for pointing fingers and criticism rather than encouragement and praise, it no longer speaks to its people . . ."

4. "When I see the words "shame culture" I think of a host of other issues, not just judgmental attitudes (e.g., there's also the way in which we obligate people to serve). (The participant went on to point out that there is an issue "of not feeling comfortable sharing real thoughts;" [he gave an example of a university-aged woman sharing and crying about her lengthy struggle with masturbation in a prayer meeting] . . . many of the congregation were very shocked and offended and she was never asked to share publicly again . . . I do think this demonstrates the judgmental nature of the church, that we have long lost our vision as a hospital for hurting people and have turned into a country-club for perfect people. They really should have been able to handle that situation better and rallied around that girl to pray for her—it is prayer meeting after all! But I think it also demonstrates something else about the church; that she hadn't felt she had a safe outlet to share her struggles within a mentorship or small-group environment of supportive accountability. She was crying out for someone just to listen to her, bottling it up inside until the day she was given a microphone and finally had a captive audience."

5. "I have not typically felt judged or criticized. It can be an important factor . . . because such thoughts ultimately result in conflicts and assumptions.

6. Case 6: On the whole, I felt accepted, even with blunders. If I was being judged, I never heard of it directly or indirectly, so I think I was protected from too-critical a tongue while growing up in my churches . . ."

7. no response

8. "This is the same as the previous question—it is a matter of culture and my answer is the exact same [as the answer given in issue #3]."

9. (participant agrees that this is an important factor). "The younger English ministry do get ideas rejected, feeling like second class. This church is working at trying to address this."

10. no response

11. "This determinant is not important and not applicable to me."

12. "[This is] not too much of an issue at our church in recent years as more emphasis is placed on the English ministries . . . This can be another important issue to address in order to keep the CBCs. Everyone wants to feel safe and not be rejected by anyone. If the Chinese churches uphold the shame culture, they will lose the CBCs because they are not agreeable to such culture. They grew up in an environment where there is freedom of expression and acceptance . . . I think a church which promotes love, forgiveness and acceptance will be an important factor for the CBCs."

13. (participant spoke of his church) "Over the last 40 years, the OBC congregation has developed a very complex love-hate relationship with the CBC leadership in their church. They wish they could control the CBC but also realize it will be the CBC who will guide the next generation, their children, to either a functional relationship with the Lord (and the church) or simply lose them to "the world." So the OBC has made many concessions over the years and increasingly one hears of English department leaders having more autonomy. But for the time being it will be an autonomy that goes as far as what a parent will give an independent child; rope that definitely has a restricted distance. But the growth of the English ministry in large centers like Vancouver means that there is a greater network of support among English ministers. Continued lack of understanding, autonomy and often respect ultimately means a short stay for many English pastors in a given congregation but over time, the role and general status of the English pastor and his in-house leadership is increasingly, perhaps reluctantly, being accepted . . . (Participant notes the lack of female English pastors)..We often used to talk of the "old school" Chinese pastors, those who ruled with an iron fist in a patriarchal, totalitarian church structure, but today that is giving way to a new generation of OBC pastors who are increasingly well versed in intercultural understanding. Many of these studied at the university level in western seminaries and were therefore more exposed to western thought and processes. I don't know that the average congregant would find "being shamed" as a reason for leaving the bicultural church. But certainly I know many

in leadership who have given up and moved away from the bicultural church because of the lack of respect shown by OBC leadership."

14. "It has to do with how people take criticism and how people give out criticism; it is more the individual themselves and how they try to solve their problems."

15. "The Chinese side is viewed as conservative and traditional, so CBCs wanting to introduce more contemporary ideas and programs automatically feel discouraged."

16. "I have not encountered this at this church . . ."

17. ". . . a respect issue . . . this is a real situation but it is a two-way street. Some young adults that I have come across demanded no criticism from the Chinese ministry while giving criticism themselves . . . without respect how can one expect to serve under the same roof?"

18. "Some feedback I have gotten from some in the early 20's is that they have felt there are too many expectations to help out—so they opt out of participation; they seem to lose belongingness by their lack of involvement. Dropping out may be linked to this."

19. "I have no thoughts on this."

20. "Yes I think this is a major weakness of the Chinese culture. And I may have to eat my previous words a little about ethnicity not playing a big part in church conflicts; yes the Chinese church imports a lot of Chinese culture and with it a tendency for judgment. I have been one of the people judging others, and I've been judged too . . . legalism and its bad . . . I think Pharisee-type people are more common in Chinese churches but I have learned to live with it . . . all of us Christians are becoming like Jesus and all of us have different starting circumstances. All the mature Chinese Christians I know are wonderful kind people. But the immature can judge and cause people to get hurt. I see this kind of thing as incurable as children's immaturity. Nonetheless I can see people leaving the church because of this. Feeling comfortable is very important to most people."

21. "No I haven't encountered such a thing in my church . . ."

22. "I definitely have felt this more so in Asian churches than anywhere else. The Chinese culture doesn't like to show emotion and is very work-money relational. You do not show you have problems as you don't want your family looked-down upon. I would definitely see how pride and society would get in the way causing CBCs to leave."

23. "... Too often traditional Chinese parents will seek to correct or change behavior that they believe is wrong in their eyes by using shame and criticism. This is the only paradigm that they have ever known."

24. "No I never felt I was being rejected or under a watchful eye, but some of my friends said they felt it, but not the friends that I grew up with. A barrier when people first start coming, I don't know if this increases."

25. "In my old church, as a pastor's kid, I must say hi to everyone, I must act my best, put on my Sunday clothes, be super nice, and lead by example. I was judged because I was a pastor's kid and the Chinese people expected too much. (Participant next speaks of his second church). Now this is a huge issue. Huge. The Chinese culture has unspoken rules or things that are expected. Even I put on my façade when I go to church because Chinese people judge and criticize everything. It is like working in the mission field . . . The Chinese culture sets people up for failure because anything under 100% is insufficient. CBC's will definitely leave because the Chinese culture is not forgiving at all and too stubborn . . ."

26. (no) ". ∴. Most of the young adults who left the church left for career or academic reasons. Our church has done an excellent job . . ."

27. "I think that people are just trying their best . . . that being said there are certain things that I would never talk about with certain people. I don't know if people will judge but there's always the fear. One friend I grew up with got into a different lifestyle (drugs, drinking, promiscuity, etc.). She would never go back to our church because she would have no one to relate to and everyone would just judge her."

28. "This is still the norm in the Chinese church. That's why I don't feel as if my faith in the church is real, I feel as if I need to go elsewhere to really think critically about what I believe in. I feel, if people really knew who I was, I would be condemned. I prefer hanging out with scholars more. I'm planning to leave because I feel as if too many people judge me in the church . . . It would be nice if there wasn't much pressure to be perfect. I like being real, but being fake just to make people happy just doesn't sit well with me."

29. participant did not answer the question

30. "Yes. This again depends on individual church culture which is affected by many factors such as average level of education, proportion of new immigrants versus old immigrants, neighborhood, pastoral team, leadership, and whether or not there is a strong youth and children ministry."

Summary on issue #4: Fourteen out of thirty (46 percent) agreed this was an issue; twelve did not feel it was an issue in their church; three did not respond to the question, one participants indicated he had no thoughts on the question. Notably several participants felt that over evaluation of the other cultural ministry was a two-way street. Some participants made reference to the EM experiencing a lack of respect and shame as a form of hegemony.

Issue #5: Western postmodern values or worldviews at conflict with Chinese traditional values manifested in the bicultural church

1. "I think it is accurate to say the young adults see their spirituality differently than the way many bicultural Chinese churches do, and it almost feels as though these churches will not accept you if you don't adhere to the Chinese traditional values that they have been instituted under for many years . . . That being said, I do not think this is a big issue and there are ways to work around this (such as an effective English ministry with core representatives who can bridge the gap and interpret values from both the post-modern and Chinese traditional side)."

2. ". . . I don't see it as a major reason for people leaving."

3. not a applicable response

4. "I think Christ has called us into community and it is impossible to live the Christian life alone. First Corinthians chapter twelve makes it clear that we need one another. I think our modern individualistic society [is] filled with suburban enclaves where we don't even know our neighbors; it has left us quite lonely. On the other hand, I think we need a more flattened view of authority in the church—there is one Lawgiver and Judge, and we all submit to God's authority, exhorting one another in His truth. We do not wish to reproduce the hierarchy of the Catholic Church with our senior pastor placed on some papal pedestal. We do not wish to emulate the controlling small groups of cults like the International church of Christ, where members confess their sins to their small group leaders and are trapped, essentially blackmailed, by them."

5. "Absolutely not; the Christian journey is to be taken with fellow believers . . . (however the participant felt that post-modern values "are very important in determining whether people will leave) . . ."

6. no response

REMAIN-IN DATA 307

7. no response

8. "I agree this is important as an issue, but I also know that both sides are wrong, and it is incorrect to state it in either/or rather a both/and type of dichotomy. I think that Chinese churches need to address that there are other values aside from their own, and that they have worth and are not garbage just because they are different. This has been a growing issue for me to wrestle with."

9. "Not sure about this question."

10. "Yes as I have mentioned before, the sense of Confucianism might override Christianity in practice for the older Chinese generation. Confucianism is not bad in itself, it is a way of life which emphasizes: respect and honor your parents, good conduct and manners, family is important, humility, etc. But it can become an idol when the parents are trying to uphold these values more than practicing Christ's grace and mercy and forgiveness. Humility can become false humility if it is all about face and shoving the real problems under the rug which happens in Chinese families . . . real problems or tensions are not resolved but on the outside we must look good as a family. The older generation expects the younger generation to understand their ways but they do not do the same for the next generation. There is a sense that the parents or the Chinese elders in the church are always right even if they make mistakes. And the unwillingness to learn from the younger generation or apologize when they make a mistake is hypocrisy. The younger generation can see through talk and practice . . . raised in the western culture [they] will always ask "why do I need to do this" instead of "yes I will do as I am told," or "I will do it even if I don't understand it.""

11. "I do have a friend who had this explanation for her leaving the church. She thought that there were a lot of hypocrites in her church and that going to church made her feel very negative because the people were all fake. They would be the Sunday Christian and have superficial conversations. Obviously not all members are like this, but she decided that her faith would be better preserved if she did not expose her ideas in that atmosphere. Therefore she told me she's a believer, but the church is just not for her. I do think this is an important factor in CBCs leaving the church."

12. "I do agree that some CBCs are more prone to western values and more individualistic in terms of actions and thinking. They are less receptive to traditional cultural practices of the Chinese churches. For

instance, singing hymns and no drums playing during praise and worship sessions. Another example is the type of clothing to wear when going to church . . ."

13. "The absorption of post-modern values goes beyond the bicultural church and permeates all institutions in our society. Fighting it within the bicultural church is all the more heightened because of the values of the traditional OBC. Whether OBC or CBC, one's values ought to be Christ-centered and community oriented to promote healthy relationships. This needs to be promoted simultaneously to both the OBC and CBC with consensus by both leadership."

14. "This is interesting because it has to do with education. It becomes an issue when people bring it up as an issue. The English ministries tend to change faster; they are more susceptible to change to a different approach."

15. "Certainly some members who left felt this way, citing that it seemed their spiritual growth was being monitored by elders on the Chinese side.

16. "This has not been a problem at this church . . ."

17. ". . . not an issue at our church . . ."

18. "I don't think that's an issue."

19. "I have this vague feeling the postmodern values are a problem creeping into the church but I don't see it . . ."

20. "I personally strongly disagree with people who leave the church to pursue independent spirituality . . . hierarchy has its good forms and it cannot be written off as always bad. The bible says much about submission—not only to God but to leaders . . . I once . . . pursued my own spirituality with other Chinese Christian friends from other churches that seemed dissatisfied with their churches. And we were partially right but we were also naïve . . . It's only by tradition that we don't live in caves. Postmodernism it seems denies the work and values of the previous generation in order to pick and choose what seems good to the current generation. But the current generation's youth and lack of wisdom do not allow them to discern what is best . . . and I think postmodern thinking, in the sense of, "I can do better than the church that brought me up" is perhaps behind all church leaving."

21. "No I've never encountered this in my church . . ."

22. "I don't believe this is applicable or that I have ever encountered this."

23. "Again we have another clash of cultural values. Chinese culture tends to be more hierarchical and possess a group think mentality that defers to authority. You can imagine the Chinese youth who are brought up on a steady diet of western individualism (Think of the Declaration of Independence: "We hold these truths to be self-evident, that all men are created equal, that they are endowed by their Creator with certain unalienable rights, that among these are Life, Liberty, and the pursuit of Happiness") would not automatically defer to authority figures."
24. "No I don't think this is an issue for my church. I think this is an issue for the whole Church in general, not mine in particular."
25. ". . . I don't think this is a very large issue in CBC's leaving the church . . ."
26. no response
27. "I haven't really seen this . . ."
28. participant wrote but didn't answer the question
29. no response
30. "Yes . . ."

Summary on issue #5: Twelve out of thirty (40 percent) participants felt this was an issue, ten did not feel it was an issue in their church. Four did not respond to the question, one was not sure about the question; two wrote but did not answer the question.

Issue #6: Over-emphasis on Chinese cultural identity and ethnocentrism

1. "I don't see this as an issue that would cause CBC's in general to leave . . . especially if the church has specified that they are a bicultural church and I would think a balance of the Chinese and Western gospel teachings would be expected in such a church."
2. "I believe that because the Chinese congregation is senior to the English congregation their focus/passion/ ministry is often not the same as the English congregation . . . as a result, when there is a focus in an area, for example—missions—it often reflects the focus of the Chinese congregation rather than the English congregation. However, it is not a major cause for established members to leave."
3. not an applicable response

4. no response

5. "I agree with saying that sometimes there is an over emphasis on Chinese cultural identity; it has not been a major issue; it is an important issue. It's important because it affects what CBCs think of bringing non-Chinese friends to church (which can be an individual's primary core group of friends)."

6. "Only if protocol followed tradition rather than what was taught in the Bible to the detriment of congregation members . . ."

7. no response

8. "This is a minor issue, but it is tied in with the value question and the question of culture. I think that as CBCs become more multicultural, the existence of a single ethnic church becomes odd, repugnant, rude, disrespectful, antiquated, etc . . . And they don't want to be associated with such a close-minded set. However many CBCs still primarily associate with other Asians . . . so this is something to consider as well, and if so, they are not as uncomfortable in a Chinese church as others who are "white-washed.""

9. "Because the majority of our church is Chinese, only one or two are Vietnamese . . . I'm not quite sure . . . the preacher is Singaporean, she will bring in her culture; I'm not sure that would be too much of a problem. If you're talking about non-Asian it could be overpowering."

10. "Yes I agree. Some church have big fights over switching their name to take out the word "Chinese" to be more welcoming to the community (not my church yet, we haven't changed the name). Also it may happen when planning a mission's trip. The Chinese side might not be as excited about [people in the English ministries] going to Africa rather than China. Or even their own children dating someone who is white or black rather than Chinese. So yes this is very much a cultural identity. But I do think parents should know that when they made the decision to bring their kids over to North America that is what they should expect. They can lovingly teach them Chinese cultural stuff but at the end the kids will make their own choice of how much of Chinese culture they embrace . . . I like to see Chinese culture being treasured and valued, but it cannot overrule Christ's teaching on loving each other's differences. It is all in the art of embracing diversity but still in unity."

11. "I guess I'm less of a CBC in this sense because I believe that we are Chinese and there are certain issues that our culture focuses on, therefore our preachers focus on teaching us those lessons. It is not

ethnocentric; it's mostly catering the sermon to the congregation's attention and focus. That's more of the sermons in the Chinese congregation, but on the English side, there is a western approach to our topics, therefore I do not think this is an important factor."

12. "This is an issue that [church name] has to deal with over the years. Some CBCs found it hard to fit in the Hakka based church. At times, only the Hakka language is spoken at church services and functions. The CBCs sometimes felt left out rather than being part of the family of God. This is an important issue . . . the church needs to be more sensitive and not neglect any groups. It needs to consider ways to accommodate the CBCs so they feel part of the services or functions."

13. "Ethnocentrism, like postmodernism thought goes beyond the OBC/CBC question. All peoples must learn to live with all peoples. So yes, this is a huge problem with the bicultural church. While it is understandable that people in Canada who speak Mandarin may have a heart and a natural connection with the Chinese in China and would wish to do missions there, an active development of missions to other cultures needs to be fostered. Many I know who have seen the ethnocentric values of bicultural churches, especially those that are content to wallow within this pond, have left the bicultural church. That said, the CBC church within many bicultural churches has done wonderful things in teaching the OBC to go beyond their own boundaries. Some churches, like my C&MA churches, promote a global perspective and have therefore done a much better job. This is one of the reasons I am well supported by the OBC congregation in my church. As they are open to me sharing about church development in Africa, I am more than happy to feed that education."

14. "It is one for parents who have children attending the English side; there is an emphasis on culture but I don't know if it is in the preaching . . . naturally there is a mission emphasis on China. In Vancouver people are likely to shop around for a different model of church. Those who grew up in the church, the neighborhood will factor into this (if it is a Chinese area, there is not an issue; if [the church] is in a multi-ethnic neighborhood, there's more pressure)."

15. "Another huge factor. Friends who wanted to bring their non-Christian friends of other races don't feel comfortable bringing them because of this."

16. ". . . some have commented . . . we have an overemphasis on resources set aside for missions work in China. Some of the CBCs felt there was a

complete lack of consideration for worthy missions work in other parts of the world. I do think this could be a big factor in some CBCs leaving because many 2nd or 3rd generation CBCs have lost touch with their Chinese roots and identify more so with the western culture. This type of ethnocentrism might come across as cultural arrogance."

17. "I think this issue is more predominant in a joint-service . . . I believe that a certain aspect of ethnocentrism is good. For example, there is no denial that I am a Chinese and that I am better equipped for ministries in China/Taiwan because I look like them, I understand (at least part of) their traditional culture, and I can speak to them (at least in some form of broken Chinese). While we are not called to serve the Chinese people only, why not take advantage of the tools that we have and take on the burden of the Chinese people? . . . while we cannot force all CBCs to embrace their own culture, I feel that there are only small percentages that leave the church because of this factor."

18. "I either don't know of it or can't think of anything. I think it is easier for a CBC who has family in the church. In a bicultural church they accept it."

19. "I know there are certain Chinese traditions and things that come with it—sometimes in the English congregation it feels like overkill (there's some of that feeling). I understand that' important for someone else, yeah let's do it."

20. "I have never encountered this."

21. "I've never encountered or even heard of this issue before. Faith is faith, regardless of what culture/race you belong to. There shouldn't even be such thing as a Chinese gospel because the gospel is universal."

22. "I agree with this statement as sometimes we end up valuing culture over religion. This is an issue with all the Asian churches I have attended."

23. "Chinese people are rightly proud of being Chinese. But the problem arises when our nationalism becomes our blind spot. I think many Chinese Christians and Chinese church leaders forget that the gospel is for all people and we are called to be a 'light to all nations,' not just to Chinese people."

24. "No I don't think I've felt that issue in my church (noted: this church formed in 1988, most parents in North America)."

25. "Chinese people over emphasize bible knowledge and Chinese culture in Canada . . . traditional Chinese culture will push CBCs away in a

heartbeat. Ethnocentrism in Chinese churches comes from the Chinese people. It therefore makes it difficult to bring in other races into a Chinese church."

26. no response

27. "A Chinese gospel? I've never heard of such a thing. The gospel is the gospel."

28. "The Chinese and English congregations almost never mix . . . the emphasis on family is very Chinese and doesn't recognize that CBC's are more individualistic . . . When I first left my church some peers in the English congregation came up to me and said, "We're one family. If you're leaving us you're leaving your family, and that isn't right." They knew that I was trying to find another church, but there wasn't support, rather misunderstanding."

29. no response

30. "Actually many CBCs feel more comfortable in a CBC church than a mostly white church, so what does that say? Also in large bilingual churches the different congregations are pretty self segregated anyways so there are ways to avoid being embarrassed or made to feel uncomfortable by someone who's speaking loudly in Cantonese or Mandarin or English."

Summary on issue #6: Fourteen out of thirty (46 percent) participants felt this was an issue, two of the fourteen felt it was only a minor issue. Eleven did not feel this was an issue in their church. Five did not respond to the question. A notable repeated comment was that this issue is a factor in CBCs not bringing friends of other races to the Chinese church.

Issue #7: Personal choice of a secular lifestyle versus Christianity

1. "I believe this could be the main issue in terms of why people (especially young adults) leave the Chinese church . . ."

2. "In Chinese churches, the faith is closely tied and/or confused with culture . . . I think at times, when people choose the secular lifestyle, it is more a rejection of their own culture and its perceived oppressiveness rather than rejection of faith.

3. "I don't think that choosing a secular lifestyle would be an issue for leaving a Chinese church. If a Christian chose to abandon their faith

to pursue a secular lifestyle, he/she would do so regardless of what church he/she belong to, whether it be Chinese, Western, or Korean."

4. no response

5. "Very valid point again—it's true that some people decide they don't want the whole burden of being a Christian. I don't think this concern is specific to CBCs but can be an important issue . . . because often time's people perceive Christianity as out-of-date; what needs to be addressed is relevance . . ."

6. "Perhaps if you were used to living the secular lifestyle your entire life, and church culture was so foreign and uncomfortable that you would revert back to the old life, you are not entirely convinced that . . . Jesus is truth, and therefore you are not willing to bank your entire life and choices on this Jesus . . . you might never have encountered God's work in your life, or you don't recognize any of it as God's work . . ."

7. no response

8. "I think this choice is made because they see NO difference between these two lifestyles. Or because of too much separation to the point where Christianity basically calls everything from itself evil and hateful . . . two extremes" (participant is referring to the segregated nature of the ethnic church).

9. "Yes. I think this issue is more a personal choice, whether they need God or not."

10. "I was really rebellious during my teenage years, but I still stayed in the church and became a two-faced Christian. I would lie and go out to parties on Saturday and play piano on Sunday service. But deep down inside I always knew God is real and I know what I was doing was wrong. And it is because somehow I stayed; eventually I came back to Christ and repented of my sings and surrendered my life step by step to God. I think for the CBCs that leave the church for secular lifestyle [there are] two main reasons: 1) seeing hypocrisy/gossip in church 2) they have been hurt by and bitter about the church" (either by leaders in the church or from a broken romantic relationship).

11. "Now more than ever, the secular lifestyle is very tempting to the young Christian and may be the main factor for someone to leave the church . . . friends outside the church who will invite to parties and activities that are part of popular culture. This may include alcohol, gambling and smoking, all activities that may slowly drag the Christian

into secular ways. Although fellowship and other church activities try to keep [youth] out of these crowds, it is very difficult for someone not to experience these activities now."

12. "This is another factor [why] some people left the church. CBCs grew up with a media saturated culture and materialistic world. They find it more fun and entertaining living a secular lifestyle over a Christian one. They want to explore and experience various things in life rather than being restricted. Those who are less connected with the people at church tend to leave for this reason. They find it more attractive to be with their non-Christian friends."

13. "This is typically the same as in all churches, the phenomena of children going through the stages of either embracing the faith for themselves or rejecting what they perceive to be the faith of the parents. CBC and OBC may face this in slightly different ways but a lack of depth of faith in high-schoolers' and young adults is fairly universal."

14. "This issue applies to anybody, not just a CBC. There is a certain Chinese value expectation on success that can factor into a secular direction."

15. "Naturally some members simply fade away; where we've failed as a church is when we don't encourage them to come back; we don't have a 'Caring Department' that follows up with them periodically."

16. "I don't think this is a factor . . ."

17. "I think this is the most important of all factors and issues. In my experience of the many CBCs that left the bicultural church, only a small percentage went on to a non bicultural church . . . most simply abandoned the church in general . . . [some] simply grew up in a church because they have to when they were young . . . left when they had a chance . . . I believe because of the Chinese culture where the parents are more authoritative, there are more CBCs that fit in this category . . ."

18. "It's definitely an issue—I'm not sure it is a CBC issue or not."

19. "It is a problem—but I do not know to what extent it is a CBC problem. I would compare more between young adults and the immigrant parents; the parents are more likely to stay with the church even just for the Chinese culture."

20. ". . . I think a CBC would choose a secular lifestyle after giving up on the church. If the church, after bringing them up, has repeatedly disappointed them and failed to meet the CBCs needs. The CBC could deny

the faith to live like a non-Christian. I've seen it happen to one of the guys I mentored. He was the leader of his high school fellowship, and then a couple years and probably many disappointments later, he does not want to talk to Christians . . . I think secular culture is one of the biggest reasons why we lose so many CBCs."

21. "In my experience . . . they have a lack of support in the church or their group of friends is non-Christian and influencing them away from the faith. If they are not well connected in the church no one will notice that they are slipping away . . ."

22. "I have seen this happen, young professionals wanting to 'live-it-up,' make money and have fun first . . . it does happen—as living a Christian walk is tough. It's easier living a secular life. I believe it's an important issue."

23. "Not having to live with the burden of a God to whom one is accountable is an attractive option. Especially if you associate your unhappy relationship with your parents and with the Christian god [sic]."

24. "Yes I saw this for sure—I think this is one of the main issues—this one stands out the most. Secular lifestyle is more exciting to some of those who have left."

25. "Ah, this is exactly what exactly happened in my old church. The secular lifestyle was more attractive than Christianity. This is because they had no solid Christian influence when they were growing up. (Participant then speaks of his second church). ". . . CBC's from a church would choose a secular lifestyle because it offers more freedom than Chinese Christianity. Chinese culture would suffocate growing Christians rather than helping them along with their faith . . . overly strict . . . You get church zombies who are trapped in the bubble . . . who don't know how the real world is . . . when Chinese churches say, "don't do___" they don't give a good enough explanation, they expect obedience. That's not how CBC's roll."

26. ". . . for CBC's the transition from living in a Christian lifestyle under their parents influence to living in a secular and postmodern lifestyle is a gradual, painful, and falsely liberating one, in the sense that they feel being freed from, what is, in a very stereotypical view, a strict and unsympathetic Chinese family. As CBCs grow in body and mind under this environment, they may come to associate these painful experiences in their Chinese families with . . . Christ and the church. Although family environment should not replace the faith, the family shoulders the responsibility in building their [young people's] faith

with understanding, care, encouragement, and love, rather than rules, family authority, and obligation."

27. CBCs would choose a secular lifestyle because its fun, you can party all you want and not feel guilty for it. It's important because it shows that people view Christianity primarily as restricting and full of laws and commands. They don't see its benefits. It's tough to be a Christian and in a way that's true."

28. "... I don't think people really truly want the secular lifestyle. It leaves you empty ... The ones I knew that left the church, left because the church wasn't relevant in their lives anymore ... They tried suggesting many ways the church could change to grow but these ideas were rejected ... they didn't feel appreciated. Now the real world appreciates them and they're sitting as directors, chairpersons and such ... These friends now no longer go to church but are focused on their careers."

29. "not at this church."

30. "Of course it could be important, if the whole point of church is to find a comfortable community to hang out with than what difference does it make if it's outside or inside the church? As long as the young person attains straight A's throughout school, gets a degree in a respectable profession, gets a good paying job and marries a respectable, also well educated spouse and buys a nice house and starts producing pretty children, who cares?"

Summary on issue #7: Twenty-four out of thirty (80 percent) felt this was an issue; four did not feel it was an issue at their church; two participants did not respond to the question. Notably, of the twenty-four who felt this was an issue, four of them expressed they thought it was a universal problem with all churches. A couple felt it might be more a rejection of some elements of the Chinese church culture and a confusion of faith and culture (e.g., the segregated nature of some ethnic churches). Many felt leaving the church was the culmination of many disappointments, lack of support, lack of discipling, and irrelevant ministry (caring) to some English congregants. Of concern is the statement that many totally abandon the church.

Issue #8: Perceived problem with church beliefs, theology, or hypocrisy

1. "I think this issue has been a problem in the churches that I've been too. I think people believe in God in different ways ... Certain types of

theology or lifestyles may be encouraged in the church and imposed on the young people, but then the older generation may stumble, and the young people feel betrayed by the standards that were imposed on them when the ones imposing those standards could not meet with it themselves . . ." (This participant expressed the confusion the church can leave a CBC in being ill equipped to address some topics such as homosexuality) . . . If they don't feel that the church is being accepting to whoever walks through the doors of church, they may have a problem with settlement in a church."

2. "I have been fortunate to be a part of a church that I believe did its best to teach with a strong bible basis . . ."

3. "Not a problem in my church."

4. no response

5. "[The] question of theology has affected me personally. Church beliefs and theology (especially in a Chinese church) is often mixed with tradition and as a consequence when they are challenged regarding a certain issue the general rule is that its "the way its always been," which is not a satisfactory answer when we're talking about Scripture. Perceiving this problem is not completely an important issue for everyone . . ."

6. no response

7. no response

8. ". . . minor issue . . . belief and theology. I do think hypocrisy has a big part to play. If anything, a perception that church beliefs are judgmental, not loving and not accepting may be those problems that people have. But I think those are valid complaints and issues about the CBC church."

9. "I think every church has this (hypocrisy), if what is being taught versus what they don't do [don't correspond]."

10. "I don't think this is an important issue for CBC's in general . . . though worship and community is a big issue among the CBC. CBCs need to have authentic, genuine times of praise and worship, not just singing songs. CBCs need to see the church care for the community within and outside the church. Sometimes the Chinese side might only focus on our own members . . . CBCs would be more willing to explore the idea of serving the community [even if it] does not bring in numbers for the congregation . . . A relationship between the church and community is important to the CBC. Whereas the Chinese congregation

might care less about that and care more about what people within the church thinks . . . contributing back to and respecting the community around the church is very important for the CBCs."

11. "This is an important factor . . . more and more documentaries are being recorded about the negative sides of religion . . . church and theology is challenged by the media and young people are being persuaded. Fellowships should take time to dissect these films so that arguments can be heard from the church side."

12. "This has not been an issue for our church. With the ongoing battle in the theology on blessing of same sex marriages and ordination of gay pastors, the stand of the church may determine if the people will remain or leave."

13. "Hypocrisy? This goes to pastors, teachers and parents living out what they teach and preach."

14. "It really focuses on the core leadership. One big one is whether they can acknowledge their faults and whether they are honest and truthful (genuine—genuinely care for people or not)."

15. "Not an issue . . ."

16. "Yes this was a problem" (Participant cited an example).

17. "Yes we had a problem with our ex-senior (Chinese ministry) pastor in regards to hypocrisy and he was let go by the church . . . hypocrisy is a major stumbling block in any church . . ."

18. "I haven't seen it."

19. no comment.

20. "Hypocrisy I think has been a problem . . . Theology not so much a problem for a mainstream denomination. I think it's pretty refined."

21. "I've never encountered this problem in my church . . ."

22. "I have seen this in my previous churches and family. It happens and it's unfortunate. If nobody speaks up the whole congregation is at a loss. I have left a church over this reason."

23. participant was not able to answer the question.

24. "No"

25. ". . . theology and church beliefs were not a huge issue in my opinion . . . However I do see that Chinese churches are much stricter in their set theology than other churches. They have many rules and

regulations which are unbiblical but traditional but I feel that it's not a huge issue for most people . . ."

26. ". . . I think the most prevalent problem with regards to hypocrisy in a CBCs belief and theology is tolerance and conformity to sins such as theft and idolatry that is actually encouraged in the Western culture. Examples of this include 1) Illegal viewing, downloading and usage of information, music, videos and software, and 2) excessive occupation of belonging and worldly values that interfere and replace the worship of God. Without acknowledging the CBC's perspectives and values the Chinese way of parenting fails to recognize the struggle in the CBC's faith, and also pushes them away from their church and faith by dealing with issues of disobeying parents rather than the important issue of disobeying God."

27. (participant noted experiencing the congregation's perception of the pastor making a sexist remark during the sermon) ". . . it was something about what a woman should/ shouldn't do. It really turned me off . . . Some people say if there's something you don't understand or agree with then just bring it up with the pastor but I didn't. This factor is probably important. How can someone go to a church and disagree with the beliefs/theology."

28. "I haven't met someone who left because of theology or hypocrisy . . ."

29. no

30. "Yes this is important for whatever kind of church. Relevance is key; when we lose our relevance, we've lost our saltiness and are good for nothing but landfill."

Summary on issue #8: Eleven out of thirty (36 percent) participants expressed that this was an issue; ten did not feel it was an issue in their church, five participants did not respond to the question; one wrote but didn't answer the question; one participant expressed not being able to answer the question; two participants were not clear in their statements.

Issue #9: Control issues with church power and politics

1. "I believe this is another main issue with young adults leaving an older-generation led bicultural church. Young adults . . . want to be . . . treated as equals. Sometimes the church structure makes it difficult, or intimidates young people to speak up regarding certain decisions or

plans for the church." (The participant laments his experience with church politics, something that leaves a negative lasting impression on the CBC generation).

2. "I think that control issues is huge . . . often the Chinese leaders are afraid of losing control and therefore make decisions that maintain that control . . . rather than empowering the English congregation to grow and make important decisions; the English congregation is not given any significant opportunity to grow and formulate its own identity. Hence the control and politics, I believe, center on this central aspect of growth . . . for established leaders, this is a key area where the decision to leave or stay lies."

3. "Yes I believe there are power struggles/politics in all churches. Particularly in the Chinese culture where power, social status, economic wealth and pride are highly valued . . . In the Chinese churches we see a struggle for or lack of leadership in young adults. Older Chinese generations tend to hold on to their children with a sincere desire to reserve the best for their children. They make many sacrifices in hopes for brighter and more promising futures. However, this can often relate to disabling many young adults. An overdependence on our parents provisions combined with overbearing parental control can lead to problems with the passing of leadership and empowerment within the church."

4. no response

5. ". . . I have not observed this to any significant extent; control issues can be important . . . because CBC young adults do have some inherent desire to go against control."

6. "It seems that [names a church] recently dealt with this issue. I'm not entirely clear on all the details, but it was an English congregation and Chinese congregation conflict. Some members also dealt with disillusionment over pastor's compensation (salary) (a cultural attitude differentiation here, where Cantonese mentality sometimes might feel that to be a pastor should mean a lifestyle of semi-poverty, whereas a more Canadian view might be that a pastor should be properly compensated, that to live in poverty is unfair suffering), but it usually isn't enough to make them get up and leave the church."

7. no response

8. "I completely agree. This is the issue that often has me on the verge of leaving, because these control issues also speak to the respect issue,

or lack of one. Power and politics are always an issue, but they can be dealt with in a harsh or tension building way, or be dealt with in an encouraging, building up way. Unfortunately it is likely the former rather than the latter which we see in the Chinese churches. This is important because it ties in with respect/face-shame and also hypocrisy. These issues are in the mind of the CBC who sees power politic struggles and that affects his view of the Chinese church."

9. "Yes, definitely it's very true. A lot of the council members and leaders are the parents and it's easy for them not to listen. Because of this a lot of younger people (in English ministries) refuse to step in. The older generation can hinder by being very controlling."

10. "Yes politics in church turns CBCs off because it seems far away from being spiritual and relational. I've experienced this shock when I go to council meetings and see how little we pray and how people make decisions based on a business model rather than biblical model. In church we were taught to be different than the world, but how come in church ministry we practice the business model of the world? . . . having meetings for the sake of meetings is not attractive to young people. My favorite times with the council members is when we have retreat and we just shared from our hearts and struggles—that was refreshing and meaningful and helped me grow as a leader."

11. "I was not involved enough at my church to experience power and politics."

12. "To some extent, this is an issue at [church name] . . . Most of the power lies in the hands of the Chinese congregation. To some degree they control the finances and policies of the church. The majority of the council members are from the older generation. Many young people lack proper representation and the power to make decisions at that level. This can be due to the lack of experience on the part of the [English congregation]. Depending on who is running the church, this can be a determining factor for some people to stay or leave. Church politics are more apparent if there are many groups of people fighting for certain issues. Sometimes it can be the Chinese congregation versus the English congregation or pastors versus pastors."

13. "Certainly power, politics and autonomy were issues within leadership. But so is respect, humility and patience. Too many CBCs fought leadership like irked teenagers demanding respect and freedom. It has to go both ways. If maturity in developing Christ-like relationships

is lacking on either or both sides, proper leadership and governance cannot happen."

14. "For those in their early twenties and late teens—they perceive this to be an issue; but I see when they get older some of these issues become irrelevant if it is for the greater good of the body—if they value the larger church family context. It really depends on the age if they decide to leave or stay—that moving elsewhere won't solve their problem . . ."

15. "Until the English department has full autonomy this will continue to be an issue. At [church name] because of the perceived image that "the Chinese department" controls the 'English department.' Having served in the English department committee, I would say this is more of an image than reality, but overcoming this image would help a lot."

16. (participant likens the issue to the CBC seeking steps towards independence; he speaks of where he most witnessed power struggles in his Chinese MB church) ". . . early on the English side was dependent on the Chinese congregation for assistance, especially financial. The power struggles that existed were more so between the senior pastor and the English pastor. In my 12-13 years at this church, the English congregation has had four different English pastors, and in its 15-16 years, there have been six. I have had close relationships with all four that I knew, and I know for a fact they have all had difficulty in forming a constructive relationship with the senior pastor. I absolutely think CBCs would find it difficult to stay in a church that had some issues with power and politics because these issues would seem to indicate an inability and perhaps even a lack of desire for the church leadership to practice what it preaches."

17. "I have experience with power and politic struggles in our church. Because a bicultural church usually consists of parent-child serving in both ministries, the autonomy/paternal control issue is more prevalent . . . I have to say that our church has grown and improved in accepting . . . changed in involving more English ministry and respecting our ideas in their decision making. However at this time they still have the bigger congregation and are more financially solid and so are still the more affluent group in the church. I can see how some CBCs may leave the church because they do not get their way at times."

18. "I don't think it is a serious issue yet; our rector is very free in handing control over; at this point our EM is not demanding a lot. At present the EM congregation is 40-50 people; the age group is between 14 and 70."

19. "I don't think it's an issue where people leave, but our English ministry has a tendency to feel like kids—it goes both ways, we act like kids, the Chinese side decides."

20. "I heard that behind the scenes in my church there was a huge drama of church politics. And I believe it, and I think we have lost at least one pastor this way . . . I think if people get burned by power games or see how ugly it gets they may be disgusted with the way things are and leave the church. I think it's important in some cases—a small fraction."

21. no clear response

22. (participant noted he had seen this and left a previous church over it).

23. "As my pastoral care professor told our class, "When intimacy is lacking in relationships people will play power games.""

24. "I didn't see anything really big; for sure there were small things."

25. "Control issues are very important. Parental control is the biggest concern at my church . . ."

26. "I do see this phenomenon take place with the younger CBC generations as they grow up and gain some independence from their families . . ."

27. "Yes this is an important issue" (participant gave an example from her church).

28. "I think control issues are pretty big. The Chinese congregation has more direction on where the church goes than the English congregation for sure. There are four deacons that have left our church so far who were part of the English congregation . . . there is only one other person from the English congregation who currently serves as a deacon. That shows me that were perhaps not that attractive a church . . . it's discouraging. I may refer to my church as the church I grew up in . . . it might be a detachment thing."

29. "This war still needs to be won. We spoke our minds during the forum I will . . . let God handle the logistics . . . I think there is a power struggle between the two congregations. I think the Chinese congregation does not want to let go of this power (deacon board) because you can find deacons that have been serving the same area for 7-8 years . . . On the other hand I think the English congregation is being too passive . . . the Chinese side wants the power and the English side is not willing to fight the battle."

30. "I felt the same way when I was immature in Christ."

Summary on issue #9: Eighteen out of thirty (60 percent) participants indicated that this was an issue; seven did not think it was an issue in their churches—two of the seven felt that it was just a perception stemming from CBC immaturity. Two participants did not answer the question. Three responses were not clear enough in their statements to determine clarity. Notably participants commented on OBC leadership making decisions to control the EM rather than empower them. Problems with empowering EM leadership were stated; EM is the weaker congregation and seeking more respect and autonomy, not being disabled by being put in an over dependent position; one participant indicated they want to be treated as equals, another survey case stated, "this issue has me on the verge of leaving."

Issue #10: Church leadership,
organizational structure and program issues

1. "I think this is a factor for smaller congregations than larger ones..."
2. "...those who are part of a church and have formed connections with people... are more inclined to try to make it work... programs are just the icing... core members recognize that relationships are central to their decision to stay or go."
3. "Yes this is common with many Chinese churches as well as the church I attend. Commonly, English ministry is the result of a need for programs for the children of Chinese parents. It starts out with baby-sitting programs and often fails to launch into the next stage of strategic vision with long term plans/goals. I do believe it is an important issue for CBCs because as they mature from their youth ministry, there is a void of programs/structure to equip them for the next stage in their lives."
4. no response
5. "this issue can be important—if people feel they are not heard they may be less likely to work with leadership..."
6. "The biggest thing I've noticed is people leaving churches due to lack of or insufficient or ineffective youth programming. Usually though, they leave the church to attend a larger church with better children's programming. I have seen CBCs burnt out doing youth ministry over and over again with insufficient support/ mentorship/leadership.

Usually these CBCs are in high school, then university, and as a result they might miss their own peers' activities/fellowship. Some CBCs end up leaving that church because they feel over used, under supported, and under appreciated."

7. no response
8. ". . . Yes it is very important to CBCs to feel that they are treated like equal people and to be given appropriate funding and support for ministry initiatives, both of which are often lacking."
9. "True—frustrating for the English congregation at the moment" (speaking of the participant's present context).
10. "Yes I do agree. But also I think this is where CBCs can learn to be less selfish about ministry and step in and take leadership roles. If you want change be a part of it! Giving up easily and leaving is the easy and selfish way out. That is how I found my role in church and I grew so much from it, though it totally depends if the older generation allows it or encourages it to happen. I was blessed to have leaders that recruited me, encouraged me and allowed me to go for it. Sometimes there might be fear from the older generation to let the young try new things on their own. So there is a sense of caution, but if too much protection it can become suffocating and deters growth of the CBCs . . . CBCs . . . should think of ways to serve and help the church rather than criticize and leave unless it is a very extreme case. Because in every bicultural church, eventually they have to face the issue of next generation and develop English ministries for the next generation. Churches need to wake up if they still don't think sowing in to the next generation is a must! And the Chinese leadership have to learn how to mentor letting them fly on their own . . . I became involved and part of the solution rather than just complaining and leaving . . ."
11. "Our English congregation was well respected from the church, therefore this was a nonfactor. There have been some inadequate programs for after university and career English young adults, but now the church has taken steps to develop programs in leadership and personal growth. The church should focus on these topics because [they] have a real interest from this generation . . ."
12. "Yes this is also another issue that [church name] has to deal with. Sometimes lack of leadership and proper representation from the English ministry restricted the growth of the English ministry. Decisions sometimes were made based on the needs of the Chinese ministry and without proper consultation from the English side. The high turnover

of English pastors also contributed to the instability of the English congregation. It is hard for a bicultural church to have the same vision and goal for both the Chinese and English ministry. The needs of each one are very different when they grow to a certain size . . ."

13. "Many English ministries were basically budding churches within a larger church. One does not build a church by first building programs and structure. English ministries and English pastors must not demand that which they are not ready to handle. Rather they should see themselves as a church plant that will grow with the people in a relational way where programs follow people as they grow, not the other way around. Here the English are often too impatient and demanding. But that said, the OBC must be nurturing and understanding of this church plant and do all it can to nurture it as a budding independent church."

14. "This issue is definitely a challenge for the church as a whole. This continues to be an area we talk about mainly because of the age stage we are in (Participant is in an English ministries that ranges in age from 18 into their 50's). Has to do with a cohort group of a dozen or so, because they serve together as a cohort (they have shared events and friendship together)." (Participant noted the church's demographic are is very multi-ethnic and Chinese, this affects the church's purpose and approach; they are in a new building and geographic area).

15. "CBCs are unwilling to serve alongside of Chinese members (i.e., deacon board) due to many reasons and until this attitude reverses we will always be caught in this vicious cycle."

16. ". . . The Chinese ministry is of course interested in growing its Chinese speaking members. Under the guise of partnership in the work of the Lord, the Chinese ministry uses the English and children's ministry as a 'babysitting' program which makes the Chinese ministry more attractive to newcomers . . . The problem I have is with the babysitter now being allowed to grow beyond this role into what the Chinese side claims it will be one day—its independent successor. With no hope of growth, I believe CBCs will definitely leave their bicultural church."

17. ". . . definitely the issue for newly formed bicultural churches . . . the babysitting concept was the initial reason for the establishment of the English ministries in Chinese churches . . . If the bicultural church continues to buy into this concept then certainly there is no reason why the young people/CBC should stay in this church . . . It is important that the bicultural church outgrow this concept and understand that a

parallel ministry is needed to enhance the growth of the church . . . to set up a vision, purpose . . . groom leaders . . ."

18. "Everything here is true and I have felt at times, those are the things we complain about. But they may not be fair complaints. We don't like what we see but we don't know what we want."

19. "I can't think of anything."

20. ". . . I see the problems and I see the consequences and it disturbs me. Programs can always be better and more effective and we who serve are always somewhat responsible for people leaving the church. But it has not been a debilitating problem in the churches I have settled in."

21. "If leadership is lacking in the English ministry, there should be a push by the congregation for a stronger leadership, perhaps a new English pastor or youth leader. There should be much prayer involved with something like this . . . if people are frustrated with what they perceive as inadequacy in the church they should push for change . . ."

22. "This does happen, but I've never really experienced it."

23. ". . . this is a lack of vision and understanding about the nature of ministry to English speaking Chinese. There is no blue print about doing English ministry . . ." (participant notes that methods must change with the times).

24. "Yes this is an issue now in my church; people are leaving over a stagnation of growth (it has caused older CBCs to leave)—the church has started to realize we do lack leadership and its starting to go in a right direction. A lot of people also left because of mobility—going to university in other parts of the country."

25. "Pretty big issue. Inadequate programs (untrained parents), lack of response from CM pastor to care for EM (because CM pastor has no clue what's going on with EM or Canadian culture for that matter); EM started as a youth ministry because none of the kids could stand sitting in a boring traditional service . . . when you have CM trying to create an EM its problem filled. You need someone who knows CBCs to run EM, but you can never find those people in CM. (Participant gives a recommendation); ". . . CM needs to suck it up and hire a white person (or CBC, but those are few) and just totally convert their youth ministry into an English ministry. Of course, EM and CM are going to do things completely different, but both reaching the same goal. Chinese people need to shed their ethnocentrism and be more open."

26. "... our English ministry does not seem to suffer this problem because we encourage each member to serve in at least one capacity and by God's grace we somehow have enough openings and leadership to encourage members of the ministry to serve in various aspects of worship, fellowship, ministry and outreach..." (Participant notes that this perspective is a grace that keeps CBCs worshipping and serving the Lord "under the guidance and encouragement from older members...").

27. "I can see this as an opportunity to serve... [however] people sometimes get burnt out when they're always the one to serve. I know people that have left church to seek this type of change."

28. "This is a sensitive issue and something I am not too interested in talking about..."

29. "Absolutely true! It is all right when you are young and believe what people tell you and be obedient. However as you grow older, and when you have your own ideology and when people (Chinese side) do not agree with your ideology, then conflict will arise. When the Chinese side always thinks the church must be united under one roof, then the English side will never flourish with their ideology and vision, since the Chinese side is always entrapped by spreading the gospel to the Chinese... I also think that this issue is the cancer in the Chinese congregation and that is why they are not growing in numbers and in members."

30. "Again this is true for all churches."

Summary on issue #10: Twenty-one out of thirty (70 percent) participants felt this was an issue in their church; two out of thirty did not feel it was an issue, two participants did not respond to the question and five participants wrote but clarity could not be determined by what they wrote. Some recognition was given to the high turnover with EM pastors and how that contributes to instability; others highlighted the lack of relationship, funding and support that can exist from a Chinese OBC board and leadership. Notably a number of participants highlighted a concern over a lack of strategic vision and long term goals for the EM that could factor into a budding independent parallel ministry/congregation or potential for a church plant. Some indicated that independence for an equivalent congregation was needed and that the EM should push for change. One participant (case 29) was bold enough to say that "the EM will never flourish with their [OBC] ideology and vision."

Issue #11: Intellectual, rational and pragmatic issues

1. "This issue wasn't as common among the CBC's who left the church in my experience..."
2. "I have known people who have decided to reject Jesus and Christianity and as a result left the church... but I can't comment on how prevalent that is."
3. N/A
4. no response
5. "Doubt in the Christian faith was not common among CBCs who left the Chinese bicultural church. It has not been a major issue for me. The main doubts and lack of faith come from inadequate understanding of the philosophical ideas first of all, and also inadequate understanding of what the bible says." (Participant is expressing that people who leave are missing a correct understanding).
6. no response
7. no response
8. "Not very common. But I know that the Chinese church is not able to engage and interact with these issues in a meaningful and intellectual way, instead of choosing to dismiss it and condemn any who want to be critical. This leads to an anti-intellectualism about the faith, even though there is a strong emphasis on education, it is often only purely as a means to an end, much like faith."
9. "Has not seen this at his church."
10. "I don't think this is very common... I think it is more about relationships than intellectual differences..."
11. "I am currently struggling with this exact issue after being challenged by the documentaries... I do think this is a big issue because there is a strong focus on faith instead of realistic solutions..."
12. "This has not been an issue for the people leaving our church..."
13. "This is church specific and goes to the heart of maturity of leadership on spiritual matters within any given church. Any church of any ethnic background can get this wrong or get this right."
14. "It would have to do with the pastoral and lay leaders and the preaching. Not being consistent, honest and truthful; too much focus on programs and numbers..." (Participant noted that the preaching and

teaching is more solid the past four years and a greater focus on discipleship is in effect).

15. no response
16. "To my knowledge, these are not a problem."
17. "I don't think this is a big issue . . ."
18. "I have seen some cases of this but not so philosophical—it's more about them, what is best for them."
19. "I feel like it probably is—especially with my friends outside the church, but I don't know if this is the case for any who left from my church."
20. ". . . I really don't know how common this kind of intellectual crisis is, but it was certainly a bad one for me."
21. "I am currently experiencing this in my university fellowship. But we choose to discuss it and look for biblical answers to try to understand what we believe and why we believe it . . . I think if people have questions about their faith they should pursue answers and do their research before they conclude that they cannot agree with the faith."
22. "This does happen but I've never really experienced it."
23. "I began my theological studies at Regent College because I was not able to find mature Christians at my church who would help me in finding answers to deeper spiritual and theological questions. In doing so I have become even more of a misfit at my church . . ." (participant expressed that people at his church are not open to questions and dealing with grey areas).
24. "I can see this being an issue; I don't think our church talks about the harder issues. We have talked about evolution and materialism, but in a one-sided manner . . . we haven't dealt with this enough."
25. "Not very common."
26. "I have not known anyone among our CBCs who left the church for this reason . . ."
27. "I haven't really seen this."
28. "This isn't too common for those that left . . ."
29. "Not common."

30. "Yes, lack of good teaching. But that's true for most [incomplete sentence]. Lack of discipleship and mushy, wishy washy thinking characterizes most Christians today whatever their ethnic background."

Summary on issue #11: Nine out of thirty (30 percent) felt that this was an issue; fifteen out of thirty did not feel this was an issue. Five participants did not respond to the question; one participant felt this issue depended on the church. One notable comment was that, leaving is more about relationships than intellectual differences.

5. Tying it up
If the bi-cultural Chinese church you are attending for a majority of the time were a car, how would you describe it?

1. "It would be an old car but modified with a new sound system, new paint job, and new wheels, but the engine is still the same old engine."
2. "It's a big clunker . . . there are many issues that are weighing it down, more often than not, these issues are culturally imposed . . . and they add baggage to the Christian faith/belief."
3. "It would be a hybrid car. It is on the brink of new technology; it is still being tested and approved for its benefits. It is great for the environment but not quite enough strength for the needs of all car users."
4. no response
5. no opinion
6. "It runs, but its exterior probably has different non-matching pieces holding it together."
7. no response
8. "Old, damaged, barely kept alive by the blood, sweat and tears of many who are dedicated to something that needs to be replaced."
9. "Very indecisive when traveling; traveling a longer journey to reach the goal (no shortcut); have to go back and forth to satisfy the congregations."
10. "It does not run really fast, but it feels very comfortable to sit in it. The best is when everyone sits in the car together. But it seems only certain older Chinese people (elders) with authority were allowed to drive it, not even the pastor sometimes."

11. "Strong tradition; safe/reliable; strong management team; powerful union; good benefits."
12. "I see the Chinese as the driver while the English young adults are the passengers."
13. "It would be a decent, pragmatic car (like a Volkswagen) that has been given outer body-work and fancy rims. It ought to see itself for what it is and not try so hard to be outwardly fancy trying to appear better. This attitude fosters a somewhat hard veneer and muddles it for people who simply want to come alongside and find community."
14. "We would look at it as a minivan, because it is a family."
15. no response
16. "... as an older model Honda with a refurbished engine, nice new seats in the front seat for the adults and ripped seat cushions in the rear for the kids to sit in. The visible portions of the rear seat however are in pristine condition."
17. "It is a car that works relatively well to accomplish the needs of various drivers of the car. Compromises are needed to ensure the efficiency of the car. Both drivers must respect and discuss the use of the car with each other and appreciate the existence of each other. The car can go far away if both drivers can work together and drive this car in the same direction."
18. "Like a truck carrying a boat trailer (the English thing is the boat trailer), at the right time it will be put down on a nice site."
19. "Like a family minivan with lots of screaming kids and yelling adults."
20. "A dodge ram pickup, because it's powerful and inefficient, but still good."
21. "A double-sliding door mini van."
22. "An older-model clunky car, with a decent engine and a lot of rust but repairable."
23. "Toyota-Corolla, dependable and stable but not flashy."
24. "Like an old Ford mustang (American classic car); its not brand new but there is this classic feel—its not kept too clean but it has this power to it—it its well kept it can really be something."
25. "The engine is the EM deacons and CM deacons. The wheels are me, because I have contact with the road (which is the people). It is burning oil and smoking; because the piston rings are worn out (we're missing

college age group). It is becoming over heated (because we lack resources). The color is yellow (because we are mellow and Asian). The driver is God (at least that's what we hope), the windows are tinted (we have little outward focus and now one can see inside), the headlights are off (because we can't see where we are going), the seats are cold (because we don't have a lot of growth, no passengers), the rear window is blurry (because I don't really know the history, and people seem to keep it hush hush), the congregation is the body. But it's rusted . . ."

26. ". . . my church would be a Toyota Sienna: Asian, dependable and relatively outgoing but slightly restricted in its range (scope) and function (activities)."

27. "A Toyota with 300,000 klms; [it] has been running for awhile, pretty safe and reliable, needs some fixing to perform at its best."

28. "It's an old car that's running out of gas that will slow down and eventually stop. It'll need an intervention or wake-up call of some kind, maybe a *'pimp my ride'* [sic] type of deal."

29. "God is the driver, and we are the parts for the cars. Chinese side is the engine because they are the money provider. We are the essential parts that make the car run."

30. "An Integra, Acura—middle class, materialistic, uncomfortably complacent, wanting more but not knowing how to get up there with the 'big boys' (mega churches); educated but fearful of getting messy if mind is engaged too much and thinking is challenged so just dabble with a bit of social concern and a bit of biblical scholarship and a lot of feel good self-concept building. The key concern is to look good and be hip but not to be seen as too flashy."

If the bicultural Chinese church you are attending for a majority of the time were a household, how would you describe it?

1. "It would be one with many children, and the children are old enough to move out of the household and form their own, but they are not resourceful enough as the parents are . . ."

2. "It's a Chinese household, there are things wrong, but people are more committed to looking like they have it all together and will do what it takes to look like nothing is wrong."

3. "It is a warm household. Often everyone is busy with their own activities. But when it comes to occasions, everyone unites for a big Thanksgiving feast."
4. no response
5. "Children going against parents because they disagree with what the parents have implemented."
6. "Agreeing to disagree in some aspects. Household members treat the house like a hotel or convention center; you're in for what you need to get done, and other guests can use the same rooms, but for perhaps different reasons. However you have no idea what other members/guests are doing, since there's no need to ask."
7. no response
8. "Dysfunctional"
9. "The younger generation will be staying in their room for quite some time; they'll probably go downstairs to raise up some issue, the parents would say you have to live by my rules—[the] young generation would try to express [themselves]—limiting development."
10. "It was a tight knit family, but not necessarily everyone's needs are met. But we have a good relationship with most people in the family."
11. "Welcoming; conflict between family members."
12. "The Chinese congregation controlling the power and finances of the household while the young ones do the chores (keeping the household alive and active)."
13. "It's generally well put together, with mostly sincere folks."
14. "It's like a triplex (EM, CM, MM). Pastors preach in all three congregations, yet its one church body."
15. "Parents are Chinese department; teenagers fighting for independence in the English department."
16. "I would describe it as somewhat dysfunctional. The parents work long hours and do not see or relate to their children much yet demand perfect obedience. The parents often invite strangers in for a meal but often neglect the needs of their children."
17. "A typical parent-child relationship where under the proper setting the child will grow to appreciate all that the parent has done for him and will become his best friend. The parent should treasure the gift of this child from God and give the best he has for him. The parent must

exercise cautious control over the child as over control will lead to a rebellious child while lack of control will lead to a wild child. Their relationship will yield either a harmonious relationship which will benefit all who visit the household as well as serve as model citizens in its community or a destructive relationship which leads to domestic disputes."

18. "Like living with your in-laws—you're in the basement, if you need something (i.e., meal) you can call."
19. "Having three generations living together (grandparents, parents, kids); different kinds of good and bad come with it."
20. "A really nice one actually."
21. "Children get input into family decisions, but parents make the final decision."
22. "A typical Asian family—proud dad, quiet gossiping mother, older rebel daughter, younger spoiled son."
23. "Caring, well meaning and busy with running church programs. Needs to learn to rest and understand more about God's grace and love."
24. "Like a happy suburban home that gets along in general but isn't comfortable enough to talk about a lot of the harder issues."
25. "God is the load bearing beams (at least that's what we hope), I as the EM intern am the heater (I bring a revival from tradition), the Chinese deacons are the next door house (not involved with EM), the EM support group is the floor, the congregation is the walls. Some kids are the chimney valve (sometimes they let the smoke go through the whole house causing a ruckus)."
26. "I would describe it as a giant family separated by various distinct generations and two distinct cultures who the heads of the family (pastors and leaders) are trying to join together."
27. "The nuclear family. Dad makes the decisions; mom does the cooking and cleaning. Kids have some freedom and are obedient."
28. "Chinese with different ages."
29. no response
30. "A big house with two floors and an attached suite. The English speaking in one part; the Cantos in another and the Mandos in the suite."

If the bicultural Chinese church you are attending for a majority of the time were a person, how would you describe it?

1. "It would be a person who is physically fit, but is struggling to find its identity on the inside."
2. "A person who has a lot of internal conflict."
3. no response.
4. no response
5. no opinion.
6. "Friendly, but in different ways."
7. no response
8. "Socially unaware, self-absorbed, and rude."
9. "I think that person would have a split personality. It is quite hard to have both congregations thinking the same way."
10. "The person can develop more in using their hands and feet, not every part of the body is being utilized. Some parts of the body are waiting for other parts to tell them what to do. The eyes and head need to be more focused on Scripture. The person is like a teenager, still finding its identity and he/she can go many different directions in the journey of life."
11. no response
12. "The Chinese congregation is the body and brain because they are more dominant and decide on more things. The English congregation will be the hands and feet because they are doing and running more ministries at church. They are in charge of running the Sunday school and youth ministries."
13. no response
14. "A person wearing multicolored clothing; probably your average looking individual, nothing too extravagant or too poor. A focus on trying to be authentic and real."
15. no response.
16. "I would describe it as too concerned with their appearance and not enough with their character. Naturally gifted in relating to people, but trying to impress people with outward beauty than inner beauty."

17. "It is a person that has grown up in different cultures and must find a balance between both cultures to establish a new identity. He must embrace and appreciate both the Chinese and western cultures as both have its advantages and shortcomings."
18. "I would describe that person as me."
19. no comment
20. "A very friendly person who could brush up on the faith, but all around quite good and very sociable."
21. "no clue"
22. "Healthy person that was in a fight—with scrapes and bruises but relatively okay.
23. Case 23: A faithful friend who is dependable and reliable, but he is not ready to take up new ideas or will find it easy to step out of his comfort zone. Intellectual but lacking depth. Ready to quote bible verses, but unable to deal with complex issues theologically. Simple and somewhat naïve about the world outside the church (looks at the world fearfully)."
24. "It would be a Chinese person like me who likes to hold traditional values but is uncomfortable with breaking out of its shell in talking about areas afraid of in order to grow (i.e., reaching out to the community, being more involved in society); I have a hard time in connecting to white people and I think in order to grow I have too and it is the same thing with my church."
25. "God is the head (at least that is what we hope), Jesus is the heart, college age is the right arm (dominant arm we are missing), youth congregation is the body, parent support group are the lungs, CM is the legs (because we still need them financially), guest speakers make up the other arm, I am the blood vessels."
26. "To me the church would be a person like Paul of Tarsus."
27. "Someone that needs understanding. Someone that is complicated. Someone that does not always say what he/she feels."
28. "Not the coolest kid on the block, but one that knows its values."
29. no response.
30. "It's a typical bilingual Canadian trying to stay politically correct in a pluralistic society."

6. Let's talk about your overall experience and spiritual journey within a bicultural Chinese church environment

   1. "I have been in a bicultural Chinese church environment for over 15 years. My spiritual journey . . . steady . . . I enjoy being in a bicultural Chinese church . . . fitting for me. I enjoy the different celebrations and worship styles of both cultures (friends, support) . . . it's the people who give meaning to my experience in church and not so much its unique culture."

   2. "There have been positive experiences . . . namely my discipleship by an older couple and also the actions a deacon took to support growth in the English ministry (drums in worship) . . . they have shown me what compassion is and how joyful it is to pursue God and to learn how rich life is when lived under His principles. In some ways it has been fulfilling, the people that I have come to know, the shared experiences—joys and struggles. A major growth lesson that I am learning and processing . . . is that I can no longer rely on the church to have it all together . . . it is messed up, just like me . . . if I take ownership and responsibility for my own pain and stop relying on the church to heal [me], I will be able to better engage with the members of the church . . . in the midst of our struggle [referring to her church], there are people who are genuinely struggling to help make things better . . . to wrestle with how to help the English ministries grow, how to empower the English congregation to make choices that are more in tune with its passions and maturity . . . it is these people who are wrestling with our current problems that are showing me hope. My decision to stay or leave will ultimately rest in how the leadership will respond to the growth of the English congregation . . . the leadership needs to take responsibility . . . I am hoping that the leadership will make a change . . ."

   3. no response

   4. no response

   5. "I have remained in a bicultural Chinese church environment for over 15 years. The experience has been fulfilling. I find fulfillment in being able to worship in an environment I'm used too. The main thing missing or lacking is sound biblical training that is relevant and can be applied to daily life—its probably a difficulty in gearing things to broad audiences, but at least these concerns can be addressed on a more one-on-one level or in small groups . . . Hope is that culture will

become less and less important because ultimately its our walk with God that counts."

6. "Twenty five years. I enjoy interacting with the Chinese side; they give me a sense of my roots and they also provide love in a way that I might not get from CBC adults in my congregation. The Chinese auntie's love is more . . . oppressive . . . but it is well-meaning, and you get some really awesome Chinese culinary treats (hello soups and steamed fish) that you might not get elsewhere. (Participant answers if the Chinese church experience has been fulfilling); Yes (fulfilling). (Participant indicates what was lacking in the Chinese church); I have not grown up to interact easily or comfortably with people of other races. I had to work at it when I was in university and when I graduated. Attending a more multicultural church would probably have opened me up to a more global experience. (Participant speculates on the future of the Chinese church); I think the Cantonese side (represented by an older generation), will slowly die down, and the mandarin side . . . will start to grow (looking at immigration trends). Both Mandarin and English speaking sides will probably start to think more alike than the Cantonese and English side did . . ."

7. no response

8. "I have been in the Chinese church seven-eight years. My growth has been despite being in a Chinese church environment I believe, not due to it. It has been fulfilling in giving me opportunities to lead but that has turned bitter when I am often forced to do much more than I should be—"intern abuse." It has given me meaning that despite all these restraints people are faithfully seeking God and he is turning their hearts to him and responding with the Holy Spirit. My hope is not in the Chinese church, but in a God who will work despite this broken structure. I hope that in time the church will learn to listen and work alongside WITH God instead of insisting solely upon its own way and refusing to listen to other voices—especially those of the past—which we relegate to "back then . . ." But as it is? It will die, people will leave for church atmospheres that can engage with their world, not separate and attack it. And if this is what the church is it deserves this fate."

9. (18 years there). "An extended spiritual family has given the most meaning; a supportive community."

10. Case 10: no response

11. "I have not grown up or matured as much as I envisioned myself because there is always something stopping me from pursuing further . . . whenever I study the bible . . . I find myself doubting truth. I look for concrete things like, how does a man stay alive in a big fish for three days? There's no food/air, how can he survive in the stomach acid of a fish? But I have to brush aside these ideas and just have faith in the miracle. The church has done everything to push me to go further into topics, therefore it s not that there is something missing or lacking in the church. (Participant expressed that he anticipates a drop in church attendance) . . . The Chinese church will grow faster than Caucasian churches because less Caucasians seem to be attending church now. The Chinese church will stay strong and will still put their children into church because they know it will teach good fundamentals and morals (notes that the Chinese school will still be a part of the Chinese church "because we value tradition"). The church will continue to use these ways to influence Chinese parents and encourage them to attend fellowship. The kids will grow up in the church but will be challenged by the time they reach the teen years. Some will leave, some will stay. But I hope that the new ones who stay will have the support of the older generation. There should be more of a merge between fellowships, encouraging mentorship and personal coaching. We've all been through the problems, and teens may not want to discuss the problems to their parents. But through mentorship church relationships will grow. I hope to see our church encourage the study of music for members to help out during praise and worship. I hope to see a growth in sports ministry where people can join a sports team and play . . . we should ask the 'dangerous questions' to stimulate their thoughts about life and religion . . ."

12. "I have been in a bicultural church environment for 20 years. For the most part my spiritual journey has been positive. I was given an environment where I can serve and grow spiritually. I tend to give more than I receive. Knowing the culture and values of the traditional church helps me to understand why certain things are done. One thing I found missing is the lack of families to anchor the English ministry. Most of our English ministry people are youth or young adults. There are not too many programs that are geared towards young families in English ministries. We are also lacking English speaking elders or adults attending and serving in the English congregation. The outlook of a bicultural Chinese church will continue to be bright if properly

managed. God will lead the way as long as these churches seek after his will."

13. "... I am optimistic for the bicultural church. As long as there remains immigration and movement between nations there will be a place for bicultural churches. I believe they will increasingly be better at what they do as evolving 'senior' leadership understands what it takes to pastor a multicultural church. I think bicultural churches should not feel in competition with non-bicultural churches and come to realize that it takes all kinds of bodies of believers for all different kinds of people."

14. (Participant noted he grew up thirty years in his church. He felt his experience has been one of reflecting on the differences of living in a materialistic society and trying to understand his role as a Christian. The Chinese church has shown him there's the continual tie to the Chinese culture. He sees lacking mainstream societal interaction. His outlook/hope is that the bicultural church would provide or allow CBCs to grow in their relationships to each other and be encouraged in their relationship with God."

15. "Ultimately we are caught in a vicious cycle where the Chinese department wants more English department members to share leadership duties; English department members will not step up because of the reasons cited in this survey. Until the cycle is broken, no progress will be made in the foreseeable future."

16. "My overall experience over the last 12-13 years is positive. I have been able to serve in a unique environment and share my life . . . I grew up in this church and learned how to put others first and put a cause ahead of my own physical needs. My frustration was not being able to make a permanent impact on this church in the form of increasing the number of members like myself. I felt God's role for me at this church was to grow, teach, mentor and make disciples of other CBCs. These types of churches however seem to be best suited for either Chinese speaking only or those English speaking who are truly bilingual. My hope for this church is a change in the church leadership either personnel or structure."

17. "I have stayed in this particular bicultural church for over 15 years and in a bicultural Chinese church environment for 22 years. My overall experience is that we as CBCs (and younger members of the congregation) need to earn our respect. If we act responsibly and serve the church responsibly, the elders and Chinese congregation will

appreciate what we have done and respect our opinion and suggestions. When we have conflicts our view will be recognized and compromise can be reached so that the harmony of the church will not be affected. The experience has been fulfilling as I have grown a lot in Christ and have also grown to appreciate my identity (Chinese culture) even more. I wish that we would be able to accommodate more people from different nationalities but I understand it may be difficult for them to fit in. My hope for the bicultural church in the future is to allow for more control to go in the hands of the up and coming young leaders (mostly from the English congregation). It is a tough thing to surrender control in any setting in life, but for the betterment of the bicultural church, a proper transfer of power must be in place to ensure the growth of a healthy church."

18. "Overall it's been very fulfilling . . . I treasure being in a bicultural church—I keep ties, and I'm near my parents. I can speak both languages quite fluently (benefits from both Cantonese and English side mentors). Being bicultural allows me to serve on both sides; I learned a lot from serving."

19. "I had less awareness when I was younger—I have grown up to appreciate the Chinese church; joint things/links with the Chinese congregation has been really important to me."

20. "I have been 24 years in a bicultural Chinese church environment. My experience so far has been sufficient to develop a strong relationship with God, going on to greater maturity. It's been a good and fulfilling experience . . . because I owe my spiritual life to the church. Without the church I would be long gone, and with the church I am healthy. I think the bicultural Chinese church is disappearing because the children are all English speaking. As I see it, the next generation will feature English churches, with perhaps a small Chinese outreach. So I think the bicultural Chinese church is fast becoming English speaking (highly educated) church which will be more and more able to integrate with other English speaking churches and lose its ethnicity. And I think the faster that happens the better. I only hope to keep that which is Christ like and godly in our Chinese church heritage."

21. "My whole life I've grown spiritually in my home church, but as I left for university I grew exponentially more. That was due partly due to the stretching of the mind that university does to you [and] partly due to my on campus Christian fellowship that I was heavily involved in, and also due to the Caucasian church I attend while at university . . ."

22. "I've been in a bicultural church for 22 years. My overall experience hasn't been too good or fruitful, but the past few years have been amazing, one hundred fold better than the rest of my life . . . Until a few years ago I wasn't growing, spreading the Word or maturing into a man of God. I merely attended and did some faithless serving. However in the past few years I've been growing, serving with purpose and realizing some of my callings for my life. God and worshipping Him has given me purpose. I haven't found anything missing or lacking but what I have noticed is how most people don't actually serve at church. My hope is that everyone eventually will step up and take responsibility of the church, serving and doing what we've been called to do—spread the Word of God."

23. No response

24. "I have remained all my life in a bicultural Chinese church environment and while studying in university; currently I am going to a mainstream church."

25. "All my life I've been in this environment. My experience is that it is a part of who I am, CBC for life. The experience has just begun to be fulfilling and meaningful. Both I and my brother are studying to be in ministry and we came from a church that was basically nothing . . . maybe it has everything to do with God. Chinese people need to lighten up; everyone's so stiff and serious. The church environment with a CM and EM are better off than if they only had one congregation because there is no way CBCs and straight up Chinese people would get along perfectly. What is lacking are people who are able to bridge both cultures. I would consider them missionaries because this is not an easy place to be in. My hope is that bicultural Chinese churches become multicultural churches. Thinking ahead, what happens if I'm in ministry in a Chinese church and I marry a white girl? Wow what a thought. There is no other way but to go multicultural. We must change. Chinese people must give up their tradition for something that adapts to the culture here. They must be willing to have the younger culture take some leadership. They must accept that they are not in China anymore. If not, goodbye church."

26. "I have remained in a bicultural Chinese church for nine years . . . my spiritual journey so far is one of wandering between ministries and marked by sequences of success, struggle, change, and growth. My experience at my church has been fulfilling . . . I grew with other members of my church in fellowship, in joys and struggles. A particular

meaning that I derive from my experience . . . is the idea of integrating two generations and two cultures embedded in two ministries by engaging in joint activities that encourage awareness and understanding in two very different perspectives, traditions, and values through joint liaison, joint fellowship, and joint services . . . my outlook of the bicultural Chinese church [is that] members of such churches will grow steadily as one body in Christ through intergenerational and intercultural programs developed by Christian organizations guided by Christian leadership."

27. (Participant is age 27). "It's been about 22 years. My experience has been fulfilling . . . I have established relationships, learned a lot about God and experienced spiritual growth. Sometimes I feel that congregations at other churches are more alive. The programs/classes are more modern and appealing elsewhere. I hope that the Chinese church will be more open to new people with different lifestyles, new ideas and ways of doing things."

28. "Nearly 25 years . . . The Chinese church experience has sometimes been fulfilling (during special events), but usually not. It's unfulfilling when people realize that these traditions and structures are holding us back from experiencing God . . ."

29. "Yes this church has been fulfilling . . . I do hold ownership to my own Chinese culture . . . Jesus is real and I have experienced him through attending this church, meeting friends, being taught by pastors and teachers . . . I want to give back to the younger people attending this church. I want them to experience what I have experienced . . ."

30. (Participant is age 46). "I've spent 40 years in a bilingual church environment. The biggest regret is that I am contributing to the segregation of the body of Christ rather than the unifying of the body here in my city."[/NL 1-30]

Summary on Section 6: Most participants used the key descriptive words—*meaningful* and *fulfilling*—to express their overall experience in positive terms. Many commented on how appreciative they were in being given opportunities to serve, finding an extended family and supportive community; participants were thankful for their spiritual growth and being helped to develop and mature in their relationship with God. One participant commented that it has been both fulfilling and unfulfilling realizing that some traditions and structures hold us back from experiencing God (case 28). Participants gave a list of things they felt were lacking which included: the need for a greater focus to listen and work with God; focus on biblical training with relevant application. Focus on a process of transferring (empower) leadership to the EM; address segregation (case 30) and have more openness to new people with different lifestyles, ideas, and ways of doing things. Equip the church to interact easily and comfortably with other races. Seek out more people who can bridge both cultures. Encourage more intercultural and intergenerational programs. Encourage a multicultural vision and support more interaction with other nationalities and mainstream society. Cultivate more mentorship and personal coaching; encourage more people to serve in their calling. Leadership needs to take responsibility to make change.

7. Hindsight can be 20/20

1. "... I believe acceptance and friendship will determine whether you stay in church or not ... If I were the bicultural Chinese church I would bring a CBC youth pastor in, someone who can relate ... is passionate about development."

2. "I think there needs to be a change in mentality ... the parent congregation needs to see their role differently ... from being overseers and minimize change to people who empower and prepare individuals to make the right choices in change ... there needs to be trust ... sure its scary ... but it is the reality of growing up."

3. no response

4. no response

5. "If the situations leading to my contemporaries' departure happened differently, they would likely still be in the church. To provide young CBCs the place to grow up and mature and find a real and fulfilling Christian life, its necessary to be relevant, something that people can relate too, but also the realization that the Christian walk is challenging, never underestimating that fact and hence preventing people from becoming complacent. To prevent younger generations from leaving, I don't think I would be equipped of making such a change."

6. no response.

7. no response

8. "Improving communication on both sides so that they dialogue rather than merely report to one another. Share thoughts, pray with each other—ask and give forgiveness. Essentially I am advocating that

the Chinese church be Christian. To respect ALL people, regardless of race, social status, looks, etc . . . these are all heart issues they require hearts to take seriously God's call to follow and pick up our crosses—which in this case, is our race and racial baggage that comes with it."

9. "People being sensitive to one another in remarks; people's vulnerability, confidentiality needs to be protected. Need to think of the consequences of being insensitive" (wide range of things here).

10. no response

11. Ways to prevent younger generations from leaving: encourage mentorship; encourage sports involvement; begin praying partner system (which forms close friendships, in-depth discussions over shallow conversations).

12. "The church needs to be more sensitive to the needs of the younger generations. The older generations need to set good examples and serve together with them. Properly trained pastors who understand such environments will also help with the process. We need to have proper programs and people in place to deal with younger generations so they don't have to seek help elsewhere all the time. The church should be a safe environment for them to grow in. Helping the younger generations to involve God more in their lives would encourage them to stay in their home church."

13. "Too big a question to answer here! It deserves a thesis all on its own!" (Note: participant perhaps has anticipated the findings of this book).

14. (Participant feels the model will flourish if . . .) "all the generations serve and support each other. Being open and honest is very important to be able to adapt to the societal influences. Its important for the leaders to realize its one church; that individuals approach decisions together as a group; over time allow for intergenerational leadership and allow room to make mistakes—allow for individuals to grow in their understanding of what it means to be on a life journey with God—whether they stay in the bicultural model or not, that CBCs [grow in] a deeper relationship with God."

15. "If my CBC friends were still here, I would feel more attached to the church and the issues would be less apparent. CBCs will continue to leave unless the English department has more motivated leaders and this includes myself."

16. "I think those contemporaries would still be in church today and thriving spiritually. If the Chinese side had more respect for the English

side, I think things would've been much better. We would've had sufficient manpower, avoided burnout and avoided long lapses without a pastor. Ultimately we would've grown in quantity and quality of Christian members."

17. "I don't know if anything that could have saved the ones that had left. Some have left because they just strayed from the Christian walk, and the ones that have gone on to different churches left for personal reasons or for reasons that would need the whole church to change for him/her. The bicultural church could learn to be more sensitive when making decisions for the church and can certainly learn to respect each other more . . ."

18. ". . . have a consistent clear vision for English ministry. When an English pastor departs things can get flakey and unclear. To have spiritual mentors for CBCs to help people grow (I try to keep contact with former Sunday school students—its very important to keep in contact with them—have that link to keep the momentum going). Have people who know how to do the ministry and what not to step on (know what others didn't like)."

19. "The biggest common factor of people leaving is they didn't have any deep discipling or accountability relationships; if they had it they may have stayed. The preventive measure is for someone to invest in their lives—ideally in the teen years (older mentors) . . . we have a lack of people to do this on the CBC side, people slip through the cracks."

20. ". . . I know my parents generation worked hard to build the church. And I know those involved in service work hard and I think they've done well with what they were given. The church has deficiencies in all kinds of areas. If I were to pick one, I would choose to increase the quality of teaching—increase it so that through the church service we can hear God more clearly. My guess is that with good teaching comes instruction for balanced spiritual growth leading to joy and contagious faith and deep relationship with God . . ."

21. ". . . If I was part of the older generation, I would have tried to get to know them more, talk to them more, and try to understand their viewpoint. Better communication in general all around in the church between generations would be greatly helpful."

22. ". . . A lot has to change but it's really dependent on each individual's needs and each church's needs. To prevent younger generations from leaving leadership needs to step up, there needs to be suitable

programs, sermons need to be more geared to the general congregation not a particular generation or age group."

23. No response

24. "... serious study and emphasis on God's word leading to true worship. This breaks through cultural biases to true sight of the church and its purpose and opens up a view of God's glory. The truth will set us free! The studying of God's word and prayer are a good thing to focus on because they are very tangible. With a functional church that knows the word of God, race should never be an issue . . . In a Chinese church we tend to avoid confrontation and we deal very loosely with many of the harder issues. Preaching I have found emphasizes analogies rather than in depth look at Scripture. Many who attend do not know where to find answers in Scripture to many topics. The hard topics must be faced . . . (participant further emphasized the need for truthful preaching that causes one to face sin in their life) . . ."

25. "We just need resources to keep people from not leaving. RESOURCES!!! A good English pastor can make all the difference. A good youth worker can make a huge difference. Finding people who understand CBC culture is so difficult, but those are the people we need. We need people to get out of their Chinese minds and start thinking Canadian. We need old Chinese men to set aside their pride and to learn something new. We need a willing younger generation to be patient and work with the older generation. We need to teach old dogs new tricks . . . now how would you do such a thing?"

26. "I cannot recall particular situations due to cultural or generational differences . . . that led to the departure of my contemporaries . . ."

27. ". . . church experience needs to be more relevant to our lives . . . the connection needs to be emphasized in a greater way. Reach out to younger generations in the most effective way. There are so many ways people can praise God."

28. "I think they would still be in this church. What needed to change? Stronger leadership and a breakaway from the Chinese congregational governance. I don't mind if people leave our church to go to another church . . . as long as they can grow in their relationship with God there."

29. No response.

30. (Participant expressed that she would like to complete a MCS degree and teach) ". . . We need solid bible teaching, not the watered down stuff we normally get."

Summary on Section 7: CBC participants provided a list of preventative changes they would have liked to see in their churches that might have detoured CBCs who left their English congregations. Top of the list was (*public ministry-prophetic leadership*) the need to increase the quality of preaching and teaching (be relevant) to hear God more clearly. The need to improve communication (*reconciling relationships-shalom leadership*) between the OBC and CBC congregations—and to be sensitive to one another when making decisions; be Christians, share thoughts, pray with each other, ask and give forgiveness. Serve and support each other; be open and honest. Encourage mentorship, prayer partners, in-depth discussions, invest in discipling and accountability relationships, provide needed resources. Several summed up their perception as a need for proper respect towards the EM. One participant advocated for respect for all people regardless of race or social status. Participants want this environment to be a safe, welcoming context where people can find acceptance and friendship. A number of participants made recommendations for the leadership structure (*leadership model*). Some were comfortable with the current dependent model but calling for improvements in intergenerational leadership and to ensure that a good EM pastor was in place that is passionate about development. Other participants were calling for the Chinese leaders to empower and trust the EM to operate more independently and to have a more consistent clear vision for EM. One participant felt that what was needed is "stronger leadership and a breakaway from the Chinese congregational governance."

Appendix G

Letter to Focus Group Leaders / Focus Group Responses

Letter to Focus Group Leaders

(Abstract was attached to this correspondence)
Matthew Todd
BGU doctoral student.
January 4, 2014

Open Letter to Church Pastor and Leadership Focus Group:
    I am a doctoral dissertation student with BGU in transformational leadership. I approached your pastor in 2013 for consent to gather a leadership team / focus group (a group of leaders either in a Chinese bicultural church or who have come from a Chinese bicultural church) to seek your permission if you would participate in reading a *very brief* review of one of the key survey data findings with CBC adults. This is intended to be a concise read and short exercise for you the participant. Your representative pastor signaled that the focus group was in agreement to receive the *confidential* data upon my completion of the findings. The data stems from a summary of qualitative research done with 60 CBC adults and 30 English ministry pastors over a three-year period as to a few top reasons why CBC adults leave Chinese churches in BC and Alberta. The quantity of responses makes the findings statistically significant. In brief, I also include a condensed form of my hypothesis and present one of the optional recommendations. My aim is to create a way to possibly change some of the *culture* of

congregations experiencing this type of attrition in hopes of minimizing the "exodus" trend. Your focus group contribution represents a tiny action-oriented step; I am requesting if you would confidentially read the one of the findings (*I make a polite integrity request that you please do not forward my research findings as they will be copyrighted and published in their entirety in late summer*) and provide a little feedback or critique. Your comments, critique and recommendation to the action plans do not have to be long; half to one page of feedback is more than sufficient. Reflect on what you are succinctly reading and what you might suggest. I am seeking your advice and wisdom on the motif of *giving permission* to English ministry congregations in Chinese churches to *be given decision making powers*. What might your leadership team recommend, in brief, to an action plan? Late summer 2014 a published volume of the entire 384-page research will be in circulation and made available to the churches.

Starting Point for Investigation / Hypothesis

The intention of this study has been to identify key factors why English-speaking Chinese adults exit (defect, apostatize, leave) Canadian Chinese bicultural churches in BC and Alberta areas and recommend some leadership strategies towards the longitudinal retention of these adults with English-ministry congregations, so that transformational leaders can strategize towards developing healthier congregations that maximize missional capacity. My hypothesis at the start was that, besides cultural, theological, and discipleship topics, the model and structure for English ministries could likely be an area of concern to be addressed.

Purpose Statement

This research on the "silent exodus" is comprised of a qualitative study with sixty in-depth open-ended emailed questionnaires of former church dropouts and remain-ins selected from a wide spectrum of circumstances and bilingual church affiliations. The purpose was to identify and establish certain common patterns and risk factors (i.e., cultural, organizational, spiritual, and personal) that may contribute to the occurrence of a silent exodus. It is recognized that there will likely be multiple "causes" or factors; each church may have its own unique circumstances due to its own history and cultural practices. However, the measurable outcome for this proposed project is: (1) the successful attempt to identify and articulate patterns and common dynamics pertinent to the Chinese bicultural churches that are contributing to a silent exodus, and (2) the formulation of a list of potential risk factors. The ultimate ideal goal of learning from past unfavorable experiences is to prevent history from repeating itself and to go forward with healthy transformational leadership insights into the future. The intended outcomes of producing a self-diagnostic checklist of potential risk factors for churches to use are: some healthy leadership recommendations for change and the potential articulation of alternative Chinese bicultural church models based on research.

Conclusions of the Study

Because this is an extensive dissertation, my statements regarding the conclusions and findings are economized and parsimonious. I only focus on one cluster of findings with CBCs who dropped out of Chinese churches as that is sufficient enough to warrant pursuing one recommendation.

This research was able to factually substantiate anecdotal reporting of a silent exodus of CBC adults from Chinese churches in the greater Vancouver BC and Alberta regions. The dissertation did explore and propose a number of transformational leadership strategies towards longitudinal retention of CBC adults so leaders could strategize towards community transformation and lasting congregations that maximize missional capacity. The literature review explored historic and present Chinese church models that have provided solutions to retain English-speaking congregants. Mindful of some of the deficiencies of such models with an aging and acculturating English ministry demographic, the dissertation investigated research on leading change and transformational leadership. It is clear that most (not all) current English ministries have been structurally bequeathed an associated dependent English congregational model. The dissertation further explored a theological basis for empowerment and why there can be a necessity for a paradigm shift to facilitate expanded mission, growth and leadership capacity for the English congregation. Core qualitative research design and fieldwork execution required gathering and subsequent processing and analysis. The qualitative research conducted with participants from diverse Chinese church affiliations produced survey findings that have established the factual grounds and key factors of why CBC adults exodus; here is one portion of those findings—as to why CBCs leave—in priority descending order:

1. Their life stage transition needs were being unfulfilled within a Chinese church.
2. The overemphasis on Chinese cultural identity and ethnocentrism.

3. Issues with Church leadership, organizational structure, and program issues.
4. Control issues with church power and politics.
5. Loneliness and the attempt to seek friends, fellowship, and relationships.

The results of the qualitative research also identified patterns and common dynamics with Chinese bicultural churches that contribute to a silent exodus and potential risk factors. Based on the examination of the research findings (with clergy, remain-in CBC adults, and dropout CBC adults), CBC adult recommendations, theological reflection, transformational leadership studies, and the sociological impetus for cultural integration, one key strategy towards the retention of English-speaking adults from Chinese Canadian churches could be through establishing parallel associated *independent* English congregational models;[1] this recognizes a linkage between the process of acculturation and the imperative to authentically leverage mission and growth potential. The recommendation requires a courageous negotiation with the Chinese church leadership to give power away to (empower) the English ministry leadership/congregation so an alternative associated model can be established. It is anticipated that this would free up a governance framework for strategizing, reducing the exodus, and permitting transformational leadership practices that contribute to shalom. As a member of a focus group, *you the reader* have a part in the action-oriented step of providing a brief feedback on the hypothesis, one cluster of survey findings, and one provided recommendation.

I want to thank you in advance for your response and look forward to hearing back a summary from your leadership focus group. Please note that I included a rough copy of an abstract on page five if that is helpful. Unfortunately, the nature of this exercise does not go beyond this framework; however, I did indicate to your pastor/leader/coordinator that after you have completed the short feedback, I would be open to meeting with your group to field questions or simply share.

In conclusion I would request if you could have your summary feedback back to me by or before the end of January 2014.

1. Parallel associated *independent* English ministries congregation. Parallel refers to sharing (being sponsored, negotiated rental costs) a facility or congregational meeting place in or adjacent to the Chinese church congregation of origin. Associated refers to the family, cultural heritage, sense of affinity, and intentional voluntary mutual joint ministry and relationship linkages. It reflects the mutual retention of healthy long-term ties and a form of unity in the body of Christ. Independent refers to being registered as a separate legal-constitutional entity in all matters of governance; full autonomy in operational, financial, structural, and ministerial (with a multiethnic/multicultural inclusive mission and vision). This is a fully empowered, autonomous, self-managed model.

Appreciative
Matthew Todd

Three Church Focus Group Responses in Their Entirety

CBC Focus Group Feedback from a Multicultural Church Plant Model[2]

January 16, 2014

Response to Matthew Todd's "Silent Exodus" Thesis
Four of us (all men; pastor, two board members, lay leader) met on January 15 to talk about the ideas presented in the subject thesis that CBCs are leaving Chinese Churches because:

1. Their life stage transition needs were being unfulfilled within a Chinese church.
2. The over emphasis on Chinese cultural identity and ethnocentrism.
3. Issues with Church leadership, organizational structure and program issues.
4. Control issues with church power and politics.
5. Loneliness and the attempt to seek friends, fellowship and relationships.

And that that Chinese Churches can curb their departure by setting up "parallel associated independent English ministries congregations," defined as:

> Parallel associated independent English ministries congregation. Parallel refers to sharing (being sponsored, negotiated rental costs) a facility or congregational meeting place in or adjacent to the Chinese church congregation of origin. Associated refers to the family, cultural heritage, sense of affinity, and intentional voluntary mutual joint ministry and relationship linkages. It reflects the mutual retention of healthy long-term ties and a form of unity in the body of Christ. Independent refers to being registered as a separate legal-constitutional entity in all matters of governance; full autonomy in operational, financial, structural and ministerial

---

2. In a follow-up dinner with this focus group, I asked if any of them would go back to an arrangement where my recommended model was in effect with the Chinese church. Conditionally, half the responses were affirmative.

(with a multiethnic/multicultural inclusive mission and vision). This is a fully empowered, autonomous, self-managed model.

1. The group (all have left a Chinese Church and are currently attending the same multi-ethnic church plant) resonated generally with the reasons for the silent exodus,
   a. except (2). No one left their church because of an over emphasis on Chinese culture and identity
   b. more people identify (1) and (5) for their reasons for leaving.
2. One person in the group feels a "parallel associated independent EM congregation" can work if the expectations are clearly set out at the onset.
3. The others in the group are less optimistic. They feel the cause of the silent exodus is born out of differences and conflicts in core values and way-of-doing-things, and they ask "how does this model eliminate these conflicts?"

   For example, in spite of the parallel independent structure, conflicts over use of facility are inevitable—especially if the CM feels they "built" the building. Furthermore, if children of the CM are "sent" to the EM, there will also be inevitable conflicts over "what" and "how" the kids are being taught. If these conflicts cannot be resolved, then history will repeat itself as the CM develops its own English ministry. Then conflict over schedules will emerge, and the EM will need to find its own facilities.
4. One person points out that at issue is also the EM sense of "identity," and much like when a CBC marries, "leaving" may be necessary for them to develop their own identity.
5. And one person points out that for the Kingdom, dispersing CBC disciples to the rest of society may not be bad for the Gospel. It may be an act of God for evangelism. And the exodus is not a problem that needs solving.

CBC Focus Group Feedback from a Mature Dependent English Ministry Model

February 4, 2014

Your recommendation that historically ethnically Chinese Church leadership to allow English ministry congregations decision making powers is one key track on the road to healthiness in CBC English ministries. You have correctly identified key factors on why English speaking Chinese adults leave traditionally Chinese churches. Thus, in our community, our senior leadership (Board of Elders) has even tried to de-emphasize the word "Chinese" in [church name mentioned] by transitioning to the term [various generic church names were given deemphasizing ethnic exclusivity] (much like how the Hong Kong Shanghai Bank of China has been shortened to "HSBC")

We have also moved to a multi-site, multi-congregational model. Each site and congregation has been given since the inception of this model, a fair bit of autonomy and oversight through the leadership of a key "Congregational Pastor" (CP) with his own leadership team. Thus it is up to the CP to lead change and transform existing leadership. Key leadership traits of CPs are: spiritual and emotional maturity, patience, a very strong cultural intelligence, wisdom in leadership, among others. Therefore, I agree that your submission of parallel associated independent English congregational models would be a good beginning. This though needs to be well supported and endorsed by senior leadership, senior pastor and any other supervisory pastors. I, for example, support our English ministries as a coordinator and also general Pastor of [office title the pastor holds currently]. All ministries need to be funded fairly and well, for example. You are preaching to the already converted in this case. I need to emphasize that not every pastor, be they from a Chinese, Western Caucasian, European, Singaporean, Korean, or other Asian background, by their very ethnicity, is able to be the change agent in transitioning English ministries to a healthy autonomy. Their cultural intelligence, spiritual and emotional maturity, character, chemistry with team and congregation, prayer life, people skills, and many other intangibles are a real key to changing the CULTURE of their own congregation and well as the whole church in general. To empower English congregations or any other congregation requires a general cultural shift for the entire church.

This said, there are many other factors that glue a community together. People will still come and go. Issues of relationship within a community, seeking life partners, healthy or unhealthy dating and marriage relationships, lack of wooden dogmatism ... the willingness to accept, live with and receive various theological positions (e.g. young earth, old earth creation, various views of creation or the end times), sense of belonging, purpose, community, engaging one's spiritual gifts, preaching and teaching style and culture, sense of being loved and cared for, one's acceptance no matter where he/she is on the faith spectrum, etc. all have a bearing on one's connection with the local church community.

Those are some of my thoughts for now on your materials, Matthew. Hope this helps.

Blessings always, [focus group leader's name]

Focus Group Feedback from a Mature Interdependent/Dependent English Ministry Model

January 29, 2014

I want to respond to your request. As I have already told you that four people from our English congregation agreed to be part of your Project. Maybe I should give you a bit of their background before I continue.

 A. [Female focus group leader's name]—in her late 70s and is 2nd or 3rd generation CBC. She became Christian through [church name] and has been attending [church name] ever since her early days. She has three grown daughters in their 40s (?) and all married to Scots!!! One of them doesn't go to church. The other two used to attend [this church] and now attend [a multicultural church] in Richmond. Please see their responses as attached.

 B. [Male focus group leader's name]—in his early 60s and 3rd or 4th gen CBC. Also, [name] was raised in [this church] as his grandparents were faithful church anchors. He is one of the elders and plays in the music team. He already replied to you earlier.

 C. [Male focus group leader's name]—in his early 60s. A 2nd gen ABC from [United States] (I think). He is a [university professor] and also an elder. He has two young adult daughters, both working in Vancouver. They (daughters) used to attend [this church] but now attend other churches. He won't have time to reply to your question until this weekend. I will forward his answer to you once I receive it.

 D. [Female focus group participant's name]—in her mid or late 20s. Graduated from [university] a few years ago. Both parents and two younger sisters also attend [this church]. Father is a 2 gen ABC and mother a 2 gen CBC. So, it makes her a 3 gen CBC. She is active in [music ministry] ... She has not replied to me yet. I asked her because she may have some insights as why her peers who left [this church].

Hope it gives you some background info and you can put the puzzles together.

Cheers and happy Chinese New Year!

[Focus group pastor/leader's name]

Email from B. focus group member

January 6, 2014

Having read your abstract and attached memo from [Lead pastor / focus group leader], I feel a small focus group from our church membership might be a good idea. I know Pastor [name] has also suggested [other names of group members who were part of this focus group] to give feedback, but there may be others . . . and our Young adults who could contribute to providing feedback to your study.

My initial reaction to your study was that it seems that this is exactly what our church is going through. I just had drafted a business case for our Session to review to present to the members of our Chinese Speaking Elders about the need to change our English name of the church, as in a sense it is self-limiting. We have cross this road a few times in the past years and each time the members of the Chinese Congregation did not support the need to change from [Chinese church name] to a more community focus name like [gives an example of a community church name].

It seemed more important and significant to the Chinese speaking members to maintain our cultural identity, however, there were others who also wanted to preserve our cultural heritage even though they were CBC, but had strong family links and history with the church when we were in China town.

In the business case I have drafted, the strategy is to maintain our name as Chinese [name of church] church but have a sub-branch giving the English Ministry a separate name under [new English church congregation name]. So our tact is not to eliminate the original name but to give a name as a ministry of [Church name]. For example [new church name] English Ministry Service.

I was raised and baptized in our church and attended it when I was three years old to now that I am 63 this year. During those years I had also come and gone. I have watched the changes occurred through the decades and noticed that our church tends to be one that support young (in terms of maturity) Christians or those going into the Ministry and when they get to a certain stage of growth they move on, but the members still keep in touch periodically as they sense their roots are still with our church.

I am not sure if breaking away from the mother church, which is ethnocentric, is the best way of retaining CBC membership. I think it has to do more with how the leadership can work with both congregations and servicing their specific needs. At one time I would tend to agree with your recommendation but as I have grown in our church and watched people come and go, I think what is more important is not to think of our church as being limited to four walls, in fact our church may be the larger community of members who have moved on to other churches and still maintaining a sense of connectedness with us. Even those members or adherents who have moved to other countries like Australia, Singapore or Hong Kong or United States still stay in touch with us and often ask how our church is managing. People who I have not seen every Sunday, often come back when we have major fund raising events, they do come to support us.

I think how we conduct our services including worship, and how well the ministers connect with our English congregational members *is more important in the sense of retention than having a separate parallel church within a church.*

These are just some of my initial thoughts, although I know this is a very complex issue, therefore I think to hear directly from other members in the English Service in a small focus group may be worth your while.

[Leader's name]
Elder [church name]

Email forwarded from focus group leader A.

(Note: this CBC focus group leader felt it was important to communicate the factors as to why her mature adult daughter's families were no longer attending their English-language congregation—in other words, why they exited the Chinese bicultural church. Some of the transcripts are included here of two of her daughters).

Email from daughter number #1 to mother:

January 9, 2014

[Mother's church name] has a strong cultural focus, [daughter's current multicultural church] has *more community-based focus*. [Multicultural church's name] emphasizes on leaving your personal comfort zone and taking chances in ways that positively change the world [that] challenged us in important ways.

Our level of *service was very high* at [mom's church]. It had become tiresome instead of joyful and were still receiving multiple requests to take on new projects. In our last year we were involved in four areas (youth, Sunday school, board of Mgrs, music team) and over the six months we were invited to take on / start up three other ministries. In a way, it feeds into the first point, as everything was designed to sustain the inner circle without having any real impact on life outside [the ethnic church].

[Daughter discussed that commuting became an issue] . . . Personally I was struggling with the idea of taking on greater responsibility at work. [My new multicultural church] after the SOUL of Leadership mentoring program which *empowered me to employ my God-given talents more visibly in the marketplace.*

Regarding the thesis topic . . . the phrasing assumes that migration of 2nd generation believers is a problem that needs to be resolved. [My husband] and I moved our family to a church that allows us the freedom to focus on teaching our kids that we are called to share His love with the whole world. We did not leave the church altogether, nor has our faith commitment to Christ suffered. *I cannot say that I see it as a "problem."*

Email from daughter number #2 to mother:

January 10, 2014

For me [leaving] wasn't about leaving an ethnic church so much as going to a church that had a place for young mom's and where others we might invite to church would feel comfortable going to (e.g., the nannies next door to us—one white, one Trinidadian). I suppose being 3rd and 4th generation in Canada there is less of a felt cultural need to be with Chinese, especially as in our family Chinese language and cultural practices ties are not highly prized or seen as necessary or important and have been emphasized less with each succeeding generation (in Richmond and RCS, many families celebrate Chinese New Years in a big way and their kids must go to Chinese school). Interestingly when we moved to Richmond some churches were too Chinese for our kids—even if they had a English speaking service . . . for me I could go either way but I want my family to feel at home in the church they go to. Sometimes people can be speaking English but still perhaps be thinking/communicating/relating in Chinese ways (e.g., saving face, teaching/learning style). On the other hand perhaps part of the reason I feel more at ease at [names a multicultural church] is that there area a lot of Asians and a good mix of various generations of Asian-Canadian (i.e., some recently moved to Canada and some who've been here a long time but many are fluent in English) and different cultures are celebrated (e.g., outreach events making laksa [Malaysian curry] or watching "jiro dreams of sushi" [movie about a sushi maker]. Whereas I see more of a separation at [names a church] between recent arrivals and a largely white population . . . once a year the [names the same church] has an international potluck lunch because it is missions month but at [names her present multicultural church] every community potluck is international just by the very nature and makeup of the congregation. Mind you I am married to [names her Caucasian husband], who felt awkward at first at [names mom's church] when everyone except the [English pastor's family] and [one lay person] was obviously Chinese . . . [she spoke highly of a multicultural congregation that helped her with her life stage needs as a young mother].

Bibliography

Aikman, David. *Jesus in Beijing*. Washington, DC: Regnery, 2006.
Alumkal, Antony W. *Asian American Evangelical Churches: Race, Ethnicity, and Assimilation*. New York: LFB Scholarly, 2003.
Anderson, Ray S. *The Soul of Ministry: Forming Leaders for God's People*. Louisville: Westminster John Knox, 1997.
Bakke, Dennis. *Joy at Work*. Seattle: PVG, 2005.
Bakke, Ray. "Ethnicity in the Church—Is It Still Okay to Be Jewish?" In *A Theology as Big as the City*, 172–77. Downers Grove: InterVarsity, 1997.
Barro, Antonio C. "Unity and Diversity in the Family of God." Faculdade Teologica Sul Americana. Londrina, Brazil, 2003. http://www.ediaspora.net/ACB_article3.html.
Bays, Daniel H., ed. *Christianity in China: From the Eighteenth Century to the Present*. Redwood City, CA: Stanford University Press, 1996.
———. *A New History of Christianity in China*. Chichester, UK: Wiley-Blackwell, 2012.
Bibby, Reginald. *Restless Gods: The Renaissance of Religion in Canada*. Toronto: Stoddart, 2002.
Blackaby, Henry T., and Richard Blackaby. *Spiritual Leadership*. Nashville: Broadman & Holman, 2001.
Booth, Wayne C., et al. "The Ethics of Research." In *The Craft of Research*, 285–88. Chicago: University of Chicago Press, 2003.
Bramadat, Paul, and David Seljak, eds. *Christianity and Ethnicity in Canada*. Toronto: University of Toronto Press, 2008.
———. *Religion and Ethnicity in Canada*. Toronto: Pearson Education Canada, 2005.
Branson, Mark Lau, and Juan F. Martinez. *Churches, Cultures and Leadership: A Practical Theology of Congregations and Ethnicities*. Downers Grove: InterVarsity, 2011.
Breaux, Mike. "A Mad Multi-Gen Strategy That Works, Dude." *Leadership*, Spring 2005, 44. http://www.christianitytoday.com/le/2005/spring/6.44.html.
Brueggemann, Walter. "Preaching to Exiles." In *Cadences of Home: Preaching among Exiles*, 1–14. Louisville: Westminster John Knox, 1997.
Busto, Rudy V. "The Gospel according to the Model Minority? Hazarding an Interpretation of Asian American Evangelical College Students." Chap. 5 in *New Spiritual Homes: Religion and Asian Americans*, edited by David K. Yoo. Honolulu: University of Hawaii Press, 1999.

Cairns, Earle E. "To the Jew First." Chap. 5 in *Christianity through the Centuries: A History of the Christian Church*. Grand Rapids: Zondervan, 1981.
Carlson, Kenneth P. "Patterns in Development of the English Ministry in a Chinese Church." Chap. 8 in *Asian American Christianity Reader*, edited by Viji Nakka-Cammauf and Timothy Tseng. Castro Valley, CA: ISAAC, 2009.
Cha, Peter. "Finding a Church Home." Chap. 10 in *Following Jesus without Dishonoring Your Parents*, edited by Jeanette Yep et al. Downers Grove: InterVarsity, 1998.
Cha, Peter, et al., eds. *Growing Healthy Asian American Churches*. Downers Grove: InterVarsity, 2006.
Chai, Karen, J. "Competing for the Second Generation." In *Gatherings in Diaspora: Religious Communities and the New Immigration*, edited by R. Stephen Warner and Judith Wittner, 295–331. Philadelphia: Temple University Press, 1998.
Chan, Joyce. *Rediscover the Fading Memories: The Early Chinese Canadian Christian History*. Burnaby, BC: Chinese Christian Mission of Canada, 2013.
Chan, K. K. "Christianity in China." Lecture from the Overture 2: China course at the Bakke Graduate University, Hong Kong campus, April 12, 2012.
Chan, Yuet Ming. "The Challenge of Reaching Canadian Born Chinese." *Challenger*, December 1980, 5–6.
Chin, Steven. "God's Double Blessing on a Church." In Yau, *Winning Combination*.
"Chinese Canadian Teenagers 1910–1947." Critical Thinking Consortium. Source Docs, online resource for teachers. http://sourcedocs.tc2.ca/history-docs/topics/chinese-canadian-history/chinese-canadian-teenagers-1910-1947.html.
Chinese Coordination Center of World Evangelism–USA & Canada. Conference on the Challenges and Future of English Ministries, Tuscarora Inn & Conference Center, Mt. Bethel, Pennsylvania, November 30–December 4, 2009. http://l2foundation.org/2009/conference-on-the-challenges-and-future-of-english-ministries.
Chua, Amy. *Battle Hymn of the Tiger Mother*. New York: Penguin, 2011.
Chuang, D. J. *Asian American Churches: An Introductory Survey*. Leadership Network, April 16, 2007. http://leadnet.org/report_on_asian_american_churches.
———. "Next Gen Multi-Asian Churches." http://djchuang.com/church-directory/next-gen-multi-asian-churches.
Citizenship and Immigration Canada. "Annual Report to Parliament on Immigration, 2012." http://www.cic.gc.ca/english/pdf/pub/annual-report-2012.pdf.
Clark, David K. "Theology in Cultural Context." In *To Know and Love God: Method for Theology*, 99–131. Wheaton, IL: Crossway, 2003.
Clements, Rob. "The Segregated Church." *Faith Today*, July/August 1997, 28–32.
Collins, Jim. *Good to Great: Why Some Companies Don't Make the Leap*. New York: HarperCollins, 2001.
Creswell, John. *Research Design: Qualitative and Quantitative Approaches*. London: Sage, 1994.
Crouch, Andy. *Culture Making: Recovering Our Creative Calling*. Downers Grove: InterVarsity, 2008.
Dennis, Rutledge M. *Biculturalism, Self-Identity and Societal Transformation*. Research in Race and Ethnic Relations 15. Bingley, UK: Emerald, 2008.
De Pree, Max. *Leadership Is an Art*. New York: Doubleday, 2004.
Der, Justin. "ABC Pastor Discouragement and Drop Out: A Study Based on the Responses of 64 Pastors." Stanford University, 2001. http://cacforum.files.wordpress.com/2011/02/abcpastors.pdf.

DeVries, Larry, et al. *Asian Religions in British Columbia*. Vancouver: University of British Columbia Press, 2010.
Dey, Ian. *Qualitative Data Analysis: A User-Friendly Guide for Social Scientists*. London: Routledge, 1993.
DeYoung, Curtiss Paul, et al. *United by Faith: The Multiracial Congregation as an Answer to the Problem of Race*. New York: Oxford University Press, 2003.
Di Giacomo, Michael. "Identity and Change: The Story of the Italian-Canadian Pentecostal Community." *Canadian Journal of Pentecostal-Charismatic Christianity* 2 (2011) 83–130.
Dueck, Dora. "Bridging Cultures in the Church." *Mennonite Brethren Herald* 44, no. 1, January 2005, 4–6.
Durkhiem, Emile. *The Elementary Forms of the Religious Life*. 1912. English translation by Joseph Swain, 1915. New York: Free Press, 1965.
Ebaugh, Helen Rose, and Janet S. Chafetz. *Religion and the New Immigrants*. Walnut Creek, CA: AltaMira, 2000.
———. "Structural Adaptations in Immigrant Congregations." *Sociology of Religion*, 61 (2000) 135–53.
Ediger, Gerald C. *Crossing the Divide: Language Transition among Canadian Mennonite Brethren 1940–1970*. Winnipeg: Centre for Mennonite Brethren Studies, 2001.
Emerson, Michael O., and Christian Smith. *Divided by Faith*. New York: Oxford University Press, 2000.
Eng, Daniel K. "Duplex: Asian American Church Models." Daniel K. Eng's blog, posted July 21, 2013. http://aapastor.wordpress.com/2013/07/24/duplex-asian-american-church-models.
———. "Room for Rent: Asian American Church Models." Daniel K. Eng's blog, posted July 21, 2013. http://aapastor.wordpress.com/2013/07/21/room-for-rent-asian-american-church-models.
———. "Townhouse: Asian American Church Models." Daniel K. Eng's blog, posted August 10, 2013. http://aapastor.wordpress.com/2013/08/10/townhouse-asian-american-church-models.
———. "Triplex: Asian American Church Models." Daniel K. Eng's blog, posted July 21, 2013. http://aapastor.wordpress.com/2013/07/31/triplex-asian-american-church-models.
Erickson, Millard J. *Christian Theology*. Grand Rapids: Baker, 1990.
Evans, James Andrew. "The Impending 'Silent Exodus' of Canadian-Born Chinese Christians from the Canadian Chinese Church." DMin dissertation, Fuller Theological Seminary, 2008.
Faith Werks. http://faithwerks.org.
Fong, Kenneth. *Pursuing the Pearl*. Valley Forge, PA: Judson, 2000.
Foster, Richard J. *Celebration of Discipline: The Path to Spiritual Growth*. San Francisco: HarperCollins, 1998.
Friedman, Edwin H. *Generation to Generation: Family Process in Church and Synagogue*. New York: Guilford, 1985.
Garrod, Andrew, and Robert Kilkenny, eds. *Balancing Two Worlds*. Ithaca, NY: Cornell University Press, 2007.
Gordon, Milton M. *Assimilation in American Life: The Role of Race, Religion, and National Origins*. New York: Oxford University Press, 1964.

Greenleaf, Robert K. *The Power of Servant Leadership.* San Francisco: Berrett-Koehler, 1998.
Grudem, Wayne. *Systematic Theology.* Grand Rapids: Zondervan, 1994.
Guder, Darrell L., ed. *Missional Church: A Vision for the Sending of the Church in North America.* Grand Rapids: Eerdmans, 1998.
Guenther, Bruce L. "Ethnicity and Evangelical Protestants in Canada." Chap. 10 in *Christianity and Ethnicity in Canada*, edited by Paul Bramadat and David Seljak. Toronto: University of Toronto Press, 2008.
———. "From Isolation and Ethnic Homogeneity to Acculturation and Multicultural Diversity: The Mennonite Brethren and Canadian Culture." *Direction* 39, no. 2 (2010) 138–61.
Guest, Kenneth J. *God in Chinatown: Religion and Survival in New York's Evolving Immigrant Community.* New York: New York University Press, 2003.
Guinness, Os. *The Call.* Nashville: Nelson, 2003.
Halverstadt, Hugh F. *Managing Church Conflict.* Louisville: Westminster John Knox, 1991.
Ham, Ken, et al. "Are Black People the Result of a Curse on Ham?" In *One Blood: The Biblical Answer to Racism*, 99–103. Green Forest, AR: Master, 1999.
Heidebrecht, Doug. "Culture Clash: What Do We Mean by 'Culture'?" *Mennonite Brethren Herald* 46, no. 9, September 2007, 9.
Herrington, Jim, et al. *Leading Congregational Change: A Practical Guide for the Transformational Journey.* San Francisco: Jossey-Bass, 2000.
Ho, Koon-Ming, and Yuk-Shuen Wong. "Searching for Manhood: Reflecting Growing Up in a Chinese Way." *Asian Journal of Counseling* 13, no. 2 (2006) 207–34.
Hor, Eugene. "Reforming Church, Culture and our City: The Second-Generation Leadership Diaspora." Eugene Hor's blog, posted November 5, 2007. http://eugenehor.wordpress.com/2007/11/05/the-second-generation-leadership-diaspora.
Hsu, George. "A Question of Identity." Chap. 2 in Yau, *Winning Combination.*
Huang, Jennifer C. "Chinese American Christianity and the Challenges of Diversity." *Chinese around the World*, January 1996, 3.
Intentionally Multicultural Churches Conference. "Continuum on Becoming an Intercultural Church." Conference handout, Richmond, BC, March 30–31, 2001.
———. "Responding to the 'New Reality': Core Values of Intentionally Multicultural Churches." Conference handout, Richmond, BC, March 30–31, 2001.
Jenkins, Orville B. "People Groups and the Homogeneous Unit Concept." Strategy Leader Training, posted March 12, 2003, revised December 7, 2006. http://strategyleader.org/articles/homogeneousunity.html.
Jenkins, Philip. *The Next Christendom: The Coming of Global Christianity.* New York: Oxford University Press, 2011.
Jeung, Russell. "Asian American Pan-Ethnic Formation and Congregational Culture." Chap. 8 in *Religions in Asian America: Building Faith Communities*, edited by Pyong Gap Min and Jung Ha Kim. Walnut Creek, CA: AltaMira, 2002.
———. "The Emerging Second Generation." Lecture at ISAAC Pacific Northwest Asian American Ministry Symposium on Generating Faith: Reaching and Retaining Future Generations, Seattle Pacific University, February 27, 2010.
———. *Faithful Generations: Race and New Asian American Churches.* Piscataway, NJ: Rutgers University Press, 2005.

Johnstone, Meg. "Chinese Churches Thrive." *BC Christian News*, April 2002, 4–5.
Jue, Dan. "An Appeal to Sacrifice." Chap. 6 in Yau, *Winning Combination*.
Kang, K. Connie. "Asian American Churches Face Leadership Gap: Pastors Aren't Being Prepared to Handle Congregational Conflicts over Cultural and Generational Issues, Experts Say." *Los Angeles Times*, March 3, 2007. Excerpts reposted by L2 Foundation, March 5, 2007. http://l2foundation.org/2007/asian-american-churches-face-leadership-gap.
Kasinitz, Philip, et al. *Inheriting the City: The Children of Immigrants Come of Age*. New York: Russell Sage Foundation, 2008.
Kersten, G. H. *Reformed Dogmatics*. Vol. 1. Grand Rapids: Eerdmans, 1981.
Kim, Mitchell, and David Lee. "Intergenerational Ministry: Why Bother?" Chap. 2 in *Honoring the Generations*, edited by M. Sydney Park et al. Valley Forge, PA: Judson, 2012.
Kinnaman, David. *UnChristian: What a New Generation Really Thinks about Christianity . . . and Why It Matters*. Grand Rapids: Baker, 2007.
Kong, Edwin. "The English Speaking Ministry in the Chinese Churches in Canada." *NACOCE Bimonthly*, December–February 1985–1986, 1–7.
Kotter, John P. *Leading Change*. Boston: Harvard Business School Press, 1996.
Kuhn, Thomas S. "Revolutions as Changes of World View." Chap. 10 in *The Structure of Scientific Revolutions*. Chicago: University of Chicago Press, 1962.
Lai, David Chuen Yan, et al. "The Chinese in Canada: Their Unrecognized Religion." Chap. 5 in *Religion and Ethnicity in Canada*, edited by Paul Bramadat and David Seljak. Toronto: University of Toronto Press, 2008.
Lam, Alfred. "The Backwards Way of Developing English-Speaking Ministry." *English Parallel Track of the 7th Chinese Coordination Center of World Evangelism* 194, July 2005. http://www.cccowe.org/content_pub.php?id=catw200507–9.
Law, Gail. "A Model for the American Ethnic Chinese Churches." *Theology, News and Notes*, December 1984, 21–26.
———. "A Model for the American Ethnic Churches." Chap. 12 in Yau, *Winning Combination*.
Lee, Helen. "Silent Exodus: Can the East Asian Church in America Reverse the Flight of Its Next Generation?" *Christianity Today* 40, no. 12, August 12, 1996, 50–53.
Lee, Sang Hyun. *From a Liminal Place: An Asian American Theology*. Minneapolis: Fortress, 2010.
———. "Pilgrimage and Home in the Wilderness of Marginality: Symbols and Context in Asian American Theology." Chap. 8 in *New Spiritual Homes: Religion and Asian Americans*, edited by David K. Yoo. Honolulu: University of Hawaii Press, 1999.
Lee, Victor. "Models of Ministry in Chinese Churches." Toronto Chinese Community Church, 2003.
Leonard, Karen Isaken, et al. *Immigrant Faiths: Transforming Religious Life in America*. Lanham, MD: AltaMira, 2005.
Leong, Russell C. "Asian Americans: Now Becoming Aware of Their Own Personality." Introduction to *Balancing Two Worlds: Asian American College Students Tell Their Life Stories*, edited by Andrew Garrod and Robert Kilkenny. Ithaca, NY: Cornell University Press, 2007.
Lewis, Phillip V. *Transformational Leadership: A New Model for Total Church Involvement*. Nashville: Broadman & Holman, 1996.

Ley, David. "The Immigrant Church as an Urban Service Hub." *Urban Studies* 45 (September 2008) 2057–74.
Lim, Peter, and Karen Quek. "The Silent Exodus of 2nd-Generation Chinese-Americans from the Chinese Church." http://www.ncfr.org/sites/default/files/downloads/news/229-22%20The%2520Silent%2520Exodus%2520of%25202nd%2520Gen%2520Chinese%2520Americans_0.pdf.
Lin, Jireh. "Selected Case Studies in How Traditional Chinese Churches Can Have an Effective ABC Ministry." DMin dissertation, Dallas Theological Seminary, March 2012.
Ling, Samuel. "Beyond the Chinese Way of Doing Things: The Continued Search for a Theology of Culture." Chap. 5 in Yau, *Winning Combination*.
———. *The Chinese Way of Doing Things*. Vancouver, BC: China Horizon and China Horizon Ministries Canada, 1999.
———. "The Chinese Way of Doing Things: Contours of OBC-ABC Cultural Differences." In Yau, *Winning Combination*, 38–58.
Ling, Samuel, and Clarence Cheuk. *The Chinese Way of Doing Things*. San Gabriel, CA: P&R, 1999.
Lingenfelter, Sherwood G., and Marvin K. Mayers. *Ministering Cross-Culturally: An Incarnational Model for Personal Relationships*. Grand Rapids: Baker, 1986.
Liu, Esther. "Cultural Tensions within Chinese American Families and Churches." Fullness in Christ Fellowship. http://www.ficfellowship.org/cultural-tensions-e.html.
Lu, Henry. "Silent Exodus Discussion." *Link* (newletter of the Chinese Overseas Christian Mission), 2011, issue 3. http://cocm.org.uk/en/publications.
Mak, Chadwin. "The Growth of Chinese Churches in Canada." *Chinese around the World*, April/May 1994, 1–4.
Mak, Wing H. "Embracing the English-Speaking Ministry in Canadian Chinese Churches." Paper presented at the Second Consultation on English-Speaking Ministry in the Canadian Chinese Churches, Eastern Pentecostal Bible College, Peterborough, ON, June 19–22, 2000.
Malphurs, Aubrey. *Advanced Strategic Planning*. Grand Rapids: Baker, 2005.
Mark, Kai. "English-Chinese Working Relationships in Churches." Talk at the Greater Vancouver English Ministries Fellowship, Chinese Presbyterian Church, Vancouver, BC, November 19, 1999.
Mathabane, Bruce."Taking the Measure of American Racism." *Time*, November 12, 1990. http://www.time.com/time/magazine/article/0,9171,971670,00.html.
Matsuoka, Fumitaka. *Out of Silence: Emerging Themes in Asian American Churches*. Cleveland: United Church Press, 1995.
Matthews, Larry. "Poised for Impact." *Faith Today* 15, no. 4, July/August 1997, 14–24.
McGavran, Donald A. *The Bridges of God*. London: World Dominion, 1955.
Mennonite Brethren Herald. "We Are in the Same Family: The Growth of Chinese MB Churches." *Mennonite Brethren Herald* 40, no. 21 November 9, 2001. http://www.mbherald.com/back/2001.en.html.
Middleton, J. Richard, and Brian J. Walsh. *Truth Is Stranger Than It Used To Be*. Downers Grove: InterVarsity, 1995.
Min, Pyong Gap, ed. *Second Generation: Ethnic Identity among Asian Americans*. Walnut Creek, CA: AltaMira, 2002.

Min, Pyong Gap, and Jung Ha Kim, eds. *Religions in Asian America: Building Faith Communities*. Walnut Creek, CA: AltaMira, 2002.

Mullins, Mark. "The Life-Cycle of Ethnic Churches in Sociological Perspective." *Japanese Journal of Religious Studies* 14 (1987) 321–34. http://www.stvolodymyr.ca/Documents/Japan%20ethnic%20religion%20study.pdf.

Murren, Doug. "The Leader as Change Agent." In *Leaders on Leadership*, edited by George Barna, 199–212. Ventura, CA: Regal, 1987.

Nakka-Cammauf, Viji, and Timothy Tseng, eds. *Asian American Christianity Reader*. Castro Valley, CA: Institute for the Study of Asian American Christianity, 2009.

Ng, John L. "Church Models for Chinese Ministry." Chap. 13 in Yau, *Winning Combination*.

Ng, Kwai Hang. "Seeking the Christian Tutelage: Agency and Culture in Chinese Immigrants' Conversion to Christianity." *Sociology of Religion* 63, no. 2 (2002) 195–214.

Ng, Ted. "Is There a Future in the Chinese Church for the Next Generation in Vancouver? An Analysis of the Silent Exodus and the Options to Address the Issue." Unpublished paper, 2011.

Ng, Wing Chung. "Becoming Chinese Canadian: The Genesis of a Cultural Category." Chap. 12 in *The Last Half-Century of Chinese Overseas*, edited by Elizabeth Sinn. Hong Kong: Hong Kong University Press, 1998.

———. *The Chinese in Vancouver, 1945–80: The Pursuit of Identity and Power*. Vancouver: University of British Columbia Press, 1999.

Niebuhr, Richard. *Christ and Culture*. New York: HarperCollins, reprint 1996.

Nouwen, Henri J. M. *In the Name of Jesus*. New York: Crossroad, 1989.

Ong, Peter. "Silent Exodus." Peter Ong's blog, posted August 29, 2006. http://peterong.wordpress.com/2006/08/29/silent-exodus.

Oppenheim, A. N. *Questionnaire Design and Attitude Measurement*. London: Heinemann Educational, 1976.

Park, David. "A Silent Exodus Leads to Freedom." *Next Gener.Asian Church* (blog), posted September 6, 2006. http://nextgenerasianchurch.com/2006/09/06/a-silent-exodus-implies-wandering-in-the-desert-but-also-freedom.

Park, M. Sydney, et al., eds. *Honoring the Generations: Learning with Asian North American Congregations*. Valley Forge, PA: Judson, 2012.

Park, Robert Ezra. *Race and Culture*. Glencoe, IL: Free Press, 1950.

Paul, Bob. "Leadership Integrity." Class lecture in DMPM 922 Leadership Theory, Theology and Practice, Carey Theological College, Vancouver, BC, January 18, 2013.

Penner, James. *Hemorrhaging Faith Report*. Commissioned by the Evangelical Fellowship of Canada Youth and Young Adult Ministry Roundtable, 2012. http://tgcfcanada.org/hemorrhagingfaith.

Perkins, Dennis N. T., et al. "Resolving Conflicts: Lessons from the Martial Arts." In *Leading at the Edge*, 221–25. New York: AMACOM, 2012.

Peterson, Eugene. *A Memoir: The Pastor*. New York: HarperCollins, 2011.

Ping, Willard. "Why Stay in the Chinese Church?" *About Face*, February 1985, 1–2.

Pollock, David C., and Ruth E. Van Reken. *Third Culture Kids: Growing Up among Worlds*. Boston: Brealey, 2009.

Quan, Isaac. Reaching Second Generations Workshop: A31, 46th Chinese Coordination Center of World Evangelism, December 30, 2006.

Quinn, Robert E. *Deep Change: Discovering the Leader Within.* San Francisco: Jossey-Bass, 1996.

Rah, Soong-Chan. *Many Colors: Cultural Intelligence for a Changing Church.* Chicago: Moody, 2010.

———. *The Next Evangelicalism: Freeing the Church from Western Cultural Captivity.* Downers Grove: InterVarsity, 2009.

———. "A Theology of Culture." In *Cultural Intelligence for a Changing Church.* Compact disc. Regent College, 2013.

Rainer, Thom S. "The Millennials Are Rejecting Fighting." Thom S. Rainer's website, posted October 21, 2013. http://thomrainer.com/2013/10/21/the-millennials-are-rejecting-fighting-churches-and-christians.

Redekop, John H. *Ethnicity and the Mennonite Brethren: A People Apart.* Winnipeg: Kindred, 1987.

"Responding to the 'New Reality': Core Values of Intentionally Multicultural Churches." Intentionally Multicultural Churches Conference, Richmond, BC, March 30–31, 2001.

Roy, Patricia E. *A White Man's Province: British Columbia Politicians and Chinese and Japanese Immigrants, 1858–1914.* Vancouver: University of British Columbia Press, 1989.

Ruokanen, Miikka, and Paulos Huang, eds. *Christianity and Chinese Culture.* Grand Rapids: Eerdmans, 2010.

Sawlers, David. *Goodbye Generation.* Glace Bay, Nova Scotia: Ponder, 2008.

Schein, Edgar H. *The Corporate Culture Survival Guide.* San Francisco: Jossey-Bass, 2009.

Sheffield, Dan. *The Multicultural Leader: Developing a Catholic Personality.* Toronto: Clements, 2005.

Shenk, Sara Wenger. *Thank You for Asking.* Waterloo, Ontario: Herald, 2005.

Shi, Yang. "Chinese Cultural Traditions: A New Interpretation of Chinese Culture." *Regent Chinese Journal* 5, no 2 (1997) 19–22.

Shoemaker, Ken, and Peter Trieu. "Moving from Chinese Church to Multicultural Church." English symposium at the 48th annual Chinese Winter Conference, Calgary, Alberta, December 29, 2008.

Silverman, David. *Interpreting Qualitative Data: Methods for Analyzing Talk, Text and Interaction.* London: Sage, 1993.

Smalley, Gary, and John Trent. *The Blessing.* New York: Pocket, 1986.

So, Wing Y. "Identity and Identification." Chap. 3 in Yau, *Winning Combination.*

Statistics Canada. "Immigration and Ethnocultural Diversity in Canada." 2011. http://www12.statcan.gc.ca/nhs-enm/2011/as-sa/99-10-x/99-10-x2011001-eng.cfm#a3.

———. "Persons in Mixed Unions by Place of Birth and Visible Minority Group." 2006 census. http://www.statcan.gc.ca/pub/11-08-x/2010001/t/11143/tbl003-eng.htm.

Sugikawa, Nancy, and M. Sydney Park. "Formation of Servants in God's Household." Chap. 7 in *Honoring the Generations*, edited by M. Sydney Park et al. Valley Forge, PA: Judson, 2012.

Sugikawa, Nancy, and Steve Wong. "Grace-Filled Households." Chap. 1 in *Growing Healthy Asian American Churches*, edited by Peter Cha et al. Downers Grove: InterVarsity, 2006.

Tan, Jonathan Y. *Asian American Theologies.* Maryknoll: Orbis, 2008.

Tan, Joshua Weichong. "Cross, Culture, Confusion: Conflict and Community in a Chinese Church in Canada." MA thesis, Simon Fraser University, Burnaby, BC, 2010.
Tanner, Kathryn. *Theories of Culture: A New Agenda for Theology*. Minneapolis: Fortress, 1997.
To, Jack, and Rose To. "Exodus: A Pilot Study on Why English-Speaking Adults Leave the Bilingual Church." *Challenger*, April/May 2000, 1–3.
Todd, Douglas. "Immigrants' Religions Tied to Their Asian Identities." *Vancouver Sun*, June 7, 2008. http://www.canada.com/story.html?id=411b9d97-edba-464a-9495-151fe8b275b8.
Todd, Matthew. "The Development and Transition of English Ministry in the Chinese Canadian Church." *MB Chinese Herald* 72, October 2009, 16–18.
———. "Embracing an Advisory Role." *MB Chinese Herald* 66, October 2008, 12–13.
———. "Scripture That Guides a Bi-cultural Church." *MB Chinese Herald* 70, June 2009, 21–23.
Top Achievement. "Creating S.M.A.R.T. Goals." *Top Achievement: Self Improvement and Personal Development Community* (website). http://topachievement.com/smart.html.
Tsang, Gideon, and Soong-Chan Rah. "The Disillusioned Generation." Chap. 3 in *Honoring the Generations: Learning with Asian North American Congregations*, edited by M. Sydney Park et al. Valley Forge, PA: Judson, 2012.
Tsang, Gladys Lee. "Churches in Ethnic Transition: The Surge of the Ethnic Chinese in Vancouver and Its Impact and Implication on the Christian Mission." MTh thesis, Regent College, 1990.
Tseng, Timothy, et al. *Pulpit & Pew Research on Pastoral Leadership: Asian American Religious Leadership Today; A Preliminary Inquiry*. Durham, NC: Duke Divinity School, 2005.
Tso, Marcus. "English Adult Ministry in the Canadian Chinese Churches." *MB Chinese Herald* 48, August 2005, 6–8.
Uhalley, Stephen, Jr., and Xiaoxin Wu, eds. *China and Christianity: Burdened Past, Hopeful Future*. Armonk, NY: Sharpe, 2001.
University of British Columbia Library. Chinese Canadian Stories. http://ccs.library.ubc.ca/en/chronology.
Verkuyl, Johannes. *Break Down the Walls: A Cry for Racial Justice*. Edited and translated by Lewis Smedes. Grand Rapids: Eerdmans, 1973.
Wahler, Leon. "Conducting Research on Sensitive Subjects." *Vue: The Magazine of the Marketing Research and Intelligence Association*, November 2008.
Wan, Enoch. *Diaspora Missiology: Theory, Methodology, and Practice*. Portland, OR: Institute of Diaspora Studies, Western Seminary, 2011.
Wang, Jiwu. *"His Dominion" and the "Yellow Peril": Protestant Missions to Chinese Immigrants in Canada, 1859–1967*. Waterloo, Ontario: Wilfrid Laurier University Press, 2006.
Wang, Paul C. "A Study on Cross-Cultural Conflict Patterns and Intervention between Two Generations of Leaders in Two Chinese Churches in Vancouver: Toward a Vibrant Intergenerational Partnership in Ministry." DMin diss., Trinity Evangelical Divinity School, Deerfield, IL, 2003.
Weems, Lovett H., Jr. *Church Leadership*. Nashville: Abingdon, 2010.

White, Randy. "Debriefing." Lecture, Overture 1, Bakke Graduate University, Fresno, CA, October 19, 2012.

———."Eight Perspectives on Transformational Leadership." Lecture, Overture 1, Bakke Graduate University, Fresno, CA, October 20, 2012.

———. "Eight Qualities of Transformational Leadership." Lecture, Overture 2, China Course, Hong Kong, April 11, 2012.

———. *Encounter God in the City: Onramps to Personal and Community Transformation*. Downers Grove: InterVarsity, 2006.

Whitehead, Evelyn Eaton, and James D. Whitehead. *Christian Life Patterns: The Psychological Challenges and Religious Invitations of Adult Life*. New York: Crossroad, 2003.

Wickberg, Edgar, ed. *From China to Canada: A History of the Chinese Communities in Canada*. Toronto: McClelland & Stewart, 1982.

Wilson, Bryan. *Religion in Sociological Perspective*. New York: Oxford University Press, 1982.

Witham, Larry A. *Who Shall Lead Them? The Future of Ministry in America*. New York: Oxford University Press, 2005.

Wong, Daniel L. "Toward a Theological Foundation for English Ministry in the Canadian Chinese Churches." Paper presented at the Consultation for English Ministry in the Canadian Chinese Churches at Fair Havens Retreat and Conference Centre, Beaverton, Ontario, September 25, 1995. Later published in *Consultation for English Ministry in the Canadian Chinese Churches Compendium*, by the Chinese Co-ordination Centre of World Evangelism, Canada, 1995.

Wong, Hoover. "Contextual or Evangelical?" Chap. 16 in Yau, *Winning Combination*.

Wong, Joseph. "Bridging the Gap." *About Face*, February 1990, 1–2.

Wong, Morgan. "NACC Church Models." Lecture, Leadership Issues in North American Chinese Churches, Carey Theological College, Vancouver, BC, February 18, 2012.

Wong, Wayland. "Reaching ABC's . . . Who Are We Working With?" Chap. 10 in Yau, *Winning Combination*.

———. "Towards a Mature English Ministry: The Canadian Chinese Church in Transition, Exploring Structures and Strategies." Lecture at the Spring Chinese Conference, Regent College, Vancouver, BC, April 20, 1996.

Wong, Wayne. "The Current Challenges of Doing Inter-Generational Chinese Ministries in Greater Vancouver: A Reconciliation Ministry." Master's thesis, Northwest Baptist Seminary, Vancouver, BC, 1998.

Wong, William. "Establishing the Need for English Ministry." Handout at Spring Chinese Conference, Regent College, Vancouver, BC, 1996.

Woo, Terry. *Banana Boys*. Toronto: Cormorant, 2005.

Wu, Frank H. *Yellow: Race in America Beyond Black and White*. New York: Basic, 2012.

Wu, Jonathan. "Trusting Households." Chap. 5 in *Growing Healthy Asian American Churches*, edited by Peter Cha et al. Downers Grove: InterVarsity, 2006.

Yancey, George A. *One Body, One Spirit: Principles of Successful Multiracial Churches*. Downers Grove: InterVarsity, 2003.

Yang, Fenggang. *Chinese Christians in America: Conversion, Assimilation, and Adhesive Identities*. University Park: Penn State University Press, 1999.

———. "Chinese Conversion to Evangelical Christianity: The Importance of Social and Cultural Contexts." *Sociology of Religion* 59, no. 3 (1998) 237–57.

———. "Religious Diversity among the Chinese in America." Chap. 3 in *Religions in Asian America: Building Faith Communities*, edited by Pyong Gap Min and Jung Ha Kim. Walnut Creek, CA: AltaMira, 2002.

———. "Tenacious Unity in a Contentious Community: Cultural and Religious Dynamics in a Chinese Christian Church." In *Gatherings in Diaspora: Religious Communities and the New Immigration*, edited by R. Stephen Warner and Judith G. Wittner, 333–61. Philadelphia: Temple University Press, 1998.

Yang, Shi. "Chinese Cultural Traditions: A New Interpretation of Chinese Culture." *Regent Chinese Journal* 2 (1997) 19–22.

Yau, Cecelia, ed. *A Winning Combination: ABC/OBC; Understanding the Cultural Tensions in Chinese Churches*. Petaluma, CA: Chinese Christian Mission, 1986.

Yee, Paul. *Salt Water City*. Seattle: University of Washington, 1988.

Yep, Jeanette, et al., eds. *Following Jesus without Dishonoring Your Parents*. Downers Grove: InterVarsity, 1998.

Yetman, Norman R. "Historical Perspectives: Asian Americans." In *Majority and Minority: The Dynamics of Race and Ethnicity in American Life*, 87–121. Needman Heights, MA: Allyn & Bacon, 1999.

Yeung, Alexander K. W. "Toward a Strategy for Developing Ministry to the Canadian Born Chinese in the Context of the Chinese Immigrant Family." DMin diss., Fuller Theological Seminary, 1987.

Yeung, Clement S. L. "Project Contempo." Paper presented at Project Contempo, held at the Hilton Hotel, Metrotown, Burnaby, BC, spring 2005.

Yew, Wally. "Postscript: A Personal Appeal." In Yau, *Winning Combination*, 173–74.

Yin, Robert. *Case Study Research: Design and Methods*. London: Sage, 1994.

Yongtao, Chen. "Christ and Culture: A Reflection by a Chinese Christian." Chap. 17 in *Christianity and Chinese Culture*, edited by Miikka Ruokanen and Paulos Huang. Grand Rapids: Eerdmans, 2010.

Yoo, David K. *New Spiritual Homes: Religion and Asian Americans*. Honolulu: University of Hawaii Press, 1999.

Young, William P. *The Shack*. London: Hodder & Stoughton, 2007.

Yu, Li. "Christianity as a Chinese Belief." Chap. 11 in *Asian Religions in British Columbia*, edited by Don Baker and Larry DeVries. Vancouver: University of British Columbia Press, 2010.

Yuen, Esther. "Mass Exodus." *Pacific Rim Magazine*, 2011. http://www2.langara.bc.ca/prm/2011/articles/exodus.html.

Yuen, Peter. "Parallel Ministry and Oneness in the Church." *About Face* 7, May 1985.

Zhou, Min. "Conflict, Coping, and Reconciliation: Intergenerational Relations in Chinese Immigrant Families." Chap. 1 in *Across Generations: Immigrant Families in America*, edited by Nancy Foner. New York: New York University Press, 2009.

Index

Note: page numbers with n indicates notes at bottom of indicated page, t indicates a table, and f indicates a figure

ABCs (American Born Chinese). *See* CBCs (Canadian Born Chinese)
Absorbing House development model, 13
acculturation, assimilation
    and appeal of multi-cultural churches, 123–24, 123n3
    by CBCs, identity struggles, 44n3, 47n28, 52n56
    as a continuum, 12n2, 63, 130n38
    defined, xiii
    and intergenerational conflicts, 6n17, 25, 47–48, 47n28, 49n37, 51–52, 52n56, 89–90
    and minority religious traditions, 50n88
    resistance to, among OBCs, 19–20, 25, 33n133
action plans, as guide to transition to independence, 143–44
Aikman, David, 51n52, 147
alienation. *See also* ethnocentrism, Sinocentrism
    among young English-speaking adults, 20, 52nn55–56
    cultural rigidity and, 52n55, 52n56, 114
    defined, xiii

    ethnocentrism and, 52nn55–56, 54n65, 114, 114–15n54, 115n53
American Chinese Churches, Second Generation Hybrid Model for, 28, 28n104
American-born Chinese (ABC). *See* CBCs (Canadian Born Chinese)
assimilation. *See* acculturation, assimilation
associated congregations., defined, xiv–xv, 129n30. *See also* parallel associated dependent English Ministry congregations; parallel associated independent English Ministry congregations
authoritarian decision-making styles, 30, 87, 161
Autonomous House Model, 13–14

Banana Boys (Woo), 98n26
biblical theology
    as basis for Chinese, 136
    need to accommodate to needs of each generation, 108n39
    vision of inclusiveness in, 65–67
bicultural churches. *See also* CBCs (Canadian Born Chinese); EM (English Ministry); monoethnic/monocultural churches, OBCs

bicultural churches *(cont.)*
(Overseas Born Chinese); silent exodus
  affection for, among study respondents, 116
  associated relationships, 129n30, 135
  colonizing *vs.* kingdomizing, 59
  culture of empowerment, 27, 27n94, 60, 68–69, 136
  defined, xiii
  development from monocultural churches, 2, 12n2, 13–14
  efforts to avoid divisions related to cultural differences, 16
  ethnocentrism and intergenerational conflicts in, xvii, 16, 52n56, 73, 89–90, 107, 107n36, 115, 123–24, 123n3
  exclusion of non-Chinese from, 91–92, 91–92n18, 91n17
  exodus of second generation English-speakers from, 1, 28, 57–58, 79, 95, 108, 110, 120–21
  exodus from, parallels to other churches, 80–81, 80n3
  expanded capacity for mission, 9n38, 62, 68–69, 116–17n63, 117, 133–34, 136
  growth of, in Canada, 125–26, 125n14
  hypocrisy in, as a reason for exodus, 80, 98, 101n31, 108, 159, 161
  identifying when model change is needed, 127–28
  independent congregations as one option for, 127, 127n20
  problems associated with, 57
  recommendations for improvement, xviii, 100–101, 102–3t
  shame culture, 72–73, 107, 159–60
biculturalism. *See also* acculturation
  advantages, 124, 126, 130
  bicultural continuum scale (Law), 8n31
  defined, xiii, 1n1
bilingual services, 21
blessings, intergenerational, importance, 132–33, 132n44

boards of directors. *See* church boards
Bramadat, Paul, 5, 43, 44n3, 47n28, 60nn87–88
Branson, Mark Lau, 23–24, 23n64
British Columbia, Canada, 46–47n26, 49n36, 125n14, 131
Brueggemann, Walter, 43–44n2, 62
burnout, as reason for leaving church, 98, 105–6
Busto, Rudy V., 31n122

Cadences of Home (Brueggemann), 62
calling-based leadership, xvi
Canada
  discrimination against Asians in, 48–50, 49nn37–38
  emphasis on multi-culturalism, 19
  growth of bicultural Chinese churches in, 28–29, 125–26, 125n14
  immigration from China and Southeast Asia, 60, 60nn87–88
Canadian Born Chinese (CBCs). *See* CBCs (Canadian Born Chinese)
Canadian Chinese Christian Business and Professional Association, 52n58
Canadian Chinese Christian identity, 125–26, 125n14
Canadian Chinese churches. *See* bicultural churches; Chinese culture; monocultural churches
  emphasis on harmony and unity, xiv, 13, 16, 23nn62–63, 27n94, 28, 34–35n151, 45n20, 46–47, 71, 129
  as inclusive faith communities, 109, 135–36
  as mature organizations, 12, 54n71
  need for institutional revisioning and transformation, 136, 140
Carlson, Kenneth P., 22
Catherine the Great, 43
CBC/OBC models, effective, examples, 25n83
CBCs (Canadian Born Chinese). *See also* acculturation; drop-out study participations; OBCs (Overseas

Born Chinese); remain-in study participants
   adults among, as high-risk ground, 117
   defined, xi
   enhanced capacity for mission, 124, 126, 130
   experiences in dependent English ministries, xv, 24, 115–16n60
   experiences after leaving church, 100
   conflicts within bicultural church, xvii, 16, 22, 29, 29n110, 33n134, 52nn,55–56, 53, 72–73, 72n3598n26, 107, 107n36, 115, 130, 159–60
   interracial marriages among, 124n4
   life stage transition needs, lack of support for, 22, 92–94, 93–94n20, 98, 105, 107, 111, 113, 139
   marginalization of, xv, 47–48, 47n28, 89–90
   and multi-ethnic, pan-Asian ministries, 16n18, 30, 123n3
   multiple identities of, 31–32n123, 52n56, 53n62, 55–56n76, 130
   retaining through empowered congregations, 52n58, 57–58, 70, 133n49, 138
   view of as threat by OBCs, 49n37, 51–53, 55
Chafetz, Janet Saltzman, 44, 52n55, 114
Chan, David, 13, 13n4, 14–15t
Cheuk, Clarence, 24–25
Chin, Steve, 128n26
China. *See also* OBC (Overseas Born Chinese)
   historical xenophobia in, 51n52
   immigration to Canada from, 60, 60nn87–88
   regions occupied by the Hakka, xiii–xiv
Chinatowns, 49
Chinese Canadian Christian identity, 53, 72–73

Chinese culture and identity. *See also* acculturation, assimilation; biculturalism; ethnocentrism/Sinocentrism; pluralism
   and authoritarian structure of traditional Chinese churches, 55n74
   and Canadian anti-Chinese discrimination, 48–50, 49nn37-38
   CBC's commitment to, 52n56, 55–56n76, 130
   CBC's struggles related to, xvii, 72–73, 98n26, 107, 107n36, 115, 130, 159
   and Chinese anti-Canadian discrimination, 49n38
   and Christian identity, 53, 65, 72–73, 108
   as a continuum, 38
   Confucian values, 16, 56, 56n81, 74, 74n40
   cultural rigidity, 19–20, 27–28, 52nn55–56, 63, 72–73, 78, 98, 105, 114, 160
   and pan-Asian congregations, 30–32, 30n112, 31n119, 31n122, 34–35n151
   shame culture, 107, 159–60
Chinese Overseas Christian Mission, 52n57
chopstick analogy for parallel associated model, 21–22n52
Christian church, as an early ethnic church, 64, 66
Christocentric identity, 53, 65, 73, 108
Chuang, D. J., 28–29
   limits placed on by OBCs, church boards, 40–42, 89–90n11, 89–91, 90n12, 106
church boards. *See also* pastors, church leaders
   authoritarian decision-making styles, 30, 87, 161
   challenges of attracting leaders, 55n74
   control issues, resistance to change, 24, 25n84, 27n94, 34, 40–42, 54–55n72, 55, 79, 87nn4–5, 89–90n11, 89–91, 90n12,

church boards *(cont.)*
  control issues, resistance to change *(cont.)*, 98–99, 106, 108, 119n69, 129n27, 139
  engaging effectively with, 9, 133n49, 143–45
  and process of transitioning towards independence, 26, 128–29, 128n26, 129n27, 142–43
church-within-a-church concept, 2
City in Focus project, 52n58
Clements, Rob, 18–19
clergy. *See* pastors, church leaders
colonizing *vs.* kingdomizing, 58–59
communication
  and inter-generational conflicts, 91, 91n15, 110
  and transformational leadership, 9, 46, 128, 128n26, 142–45, 142n16, 145n33
community centers, ethnic churches as, 44, 44n3
conflict, healthy and transformational, 9, 9n32, 23n62, 40–41, 131–32, 132n44
Confucian traditions and values, 16, 56, 56n81, 74, 74n40. *See also* ethnocentrism, Sinocentrism
Confucius, quote from, 75
congregational life cycles, 12
covenant relationship, lack of understanding among individuals leaving the church, 97, 97n24
cross-cultural mission of diaspora church, 136n60
Cultural Intelligence, 70n22
culture, Chinese. *See* Chinese culture and identity

De Pree, Max, 39–40
denominational leaders, 3, 45–46
dependent congregations, defined, xiv. *See also* parallel associated dependent English Ministries congregations
dependent relationships, limits of, 19, 30, 54–55, 54–55n72, 135

developmental needs. *See* CBCs (Canadian Born Chinese); life stage transitions; young adults
Dey, Ian, 115n59
DeYoung, Curtiss Paul, 20, 29, 34–36
Di Giacomo, Michael, 33n133
diaspora churches. *See also* monoethnic/monocultural churches
  and cross-cultural mission, 136n60
  defined, xiii, 43n1
  silent exodus as common phenomenon in, 52n57, 80–81, 80n3, 116
  theology and missiology of, 136n60
diversity, unity in, xiv, 27, 35, 69–72
drop-out study participants, findings related to
  age at leaving, 92
  appreciation for mentors and role models, 88–89, 88n7, 89n8
  baptism among, 86, 86n3
  and conflicts with OBCs, 89–90, 89–90n11, 94–95
  demographics, 81–82, 84–85t
  denominational scope, 86, 86n2
  descriptions of church cultural environments, 86–87, 87n4
  and exclusion of non-Chinese outsiders, 91–92, 91–92n18, 91n17
  impacts of leaving on individuals, 96–97, 100, 100n29
  impacts of leaving on remaining church members, 95–96, 96n23
  leaving process, 95–96, 95n21, 95n22
  levels of church involvement, volunteerism, 88, 88n6
  and move to other churches, 118–19
  parents role in early Church participation, 86, 86n1
  personal and community involvement, 87–88, 87–88n5, 88n7, 89n10
  primary issues of concern, 92–95, 97–101, 99t, 112–13, 112t, 113f
  recommendations for improvement, 100–101, 100n30, 102–3t

INDEX 379

relationship with leaders and pastoral staff, 89, 95
and understanding of covenant relationships, 97, 97n24
Dynamic-Bicultural-Continuum model (Law), 123

Ebaugh, Helen Rose, 44, 52n55, 114
"The Eight Qualities of Transformational Leadership" (White), xv–xvi
EM (English Ministry) congregations. *See also* bicultural churches; empowerment; parallel associated dependent English Ministry congregations; parallel associated independent English Ministry congregations; silent exodus
  barriers to development, 19, 25, 25n82, 27–28, 38–42, 51, 54–55, 57, 63, 74, 79, 89–90n11, 89–91, 90n12, 106 125–26, 128n26
  defined, xi
  dependent models for, 16–17, 19, 54
  empowering, benefits of and mission potential, 10, 52n55, 55–58, 55–56n76, 59, 60–61, 68–69, 74, 122, 133n49, 135–38
  establishment and development process, 1–2, 21–22, 21–22n52, 25, 25–26n84, 33, 36–37, 53, 56–57, 127–28, 128n23
  exodus of English-speaking adults from, 1, 28, 57–58, 79, 95, 108, 110, 120–21
  inheritance of dependent model by, 54
  kingdomizing *vs.* colonizing, 59
  leadership issues and needs, 21, 24–27, 57, 60, 74, 79–80, 94–95, 108, 134, 136
  limits placed on by OBCs, church boards, 24, 25n84, 27n94, 34, 40–42, 54–55n72, 55, 79, 87nn4–5, 89–90n11, 89–91, 90n12, 98–99, 106, 108, 119n69, 129n27, 139
  models for, 16–18, 17n23, 18f, 58
  pressures on remaining congregation associated with silent exodus, 106
  relevancy to youth and young adults, 56, 73, 79–80, 98, 141–42
  and retaining spiritual relationship with founding church, 132–33
  need for revisioning and change, 57–58, 116–17n63, 117, 131, 140
  suggestions for preventing further exodus, xviii, 100–101, 102–3t, 110, 135–37
  transitioning to independence, as a process, 128–30, 128n25, 133–35, 140–47
  types congregations, 17n24, 55
  view of as failure and threat to Chinese traditions, 19
Emerson, Michael O., 39, 39n175
empowerment. *See also* independent congregations
  benefits of, 52n55, 55–58, 55–56n76, 59, 60–61, 68–69, 74, 122, 133n49, 135–38
  control vs., 30, 108
  culture of empowerment, 27, 27n94
  and effective mission, xvii, 60
  as goal of transformational leadership, 39
  lack of, as a reason for exodus, 55, 79, 139n1
  legal, and independence, 14
  as positive value, 16n18, 38
  and power struggles, politics, as a prime reason for leaving Chinese church, 94–95, 98, 139
  role of shalom leadership in promoting, 10, 131
  theological basis for, 138
  working to achieve, 143
Eng, Daniel K., Triplex Model, 23
English Ministry (EM). *See* EM (English Ministry)
English-speaking Chinese. *See* CBCs (Canadian Born Chinese)

equality, promoting through shalom leadership, 10, 131
ethnic churches. *See* bicultural churches; monoethnic/monocultural churches
ethnic ghettoes, 58–59
ethnocentrism/Sinocentrism. *See also* alienation; Chinese culture; inclusiveness
   among Anglos, 48–50, 49nn37–38
   and the appeal of the monoethnic church, 26–27, 52n55, 78
   biblical proscriptions against, 66–67
   and Canadian anti-Asian discrimination, 48–50, 49nn37–38
   as cause for dissatisfaction and exodus, 98, 106, 108, 139, 160
   and Chinese anti-Canadian discrimination, 49n38
   and cultural rigidity, 52nn55–56, 63, 72–73, 114
   and feelings of marginalization and disrespect, 49–50, 89–90n11, 90, 90nn13–14
   and isolation, 52n55, 54n65, 114, 114–15n54, 115n53
   and shame culture, 107, 159–60
Evans, James Andrew, 28, 55n74, 115n53, 133n49
Evergreen Baptist Church, Los Angeles, 37n168

F3C (3 subscript) (Vancouver, B. C.), 16n18
faith communities. *See also* Great Commission; mission, evangelic
   and Chinese Christian identity, 53, 65, 72–73, 108
   disparity between words and reality, 67–68, 68n9
   lineage of faith, 16n18
   need to focus on God's love as opposed to, 116
faith in exile experience (Brueggemann), 43–44n2. *See also* diaspora churches
Faith Werks (Vancouver, B. C.), 16n18
family model, Chinese
   and dependent church relationships, 29–30
   as model for Canadian Chinese churches, 16
   as value, 20, 27–28
Filipino churches, silent exodus from, 52n57
Fong, Kenneth, 16–17, 17n22, 124n7, 143

Great Commission. *See also* inclusiveness; mission, evangelic
   advancing through effective EMs, xiv, 55–56n76, 60, 62
   global nature of, 68
   and God's multi-racial kingdom, xiv, 64, 64nn4–5, 67–68, 73, 132n44
   mission of world evangelism, 65–66
   and monoethnic churches, 46–47, 63–64, 64n4
   and pan-Asian congregations, 30
   and the vision of inclusiveness, 66–67, 70–71
Grecian Jews, 64, 66
Guenther, Bruce L., 47n27

Hakka Chinese (Hakka Han), xiii–xiv
harmony. *See* unity, as value in Chinese culture
Homogenous Unity Principle, 45n20

immigrants, Chinese. *See also* monoethnic/monocultural churches; OBC (Overseas Born Chinese)
   discrimination against, 48–50, 49nn37–38
   importance of ethnic churches to, 5, 19–20, 19n38, 43, 44n3, 63
   and secular function of ethnic churches, 44–45, 44n3
incarnational leadership, defined, xvi
inclusiveness
   and the Autonomous House Model of development, 13–14
   benefits of, 10–11, 39, 67, 70–72
   and Christ's mission, 10–11, 59, 64, 64n4, 65–67

INDEX 381

and intercultural/multicultural community, 109, 135–36
independent congregations. *See also* parallel independent English Ministry congregations
   defined, xv, 129, 129nn29–30
   pan-Asian, retention of English speakers in, 27–32
   and the Separate House Model of church development, 13
In-House Model of church development, 13
Intentionally Multicultural church movement, 12n2
intergenerational relationships
   and cultural conflicts, xvii, 22, 33n134, 52nn55–56, 72–73, 98n26, 107, 107n36, 115, 130, 159–60
   positive, as key to sustained associated independent, 38, 128–30, 132–33, 132n44, 132n45
   reconciliatory approaches, 9–10, 135
isolationism. *See* ethnocentrism
Italian Pentecostal first generation immigrants, 33n133

Jeung, Russell, 14, 28, 28n104, 30–34, 30n112, 31n119, 44, 74n40, 123n3
Jewish Christians, persecution of and scattering, 64–66
Jue, Dan, 114–15n54

Kasinitz, Philip, 130n37
Killarney Park Mennonite Brethren Church, Vancouver, 34n151
Kim, Mitchell, 36–37, 132n44
kingdomizing, theological perspective, 59
Kong, Edwin, 21, 21–22n52
Korean churches, silent exodus from, 52n57
Kotter, John P., 41
Kuhn, Thomas S., 126n17

Lam, Alfred, 9n38

Law, Gail, Dynamic-Bicultural continuum scale (DBC model), 8n31, 123
LBCs (Local Born Chinese). *See* CBCs (Canadian Born Chinese)
leadership, Chinese churches. *See also* transformational leadership
   attracting, as challenge for boards, 55n74
   autonomy issues, 25–27, 25n82, 25–26n84, 26–27, 55n72
   calling-based leadership, xvi
   in EMs, issues and needs, 21, 24–27, 57, 60, 74, 79–80, 94–95, 108, 134, 136
   empowering EM leadership, 60, 94
   frustration with, as a reason for exodus, 55n72, 58, 79, 98, 105, 139, 161
   frequent changes in, 95
   need for refocusing and rededication to mission, 74, 140–41, 140n5
leadership theory (Kotter), 41
Lee, David, 36–37, 132n44
Lee, Helen, 1
Lee, Sang Hyun, 32, 54n65, 71–72
Lee, Victor, 13, 14–15t, 20
Leong, Russell C., 31–32
Ley, David, 20–21, 33, 44–45, 53n62, 140
life-cycles of congregations, 12
Ling, Samuel, 24–25, 130n38
Local Born Chinese (LBCs). *See* CBCs (Canadian Born Chinese)
loneliness, need for fellowship, as reason for exodus, 98–99, 112, 119n69, 139
Lu, Henry, 52n57

Mak, Wing H., 25–27, 26n85
Malphurs, Aubrey, 146
Mandarin ministries, 23, 23n63
Mandela, Nelson, 138
marginal ethnics, defined, xiv
marginalization
   of CBCs by OBCs, 47–48, 47n28, 52n56, 89–90, 89–90n11

marginalization (cont.)
  of Chinese immigrants, and ethnocentrism, 19–20, 49–50, 49n38, 90, 90nn13–14
  pilgrimage as response to, 32
marriages, mixed-raced unions, 124n4
Martinez, Juan F., 23–24, 23n64
McGavran, Donald A. (*Bridges of God*), 45n20
men, predominance of among study participants, 118n67
Mennonite Brethren ministries, German-speaking, 33
Middleton, J., Richard, 116
mid-life adults, exodus from Chinese churches, 55n72
ministers. *See* pastors, church leaders
mission, evangelic. *See also* Great Commission; transformational leadership
  cross-cultural, and advances of bicultural experience of CBCs, 125–26, 130–31
  differing views about in Anglo and Chinese churches, 57n84
  importance of shalom leadership to, 10, 131
  and limits of dependent congregations, 124
  potential of EMs for, 59–60, 68, 134
  vision and vision path versus, 142n16
mixed race marriages, 123–25
monoethnic/monocultural churches. *See also* bicultural churches; CBCs (Canadian Born Chinese); EMs (English Ministries); ethnocentrism/Sinocentrism; OBCs (Overseas Born Chinese)
  and the Absorbing House Model of development, 13
  addition of bilingual services to, 21
  conflicts between identity and mission, 33–34, 33n134, 34–35n151
  Confucian-based values, 56, 56n81
  congregational life cycles, 12, 67
  connections with country of origin, 44
  defined, xiv
  exclusion of non-Chinese from, 45, 48, 71, 91–92, 91–92n18, 91n17, 126n15
  importance to recent immigrants, 19–20, 19n38, 63
  multicultural churches as reaction to negative experiences in, 34
  origins, 46, 46n23, 48–49n35
  one-roof model of development, 22
  and rigid cultural identity, 18–20, 45, 48–50, 49nn37–38, 51n51, 71, 113
  secular functions, 44–45, 44n3, 63
  spiritual limitations, 46, 51–52, 52n55, 63–64, 71
  theological justifications, 45–46, 45nn20–21, 48
multi-congregational church model, 36, 36n163
multicultural/multiracial churches. *See also* inclusiveness
  appeal to later-generation CBCs, 123–24
  arguments for creating, 34, 34–35n151
  barriers to forming, 91–92n18, 92
  defined, xiv
  leaders of, challenges faced by, 2
  and mixed-race unions, 123–25, 124n7
  new models for, 16n18
  parallel congregation model, 2–3
  steps for transitioning to, 23–24, 23n64
  study participants affiliated with, responses to study findings, 119–20
  theological vision, 34–35
  types of, 36
Murakami, Haruki, 1

New Jerusalem, integrated vision of, 48
Ng, John L., 13–14
Ng, Ted, 16n18, 26–27
Ng, Wing Chung, 72

Niebuhr, Reinhold, 69, 69n13
North America, segregation of churches in, 48

OBCs (Overseas Born Chinese). *See also* bicultural churches; church boards; monoethnic/monocultural churches; parallel associated dependent English Ministry congregations
  benefits to from cultural pluralism, 131
  Christian identity among, 60n87
  and concept of colonization, 58–59
  discrimination experienced by, 48–50, 49nn37–38
  dominance in monoethnic and bicultural churches, 16, 22, 30, 35, 108
  ethnic and cultural solidarity with country of origin, 35, 44
  fears about EMs, 73–74, 108n39, 128–29, 128n26
  immigration into Canada, 60
  negative views about CBCs, 51, 72, 72n35, 80, 89–90n11, 126, 126nn15–16
  seeking blessings from, when seeking independence, 132–33, 132n44, 132n45, 133n49, 145n30
  and conflict avoidance through dependent Chinese bilingual churches, 16, 57–58

pan-Asian churches
  appeal, 28–31, 30n112
  defined, xiv
parallel associated dependent English Ministries congregation. *See also* bicultural churches; CBCs (Canadian Born Chinese); EM (English Ministry); OBCs (Overseas Born Chinese)
  defined, xiv
  destiny vision for, 57–58
  Duplex Model, 22
  experience of CBCs in, 2, 24–25, 123–24
  forced dependency, 16–17, 19, 54, 79, 108, 120–21
  healthy models, 25–26, 26n85
  intergenerational partnerships, 23n62
  leadership and autonomy issues, 25–27, 25n82, 25–26n84, 26–27
  limited capacity for mission, 22–23, 58, 124–26
  origins, 20–22, 54
  pan-Asian churches as reaction to, 29
  Paternal (Father/Son) Model, 22
  Room for Rent Model, 21, 21n49
  steps for transitioning to, 23–24, 23n64
  Townhouse Model, 37, 37n167
parallel associated independent English ministries congregation. *See also* CBCs (Canadian Born Chinese); EM (English Ministry); multi-ethnic church; OBCs (Overseas Born Chinese); transformational leadership
  as approach to sustaining the bicultural church, 2, 28, 58, 122, 127–28, 127n20, 128n24, 139
  benefits of autonomy, 10, 135
  defined, xv
  developing, as a process, 28, 36–37, 127–30, 128nn24–25
  examples of, 37n168
  focus group participants from, response to study findings, 121–22
  importance of independence, 41–42
  legal approaches to organizing, 126
  leadership needs, 74, 131
  and pan-Asian, multi-ethnic churches, 30, 35
  potential for expanded mission, 38, 64n4, 68–69, 124–25
  recommended context for, 36, 38
  transitioning to without conflict, 131–33, 132n44, 132n45, 135, 140–47
parallel congregations, defined, xiv–xv

parent-child relationships
  as barrier to leadership development, 55n72
  and dependent church congregations, 2
  maintaining indefinitely, as barrier to maturity, 54–55
  and Paternal Model for the EM, 22, 23n63
parents, role in initiating church attendance, 86n1, 105
Park. Robert Ezra, 12n2
partnership models. *See* parallel associated inter-dependent English ministries congregation
pastors, church leaders. *See also* transformational leadership
  diversity among, 2
  in EMs, turnover among, 108
  irrelevant preaching by, and exodus from church, 106, 110
  pastoral neglect, 105
  relationship of church dropouts with, 89
  the unbusy pastor, 89n9
pastors, church leaders among study participants
  focus group feedback, 114, 119–22
  primary issues of concern, 77–81, 112, 112–13n48, 112t, 113f
  study findings, 77–81
Paternal (Father/Son) Model, 2, 22
Paterson, Eugene, 89n9
pilgrimage, as response to feeling marginalized, 32
Ping, Willard, 22
pluralism. *See also* biculturalism; diversity, unity in; inclusiveness
  defined, xiii
  healthy models, 131
  and human diversity, 71
Pollock, David C., 22
possibility leadership, 8
power struggles, church politics. *See* empowerment
Project Contempo, 52n58
prophetic leadership
  defined, xvi

desire for, among EM congregation remaining in the Chinese church, 110, 110n40
  motivational role, 9
  and speaking truth with love to power, xvi, 106, 116
Providential gifts, ministries as, 53
Pursuing the Pearl (Fong), 143

Quek, Dr. Timothy, 128n25
Quinn, Robert E., 140

racism experience by Chinese immigrants, 19–20, 49n36, 51, 90n14. *See also* ethnocentrism
Rah, Soong-Chan, 69–70, 70n22, 124–25
reconciliatory approach to independence, 9–10, 135
reflective leadership, defined, xvi
Reid, Angus, 101n31
relationships
  focusing on, vs. programmatic focus, 10, 39
  hierarchical, limits of, 25n83, 27, 39n175, 56, 90
  intergenerational, rebuilding and reconciling, 9–10, 37, 71, 110
  need for among adult CBCs, 46, 87n5, 89n10, 98–99, 99t, 108, 111, 111–12n47, 113
  and transformational leadership, xvi, 8, 39, 110
remain-in (current Chinese Church member) study participants, findings related to
  baptism among, 105
  demographics, 103, 104t, 105
  experiences within the Chinese church, 105, 109
  on impact of silent exodus on their participation, 106
  parents' role in early church participation, 105
  previous exodus from other churches, 111
  primary issues of concern, 112–13, 112t, 113f

on process involved in separating from the church, 105–6
on reasons for silent exodus, 105–8
risk of exodus among, 110–11
suggestions for preventing further exodus, 109–10
"Room for Rent" model, 21n49

Scarborough Community Alliance Church, Ontario, 37n168
scattering, as a theological concept, 116
Schein, Edgar H., 40
Scripture. *See also* Great Commission
advocacy for cultural diversity in, 71
and Christian identity and mission, 71–73, 116–17, 128n23
vision of inclusiveness in, 64n4, 65–68, 70
second generation (children) of immigrants. *See also* CBCs (Canadian Born Chinese)
appeal of pan-Asian churches, 30–32, 30n112, 31n119, 31n122
attraction to wider culture, 33n133
continuum of cultural identity, 38, 72
cross-cultural theological mission, 57–58, 136n60
feelings of isolation from both parents and mainstream culture, 53–54, 72
importance of relationship to, 46, 87n5, 89n10, 98–99, 99t, 108, 111, 111–12n47, 113
Second Generation Hybrid Model for EMs (Jeung), 28, 28n104
secular lifestyle, appeal of, as one reason for exodus, 97–98, 105, 107, 159
Seljak, David, 5, 44n3, 47n28, 60nn87–88
Separate House Model of church development, 13
servant leadership, servanthood, xvi, 39, 134
shalom leadership. *See also* transformational leadership

defined, xvi
and expanded mission of bicultural churches, 131
inclusiveness, 10–11
and intergenerational renewal and reconciliation, 9
and move towards equality and empowerment, 10, 110
perceived lack of, in existing bicultural churches, 90–91
shame culture, in Chinese bicultural churches, 107, 159–60
Shenk, Sara Wenger, 33n134
Shoemaker, Ken, 34
silent exodus
approaches to stopping, 100–101, 102–3t, 140
from bicultural churches, as common phenomenon, 52n57, 80–81, 80n3, 116
identifying reasons for, 1, 54, 57–58, 98, 139, 160
impact on those remaining in the church, 106, 108
as loss of valuable resource, 59, 131–32
as loss of valuable resources, 55
OBC attribution to CBC selfishness, 55
theological issues, 116–17n63, 116–18
young adults as predominant among drop-outs, 54n72, 55n72, 75–76
silent exodus study. *See also* drop-out study participants; pastors, church leaders among study participants; remain-in (current Chinese Church member) study participants
age of respondents, 117
comparison of findings from the three study groups, 112–13, 112t, 113f
findings from church dropouts, 82–83, 84–85t, 86–101, 102–3t
findings from pastors and EM clergy, 77–81

silent exodus study *(cont.)*
  findings from remain-in participants, 103–12, 104t, 109t
  follow-up focus groups, 118–22
  research design and methodology, 75–76, 114–15
  return rate, 116
  study weaknesses, limitations, 115–18, 115n59, 118n67
  summary of results, 115
  survey design and sampling, 81–82
Sinocentrism, defined, xv. *See also* ethnocentrism, Sinocentrism
Sinophobia, 48–49, 48–49n35
Smalley, Gary, 133
SMART goals, in action plans, 144
Smith, Christian, 39, 39n175
So, Wing, 72
social justice, CBC concerns about, 106
Southeast Asians, immigration into Canada, 60
spiritual growth needs, as reason for leaving, 98, 106, 109, 159
strategic planning, 146
Suen, Nick, 16n18

Tan, Jonathan Y, 19
Tan, Joshua Weichong, 47n27, 55–56
The Tapestry, Vancouver, B.C., 16n18
theological conflicts, as one reason for exodus, 98, 108, 161
theology, theologians
  and challenges of multicultural missions, 2
  as human-produced, 69n13
  theology of place, 136
Theresa, Mother, 12
To, Jack and Rose, 111
Toffler, Alvin, 123
Townhouse Model, 37, 37n167
transformational leadership
  and cultural change, 40
  defined, xv–xvi, 39
  educational and training role, 146
  and effective communication, conflict resolution, 9, 46, 128, 128n26, 142–45, 142n16, 145n33
  and the establishment of trust, 10
  and Kotter's leadership theory, 41
  motivational role, 9
  and need for rededication to mission, 140–41, 140n5, 141n8, 142n16, 146–47
  need for vision, vision path, 8, 8n31, 141–42, 142n16
  preparing for objections, questions, 144–45
  prophetic leadership, 42
  role in stemming silent exodus, 1, 138
  servant leadership, servanthood, 39–40, 134
  strategic planning, 146
  and transformation as a process, 11, 62, 140
  and transition to a multi-cultural church community, 23–24, 23n64
  and transition to EM independence, 128–30, 128n26, 129n27, 143–44
  types of, xvi
transnationalism
  defined, xv
  and diaspora churches, 43n1
Trent, John, 133
tricultural churches, xv, 23
Trieu, Peter, 34
Tsang, Gladys Lee, 18, 36, 36n163
Tseng, Timothy, 55n73
Tso, Marcus, 37, 55n75

the unbusy pastor, 89n9
unity, as value in Chinese culture, xiv, 13, 16, 23nn62–63, 27n94, 28, 34–35n151, 45n20, 46–47, 71, 129

Van Reken, Ruth C., 22
Vancouver, B. C., model EM ministries in, 16n18

Walsh, Brian J., 116

Wan, Enoch, 136n60
Wang, Jiwu, 48–49n35, 49nn37–38, 51n51
Wang, Paul C., 23n62, 32, 38, 72, 113
Weems, Lovett H., Jr., 42
White, Randy ("The Eight Qualities of Transformational Leadership"), xv–xvi, 127
Whitehead, Evelyn Eaton and James, 55n72
Wong, Hoover, 38
Wong, Morgan, 13, 13n3, 14–15t
Wong, Wayland, 25, 111, 111n44
Wong, Wayne, 16n18, 20, 27–28, 116n61
Woo, Terry (*Banana Boys*), 98n26
Wu, Jonathan, 140n4

xenophobia
  defined, xv
  and ethnic divisions in Chinese churches, 49–50, 49nn37–38
  historically, within China, 51n52
  in monocultural churches, 19
  as a reason for leaving the Chinese church, 98

Yancey, George A., 18, 18n25, 36, 69
Yang, Fenggang, 16, 19n38, 26n88, 28, 31n120, 31–32n123, 45, 45n21, 46n23, 53n62, 55–56n76, 56n81, 72n35
Yeung, Dr. Clement, 52n58
Yew, Dr. Clement, 147
Young, William P. (*The Shack*), 115n60
young adults. *See also* CBCs (Canadian-born Chinese)
  divergent life needs, as reason for leaving bicultural churches, 92–94, 93–94n20
  dominance of among those exiting Chinese monoethnic churches, 54n72, 55
  efforts of English Ministries to appeal to, 56
  exodus of from all churches, 80–81, 80n3
  failure of church to meet life stage needs, as reason for exodus, 79–80
youth ministries2, 56
Yuen, Peter, 21

www.ingramcontent.com/pod-product-compliance
Lightning Source LLC
Chambersburg PA
CBHW071230290426
44108CB00013B/1353